문덕 영어 독해

합격, 박문각

동영상강의 pmg.co.kr

문 덕 편저

가장 명쾌한 독해 전략, 문덕의 Signal Reading!

- 최빈출 92구문으로 구문 독해력 완성
- 공무원 독해 문제의 핵심을 꿰뚫는 전략과 해법
- 빈칸 완성 문제에 대한 혁신적 solution 제시
- [부록] 테마별 어휘 수록

PMG 박문각

이 책의 **머리말**

FOREWORD

공무원 수험생이라면 누구나 설사 독해 파트만 전문적으로 수록한 교재는 아니라도 독해 기출 문제 등이 수록되어 독해력 상승에 도움을 주는 책들이 적어도 한두 권쯤은 있으리라 생각된다. 하지만 다음과 같은 질문에 명확한 답을 내놓는 교재가 있는지 한 번 생각해 볼 필요가 있다.

1. 독해력의 체계적 상승에 대한 고민이 책 속에 제대로 반영되어 있는가?
2. 공무원 독해 문제의 유형별 전략이 구체적으로 제시되어 있고 일관된 구성을 취하고 있는가?
3. 독해 문제 중 가장 난이도가 높다고 할 수 있는 '빈칸 완성 문제'와 '순서 배열', 그리고 '문장 삽입'의 문제에 대한 실질적이고 혁신적인 공략법이 제시되어 있는가?

[문덕 영어 독해]는 이와 같은 고민에 대한 답을 제시한 교재라 할 수 있다.

첫 번째로 독해력의 체계적 상승에 대한 고민에서 본서의 Part 1 구문 독해는 '특별한' 방식을 구현해 냈다. 얼핏 보면 여느 독해 교재의 구문 편과 비슷해 보이겠지만 Check-up 문제와 정답을 통한 집중적인 '주어와 동사 찾기' 훈련과 본서에서 제시한 복잡한 문장의 원리를 혁신적인 방식으로 해결하는 '앞의 콤마'와 '뒤의 콤마', '명사 후치 수식어구'라는 세 가지 구문 분석 장치를 통하여, 그 어느 교재보다도 탄탄한 문장 이해 능력을 제고시켜 줄 것이다.

두 번째로 본 교재는 공무원 독해 문제의 유형별 전략을 따로 마련하여 효율적인 독해 문제 풀이 전략들을 추상적인 방법론이 아닌 구체적인 문제 풀이 routine으로서 제시하였다. 이러한 문제 접근 방식은 문제 해설에도 그대로 녹아 있는데, 특히 '주제'와 '요지'를 암시하는 signal을 찾는 구체적인 방법과 실제 문제 해설은, 막연한 독해 문제 풀이의 답답한 과정이 아닌 스스로 체험하며 문제점을 인식하고 해결해 가는 자연스러운 훈련으로 수험생 여러분을 인도할 것이다. 이것이 바로 [문덕 영어 독해]가 공무원 영어 독해 실력의 획기적 상승으로 이끌 'Signal Reading'이다.

마지막으로 '논리성'과 연관된 빈칸 완성 문제와 순서 배열, 그리고 문장 삽입 문제에 대한 [문덕 영어 독해]의 전략적 해법과 훈련 과정은 그 어떤 교재와도 차별화된 본서만의 특징이라고 할 수 있다. 이미 수많은 현장 강의를 통해서 빈칸 문제를 빠른 시간 내에 풀어내는 '좁풀 – 좁게 풀기'의 비법에 수많은 찬사가 이어지고 있다. 본서가 제시하는 방법론을 충실히 따라온다면 정확한 정답을 찾는 능력의 향상은 물론 공무원 영어 수험생의 가장 큰 고민 중 하나인 문제 풀이 시간의 획기적 단축까지 가능할 것이다.

아무쪼록 [문덕 영어 문법], [문덕 영어 어휘]와 함께, [문덕 영어 독해]가 제시하는 다소 독창적이지만 가장 실용적이고 효율적인 방법론과 전략을 신뢰하고 끝까지 함께해서 완벽에 가까운 공무원 영어 실력의 토대를 구축하기 바란다.

2021년 7월

문덕

이 책의 **공부방법**

GUIDE

구문 독해 편

공무원 영어의 독해 지문은 일반적으로 길고 복잡한 문장 구조를 지니고 있습니다. [문덕 영어 독해]는 이러한 까다로운 문장 구조를 분석할 수 있는 특별한 '무기'를 제시하고 있는데, 이는 바로 문장 구조를 드러내는 '앞의 콤마', '뒤의 콤마', '명사 후치 수식어구'에 대한 공식(formula)입니다.

1. 반드시 '앞의 콤마', '뒤의 콤마', '명사 후치 수식어구'에 대한 학습을 먼저 하세요.
2. 구문 독해 본문을 이해할 때 문법적 지식을 바탕으로 문장의 주어와 동사를 찾는 훈련을 집요하게 하세요.
3. Check-up을 통해서 반드시 배운 내용을 점검하세요.

독해 전략 편

[문덕 영어 독해]는 공무원 영어 독해 문제 풀이 능력의 구체적이고도 빠른 상승을 위하여 체계적이고 짜임새 있는 전략을 문제 유형별로 준비를 하였습니다. 그러므로 유형별 독해 문제를 풀기 전에 반드시 독해 전략을 미리 공부하시기 바랍니다. 또한 문제 풀이를 하다가 종종 방향감을 잃거나 막연하게 문제를 풀어가는 느낌이 들 때마다 '독해 전략 편'으로 돌아가서 다시 한 번 전략을 점검하기 바랍니다.

유형별 독해 편

[문덕 영어 독해]는 공무원 영어에 등장하는 모든 기출문제 유형을 총망라하여 정리한 후 빈출되는 문제들을 수록하였습니다. 최신 기출문제들도 수록함으로써 실전 감각을 키우고 자신의 독해력이 실제 기출문제에서 어떻게 적용되고 반영되고 있는지를 가늠할 수 있도록 하였습니다. 다만 주의할 점은 반드시 [문덕 영어 독해]가 제시하는 문제 풀이 전략에 따라 문제를 풀려고 노력해야 한다는 것입니다. 특히 빈칸 완성과 순서 배열 등 '논리성'과 연관된 문제를 풀 때 무턱대고 풀어가던 기존의 습관을 고집한다면 실력이 더디게 는다는 점을 명심하시기 바랍니다.

부록 - 주제별 어휘 편

독해력 향상에서 가장 기본적이고도 중요한 것은 어휘력이라는 것을 누구나 알고 있을 것입니다. [문덕 영어 독해]에서 주제별 어휘 리스트를 준비한 이유는 하나의 독해 지문은 특정한 소재와 주제를 서술하는 글이므로 동일한 범주의 단어들이 집단적으로 등장하기 때문입니다. 이러한 사실에 근거하여 주제별 어휘 학습을 보충한다면 지문을 읽을 때 훨씬 자신감 있게 막힘없이 해석해 나갈 수 있는 힘을 기를 수 있습니다. 사실 이 파트는 독해 전략을 공부하고 나서 유형별 문제 풀이에 들어가기 전에 미리 공부해도 무방합니다. 스스로 공부하다가 추가적으로 발견한 주제별 어휘를 교재에 스스로 기입해서 자기만의 주제별 어휘 리스트를 채워 나가는 것도 영어 공부에 재미와 효율을 더해 줄 것입니다.

이 책의 **구성과 특징**

CONSTRUCTION

1

독해를 할 때 문장 구조를 파악하고 해석함에 있어 문법 학습이 선행돼야 한다. 따라서 [문덕 영어 독해]에서는 주요 문법 포인트를 92개로 정리하여 간단한 설명과 예문을 함께 구성하였다.

2

구문 Check-up을 통해 앞서 학습한 문법 내용을 적용하여 주어와 동사를 찾아내는 문장 구조 분석을 연습할 수 있도록 하였다.

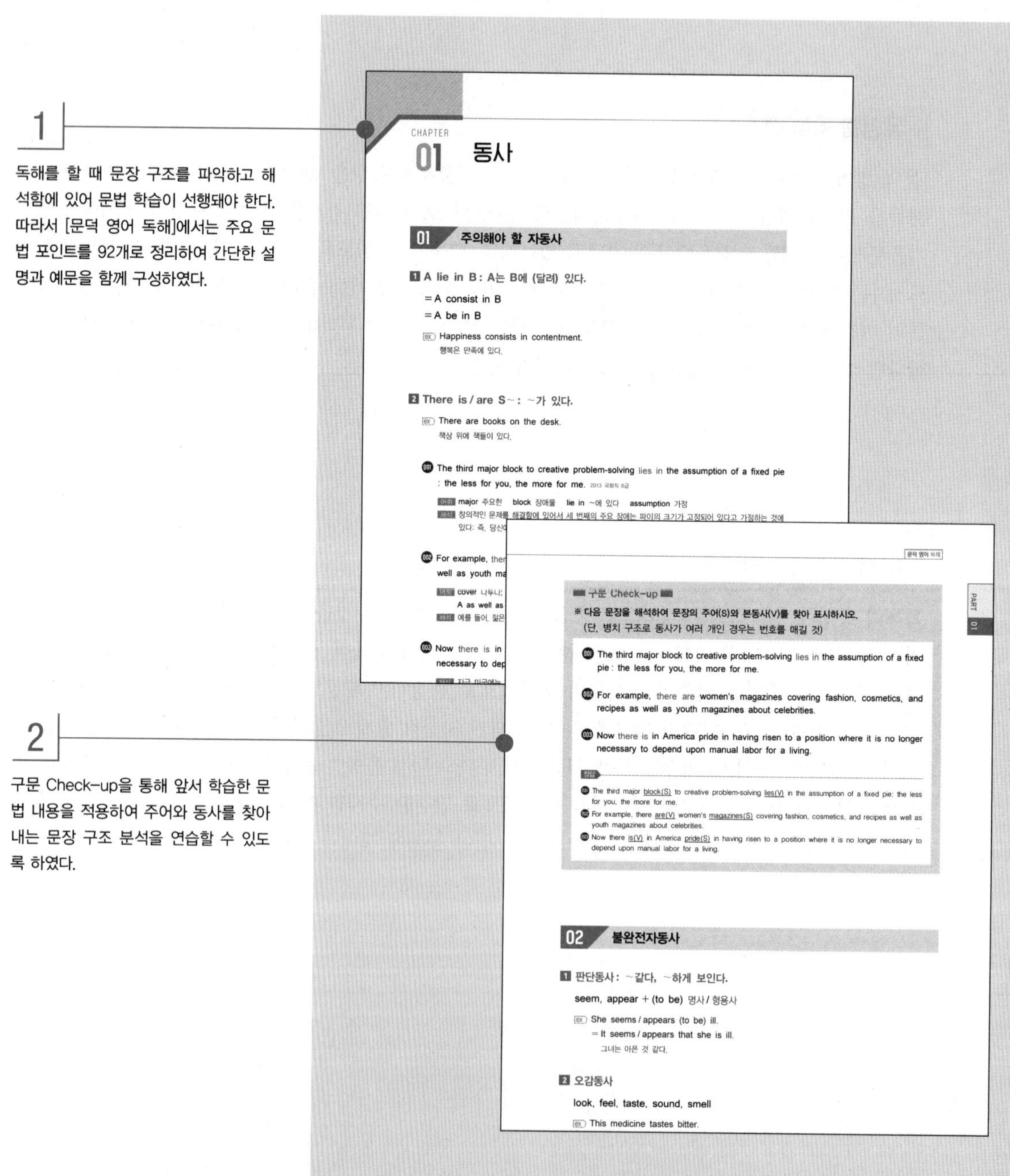

CHAPTER 01 동사

01 주의해야 할 자동사

1 A lie in B : A는 B에 (달려) 있다.

= A consist in B

= A be in B

예) Happiness consists in contentment.

행복은 만족에 있다.

2 There is / are S~ : ~가 있다.

예) There are books on the desk.

책상 위에 책들이 있다.

001 The third major block to creative problem-solving lies in the assumption of a fixed pie : the less for you, the more for me. 2013 국회직 8급

어휘 major 주요한 block 장애물 lie in ~에 있다 assumption 가정

해석 창의적인 문제를 해결함에 있어서 세 번째의 주요 장애는 파이의 크기가 고정되어 있다고 가정하는 것에 있다: 즉, 당신...

002 For example, ther... well as youth ma...

어휘 cover 다루다; ... A as well as ...

해석 예를 들어, 젊은...

003 Now there is in ... necessary to dep...

문덕 영어 독해

PART 01

구문 Check-up

※ 다음 문장을 해석하여 문장의 주어(S)와 본동사(V)를 찾아 표시하시오.
(단, 병치 구조로 동사가 여러 개인 경우는 번호를 매길 것)

001 The third major block to creative problem-solving lies in the assumption of a fixed pie : the less for you, the more for me.

002 For example, there are women's magazines covering fashion, cosmetics, and recipes as well as youth magazines about celebrities.

003 Now there is in America pride in having risen to a position where it is no longer necessary to depend upon manual labor for a living.

정답

001 The third major block(S) to creative problem-solving lies(V) in the assumption of a fixed pie: the less for you, the more for me.

002 For example, there are(V) women's magazines(S) covering fashion, cosmetics, and recipes as well as youth magazines about celebrities.

003 Now there is(V) in America pride(S) in having risen to a position where it is no longer necessary to depend upon manual labor for a living.

02 불완전자동사

1 판단동사 : ~같다, ~하게 보인다.

seem, appear + (to be) 명사 / 형용사

예) She seems / appears (to be) ill.

= It seems / appears that she is ill.

그녀는 아픈 것 같다.

2 오감동사

look, feel, taste, sound, smell

예) This medicine tastes bitter.

문덕 영어 독해 R

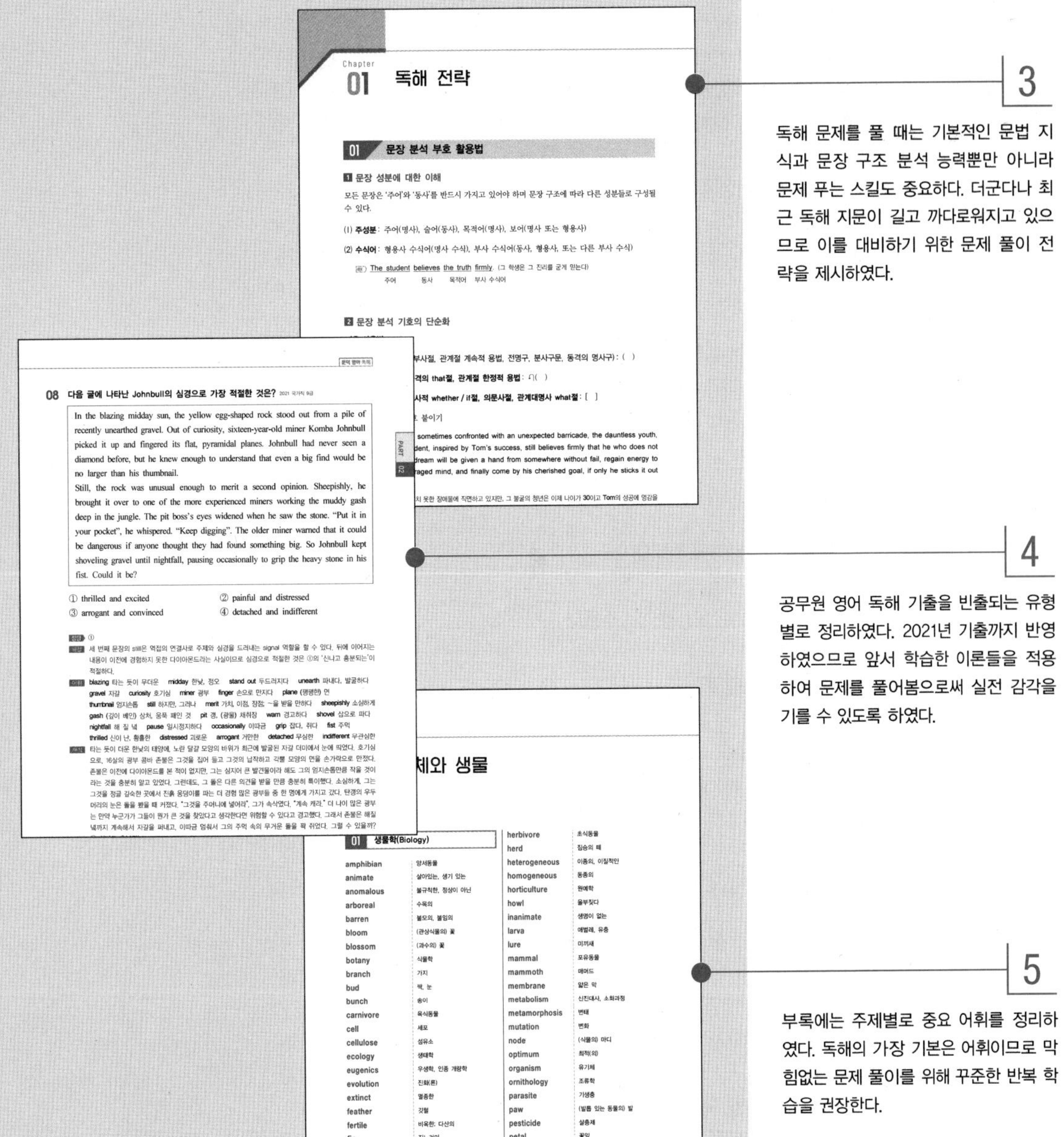
Chapter 01 독해 전략

01 문장 분석 부호 활용법

1 문장 성분에 대한 이해

모든 문장은 '주어'와 '동사'를 반드시 가지고 있어야 하며 문장 구조에 따라 다른 성분들로 구성될 수 있다.

(1) **주성분**: 주어(명사), 술어(동사), 목적어(명사), 보어(명사 또는 형용사)

(2) **수식어**: 형용사 수식어(명사 수식), 부사 수식어(동사, 형용사, 또는 다른 부사 수식)

例) The student believes the truth firmly. (그 학생은 그 진리를 굳게 믿는다)
주어 동사 목적어 부사 수식어

2 문장 분석 기호의 단순화

부사절, 관계절 계속적 용법, 전명구, 분사구문, 동격의 명사구): ( )

격의 that절, 관계절 한정적 용법: ∩( )

사적 whether / if절, 의문사절, 관계대명사 what절: [ ]

붙이기

sometimes confronted with an unexpected barricade, the dauntless youth, dent, inspired by Tom's success, still believes firmly that he who does not dream will be given a hand from somewhere without fail, regain energy to raged mind, and finally come by his cherished goal, if only he sticks it out

치 못한 장애물에 직면하고 있지만, 그 불굴의 청년은 이제 나이가 30이고 Tom의 성공에 영감을

문덕 영어 독해

08 다음 글에 나타난 Johnbull의 심경으로 가장 적절한 것은? 2021 국가직 9급

In the blazing midday sun, the yellow egg-shaped rock stood out from a pile of recently unearthed gravel. Out of curiosity, sixteen-year-old miner Komba Johnbull picked it up and fingered its flat, pyramidal planes. Johnbull had never seen a diamond before, but he knew enough to understand that even a big find would be no larger than his thumbnail.
Still, the rock was unusual enough to merit a second opinion. Sheepishly, he brought it over to one of the more experienced miners working the muddy gash deep in the jungle. The pit boss's eyes widened when he saw the stone. "Put it in your pocket", he whispered. "Keep digging". The older miner warned that it could be dangerous if anyone thought they had found something big. So Johnbull kept shoveling gravel until nightfall, pausing occasionally to grip the heavy stone in his fist. Could it be?

① thrilled and excited ② painful and distressed
③ arrogant and convinced ④ detached and indifferent

정답 ①

해설 세 번째 문장의 still은 역접의 연결사로 주제와 심경을 드러내는 signal 역할을 할 수 있다. 뒤에 이어지는 내용이 이전에 경험하지 못한 다이아몬드라는 사실이므로 심경으로 적절한 것은 ①의 '신나고 흥분되는'이 적절하다.

어휘 blazing 타는 듯이 무더운 midday 한낮, 정오 stand out 두드러지다 unearth 파내다, 발굴하다 gravel 자갈 curiosity 호기심 miner 광부 finger 손으로 만지다 plane (평평한) 면 thumbnail 엄지손톱 still 하지만, 그러나 merit 가치, 이점, 장점; ~을 받을 만하다 sheepishly 소심하게 gash (깊이 베인) 상처, 움푹 패인 것 pit 갱, (광물) 채취장 warn 경고하다 shovel 삽으로 파다 nightfall 해 질 녘 pause 일시정지하다 occasionally 이따금 grip 잡다, 쥐다 fist 주먹 thrilled 신이 난, 황홀한 distressed 괴로운 arrogant 거만한 detached 무심한 indifferent 무관심한

해석 타는 듯이 더운 한낮의 태양에, 노란 달걀 모양의 바위가 최근에 발굴된 자갈 더미에서 눈에 띄었다. 호기심으로, 16살의 광부 콤바 존불은 그것을 집어 들고 그것의 납작하고 각뿔 모양의 면을 손가락으로 만졌다. 존불은 이전에 다이아몬드를 본 적이 없지만, 그는 심지어 큰 발견물이라 해도 그의 엄지손톱만큼 작을 것이라는 것을 충분히 알고 있었다. 그런데도, 그 돌은 다른 의견을 받을 만큼 충분히 특이했다. 소심하게, 그는 그것을 정글 깊숙한 곳에서 진흙 웅덩이를 파는 더 경험 많은 광부들 중 한 명에게 가지고 갔다. 탄갱의 우두머리의 눈은 돌을 봤을 때 커졌다. "그것을 주머니에 넣어라", 그가 속삭였다. "계속 캐라." 더 나이 많은 광부는 만약 누군가가 그들이 뭔가 큰 것을 찾았다고 생각한다면 위험할 수 있다고 경고했다. 그래서 존불은 해질 녘까지 계속해서 자갈을 퍼내고, 이따금 멈춰서 그의 주먹 속의 무거운 돌을 꽉 쥐었다. 그럴 수 있을까?

체와 생물

01 생물학(Biology)

amphibian	양서동물	herbivore	초식동물
animate	살아있는, 생기 있는	herd	짐승의 떼
anomalous	불규칙한, 정상이 아닌	heterogeneous	이종의, 이질적인
arboreal	수목의	homogeneous	동종의
barren	불모의, 불임의	horticulture	원예학
bloom	(관상식물의) 꽃	howl	울부짖다
blossom	(과수의) 꽃	inanimate	생명이 없는
botany	식물학	larva	애벌레, 유충
branch	가지	lure	미끼새
bud	싹, 눈	mammal	포유동물
bunch	송이	mammoth	매머드
carnivore	육식동물	membrane	얇은 막
cell	세포	metabolism	신진대사, 소화과정
cellulose	섬유소	metamorphosis	변태
ecology	생태학	mutation	변화
eugenics	우생학, 인종 개량학	node	(식물의) 마디
evolution	진화(론)	optimum	최적(의)
extinct	멸종한	organism	유기체
feather	깃털	ornithology	조류학
fertile	비옥한; 다산의	parasite	기생충
fin	지느러미	paw	(발톱 있는 동물의) 발
fledged	깃털이 다 자란, 날 수 있게 된	pesticide	살충제
flock	동물 또는 새의 떼	petal	꽃잎
flutter	퍼덕이다	photosynthesis	광합성
		physiology	생리학
		poach	밀렵하다

3

독해 문제를 풀 때는 기본적인 문법 지식과 문장 구조 분석 능력뿐만 아니라 문제 푸는 스킬도 중요하다. 더군다나 최근 독해 지문이 길고 까다로워지고 있으므로 이를 대비하기 위한 문제 풀이 전략을 제시하였다.

4

공무원 영어 독해 기출을 빈출되는 유형별로 정리하였다. 2021년 기출까지 반영하였으므로 앞서 학습한 이론들을 적용하여 문제를 풀어봄으로써 실전 감각을 기를 수 있도록 하였다.

5

부록에는 주제별로 중요 어휘를 정리하였다. 독해의 가장 기본은 어휘이므로 막힘없는 문제 풀이를 위해 꾸준한 반복 학습을 권장한다.

이 책의 **차례**

CONTENTS

PART 01

구문 독해

CHAPTER 03 접속사와 기타 구문

이 책의 **차례**

CONTENTS

들어가기 전에

INTRO

복잡한 문장 내의 콤마 처리 방법

1. 완성된 문장의 위치를 확인한다.
2. 완성된 문장의 앞에 나오는 콤마가 '앞의 콤마' 8가지이다.
3. 완성된 문장의 뒤에 나오는 콤마가 '뒤의 콤마' 9가지이다.
4. 뒤의 콤마는 주어의 바로 뒤에 위치할 수도 있다.
5. 병치 구조에 등장하는 콤마는 '앞의 콤마', '뒤의 콤마'의 예외이다.

앞의 콤마 요소들	________ ,[S + V + O], ________ ↓ (앞의 콤마) ↓ (뒤의 콤마) *[S, (뒤의 콤마 요소들), + V + O]의 형식도 가능함.	뒤의 콤마 요소들
1. 접속사 + S + V ________		1. 접속사 + S + V ________
2. 전치사구		2. 전치사구
3. 현재분사 구문	*명사 후치 수식어구	3. 현재분사 구문
4. (being) 과거분사 구문	1. 관계대명사절의 한정적 용법	4. (being) 과거분사 구문
5. to부정사	2. 관계부사절의 한정적 용법	5. to부정사 (×)
6. (Being) 형용사	3. 전치사구	6. 관계대명사절의 계속적 용법
7. 부사	4. 현재분사	7. 관계부사절의 계속적 용법
8. 동격의 명사	5. 과거분사	8. (Being) 형용사
	6. 형용사구	9. 부사
	7. 동격	10. 동격의 명사

Though he is sometimes confronted with an unexpected barricade, the dauntless youth,
앞의 콤마(접속사+주어+동사) / 주어

a 30-year-old student, inspired by Tom's success, still firmly believes [that he (who does not
뒤의 콤마(동격) / 뒤의 콤마(분사구) / 동사 / 명사절(목적어)

give up his own dream) will be given a hand from somewhere without fail, regain energy (to
명사 후치 수식어구(관계절) / 병렬 ① / 병렬 ②

revive the discouraged mind), and finally come by his cherished goal, if only he sticks it out with MD].
명사 후치 수식어구(to부정사) / 병렬 ③ / 뒤의 콤마(접속사+주어+동사)

비록 그는 때때로 예기치 못한 장애물에 직면하고 있지만, 그 불굴의 청년은 이제 나이가 30이고 Tom의 성공에 영감을 받아서 아직도 굳게 믿고 있는 사실이 있으니 그것은 바로 자신만의 꿈을 포기하지 않는 사람은 반드시 어딘가로부터 도움을 받게 될 것이고 낙심한 마음을 다시 살려낼 에너지를 얻게 되어 마침내 소중히 품어온 목표를 얻게 된다는 것이다. 만약 그가 MD와 함께 버티어 내기만 한다면 말이다.

문덕 영어
독해

PART

01

구문 독해

Chapter 01 동사

Chapter 02 준동사

Chapter 03 접속사와 기타 구문

CHAPTER

01 동사

01 주의해야 할 자동사

1 A lie in B : A는 B에 (달려) 있다.

= A consist in B

= A be in B

ex Happiness consists in contentment.

행복은 만족에 있다.

2 There is / are S~ : ~가 있다.

ex There are books on the desk.

책상 위에 책들이 있다.

001 The third major block to creative problem-solving lies in the assumption of a fixed pie : the less for you, the more for me. 2013 국회직 8급

어휘 major 주요한 block 장애물 lie in ~에 있다 assumption 가정

해석 창의적인 문제를 해결함에 있어서 세 번째의 주요 장애는 파이의 크기가 고정되어 있다고 가정하는 것에 있다: 즉, 당신에게 돌아가는 파이가 더 작으면 작을수록, 나에게 돌아오는 파이는 커진다는 것이다.

002 For example, there are women's magazines covering fashion, cosmetics, and recipes as well as youth magazines about celebrities. 2014 국가직 9급

어휘 cover 다루다; 덮다; 보호하다; 보도하다 cosmetics 화장품 recipe 요리법
A as well as B B뿐만 아니라 A도 celebrity 명성; 유명인사

해석 예를 들어, 젊은 층이 보는 유명인에 대한 잡지뿐만 아니라 패션, 화장품, 요리법을 다루는 여성 잡지도 있다.

003 Now there is in America pride in having risen to a position where it is no longer necessary to depend upon manual labor for a living. 2008 중앙선거관리위원회 9급

해석 지금 미국에는 생계를 위하여 더 이상 육체노동에 의존할 필요가 없는 위치에 올랐다는 자부심이 있다.

■ 구문 Check-up ■

※ 다음 문장을 해석하여 문장의 주어(S)와 본동사(V)를 찾아 표시하시오.
(단, 병치 구조로 동사가 여러 개인 경우는 번호를 매길 것)

001 The third major block to creative problem-solving lies in the assumption of a fixed pie : the less for you, the more for me.

002 For example, there are women's magazines covering fashion, cosmetics, and recipes as well as youth magazines about celebrities.

003 Now there is in America pride in having risen to a position where it is no longer necessary to depend upon manual labor for a living.

정답

001 The third major block(S) to creative problem-solving lies(V) in the assumption of a fixed pie: the less for you, the more for me.

002 For example, there are(V) women's magazines(S) covering fashion, cosmetics, and recipes as well as youth magazines about celebrities.

003 Now there is(V) in America pride(S) in having risen to a position where it is no longer necessary to depend upon manual labor for a living.

02 불완전자동사

1 판단동사 : ~같다, ~하게 보인다.

seem, appear + (to be) 명사 / 형용사

ex She seems / appears (to be) ill.
= It seems / appears that she is ill.
그녀는 아픈 것 같다.

2 오감동사

look, feel, taste, sound, smell

ex This medicine tastes bitter.
이 약은 맛이 쓰다.

004 It seems to me that I can hardly pick up a magazine nowadays without encountering someone's views on our colleges. 2008 국가직 7급

어휘 hardly 거의 ~않다 pick up 집어 들다 encounter 만나다

해석 나는 요즘에는 우리 대학들에 대한 다른 사람들의 의견을 마주치지 않고서는 잡지를 거의 집어 들지 못하는 것 같다.

005 Despite the prevailing conception of science as being concerned only with facts, science seems to be full of opinions and interpretations. 2015 서울시 7급

어휘 prevailing 널리 퍼진 conception 개념 interpretation 해석

해석 오직 사실과만 연관되어야 한다는 과학에 대한 일반적인 개념에도 불구하고, 과학은 의견과 해석으로 가득 차 있는 것 같다.

006 A child who is constantly criticized or compared unfavourably to others will begin to feel worthless, and those feelings can stay with her throughout her life. 2007 지방직 9급

어휘 constantly 항상, 끊임없이 criticize 비판하다 compare 비교하다 unfavorably 불리하게, 나쁘게 worthless 가치 없는 throughout ~내내

해석 끊임없이 비난받거나 남과 나쁘게 비교당하는 아이는 스스로 쓸모없다고 느끼기 시작할 것이고, 그런 감정은 평생 그 아이와 함께 할 수가 있다.

구문 Check-up

※ 다음 문장을 해석하여 문장의 주어(S)와 본동사(V)를 찾아 표시하시오.
(단, 병치 구조로 동사가 여러 개인 경우는 번호를 매길 것)

004 It seems to me that I can hardly pick up a magazine nowadays without encountering someone's views on our colleges.

005 Despite the prevailing conception of science as being concerned only with facts, science seems to be full of opinions and interpretations.

006 A child who is constantly criticized or compared unfavourably to others will begin to feel worthless, and those feelings can stay with her throughout her life.

정답

004 It seems(V) to me that I can hardly pick up a magazine nowadays without encountering someone's views on our colleges(S).

005 Despite the prevailing conception of science as being concerned only with facts, science(S) seems(V) to be full of opinions and interpretations.

006 A child(S_1) who is constantly criticized or compared unfavourably to others will begin(V_1) to feel worthless, and those feelings(S_2) can stay(V_2) with her throughout her life.

03 목적어 앞에 전치사가 필요한 가짜 수여동사 (1)

1 통고 · 확신 동사 + 사람 + of + 사물

inform / notify 알리다, warn 경고하다, remind 상기시키다, convince / assure 확신시키다

ex) She reminds me of my dead sister.
그녀는 나에게 나의 죽은 누이를 상기시킨다.

2 제거 · 박탈 동사 + 사람 + of + 사물

rob / deprive 빼앗다, cure 치료하다, relieve 덜어주다

ex) He robbed her of her money.
그는 그녀에게서 돈을 강탈했다.

007 If readers wish to inform themselves of the pressing problems of the day, they will do better to read, not novels but the books that specially deal with them. 2008 국가직 9급

어휘 press 긴급한, 중대한 specially 특별하게 deal with 다루다
해석 만약에 독자들이 오늘날의 중대한 문제들을 독자 스스로에게 정보를 주고자 한다면, 독자들은 소설이 아니라 그 문제들은 특별히 다룬 책들을 읽는 것이 좋다.

008 News that the United States has seriously failed to achieve its goal of reducing high school smoking surprises me as there was such confidence a few years ago that we could convince kids of the dangers of smoking through education efforts. 2010 국회직 8급

어휘 seriously 심각하게 achieve 성취하다 confidence 자신감
해석 미국이 고등학생들의 흡연을 줄이려는 목표를 달성하는데 심각하게 실패를 했다는 뉴스는 나를 놀라게 한다. 왜냐하면 몇 년 전에는 우리는 너무나 자신감이 있어서 아이들에게 교육을 통하여 흡연의 위험을 확신시킬 수 있었기 때문이다.

009 In 1688, the king was generally deprived of power, and the Parliament became the actual sovereign of politics with the right to legislate laws. 2018 기상직 9급

어휘 deprive 빼앗다 parliament 의회 actual 실제의 sovereign 군주의, 주권의 legislate 제정하다
해석 1688년에, 왕은 전반에 걸쳐 권력을 빼앗겼고, 의회는 법률을 제정하는 권력을 가진 실질적인 정치 주권자가 되었다.

■ 구문 Check-up ■

※ 다음 문장을 해석하여 문장의 주어(S)와 본동사(V)를 찾아 표시하시오.
(단, 병치 구조로 동사가 여러 개인 경우는 번호를 매길 것)

007 If readers wish to inform themselves of the pressing problems of the day, they will do better to read, not novels but the books that specially deal with them.

008 News that the United States has seriously failed to achieve its goal of reducing high school smoking surprises me as there was such confidence a few years ago that we could convince kids of the dangers of smoking through education efforts.

009 In 1688, the king was generally deprived of power, and the Parliament became the actual sovereign of politics with the right to legislate laws.

정답

007 If readers wish to inform themselves of the pressing problems of the day, they(S) will do(V) better to read, not novels but the books that specially deal with them.

008 News(S) that the United States has seriously failed to achieve its goal of reducing high school smoking surprises(V) me as there was such confidence a few years ago that we could convince kids of the dangers of smoking through education efforts.

009 In 1688, the king(S_1) was generally deprived(V_1) of power, and the Parliament(S_2) became(V_2) the actual sovereign of politics with the right to legislate laws.

04 목적어 앞에 전치사가 필요한 가짜 수여동사 (2)

금지동사 + 사람 + from ~ing : 目가 ~를 못하게 하다

prevent, keep, hold, stop, prohibit, ban, bar, deter, disable, dissuade, discourage, hinder, restrain

ex The heavy rain kept me from going out.
폭우는 내가 외출하지 못하게 했다.

010 The most well-known measure is the ubiquitous holdout line which prevents ticket holders for the next showing of that weekend's most popular movie from entering the building until their particular auditorium has been cleared out and cleaned. 2016 국회직 8급

어휘 well-known 잘 알려진 measure 조치, 대책 ubiquitous 편재하는, 모든 곳에 존재하는 holdout line 대기 줄 auditorium 관람석 clear out 다 비우다

해석 가장 잘 알려진 조치는 가장 인기가 있는 주말 영화의 다음 상영을 위한 표를 보유한 사람들이 자신들의 특정한 관람석이 비워지고 청소될 때까지 건물에 들어가는 것을 막는 도처에 널린 대기 줄(holdout)이다.

■ 구문 Check-up ■

※ 다음 문장을 해석하여 문장의 주어(S)와 본동사(V)를 찾아 표시하시오.
(단, 병치 구조로 동사가 여러 개인 경우는 번호를 매길 것)

010 The most well-known measure is the ubiquitous holdout line which prevents ticket holders for the next showing of that weekend's most popular movie from entering the building until their particular auditorium has been cleared out and cleaned.

정답

010 The most well-known measure(S) is(V) the ubiquitous holdout line which prevents ticket holders for the next showing of that weekend's most popular movie from entering the building until their particular auditorium has been cleared out and cleaned.

05 목적어 앞에 전치사가 필요한 가짜 수여동사 (3)

1 설명 동사 + to + 사람 + 목적어

explain, introduce, announce, suggest, propose

ex He suggested to us that we start right away.
그는 우리가 즉시 출발해야 한다고 제안했다.

2 제공 · 공급 동사 + 사람 + with + 목적어

provide, supply, furnish, equip, present, acquaint, charge

ex They provided us with money to spend.
그들은 우리에게 쓸 돈을 제공했다.

011 In Rome, Italy, a store burglary suspect, when caught in a store after closing hours, explained to the police that he suffered from a desire to sleep constantly and had fallen asleep inside the store. 2007 국가직 9급

어휘 burglary 강도 suspect 용의자 desire 욕구, 욕망 constantly 계속해서, 끊임없이

해석 이탈리아 로마에 한 상점털이 강도 용의자가 폐점시간이 지난 후 상점에서 붙잡혔을 때 자신은 끊임없이 잠자고자 하는 욕구에 사로잡혀 그 상점 안에서 잠들고 말았다고 경찰에 설명했다.

012 Even if these measures prove insufficient, they will furnish us with better knowledge than we have now for taking the next step. 2010 국가직 9급

어휘 prove 판명되다 insufficient 불충분한

해석 비록 이러한 조치가 충분치 않다고 밝혀진다 하더라도, 이 조치는 다음 조치를 취하는 데 있어 현재보다 더 나은 지식을 우리에게 제공할 것이다.

구문 Check-up

※ 다음 문장을 해석하여 문장의 주어(S)와 본동사(V)를 찾아 표시하시오.
(단, 병치 구조로 동사가 여러 개인 경우는 번호를 매길 것)

011 In Rome, Italy, a store burglary suspect, when caught in a store after closing hours, explained to the police that he suffered from a desire to sleep constantly and had fallen asleep inside the store.

012 Even if these measures prove insufficient, they will furnish us with better knowledge than we have now for taking the next step.

정답

011 In Rome, Italy, a store burglary suspect(S), when caught in a store after closing hours, explained(V) to the police that he suffered from a desire to sleep constantly and had fallen asleep inside the store.

012 Even if these measures prove insufficient, they(S) will furnish(V) us with better knowledge than we have now for taking the next step.

06 수여동사

간접목적어(사람)와 직접목적어(사물)를 수반하는 동사들

3형식으로 전환 시 사용되는 전치사들
to : give, award, offer, bring, show, tell, lend, send, sell
for : buy, make, get, find, choose, order, cook, build, call

ex He gave me a present.
= He gave a present to me.
그는 나에게 선물을 주었다.

He bought me a present.
= He bought a present for me.
그는 나에게 선물을 사 주었다.

*수여동사 **ask**는 간접목적어 후치 시 전치사 **of**를 쓴다.

ex He asked me a question.
= He asked a question of me.
그는 나에게 질문을 했다.

013 He was the son of a wealthy man who could give him the advantages of a broad education, the opportunity to see the greatest exponents of theatre art at home and abroad. 2016 국가직 9급

어휘 advantage 이점, 유리함 opportunity 기회 exponent 대표자, 주창자
해석 그는 그에게 다양한 교육의 이점과 국내와 국외에서 무대 예술의 위대한 대표자들을 만날 수 있는 기회를 줄 수 있었던 부유한 남자의 아들이었다.

014 On my most recent visit to Iowa, my hosts showed me a churchyard offering a dramatically visible example of those soil losses. 2017 지방직 9급

어휘 churchyard 교회부지 dramatically 극적으로 visible 눈에 보이는, 명백한 soil loss 토양손실
해석 최근에 아이오와를 방문했을 때, 나의 호스트들은 나에게 토양 손실의 극적으로 눈에 띄는 예를 보여주는 한 교회 부지를 보여주었다.

015 After selling his farm, which his grandfather had bought him in the hope that he would settle down, he set sail with his family for England. 2016 기상직 9급

어휘 settle down 정착하다 set sail 출항하다
해석 그의 할아버지가 그가 정착하기를 바라는 마음에서 그에게 사주었던 농장을 팔고 난후 그는 가족과 함께 런던으로 향하는 배에 올랐다.

016 One cold day when Lincoln was walking along the Springfield road, he came up to a man who was driving by in a carriage and asked him if he would take his overcoat into town. 2010 경찰 2차

어휘 come up to ~에 다가가다 overcoat 외투

해석 링컨이 Springfield 거리를 따라서 걷고 있던 어느 추운 날 그는 마차를 타고 지나 가고 있는 한 남자에게 다가갔다. 그리고 그에게 그가 그의 외투를 도시까지 가져다 줄 수 있는지를 물어보았다.

구문 Check-up

※ 다음 문장을 해석하여 문장의 주어(S)와 본동사(V)를 찾아 표시하시오.
(단, 병치 구조로 동사가 여러 개인 경우는 번호를 매길 것)

013 He was the son of a wealthy man who could give him the advantages of a broad education, the opportunity to see the greatest exponents of theatre art at home and abroad.

014 On my most recent visit to Iowa, my hosts showed me a churchyard offering a dramatically visible example of those soil losses.

015 After selling his farm, which his grandfather had bought him in the hope that he would settle down, he set sail with his family for England.

016 One cold day when Lincoln was walking along the Springfield road, he came up to a man who was driving by in a carriage and asked him if he would take his overcoat into town.

정답

013 He(S) was(V) the son of a wealthy man who could give him the advantages of a broad education, the opportunity to see the greatest exponents of theatre art at home and abroad.

014 On my most recent visit to Iowa, my hosts(S) showed(V) me a churchyard offering a dramatically visible example of those soil losses.

015 After selling his farm, which his grandfather had bought him in the hope that he would settle down, he(S) set(V) sail with his family for England.

016 One cold day when Lincoln was walking along the Springfield road, he(S) came(V_1) up to a man who was driving by in a carriage and asked(V_2) him if he would take his overcoat into town.

07 that절을 직접목적어로 취하는 동사

다음 동사들은 that절이 목적어일 경우 반드시 간접목적어가 필요하다.

inform 알리다, convince / assure 확신시키다, remind 상기시키다, persuade 설득하다, tell 말하다

ex He told that he was sick. (×)
⇨ He told me that he was sick. (○)
그는 나에게 아프다고 말했다.

He convinced that he was right. (×)
⇨ He convinced me that he was right. (○)
그는 자기가 옳다고 나에게 확신시켰다.

017 *The Diary of Anne Frank* has been read by millions. People are drawn to the story of Anne and her family because it reminds us that the human spirit has enormous resiliency even in the face of terrifying evil. 2015 서울시 7급

어휘 draw 끌다, 매혹하다 remind 상기시키다 enormous 거대한 resiliency 탄성, 회복력 in the face of ~의 면전에서, ~에도 불구하고 terrifying 무시무시한, 끔찍한

해석 『Anne Frank의 일기』는 수백만 독자에게 읽혀져 왔다. 인간 정신이 무시무시한 악에 직면했을 때조차도 엄청난 복원력을 가진다는 것을 우리에게 상기시켜주기 때문에 사람들은 Anne와 그녀의 가족의 이야기에 끌린다.

018 This positivity had convinced the interviewers that such pleasant and socially skilled applicants would fit well into the workplace, and so should be offered a job. 2016 국가직 9급

어휘 positivity 적극성 convince 확신시키다 applicant 신청자, 지원자 fit into 적응하다, 맞다 workplace 직장

해석 이러한 적극성은 인터뷰를 진행하는 자들에게 이렇게 쾌활하고 사교성을 가진 지원자들은 직장에 잘 맞을 것이고, 따라서 일자리를 제공받아야 한다는 확신을 주었다.

019 Based on this reasoning, a researcher thought that one way to urge people to donate would be to inform them that even a small sum would be helpful. 2011 사회복지직 9급

어휘 reasoning 추론 urge 촉구하다 helpful 도움이 되는

해석 이러한 추론에 근거하여, 한 연구자는 사람들에게 기부를 하도록 촉구할 수 있는 한 가지 방법은 심지어 적은 금액이라도 도움이 된다고 그들에게 알리는 것이라고 생각했다.

■ 구문 Check-up ■

※ 다음 문장을 해석하여 문장의 주어(S)와 본동사(V)를 찾아 표시하시오.
(단, 병치 구조로 동사가 여러 개인 경우는 번호를 매길 것)

017 The Diary of Anne Frank has been read by millions. People are drawn to the story of Anne and her family because it reminds us that the human spirit has enormous resiliency even in the face of terrifying evil.

018 This positivity had convinced the interviewers that such pleasant and socially skilled applicants would fit well into the workplace, and so should be offered a job.

019 Based on this reasoning, a researcher thought that one way to urge people to donate would be to inform them that even a small sum would be helpful.

정답

017 The Diary(S) of Anne Frank has been read(V) by millions. People(S) are drawn(V) to the story of Anne and her family because it reminds us that the human spirit has enormous resiliency even in the face of terrifying evil.

018 This positivity(S) had convinced(V) the interviewers that such pleasant and socially skilled applicants would fit well into the workplace, and so should be offered a job.

019 Based on this reasoning, a researcher(S) thought(V) that one way to urge people to donate would be to inform them that even a small sum would be helpful.

08 불완전타동사

목적격보어 앞에 to be나 as를 수반하지 않는 동사

make / render ~이 되게 하다, call, name ~라고 부르다

ex) He made his wife happy.
그는 그의 아내를 행복하게 해주었다.

⇨ He made his wife to be happy. (×)
⇨ He made his wife as happy. (×)

They call him a little giant.
사람들은 그를 작은 거인이라고 부른다.

They named the child John.
그들은 그 아이의 이름을 존이라고 지었다.

020 In the 1860s, amendments to the Constitution made these former slaves free and gave them all the rights of citizenship, including the right to vote. 2010 국회직 9급

어휘 amendment 개정 Constitution (미국) 헌법 citizenship 시민권, 국적
해석 1860년대에, 헌법 수정안들은 이 과거의 노예들을 자유롭게 만들었고 그들에게 투표권을 포함해서 모든 시민의 권리를 주었다.

021 The French sociologist Emile Durkheim called this sense of disorientation and meaninglessness anomie, and he argued that it could lead to despair and even suicide.
2019 국가직 9급

어휘 sociologist 사회학자 disorientation 방향 감각 상실; 혼미 anomie 아노미, (사회적) 무질서 despair 절망, 좌절, 체념 suicide 자살
해석 프랑스 사회학자 Emile Durkheim은 이러한 방향감 상실과 무의미의 느낌을 anomie(무질서)라고 불렀고 그의 주장에 따르면 이것이 절망과 자살을 불러 올 수 있다.

구문 Check-up

※ 다음 문장을 해석하여 문장의 주어(S)와 본동사(V)를 찾아 표시하시오.
(단, 병치 구조로 동사가 여러 개인 경우는 번호를 매길 것)

020 In the 1860s, amendments to the Constitution made these former slaves free and gave them all the rights of citizenship, including the right to vote.

021 The French sociologist Emile Durkheim called this sense of disorientation and meaninglessness anomie, and he argued that it could lead to despair and even suicide.

정답

020 In the 1860s, amendments(S) to the Constitution made(V_1) these former slaves free and gave(V_2) them all the rights of citizenship, including the right to vote.

021 The French sociologist(S_1) Emile Durkheim called(V_1) this sense of disorientation and meaninglessness anomie, and he(S_2) argued(V_2) that it could lead to despair and even suicide.

09 S + V + O + to V

to부정사를 목적격보어로 쓰는 동사들

want / wish 원하다, expect 기대하다, ask / require 요구하다, enable ~할 수 있게 하다, encourage 격려하다, force / compel/oblige 강요하다, tell / order 명령하다, persuade 설득하다, allow / permit 허락하다, forbid 금지하다

ex) I want you to go there.
나는 네가 거기 가기를 원한다.

His efforts enabled him to succeed.
그의 노력은 그가 성공할 수 있게 했다.

*목적어와 목적격보어가 수동 관계일 때는 (to be) p.p를 쓴다.

ex) I want the work (to be) done quickly.
나는 그 일이 빨리 마쳐지기를 원한다.

022 The new bill obliges the public sector to reserve more than a 3-precent share for job applicants aged between 15 and 29 in hiring quotas from next year. 2013 서울시 9급

어휘 oblige 강요하다 public sector 공공분야 reserve 뒤에 남기다, 유보하다 applicant 지원자 quota 할당량

해석 새로운 법안은 내년부터 고용 할당제로 15-29세 사이의 구직자들을 위하여 3퍼센트 이상의 일자리를 유보하도록 공공부문을 강제하고 있다.

023 You don't want your writing to be too informal and colloquial, but you also don't want to sound like someone you're not — like your professor or boss, for instance, or the Rhodes scholar teaching assistant. 2018 서울시 9급

어휘 colloquial 구어체의 Rhodes scholar 로즈 장학생 assistant 조교

해석 너는 너의 글이 너무나 격식이 없고 구어체적인 것을 원하지 않지만 또한 당신이 실제로 아닌, 예를 들어, 당신의 교수나 사장 또는 로즈 장학생 조교처럼 들리는 것도 원하지 않는 것이다.

024 A technique that enables an individual to gain some voluntary control over autonomic, or involuntary, body functions by observing electronic measurements of those functions is known as biofeedback. 2018 국가직 9급

어휘 enable 가능하게 하다 autonomic 자동적인 involuntary 무의식적인 observe 관찰하다; 준수하다 measurement 측정

해석 전자계측 관측을 통해 개인이 자동적 또는 무의식적인 몸의 기능에 대한 일부 자율적인 통제력을 얻을 수 있도록 가능케 하는 기술은 바이오피드백으로 알려져 있다.

025 The emphasis on decoding, translated mainly as phonemic awareness and knowledge of the alphabetic principle, has led schools to search for packaged or commercially produced reading programs that help students master the skills of decoding. 2014 국가직 9급

어휘 emphasis 강조 decode 암호를 해독하다 phonemic 음운의, 음소의 packaged 패키지화된 commercially 상업적으로

해석 주로 알파벳 원칙의 음소별 인식과 지식으로 이해되는 해독에 대한 강조로 인하여 학교는 학생들이 해독 기술을 숙달하는 데에 도움이 될 수 있는 패키지화되고 상업적으로 제작된 독해 프로그램을 찾게 되었다.

026 Within ten years, the astronomer Edwin Hubble discovered that the universe was expanding, causing Einstein to abandon the idea of the 'cosmological constant'. 2014 서울시 9급

어휘 astronomer 천문학자 expand 팽창하다 abandon 포기하다 cosmological 우주의 constant 상수

해석 10년 이내에, 천문학자 에드윈 허블은 우주가 팽창하고 있음을 발견했고, 이로 인하여 아인슈타인은 '우주 상수'의 개념을 포기하게 되었다.

구문 Check-up

※ 다음 문장을 해석하여 문장의 주어(S)와 본동사(V)를 찾아 표시하시오.
(단, 병치 구조로 동사가 여러 개인 경우는 번호를 매길 것)

022 The new bill obliges the public sector to reserve more than a 3-precent share for job applicants aged between 15 and 29 in hiring quotas from next year.

023 You don't want your writing to be too informal and colloquial, but you also don't want to sound like someone you're not – like your professor or boss, for instance, or the Rhodes scholar teaching assistant.

024 A technique that enables an individual to gain some voluntary control over autonomic, or involuntary, body functions by observing electronic measurements of those functions is known as biofeedback.

025 The emphasis on decoding, translated mainly as phonemic awareness and knowledge of the alphabetic principle, has led schools to search for packaged or commercially produced reading programs that help students master the skills of decoding.

026 Within ten years, the astronomer Edwin Hubble discovered that the universe was expanding, causing Einstein to abandon the idea of the cosmological constant.

정답

022 The new bill(S) obliges(V) the public sector to reserve more than a 3-precent share for job applicants aged between 15 and 29 in hiring quotas from next year.

023 You(S_1) don't want(V_1) your writing to be too informal and colloquial, but you(S_2) also don't want(V_2) to sound like someone you're not — like your professor or boss, for instance, or the Rhodes scholar teaching assistant.

024 A technique(S) that enables an individual to gain some voluntary control over autonomic, or involuntary, body functions by observing electronic measurements of those functions is known(V) as biofeedback.

025 The emphasis(S) on decoding, translated mainly as phonemic awareness and knowledge of the alphabetic principle, has led(V) schools to search for packaged or commercially produced reading programs that help students master the skills of decoding.

026 Within ten years, the astronomer(S) Edwin Hubble discovered(V) that the universe was expanding, causing Einstein to abandon the idea of the cosmological constant.

10 지각동사

목적격보어로 to가 없는 원형부정사를 쓰는 지각동사들

see, watch, notice, observe, hear, feel, smell

ex I saw her cross the street.
나는 그녀가 길을 건넌 것을 보았다.

*수동태 전환 시 원형부정사가 to부정사로 바뀐다.

ex She was seen to cross the street.
그녀는 길을 건너는 것이 보였다.

*진행의 뜻일 때 현재분사(~ing)를 쓸 수 있다. 단, 목적어와 목적격보어가 수동의 관계이면 과거분사(p.p)를 쓴다.

ex I saw her crossing the street.
나는 그녀가 길을 건너가고 있는 것을 보았다.

I heard my name called.
나는 내 이름이 불리는 것을 들었다.

027 They kept on going until they heard the faraway sound of a waterfall and saw a distant column of spray rising and disappearing. 2017 지방직 9급

어휘 faraway 멀리 있는 waterfall 폭포 column 기둥 spray 물보라, 분무
해석 그들은 멀리서 들리는 폭포의 소리를 들을 때까지 계속 갔고 멀리서 물보라의 기둥이 솟아났다 사라지는 것을 보았다.

구문 Check-up

※ 다음 문장을 해석하여 문장의 주어(S)와 본동사(V)를 찾아 표시하시오.
(단, 병치 구조로 동사가 여러 개인 경우는 번호를 매길 것)

027 They kept on going until they heard the faraway sound of a waterfall and saw a distant column of spray rising and disappearing.

정답

027 They(S) kept(V_1) on going until they heard the faraway sound of a waterfall and saw(V_2) a distant column of spray rising and disappearing.

11 사역동사

목적격보어로 to가 없는 원형부정사를 쓴다.

make ~하게 만들다, let ~하도록 허용하다, have ~하도록 시키다

ex) She made me obey the rules.
그녀는 내가 규칙을 따르게 했다.

He let me use his car.
그는 내가 그의 차를 쓰게 했다.

I had him repair my car.
나는 그가 나의 차를 수리하게 했다.

*have는 무의지적인 행위 유발 또는 상태의 지속을 나타낼 때 현재분사(~ing)를 쓸 수 있다.

ex) He had us laughing all through the night.
그는 밤새 우리를 웃게 했다.

*목적어와 목적격보어가 수동관계인 경우는 과거분사를 사용한다.

ex I had my car stolen.
나는 차를 도난당했다.

I couldn't make myself understood.
나는 나를 (남에게) 이해시킬 수 없었다.

*let은 수동관계일 때 그냥 p.p가 아니라 'be + p.p'를 쓴다.

ex Let it be forgotten.
그 일은 그냥 잊혀 지게 해라.

028 In one experiment, a team of researchers injected a group of fifty students with rhinovirus, and then had part of the group run, climb stairs, or cycle at moderate intensity for forty minutes every other day, while the second group remained relatively sedentary. 2009 법원직 9급

어휘 experiment 실험 inject 주입하다 rhinovirus 코감기 바이러스 moderate 적당한 intensity 강도 relatively 비교적으로, 상대적으로 sedentary 앉아있는

해석 한 실험에서, 한 팀의 연구자들은 한 무리의 50명의 학생들에게 코감기 바이러스를 주사로 주입했다. 그러고 나서 그 무리의 일부에게 이틀마다 보통의 강도로 40분씩 달리기를 하고, 계단을 오르고, 자전거를 타도록 시켰다. 반면에 두 번째 그룹의 학생들은 상대적으로 가만히 앉아 있었다.

029 If the time comes when I can no longer take part in decisions for my own future, let this statement stand as an expression of my wishes and directions, while I am still of sound mind. 2009 국회직 8급

어휘 statement 진술 direction 지시 sound 건전한, 온전한

해석 만일 내가 더 이상 나 자신의 미래에 대하여 결정에 참여할 수 없을 때(죽을 때)가 오면, 내가 아직 정신이 온전한 동안에, 나의 바람이자 지시의 표현으로 이 진술이 유효하도록 하시오.

구문 Check-up

※ 다음 문장을 해석하여 문장의 주어(S)와 본동사(V)를 찾아 표시하시오.
(단, 병치 구조로 동사가 여러 개인 경우는 번호를 매길 것)

028 In one experiment, a team of researchers injected a group of fifty students with rhinovirus, and then had part of the group run, climb stairs, or cycle at moderate intensity for forty minutes every other day, while the second group remained relatively sedentary.

029 If the time comes when I can no longer take part in decisions for my own future, let this statement stand as an expression of my wishes and directions, while I am still of sound mind.

정답

028 In one experiment, a team of researchers(S) injected(V_1) a group of fifty students with rhinovirus, and then had(V_2) part of the group run, climb stairs, or cycle at moderate intensity for forty minutes every other day, while the second group remained relatively sedentary.

029 If the time comes when I can no longer take part in decisions for my own future, let(V) this statement stand as an expression of my wishes and directions, while I am still of sound mind.

12 사역동사의 수동태

사역동사의 목적격보어가 원형부정사인 경우 수동태 전환 시 원형부정사가 to부정사로 바뀌어야 한다.

ex) She made me obey the rules.
= I was made to obey the rules by her.
그녀는 내가 규칙을 따르게 했다.

*사역동사 have는 'be asked to do', let은 'be allowed to do'를 사용하여 수동적인 의미를 전달할 수 있으며, have와 let 자체를 수동태로 취할 수는 없다.

ex) He had me repair the door.
= I was asked to repair the door.
그는 내가 그 문을 수리하도록 시켰다.

She let me go out alone.
= I was allowed to go out alone.
그녀는 내가 밖에 혼자 외출하는 것을 허용했다.

030 Although improvements have been made to control corruption, numerous opportunities exist for deviant and corrupt practices. 2012 경찰 3차

어휘 improvement 개선, 발전 control 통제하다, 억제하다 corruption 부패 numerous 수많은 deviant 탈선적인, 일탈하는 practice 관행, 관습

해석 비록 부패를 통제할 수 있도록 많은 개선이 이루어졌지만 일탈하고 부패한 관행들을 위한 기회는 존재한다.

■ 구문 Check-up ■

※ 다음 문장을 해석하여 문장의 주어(S)와 본동사(V)를 찾아 표시하시오.
(단, 병치 구조로 동사가 여러 개인 경우는 번호를 매길 것)

030 Although improvements have been made to control corruption, numerous opportunities exist for deviant and corrupt practices.

정답

030 Although improvements have been made to control corruption, numerous opportunities(S) exist(V) for deviant and corrupt practices.

13 현재시제의 미래 대용

'시간 · 조건 부사절'에서는 will을 쓰지 않고 현재시제로 미래를 표현한다.

when, while, before, after, until / till, as soon as, if, unless

ex I will start when she will come back next week. (×)
⇨ I will start when she comes back next week. (○)
그녀가 다음 주에 돌아올 때 나는 출발하겠다.

I will not go there if it will rain tomorrow. (×)
⇨ I will not go there if it rains tomorrow. (○)
내일 비가 오면 거기에 가지 않겠다.

*when이나 if가 명사절을 이끌 때, 미래의 내용일 경우에는 will을 쓴다.

ex I don't know when she will come back.
그녀가 언제 돌아올지 모르겠다.

I don't know if it will rain tomorrow.
내일 비가 올지 모르겠다.

031 In the future, once we've become weary of our lives being visible online for all to see and our privacy has been all but lost, anonymity may be more desirable than fame. 2020 국가직 9급

어휘 weary 싫증이 난 visible 보이는 privacy 사생활 all but 거의 anonymity 무명, 익명 desirable 바람직한

해석 미래에, 일단 모두가 볼 수 있는 온라인에서의 가시적인 우리의 삶에 우리가 싫증을 내게 되고 우리의 사생활이 거의 사라지면, 익명이 명성보다 더 바람직할지도 모른다.

032 By the time we get there, having sacrificed so much on the altar of being successful, we will realize that success was not what we wanted. 2012 국가직 9급

어휘 sacrifice 희생하다 altar 제단

해석 우리가 성공이라는 제단에 많은 것들을 희생시키고서 성공에 도달할 때쯤에, 우리는 성공이 우리가 원한 것이 아님을 깨닫게 될 것이다.

구문 Check-up

※ 다음 문장을 해석하여 문장의 주어(S)와 본동사(V)를 찾아 표시하시오.
(단, 병치 구조로 동사가 여러 개인 경우는 번호를 매길 것)

031 In the future, once we've become weary of our lives being visible online for all to see and our privacy has been all but lost, anonymity may be more desirable than fame.

032 By the time we get there, having sacrificed so much on the altar of being successful, we will realize that success was not what we wanted.

정답

031 In the future, once we've become weary of our lives being visible online for all to see and our privacy has been all but lost, anonymity(S) may be(V) more desirable than fame.

032 By the time we get there, having sacrificed so much on the altar of being successful, we(S) will realize(V) that success was not what we wanted.

14 현재완료의 용법과 부사

과거부터 현재까지의 '완료 · 경험 · 계속 · 결과'

현재완료를 드러내는 부사들

완료 : just, already, yet

경험 : ever, never, before, often, once, twice

계속 : so far, up to now, until now, for, since

결과 : 특별히 수반되는 부사 없음.

ex) I have already finished the work. (완료)
나는 벌써 일을 끝냈다.

I have seen a UFO before. (경험)
나는 전에 UFO를 본 적이 있다.

I have lived here for ten years. (계속)
나는 이곳에서 10년 동안 살아왔다.

I have lost my watch. (결과)
나는 시계를 잃어버렸다(그래서 지금은 없다).

033 Science has pushed aside gods and demons and revealed a cosmos more intricate and awesome than anything produced by pure imagination. 2014 국가직 9급

어휘 push aside 밀어내다 demon 악마, 악령 cosmos 우주 intricate 복잡한 awesome 멋진, 경탄할 만한

해석 과학은 신과 악령을 밀어냈고, 상상만으로 만들어지는 그 어느 것보다 더 복잡하고 경탄할 만한 우주를 드러냈다.

034 The bee's crushed-body treatment has been standard for fifty years, but a report released recently said that it was ineffective. 2013 국가직 9급

어휘 crushed 으깨진 treatment 치료 release 발표하다, 발매하다 ineffective 효과가 없는

해석 벌의 으깬 몸통으로 치료하는 것이 50년 동안 계속된 표준이었지만, 최근에 발표된 한 연구 보고서는 그것이 효과가 없다고 말했다.

035 Many gun-rights proponents say these statistics do not indicate a cause-and-effect relationship and note that the rates of gun homicide and other gun crimes in the United States have dropped since highs in the early 1990's. 2020 국가직 9급

어휘 proponent 지지자, 제안자 statistics 통계학, 통계 자료 indicate 나타내다
cause-and-effect relationship 인과관계 note 언급하다, 지적하다

해석 많은 총기 소유권 지지자들은 이러한 통계들이 인과관계를 나타내지 않는다고 말하고 1990년대 초에 최고치를 찍은 이후로 총기 살인과 다른 총기 범죄의 비율이 계속해서 떨어지고 있다는 점을 지적한다.

■ 구문 Check-up ■

※ 다음 문장을 해석하여 문장의 주어(S)와 본동사(V)를 찾아 표시하시오.
(단, 병치 구조로 동사가 여러 개인 경우는 번호를 매길 것)

033 Science has pushed aside gods and demons and revealed a cosmos more intricate and awesome than anything produced by pure imagination.

034 The bee's crushed-body treatment has been standard for fifty years, but a report released recently said that it was ineffective.

035 Many gun-rights proponents say these statistics do not indicate a cause-and-effect relationship and note that the rates of gun homicide and other gun crimes in the United States have dropped since highs in the early 1990's.

정답

033 Science(S) has pushed(V_1) aside gods and demons and revealed(V_2) a cosmos more intricate and awesome than anything produced by pure imagination.

034 The bee's crushed-body treatment(S_1) has been(V_1) standard for fifty years, but a report(S_2) released recently said(V_2) that it was ineffective.

035 Many gun-rights proponents(S) say(V_1) these statistics do not indicate a cause-and-effect relationship and note(V_2) that the rates of gun homicide and other gun crimes in the United States have dropped since highs in the early 1990's.

15 과거완료시제

그 이전부터 과거 어느 시점까지의 '완료 · 경험 · 계속 · 결과'

ex I had finished the work when he came. (완료)
그가 왔을 때 나는 일을 끝냈었다.

I recognized her, for I had met her before. (경험)
나는 전에 그녀를 만난 적이 있었기 때문에, 그녀를 알아보았다.

I had lived here for ten years before I moved to Busan. (계속)
나는 부산으로 이사 가기 전에 여기에서 10년 동안 살았었다.

I had lost my watch when I left the train. (결과)
기차에서 내렸을 때에는 시계가 없었다.

036 By 1955 Nikita Khrushchev had emerged as Stalin's successor in the USSR. and he embarked on a policy of "peaceful coexistence" whereby East and West were to continue their competition, but in a less confrontational manner. 2019 서울시 9급

어휘 successor 후계자 USSR 구소련 embark on 착수하다, 시작하다 coexistence 공존 whereby 그것에 의해서 confrontational 대립적인

해석 1955년까지는 이미 니키타 흐루쇼프는 구소련에서 스탈린의 후계자로 떠올랐고, 그는 "평화 공존" 정책에 착수했는데, 그 정책에서 동서양이 경쟁은 계속하되, 대립은 덜 하도록 하는 것이었다.

037 Before she traveled to Mexico last winter, she needed to brush up on her Spanish because she had not practiced it since college. 2014 국가직 9급

어휘 brush up on 복습하다, 연마하다 practice 연습하다

해석 대학 시절 이후로 스페인어를 써본 적이 없었기 때문에, 그녀는 작년 겨울에 멕시코로 여행을 가기 전에 스페인어를 다시 복습해야 했다.

구문 Check-up

※ 다음 문장을 해석하여 문장의 주어(S)와 본동사(V)를 찾아 표시하시오.
(단, 병치 구조로 동사가 여러 개인 경우는 번호를 매길 것)

036 By 1955 Nikita Khrushchev had emerged as Stalin's successor in the USSR. and he embarked on a policy of "peaceful coexistence" whereby East and West were to continue their competition, but in a less confrontational manner.

037 Before she traveled to Mexico last winter, she needed to brush up on her Spanish because she had not practiced it since college.

정답

036 By 1955 Nikita Khrushchev(S_1) had emerged(V_1) as Stalin's successor in the USSR. and he(S_2) embarked(V_2) on a policy of peaceful coexistence" whereby East and West were to continue their competition, but in a less confrontational manner.

037 Before she traveled to Mexico last winter, she(S) needed(V) to brush up on her Spanish because she had not practiced it since college.

16 진행시제

특정 시점에서 일시적으로 동작이 계속되는 것을 나타낸다.

ex He is studying hard right now. (현재진행)
그는 바로 지금 열심히 공부하고 있다.

I was taking a bath when the bell rang. (과거진행)
벨이 울렸을 때 나는 목욕을 하고 있었다.

It will be raining when we get there. (미래진행)
우리가 그곳에 도착할 때 비가 오고 있을 것이다.

*왕래발착동사는 현재진행시제가 가까운 미래의 예정을 나타낼 수 있다.

ex She is leaving Korea tomorrow.
그녀는 내일 한국을 떠날 예정이다.

038 In recent years, the world has made tremendous advances in fields ranging from biology to information technology, and yet not everyone is benefiting from these innovations.

2012 지방직 9급

어휘 tremendous 엄청난 advance 진전, 발달 range from A to B 범위가 A에서 B까지다
benefit 이익을 얻다 innovation 혁신

해석 최근 몇 년 동안에, 세계는 생물학에서 정보 기술에 이르는 분야까지 어마어마한 진보를 이루었다. 그러나 모든 사람이 이러한 혁신으로부터 혜택을 받고 있지는 않다.

039 Even in rural America few children are still roaming in a free-ranging manner, unaccompanied by adults. 2019 지방직 9급

어휘 roam 어슬렁거리며 돌아다니다 unaccompanied 동행하지 않은, 혼자인

해석 미국 시골에서서도 어른과 동행하지 않고 여전히 자유롭게 돌아다니고 있는 아이들은 거의 없다.

구문 Check-up

※ 다음 문장을 해석하여 문장의 주어(S)와 본동사(V)를 찾아 표시하시오.
(단, 병치 구조로 동사가 여러 개인 경우는 번호를 매길 것)

038 In recent years, the world has made tremendous advances in fields ranging from biology to information technology, and yet not everyone is benefiting from these innovations.

039 Even in rural America few children are still roaming in a free-ranging manner, unaccompanied by adults.

정답

038 In recent years, the world(S_1) has made(V_1) tremendous advances in fields ranging from biology to information technology, and yet not everyone(S_2) is benefiting(V_2) from these innovations.

039 Even in rural America few children(S) are still roaming(V) in a free-ranging manner, unaccompanied by adults.

17 수동태

수동태의 주어는 항상 의미상 동사의 목적어이다.

ex) He was beaten black and blue by her.
I was called upon to help her with her assignments.

040 A church was built there in the middle of farmland during the 19th century and has been maintained continuously as a church ever since, while the land around it was being farmed. 2017 지방직 9급

어휘 farmland 농지 maintain 유지하다

해석 교회는 19세기에 농지의 한가운데에 지어졌으며 이후로 쭉 교회로 계속 유지되어 왔고 주변의 땅은 경작이 되고 있었다.

041 The old model, in place for over three decades, was based on industrial protectionism, foreign borrowing, the exploitation of natural resources, and domestic budget deficits. 2013 서울시 7급

어휘 decade 십년 be based on ~에 기초하다 protectionism 보호주의 exploitation 개발; 착취 domestic 국내의 budget deficit 재정적자

해석 삼십 년 이상 동안 자리를 잡아왔던 과거의 모델은 산업 보호주의, 차관, 천연자원 개발, 그리고 국내 재정 적자에 토대하고 있었다.

042 Any effects of birth order on intelligence or personality will likely be washed out by all the other influences in a person's life. 2013 국가직 9급

어휘 intelligence 지능 personality 성격 wash out 씻어 버리다

해석 지능이나 성격에 미치는 출생 순서의 그 어떠한 영향도, 한 사람의 삶에 끼치는 다른 모든 영향력들에 의하여 씻겨 사라져 버릴 것이다.

■ 구문 Check-up ■

※ 다음 문장을 해석하여 문장의 주어(S)와 본동사(V)를 찾아 표시하시오.
(단, 병치 구조로 동사가 여러 개인 경우는 번호를 매길 것)

040 A church was built there in the middle of farmland during the 19th century and has been maintained continuously as a church ever since, while the land around it was being farmed.

041 The old model, in place for over three decades, was based on industrial protectionism, foreign borrowing, the exploitation of natural resources, and domestic budget deficits.

042 Any effects of birth order on intelligence or personality will likely be washed out by all the other influences in a person's life.

정답

040 A church(S) was built(V_1) there in the middle of farmland during the 19th century and has been maintained(V_2) continuously as a church ever since, while the land around it was being farmed.

041 The old model(S), in place for over three decades, was based(V) on industrial protectionism, foreign borrowing, the exploitation of natural resources, and domestic budget deficits.

042 Any effects(S) of birth order on intelligence or personality will likely be washed(V) out by all the other influences in a person's life.

18 완료형 · 진행형의 수동태

1 완료형 수동태 : have been p.p

ex He has written a letter.
= A letter has been written by him.
그는 편지를 썼다.

2 진행형 수동태 : be being p.p

ex He must be writing a letter.
= A letter must be being written by him.
그는 편지를 쓰고 있음에 틀림없다.

3 완료 진행형 수동태 : have been being p.p

ex He has been writing a lot of letters.
= A lot of letters have been being written by him.
그는 많은 편지를 써오고 있다.

043 Soldiers who have been temporarily deprived of salt report that at its maximum intensity the craving for salt is more insistent than the desire for food itself. 2014 지방직 9급

어휘 temporarily 일시적으로 deprive 빼앗다 maximum 최대의 intensity 강도 crave 열망하다 insistent 집요한

해석 일시적으로 소금을 박탈당한 군인들이 말한 바에 따르면, 소금에 대한 갈망은 그 강도가 최대일 때 음식 자체에 대한 욕구보다 더 집요하다고 한다.

044 Such a calculation not only involves a translation process, but scientists have been handicapped by lack of knowledge of what to count. 2017 국가직 9급

어휘 calculation 계산 translation process 번역 과정 handicap 불리하게 하다, 괴롭히다 lack 부족

해석 그러한 계산은 번역 과정을 포함할 뿐만 아니라 과학자들은 무엇을 중요하게 여겨야 하는지에 대한 지식 부족으로 인해 어려움을 겪어 왔다.

045 Despite the growing sophistication of signal-detecting radio telescopes, no such signals have been found, except for a few unexpected – never redetected – anomalies. 2010 서울시 9급

어휘 sophistication 정교화, 첨단화 signal-detecting 신호를 탐지하는 radio telescope 전파 망원경 unexpected 예기치 않은 redetect 재탐지하다 anomaly 예외, 이례

해석 신호를 감지하는 전파 망원경들이 날로 정교해지고 있음에도 불구하고, 몇 개의 예상 못한 - 다시는 재탐색이 되지 않은 - 예외를 제외하고는 그런 신호들은 발견되지 않았다.

046 Until recently many experts assumed that under the influence of universal literacy and mass media, regional dialects were being leveled. 2014 국가직 9급

어휘 assume 가정하다 universal 보편적인 literacy 읽고 쓰는 능력 regional dialect 지방 사투리 level 완전히 파괴하다

해석 최근까지 많은 전문가들이 읽고 쓰는 능력의 보편적인 보급과 대중 매체의 영향으로 인하여 지역 방언 간의 차이가 파괴되고 있다고 가정했다.

047 Weekly movie and concert schedules are being finalized and will be posted outside the cafeteria every Wednesday. 2014 국가직 9급

어휘 finalize 확정하다 post 게시하다

해석 주간 영화와 콘서트 스케줄이 최종적으로 확정되는 중이며, 그리고 매주 수요일 식당 바깥에 게시될 것입니다.

■ 구문 Check-up ■

※ 다음 문장을 해석하여 문장의 주어(S)와 본동사(V)를 찾아 표시하시오.
(단, 병치 구조로 동사가 여러 개인 경우는 번호를 매길 것)

043 Soldiers who have been temporarily deprived of salt report that at its maximum intensity the craving for salt is more insistent than the desire for food itself.

044 Such a calculation not only involves a translation process, but scientists have been handicapped by lack of knowledge of what to count.

045 Despite the growing sophistication of signal-detecting radio telescopes, no such signals have been found, except for a few unexpected — never redetected — anomalies.

046 Until recently many experts assumed that under the influence of universal literacy and mass media, regional dialects were being leveled.

047 Weekly movie and concert schedules are being finalized and will be posted outside the cafeteria every Wednesday.

정답

043 Soldiers(S) who have been temporarily deprived of salt report(V) that at its maximum intensity the craving for salt is more insistent than the desire for food itself.

044 Such a calculation(S_1) not only involves(V_1) a translation process, but scientists(S_2) have been handicapped(V_2) by lack of knowledge of what to count.

045 Despite the growing sophistication of signal-detecting radio telescopes, no such signals(S) have been found(V), except for a few unexpected — never redetected — anomalies.

046 Until recently many experts(S) assumed(V) that under the influence of universal literacy and mass media, regional dialects were being leveled.

047 Weekly movie and concert schedules(S) are being finalized(V_1) and will be posted(V_2) outside the cafeteria every Wednesday.

19 수여동사의 수동태

목적어가 두 개이기 때문에 두 가지 수동태가 가능하다.

*직접목적어가 수동태의 주어로 나가고 간접목적어가 남을 때 그 앞에 전치사를 붙인다.

ex John gave Mary a watch.
= Mary was given a watch by John.
= A watch was given to Mary by John.
존은 매리에게 시계를 주었다.

*'buy, make, write, sing, sell, read' 등은 직접목적어만 수동태의 주어가 될 수 있다.

ex He bought me a book.
= I was bought a book by him. (×)
= A book was bought for me by him. (○)
그는 나에게 책을 사 줬다.

048 Hence, people should be allowed free access to such facilities. 2014 지방직 9급

어휘 hence 따라서, 그러므로 access 접근, 입장 facility 시설; 용이함; 재능
해석 따라서 사람들은 무료로 그러한 시설들을 이용할 수 있어야 한다.

049 When the children had originally been shown what we think of as an object, like the copper tee, they pointed to an object of the same shape but a different substance, such as a plastic plumbing tee, not to the same substance with a different shape, namely a pile of copper bits. 2014 국가직 9급

어휘 originally 처음, 본래 copper 구리 tee T형강 point at 가리키다 substance 물질, 재료 plumbing 배관 pile 더미 bit 조각
해석 T배관처럼 아이들이 우리가 물체로 간주하는 것을 처음 보게 되었을 때, 그들은 가령 구리 조각 더미처럼 다른 모양을 가진 동일한 물질이 아니라, 플라스틱 T배관처럼 동일한 모양이지만 다른 물질로 된 물체를 가리켰다.

구문 Check-up

※ 다음 문장을 해석하여 문장의 주어(S)와 본동사(V)를 찾아 표시하시오.
(단, 병치 구조로 동사가 여러 개인 경우는 번호를 매길 것)

048 Hence, people should be allowed free access to such facilities.

049 When the children had originally been shown what we think of as an object, like the copper tee, they pointed to an object of the same shape but a different substance, such as a plastic plumbing tee, not to the same substance with a different shape, namely a pile of copper bits.

정답

048 Hence, people(S) should be allowed(V) free access to such facilities.

049 When the children had originally been shown what we think of as an object, like the copper tee, they(S) pointed(V) to an object of the same shape but a different substance, such as a plastic plumbing tee, not to the same substance with a different shape, namely a pile of copper bits.

20 목적어가 that절인 경우의 수동태

가주어 it을 사용하여 'it is ~ that …' 구문으로 변환하거나 또는 that절 안의 주어를 수동태의 주어로 할 수 있다.

They say / think / believe / know + that S + V
= It is said / thought / believed / known + that S + V
= S + be said / thought / believed / known + to V

ex They say that she is very rich.
= It is said that she is very rich.
= She is said to be very rich.
사람들은 그녀가 부자라고 말한다.

*that절이 수여동사의 직접목적어인 경우 가주어를 이용한 수동태는 쓸 수 없고 간접목적어를 수동태의 주어로 한다.

ex They convinced me that he was right.
= I was convinced that he was right.
그들은 나에게 그가 옳다는 것을 확신시켰다.

050 It is said that a group of drugs referred to as the "anticholinergics" are risky in this age group. 2009 국회직 8급

어휘 refer to A as B A를 B로 부르다 anticholinergics 콜린 억제제 risky 위험한
해석 "콜린 억제제"로 일컬어지는 약물들은 이 나이 그룹에서 위험스러운 것으로 전해지고 있다.

051 By the 1920s it was thought that no corner of the earth fit for human habitation had remained unexplored. New Guinea, the world's second largest island, was no exception. 2016 기상직 9급

어휘 fit 적합하다 habitation 거주 unexplored 미지의, 탐험이 안 된 exception 예외
해석 1920년대까지 인간의 거주에 적합한 지구의 모든 지역에 사람의 발길이 닿았다고 생각되었다. 세계에서 두 번째로 큰 섬인 New Guinea도 예외는 아니었다.

052 For much of the history of modern neuroscience, the adult brain was believed to be a fixed structure that, once damaged, could not be repaired. 2017 사회복지직 9급

어휘 neuroscience 신경과학 fixed 고정된 damage 해를 주다, 손상을 입히다 repair 수리하다
해석 많은 근대 신경과학 역사에 따르면, 성인의 뇌는 고정된 구조로, 한번 손상을 입게 되면 회복이 될 수 없다고 간주되었다.

■ 구문 Check-up ■

※ 다음 문장을 해석하여 문장의 주어(S)와 본동사(V)를 찾아 표시하시오.
(단, 병치 구조로 동사가 여러 개인 경우는 번호를 매길 것)

050 It is said that a group of drugs referred to as the "anticholinergics" are risky in this age group.

051 By the 1920s it was thought that no corner of the earth fit for human habitation had remained unexplored. New Guinea, the world's second largest island, was no exception.

052 For much of the history of modern neuroscience, the adult brain was believed to be a fixed structure that, once damaged, could not be repaired.

정답

050 It is said(V) that a group of drugs referred to as the anticholinergics are risky in this age group(S).

051 By the 1920s it was thought(V) that no corner of the earth fit for human habitation had remained unexplored(S). New Guinea(S), the world's second largest island, was(V) no exception.

052 For much of the history of modern neuroscience, the adult brain(S) was believed(V) to be a fixed structure that, once damaged, could not be repaired.

21 가정법 과거

현재 사실을 반대로 가정할 때 쓴다.

If + S + 과거 ~, S + would / should / could / might + V : 만약 ~하면, …할 텐데

ex) If I knew the answer, I could tell you.
내가 답을 안다면 너에게 말해 줄 수 있을 텐데.

*if절의 be동사는 인칭과 관계없이 were를 쓴다.

ex) If he were honest, I would employ him.
그가 정직하다면 그를 고용할 텐데.

*if절에 조동사는 could만 올 수 있다.

ex If I could sing as well as you, I would be a singer.
내가 너만큼 노래를 잘 할 수 있다면 가수가 될 텐데.

053 If we could pull the plug on the world's oceans, it would be quite clear that Zealandia stands out about 3,000 meters above the surrounding ocean crust. 2017 하반기 국가직 9급

어휘 pull the plug on ~을 끝장내다, 마개를 뽑아버리다 stand out 우뚝 서다, 눈에 두드러지다 ocean crust 대양지각

해석 우리가 세계의 바다를 모두 없애버릴 수 있다면, 뉴질랜드가 대양지각에서 3000미터 가량 위로 우뚝 솟아 있는 것이 명확히 보일 것이다.

054 According to their belief, if the artists captured an animal's true likeness, they would be sure to capture the real thing during the hunt. 2008 법원직 9급

어휘 artist 예술가 capture 포착하다, 체포하다 likeness 유사함

해석 그들의 믿음에 따르면, 만일 그 예술가들이 동물의 진정한 모습을 포착한다면, 그들은 사냥하는 동안에 진짜 그 동물을 잡을 수 있다고 확신한다.

구문 Check-up

※ 다음 문장을 해석하여 문장의 주어(S)와 본동사(V)를 찾아 표시하시오.
(단, 병치 구조로 동사가 여러 개인 경우는 번호를 매길 것)

053 If we could pull the plug on the world's oceans, it would be quite clear that Zealandia stands out about 3,000 meters above the surrounding ocean crust.

054 According to their belief, if the artists captured an animal's true likeness, they would be sure to capture the real thing during the hunt.

정답

053 If we could pull the plug on the world's oceans, it would be(V) quite clear that Zealandia stands out about 3,000 meters above the surrounding ocean crust(S).

054 According to their belief, if the artists captured an animal's true likeness, they(S) would be(V) sure to capture the real thing during the hunt.

22 가정법 과거완료

과거 사실을 반대로 가정할 때 쓴다.

If + S + had p.p ~, S + would / should / could / might + have p.p…: 만약 ~했다면, …했을 텐데

ex If I had studied hard, I would have passed the exam.
내가 열심히 공부했다면, 시험에 합격했을 텐데.

*if절에 조동사는 'could have p.p'만 올 수 있다.

ex If he could have helped us, we would have finished it.
그가 우리를 도울 수 있었다면, 우리는 그 일을 끝냈을 텐데.

055 If he had taken more money out of the bank, he could have bought the shoes. 2013 지방직 9급

해석 만일 그가 은행에서 더 많은 돈을 인출해 두었더라면, 그는 그 신발을 살 수 있었을 텐데.

056 In most cases, primates have visible folds that they would not have if they had, even lightly, groomed the area. 2017 법원직 9급

어휘 primate 영장류 visible 눈에 보이는 fold 주름 groom 손질하다, 빗질하다
해석 대부분의 경우, 영장류는 만일 그들이 그 부위를 가볍게라도 손질했다면 가지게 되지 않았을 눈에 띄는 주름을 가지고 있다.

구문 Check-up

※ 다음 문장을 해석하여 문장의 주어(S)와 본동사(V)를 찾아 표시하시오.
(단, 병치 구조로 동사가 여러 개인 경우는 번호를 매길 것)

055 If he had taken more money out of the bank, he could have bought the shoes.

056 In most cases, primates have visible folds that they would not have if they had, even lightly, groomed the area.

정답

055 If he had taken more money out of the bank, he(S) could have bought(V) the shoes.
056 In most cases, primates(S) have(V) visible folds that they would not have if they had, even lightly, groomed the area.

23 if의 생략

if절에 were / had / should가 있는 경우 if를 생략할 수 있으며, 이런 경우 주어와 동사가 도치된다.

Were / Had / Should + S ~

ex Were he honest, I would employ him.
= If he were honest, I would employ him.
그가 정직하다면, 나는 그를 고용할 텐데.

Had I known the answer, I could have told you.
= If I had known the answer, I could have told you.
내가 해답을 알았더라면, 너에게 말을 했을 텐데.

Should it rain tomorrow, we will / would not go on a picnic.
= If it should rain tomorrow, we will / would not go on a picnic.
내일 혹시라도 비가 온다면, 우리는 소풍을 가지 않을 것이다.

057 Had the computer parts been delivered earlier, we could have been able to complete the project on time. 2009 국가직 7급

어휘 part 부품 deliver 배달하다 complete 끝내다, 완성하다 on time 제때에
해석 컴퓨터 부품이 좀 더 일찍 배달되었더라면, 우리는 그 프로젝트를 제시간에 마칠 수 있었을 텐데.

058 Should such a terrible earthquake hit the area, no one can tell how devastating the aftermath will be. 2012 서울시 9급

어휘 terrible 끔찍한 earthquake 지진 devastating 파괴적인; 매혹적인 aftermath 영향, 여파
해석 혹시라도 그토록 끔찍한 지진이 그 지역을 친다면, 아무도 그 결과가 얼마나 파괴적일지 알 수 없다.

059 Had the companies been notified of the possibility of a strike, they would have taken extra measures. 2007 국회직 8급

어휘 notify 공지하다, 통지하다 strike 파업 extra 여분의 measure 조치
해석 만일 그 회사들이 파업의 가능성을 통보받았더라면, 그들은 별도의 조치를 취했을 것이다.

구문 Check-up

※ 다음 문장을 해석하여 문장의 주어(S)와 본동사(V)를 찾아 표시하시오.
(단, 병치 구조로 동사가 여러 개인 경우는 번호를 매길 것)

057 Had the computer parts been delivered earlier, we could have been able to complete the project on time.

058 Should such a terrible earthquake hit the area, no one can tell how devastating the aftermath will be.

059 Had the companies been notified of the possibility of a strike, they would have taken extra measures.

정답

057 Had the computer parts been delivered earlier, we(S) could have been(V) able to complete the project on time.

058 Should such a terrible earthquake hit the area, no one(S) can tell(V) how devastating the aftermath will be.

059 Had the companies been notified of the possibility of a strike, they(S) would have taken(V) extra measures.

24 without / but for

'~이 없다면'의 뜻의 전치사로 if절의 역할을 한다. 주절의 가정법 과거인지 과거완료인지에 따라 다음 두 가지 의미로 해석된다.

If it were not for ~ = Were it not for ~ : ~이 없다면

If it had not been for ~ = Had it not been for ~ : ~이 없었다면

ex Without / But for water, nothing could live.
= If it were not for water, nothing could live.
= Were it not for water, nothing could live.
만일 물이 없다면, 아무것도 살 수 없을 것이다.

Without / But for your help, I would not have succeeded.
= If it had not been for your help, I would not have succeeded.
= Had it not been for your help, I would not have succeeded.
만일 당신의 도움이 없었다면, 나는 성공하지 못했을 것이다.

060 If it had not been for Newton, the law of gravitation would not have been discovered.
2012 지방직 9급

어휘 gravitation 중력 discover 발견하다
해석 뉴턴이 없었다면 중력의 법칙은 발견되지 않았을 것이다.

061 Were it not for the refraction, the sun would just then actually have its lower edge a little more than half a degree below the horizon. 2011 법원직 9급

어휘 refraction 굴절 edge 가장자리, 끝 horizon 지평선
해석 만약 굴절이 없다면, 그때 태양은 실제로 0.5도 이상 지평선 아래로 그 끝부분이 위치할 것이다.

062 Were it not for public acceptance of a single yardstick of time, social life would be unbearably chaotic: the massive daily transfers of goods, services, and information would proceed in fits and starts; the very fabric of modern society would begin to unravel. 2012 법원직 9급

어휘 acceptance 용인, 수락 single 하나의, 단일한 yardstick 기준, 척도 unbearably 참을 수 없이 chaotic 혼란스러운 massive 거대한, 방대한 transfer 이송, 운송 proceed 진행되다 in fits 간헐적으로 fabric 구조 unravel 풀리다, 혼란스러워지다
해석 단일 시간 기준에 대한 공공의 동의가 없다면, 사회적 삶은 참을 수 없을 정도로 혼란스러울 것이다. 재화, 용역, 정보의 매일 같은 엄청난 이동은 간헐적으로 진행될 것이다. 또한 현대 사회의 바로 그 기본 구조는 흐트러지기 시작할 것이다.

구문 Check-up

※ 다음 문장을 해석하여 문장의 주어(S)와 본동사(V)를 찾아 표시하시오.
(단, 병치 구조로 동사가 여러 개인 경우는 번호를 매길 것)

060 If it had not been for Newton, the law of gravitation would not have been discovered.

061 Were it not for the refraction, the sun would just then actually have its lower edge a little more than half a degree below the horizon.

062 Were it not for public acceptance of a single yardstick of time, social life would be unbearably chaotic: the massive daily transfers of goods, services, and information would proceed in fits and starts; the very fabric of modern society would begin to unravel.

정답

060 If it had not been for Newton, the law of gravitation(S) would not have been discovered(V).

061 Were it not for the refraction, the sun(S) would just then actually have(V) its lower edge a little more than half a degree below the horizon.

062 Were it not for public acceptance of a single yardstick of time, social life(S_1) would be(V_1) unbearably chaotic: the massive daily transfers(S_2) of goods, services, and information would proceed(V_2) in fits and starts; the very fabric(S_3) of modern society would begin(V_3) to unravel.

25 that + 가정법 현재

다음의 동사 또는 그 명사들처럼 '당위성'의 내용을 내포하는 단어들 뒤에 that절이 오면 가정법 현재의 '(should) + 동사원형'이 쓰인다.

insist / urge 주장하다, ask / demand / require / request 요구하다, order 명령하다, suggest / propose / move 제안하다, advise / recommend 충고하다, decide 결정하다

ex He insisted that I (should) be present at the meeting.
그는 내가 회의에 참석해야 한다고 주장했다.

He demands that she (should) help him.
그는 그녀가 그를 도울 것을 요구한다.

He made a suggestion that we (should) leave early.
그는 우리가 일찍 출발해야 한다는 제안을 했다.

063 I do, however, ask that medication be mercifully administered to me to alleviate suffering even though this may shorten my remaining life. 2009 국회직 8급

어휘 medication 약물 mercifully 자비롭게 administer 투약하다 alleviate 경감하다, 완화시키다 shorten 단축하다 remaining 남아 있는

해석 그러나 나는 비록 이것이 나의 남은 생명을 단축시킬지라도 고통을 완화시키기 위하여 약물이 자비롭게 나에게 투여되기를 진정으로 요청한다.

064 She wore one of her "outfits" — a purple pantsuit, a scarf, high heels, and sunglasses, and she insisted that I wear a white shirt and a necktie. 2009 법원직 9급

어휘 outfit 의상, 복장 purple 자주색의 insist 주장하다, 고집하다

해석 그녀는 자주색 팬츠와 스카프, 하이힐과 선글라스의 "복장"을 하고 있었고 나는 흰 셔츠와 넥타이를 입어야 한다고 주장했다.

065 An old friend suggested that rather than paying for people's coffee, Ryan put that money towards helping school students pay off their delinquent school lunch accounts. 2016 서울시 9급

어휘 suggest 제안하다; 암시하다 pay off 갚다, 변제하다 delinquent 체납된; 비행의 account 계좌

해석 오랜 친구 한 명이 사람들의 커피 값을 대신 낼 게 아니라, Ryan이 그 돈을 학교 점심 값이 밀린 학생들이 점심 값을 지불하는 데 도움이 되도록 그 돈을 내놓을 것을 제안했다.

■ 구문 Check-up ■

※ 다음 문장을 해석하여 문장의 주어(S)와 본동사(V)를 찾아 표시하시오. (단, 병치 구조로 동사가 여러 개인 경우는 번호를 매길 것)

063 I do, however, ask that medication be mercifully administered to me to alleviate suffering even though this may shorten my remaining life.

064 She wore one of her "outfits" — a purple pantsuit, a scarf, high heels, and sunglasses, and she insisted that I wear a white shirt and a necktie.

065 An old friend suggested that rather than paying for people's coffee, Ryan put that money towards helping school students pay off their delinquent school lunch accounts.

정답

063 I(S) do, however, ask(V) that medication be mercifully administered to me to alleviate suffering even though this may shorten my remaining life.

064 She(S_1) wore(V_1) one of her "outfits" — a purple pantsuit, a scarf, high heels, and sunglasses, and she(S_2) insisted(V_2) that I wear a white shirt and a necktie.

065 An old friend(S) suggested(V) that rather than paying for people's coffee, Ryan put that money towards helping school students pay off their delinquent school lunch accounts.

26 must

must는 '~해야 한다(have to)'와 '강한 긍정의 추측'의 의미를 갖는다.

066 All students who want to use the library borrowing services and the recreational, athletic, and entertainment facilities must have an authorized summer identification card. 2014 국가직 9급

어휘 recreational 레크레이션의 athletic 운동의 entertainment 오락 facilities 시설 authorized 공인된, 승인받은 identification 신원 확인

해석 도서관 대여 서비스 그리고 레크리에이션, 운동 그리고 오락 시설을 이용하고자 하는 모든 학생들은 공인된 여름용 신원 확인 카드를 소지해야 합니다.

067 James speculated that seasickness must be due to some temporary disturbance of the inner ear, a problem to which the deaf mutes were not sensitive at all. 2016 법원직 9급

어휘 speculate 추측하다; 투기하다 seasickness 뱃멀미 due ~때문인 temporary 일시적인 disturbance 장애, 방해 deaf 귀먹은 mute 벙어리 sensitive 민감한, 영향을 받는

해석 제임스는 배 멀미가 벙어리 청각 장애인은 전혀 느끼지 못하는 내이의 일시적인 장애 때문에 발생함에 틀림없다고 추측했다.

구문 Check-up

※ 다음 문장을 해석하여 문장의 주어(S)와 본동사(V)를 찾아 표시하시오.
(단, 병치 구조로 동사가 여러 개인 경우는 번호를 매길 것)

066 All students who want to use the library borrowing services and the recreational, athletic, and entertainment facilities must have an authorized summer identification card.

067 James speculated that seasickness must be due to some temporary disturbance of the inner ear, a problem to which the deaf mutes were not sensitive at all.

정답

066 All students(S) who want to use the library borrowing services and the recreational, athletic, and entertainment facilities must have(V) an authorized summer identification card.

067 James(S) speculated(V) that seasickness must be due to some temporary disturbance of the inner ear, a problem to which the deaf mutes were not sensitive at all.

27 should

1 (사회적, 도덕적) 의무: ~해야 한다

ex You should obey your parents.
너는 부모님에게 순종해야 한다.

You should not tell a lie.
너는 거짓말을 해서는 안 된다.

*'강조'의 의미를 전달할 경우 ought to로 바꾸어 쓸 수 있다.

ex You ought to obey your parents.
너는 부모님에게 순종해야 한다.

*ought to의 부정은 ought not to이다.

ex) You ought not to tell a lie.
너는 거짓말을 해서는 안 된다.

2 다음의 감정적 판단을 나타내는 형용사나 명사 뒤에 오는 that절에 should가 쓰이면 '~하다니'의 뜻이다.

surprising, strange, curious, odd, regrettable, a pity

ex) It is surprising that she should say such a thing.
그녀가 그런 말을 하다니 놀랍다.

*과거의 일은 'should have p.p'로 나타낸다.

ex) It is surprising that she should have failed in the exam.
그녀가 시험에 떨어졌다니 놀랍다.

068 Despite the fact that the priority should be to create infrastructure such as roads, schools, and hospitals, what often happens is that incompetent and corrupt officials end up misusing or stealing the money. 2015 경찰직

어휘 priority 우선사항 create 창조하다 infrastructure 기반시설, 기간산업 incompetent 무능한 corrupt 타락한 end up ~로 끝나다 misuse 오용하다, 남용하다

해석 우선순위가 도로, 학교, 병원과 같은 기반시설을 만드는 것이어야 한다는 사실에도 불구하고, 종종 발생하는 일은 무능하고 부패한 관료들이 결국 그 자금을 오용하거나 훔치고 있다는 것이다.

구문 Check-up

※ 다음 문장을 해석하여 문장의 주어(S)와 본동사(V)를 찾아 표시하시오.
(단, 병치 구조로 동사가 여러 개인 경우는 번호를 매길 것)

068 Despite the fact that the priority should be to create infrastructure such as roads, schools, and hospitals, what often happens is that incompetent and corrupt officials end up misusing or stealing the money.

정답

068 Despite the fact that the priority should be to create infrastructure such as roads, schools, and hospitals, what often happens(S) is(V) that incompetent and corrupt officials end up misusing or stealing the money.

28 조동사 + have p.p

1 과거 사실에 대한 추측

may have p.p : ~했을지도 모른다
must have p.p : ~했음에 틀림없다
cannot have p.p : ~했을 리가 없다

ex) She may have been ill yesterday.
그녀가 어제 아팠을지도 모른다.

She must have been ill yesterday.
그녀가 어제 아팠음에 틀림없다.

She cannot have been ill yesterday.
그녀가 어제 아팠을 리가 없다.

2 과거 사실에 대한 유감

should / ought to have p.p : ~했어야 했는데
had better have p.p : ~하는 게 좋았을 텐데
would rather have p.p : ~하는 게 차라리 좋았을 텐데
need not have p.p : ~할 필요가 없었는데

ex) You should have been more careful.
너는 더 조심했어야 했다.

I would rather have stayed at home.
집에 있는 게 차라리 좋았을 텐데.

You need not have hurried.
서두를 필요는 없었는데.

069 John had just started working for the company, and he was not dry behind the ears yet. We should have given him a break. 2014 지방직 9급

어휘 not dry behind the ears 풋내기인, 애송이인 give a break 기회를 주다
해석 John은 이제 막 그 회사에서 일을 시작했고, 그는 아직 풋내기였다. 우리는 그에게 기회를 주었어야만 했다.

070 More recently, some movies explored the possibility of sustaining human life in outer space, while other films have questioned whether extraterrestrial life forms may have visited our planet. 2019 국가직 9급

어휘 explore 탐험하다, 탐구하다 sustain 유지하다; 부상을 겪다 question 질문을 하다 extraterrestrial 외계의 planet 행성

해석 보다 최근에는, 어떤 영화들이 우주 공간에서 인간의 생명을 유지할 수 있는 가능성을 탐구하는 한편, 다른 영화들은 외계 생명체가 우리 지구를 방문했을지도 모른다는 의문을 던져 왔다.

071 The monastic revival, in particular, had started in France, and many English monks must have studied there. 2018 서울시 7급

어휘 monastic 수도원의 revival 부활 monk 수도승, 승려

해석 특히 수도원 생활의 부흥은 프랑스에서 시작했고 많은 영국 수도승들이 그곳에서 공부했음에 틀림없다.

구문 Check-up

※ 다음 문장을 해석하여 문장의 주어(S)와 본동사(V)를 찾아 표시하시오.
(단, 병치 구조로 동사가 여러 개인 경우는 번호를 매길 것)

069 John had just started working for the company, and he was not dry behind the ears yet. We should have given him a break.

070 More recently, some movies explored the possibility of sustaining human life in outer space, while other films have questioned whether extraterrestrial life forms may have visited our planet.

071 The monastic revival, in particular, had started in France, and many English monks must have studied there.

정답

069 John(S_1) had just started(V_1) working for the company, and he(S_2) was(V_2) not dry behind the ears yet. We(S_3) should have given(V_3) him a break.

070 More recently, some movies(S) explored(V) the possibility of sustaining human life in outer space, while other films have questioned whether extraterrestrial life forms may have visited our planet.

071 The monastic revival(S_1), in particular, had started(V_1) in France, and many English monks(S_2) must have studied(V_2) there.

CHAPTER

02 준동사

29 be to부정사

'be to'는 의미상 일종의 조동사 역할을 하여 '예정 · 의무 · 가능 · 의도 · 운명'의 뜻을 나타낸다.

ex) We are to arrive there tomorrow. (예정)
우리는 내일 거기에 도착할 예정이다.

You are to obey your parents. (의무)
당신은 부모에게 순종해야 한다.

No one was to be seen on the street. (가능)
길에서 아무도 볼 수 없었다.

If you are to succeed, you must work hard. (의도)
당신은 성공하려면 열심히 일해야 한다.

He was never to return home. (운명)
그는 고향에 돌아오지 못할 운명이었다.

072 On 26 April 2003, the civil courts of the English legal system are to undergo a huge change. 2011 법원직 9급

어휘 civil 민사의 court 법정; 궁정 legal 법률의, 법적인 undergo 경험하다, 겪다 huge 거대한
해석 2003년 4월 26일에 영국의 법률 체계의 민사 법원은 커다란 변화를 겪게 된다.

073 I am convinced that the people of this planet must ultimately and inevitably move toward a single form of world government if civilization is to survive. 2006 법원직 9급

어휘 convince 확신시키다, 납득시키다 ultimately 궁극적으로 inevitably 필연적으로 civilization 문명 survive 생존하다
해석 나는 문명이 계속 살아남기 위해서는 이 지구의 사람들이 반드시 궁극적으로 그리고 명백하게 하나의 세계 정부의 형태로 나아가야만 한다고 확신한다.

■ 구문 Check-up ■

※ 다음 문장을 해석하여 문장의 주어(S)와 본동사(V)를 찾아 표시하시오.
(단, 병치 구조로 동사가 여러 개인 경우는 번호를 매길 것)

072 On 26 April 2003, the civil courts of the English legal system are to undergo a huge change.

073 I am convinced that the people of this planet must ultimately and inevitably move toward a single form of world government if civilization is to survive.

정답

072 On 26 April 2003, the civil courts(S) of the English legal system are(V) to undergo a huge change.

073 I(S) am convinced(V) that the people of this planet must ultimately and inevitably move toward a single form of world government if civilization is to survive.

30 to부정사의 가 / 진주어 · 가 / 진목적어 용법

to부정사가 주어일 때는 보통 가주어 it과 진주어 to부정사로 바꾸어 변환하여 쓴다.

ex To speak English fluently is necessary.
= It is necessary to speak English fluently.
영어를 유창하게 말하는 것이 필요하다.

*to부정사가 불완전타동사 make, believe, consider, think, find의 목적어일 경우 반드시 가목적어 it과 진목적어 to부정사의 형태로 쓴다.

ex I think to speak English fluently necessary. (×)
⇨ I think it necessary to speak English fluently. (○)
나는 영어를 유창하게 말하는 것이 필요하다고 생각한다.

074 It is important to remember that without the greenhouse effect, life on earth as we know it would not be possible. 2008 지방직 7급

어휘 greenhouse effect 온실 효과

해석 온실 효과가 없다면 우리가 알고 있는 지구상의 생명체는 가능하지 않을 것임을 기억하는 것이 중요하다.

075 For it seems reasonable to suppose that a person who is acting in accordance with true statements, and not false ones likely to be true, has more chance of reaching acceptable goals. 2015 서울시 9급

어휘 reasonable 합리적인 suppose 가정하다 in accordance with ~에 따라서
statement 진술, 명제, 지침 acceptable 용인되는, 수용할 만한

해석 왜냐하면 사실일 것 같은 거짓 지침이 아니라, 사실인 지침에 따라 행동하는 사람이 사회적으로 용인되는 목표에 도달할 가능성이 더 많다고 생각하는 것이 합리적으로 보이기 때문이다.

076 A lot of women, however, wear sunscreen before they go out, and this often, makes it more difficult for their body to produce vitamin D — as sunscreen can block vitamin D-producing ultraviolet rays. 2015 지방직 9급

어휘 sunscreen 선크림 block 차단하다 ultraviolet ray 자외선

해석 그러나 많은 여성들이 외출하기 전에 선크림을 바르는데 이는 종종 그들의 몸이 비타민 D를 만드는 것을 어렵게 한다. 왜냐하면 선크림이 비타민 D를 만드는 자외선을 차단하기 때문이다.

구문 Check-up

※ 다음 문장을 해석하여 문장의 주어(S)와 본동사(V)를 찾아 표시하시오.
(단, 병치 구조로 동사가 여러 개인 경우는 번호를 매길 것)

074 It is important to remember that without the greenhouse effect, life on earth as we know it would not be possible.

075 For it seems reasonable to suppose that a person who is acting in accordance with true statements, and not false ones likely to be true, has more chance of reaching acceptable goals.

076 A lot of women, however, wear sunscreen before they go out, and this often, makes it more difficult for their body to produce vitamin D — as sunscreen can block vitamin D-producing ultraviolet rays.

정답

074 It is(V) important to remember(S) that without the greenhouse effect, life on earth as we know it would not be possible.

075 For it seems(V) reasonable to suppose(S) that a person who is acting in accordance with true statements, and not false ones likely to be true, has more chance of reaching acceptable goals.

076 A lot of women(S_1), however, wear(V_1) sunscreen before they go out, and this(S_2) often, makes(V_2) it more difficult for their body to produce vitamin D — as sunscreen can block vitamin D-producing ultraviolet rays.

31 to부정사의 부사적 용법

to V / in order to V / so as to V : ~하기 위하여

ex He studied hard to pass the exam.
그는 시험에 합격하기 위하여 열심히 공부했다.

*강조를 하기 위하여 in order나 so as를 붙일 수 있다.

ex He studied hard in order / so as to pass the exam.
그는 시험에 합격하기 위하여 열심히 공부했다.

*'only to부정사'는 '결과'의 의미를 전달하기도 한다.

ex He tried hard only to fail.
그는 열심히 노력했지만 실패했다.

077 The word cloning also brings to mind the possibility of headless human bodies grown only to be picked apart for their parts. 2018 서울시 7급

어휘 cloning 복제 bring to mind 상기시키다 headless 머리가 없는 pick apart 분해하다, 해체하다 part 부분, 기관

해석 복제라는 말은 또한 머리가 없는 인체가 자라나서 그 기관만을 위해 따로 분리되어질 수도 있는 가능성도 상기시킵니다.

078 The chimpanzee — who puts two sticks together in order to get at a banana because no one of the two is long enough to do the job — uses intelligence. 2015 국가직 9급

어휘 chimpanzee 침팬지 stick 막대기 intelligence 지능

해석 그 둘 중에 어느 것도 그 일을 하기에는 충분하게 길지 않기 때문에 바나나를 획득하기 위하여 그 두 개의 막대기를 연결하는 침팬지는 지능을 사용한다.

구문 Check-up

※ 다음 문장을 해석하여 문장의 주어(S)와 본동사(V)를 찾아 표시하시오.
(단, 병치 구조로 동사가 여러 개인 경우는 번호를 매길 것)

077 The word cloning also brings to mind the possibility of headless human bodies grown only to be picked apart for their parts.

078 The chimpanzee — who puts two sticks together in order to get at a banana because no one of the two is long enough to do the job — uses intelligence.

정답

077 The word(S) cloning also brings(V) to mind the possibility of headless human bodies grown only to be picked apart for their parts.

078 The chimpanzee(S) — who puts two sticks together in order to get at a banana because no one of the two is long enough to do the job — uses(V) intelligence.

32 난이형용사 + to부정사

to부정사가 어렵거나 쉬움의 뜻을 내포하는 '난이'형용사를 수식할 때 문장의 주어는 의미상으로 부정사의 목적어이다.

easy, hard, difficult, impossible, dangerous

ex This book is difficult to read.
= It is difficult to read this book.
이 책은 읽기에 어렵다.

*부정사가 자동사일 경우 적절한 전치사가 필요하다.

ex The river is dangerous to swim. (×)
⇨ The river is dangerous to swim in. (○)
= It is dangerous to swim in the river.
이 강은 수영하기에 위험하다.

079 That will teach them money is not easy to get, and they'll be more careful about spending it. 2012 국회직 7급

어휘 careful 신중한, 주의 깊은

해석 그것은 그들에게 돈은 얻기 쉽지 않다는 것을 가르칠 것이고, 그들은 그것을 소비하는데 대하여 좀 더 신중할 것이다.

080 Since what we're talking about here is the body of unspoken and unexamined assumptions, values, and mythologies which make your world go round, this kind of cultural audit is impossible to conduct without outside help. 2011 국회직 8급

어휘 unspoken 이야기되지 않은 unexamined 검증되지 않은 assumption 가정, 추정 value 가치 mythology 신화 cultural 문화의 audit 조사 conduct 실행하다

해석 우리가 여기서 말하고 있는 것은 당신의 세계를 돌아가게 만드는 거론되지 않고 검증되지 않은 가정, 가치, 신화들의 체계이기 때문에 이런 종류의 문화적 조사는 외부의 도움 없이는 수행하기가 불가능하다.

■ 구문 Check-up ■

※ 다음 문장을 해석하여 문장의 주어(S)와 본동사(V)를 찾아 표시하시오.
(단, 병치 구조로 동사가 여러 개인 경우는 번호를 매길 것)

079 That will teach them money is not easy to get, and they'll be more careful about spending it.

080 Since what we're talking about here is the body of unspoken and unexamined assumptions, values, and mythologies which make your world go round, this kind of cultural audit is impossible to conduct without outside help.

정답

079 That(S_1) will teach(V_1) them money is not easy to get, and they(S_2)'ll be(V_2) more careful about spending it.

080 Since what we're talking about here is the body of unspoken and unexamined assumptions, values, and mythologies which make your world go round, this kind of cultural audit(S) is(V) impossible to conduct without outside help.

33 to부정사 관용 구문

1 too ~ to V: 너무 ~해서 …할 수 없다

ex She is too young to get married.
= She is so young that she can't get married.
그녀는 너무 어려서 결혼 할 수 없다.

2 enough to V: ~할 만큼 충분히 …하다

ex He is rich enough to buy the car.
= He is so rich that he can buy the car.
그는 그 차를 살 만큼 부자이다.

3 so ~ as to V: 매우 ~하여 …하다

ex He studied so hard as to pass the exam.
= He studied so hard that he passed the exam.
그는 매우 열심히 공부해서 시험에 합격했다.

081 "But Daddy" he replied, "I thought Pluto was too cold for anything to live there". 2011 서울시 9급

어휘 reply 대답하다 Pluto 명왕성
해석 "하지만 아빠, 내 생각엔 명왕성은 너무 추워서 무엇도 거기에서 살기 어려울 것 같아요".라고 그는 대답을 했다.

082 Bold claims were made by critics of the day who averred that Russian technology wasn't advanced enough to perform such a feat and therefore the project was a fake.
2008 지방직 9급

어휘 bold 대담한 claim 주장, 요구 aver 공언하다, 확언하다 advanced 발전된, 진전된 feat 업적, 위업 fake 가짜
해석 러시아의 기술이 그러한 위업을 수행할 만큼 충분히 발전하지 않았고 따라서 그 프로젝트는 가짜였다고 단언했던 그 당시의 비평가들에 의하여 대담한 주장들이 제기되었다.

구문 Check-up

※ 다음 문장을 해석하여 문장의 주어(S)와 본동사(V)를 찾아 표시하시오. (단, 병치 구조로 동사가 여러 개인 경우는 번호를 매길 것)

081 "But Daddy", he replied, "I thought Pluto was too cold for anything to live there".

082 Bold claims were made by critics of the day who averred that Russian technology wasn't advanced enough to perform such a feat and therefore the project was a fake.

정답

081 "But Daddy", he(S) replied(V), "I thought Pluto was too cold for anything to live there".
082 Bold claims(S) were made(V) by critics of the day who averred that Russian technology wasn't advanced enough to perform such a feat and therefore the project was a fake.

34 to부정사의 부정

to부정사를 부정할 때는 부정어 not / never를 to 앞에 쓴다.

ex He decided to not go there. (×)
⇨ He decided not to go there. (○)
그는 거기에 가지 않기로 결정했다.

ex He promised to never smoke again. (×)
⇨ He promised never to smoke again. (○)
그는 다시는 담배를 피우지 않겠다고 약속했다.

083 Darwin decided to produce an "abstract" of a longer book on evolution that he was working on, so as not to let anyone else take credit for an idea he had been developing for more than twenty years. 2013 국회직 8급

해석 다윈은 20여 년 동안 자신이 발전시켜 온 아이디어를 다른 사람이 가로채지 못하도록 하기 위하여, 자신이 연구 중인 진화론에 관한 긴 책의 요약본을 만들기로 결심하였다.

구문 Check-up

※ 다음 문장을 해석하여 문장의 주어(S)와 본동사(V)를 찾아 표시하시오.
(단, 병치 구조로 동사가 여러 개인 경우는 번호를 매길 것)

083 Darwin decided to produce an "abstract" of a longer book on evolution that he was working on, so as not to let anyone else take credit for an idea he had been developing for more than twenty years.

정답

083 Darwin(S) decided(V) to produce an "abstract" of a longer book on evolution that he was working on, so as not to let anyone else take credit for an idea he had been developing for more than twenty years.

35 동명사의 역할

1 명사처럼 주어 · 목적어 · 보어로 쓰인다.

ex) Collecting stamps is very interesting. (주어)
우표를 수집하는 것은 매우 재미있다.
I enjoy collecting stamps. (목적어)
나는 우표를 수집하는 것을 즐긴다.
My hobby is collecting stamps. (보어)
나의 취미는 우표를 수집하는 것이다.

2 전치사의 목적어로 to부정사는 올 수 없고, 동명사만 가능하다.

ex) I'm interested in to collect stamps. (×)
⇨ I'm interested in collecting stamps. (○)
나는 우표 수집하는 것에 관심이 있다.

084 Some studies find that having a wide range of social contacts — belonging to community groups as well as having a network of friends — offers the greatest protection. 2013 서울시 7급

어휘 range 범위 belong to ~에 속하다 network 관계망 offer 제공하다 protection 보호
해석 몇몇 연구에 따르면, 가까운 사람들과의 돈독한 관계를 유지하는 것뿐만 아니라 지역 사회의 다양한 그룹에 소속되는 것 등, 광범위한 사회적 관계를 형성해 나가는 것이 최고의 안정감을 제동한다.

085 As people throughout the world strive for economic development and greater prosperity, achieving higher standards of living becomes a dominant motivation in offering attractive business opportunities in new markets. 2015 지방직 7급

어휘 throughout ~에 걸쳐서 strive 노력하다 prosperity 번영 dominant 지배적인 motivation 동기부여 attractive 매력적인
해석 전 세계의 사람들이 경제 발전과 보다 더 높은 번영을 추구하기 때문에, 보다 높은 생활수준을 성취하는 것이 새로운 시장 안에서 매력적인 사업을 제공함에 있어서의 주된 동기가 된다.

086 With the clinic's report in your hand no mechanics will be able to defraud you by telling you that you need major repairs when only a small repair is necessary. 2013 지방직 9급

어휘 clinic 진료소 mechanic 기계공, 정비공 defraud 속이다, 사취하다 major 주요한, 대규모의
해석 자동차 검사 확인서를 손에 들고 있으면, 사소한 수리만 하면 될 때 대규모의 수리가 필요하다고 당신에게 말을 함으로써 당신을 속이려는 정비공은 없을 것이다.

■ 구문 Check-up ■

※ 다음 문장을 해석하여 문장의 주어(S)와 본동사(V)를 찾아 표시하시오.
(단, 병치 구조로 동사가 여러 개인 경우는 번호를 매길 것)

084 Some studies find that having a wide range of social contacts—belonging to community groups as well as having a network of friends—offers the greatest protection.

085 As people throughout the world strive for economic development and greater prosperity, achieving higher standards of living becomes a dominant motivation in offering attractive business opportunities in new markets.

086 With the clinic's report in your hand no mechanics will be able to defraud you by telling you that you need major repairs when only a small repair is necessary.

정답

084 Some studies(S) find(V) that having a wide range of social contacts—belonging to community groups as well as having a network of friends—offers the greatest protection.

085 As people throughout the world strive for economic development and greater prosperity, achieving(S) higher standards of living becomes(V) a dominant motivation in offering attractive business opportunities in new markets.

086 With the clinic's report in your hand no mechanics(S) will be(V) able to defraud you by telling you that you need major repairs when only a small repair is necessary.

36 완료동명사

술어동사보다 동명사의 시제가 앞선 경우 having p.p를 쓴다.

ex He is proud of having been rich when young.
= He is proud that he was rich when young.
그는 젊었을 때 부자였던 것을 자랑스러워한다.

He admitted having stolen the car.
= He admitted that he had stolen the car.
그는 그 차를 훔친 것을 인정했다.

087 Although paying an additional $150 or so per extra day may seem like a lot when you're planning your trip, it will seem a relatively insignificant saving later on if you've gone to the expense and effort to start a trek and then need to come down without having reached the top. 2015 법원직 9급

어휘 additional 추가적인 per ~당 extra 추가의, 여분의 relatively 상대적으로, 비교적 insignificant 사소한, 중요하지 않은 trek (힘든) 여행

해석 여행을 계획 할 때, 추가한 하루당 약 150불을 지불하는 것이 너무 많게 보일 수도 있지만, 돈을 아껴 힘든 여행을 시작하고 정상에 오르지 못하고 내려오게 되는 것보다는 나을 것이다.

구문 Check-up

※ 다음 문장을 해석하여 문장의 주어(S)와 본동사(V)를 찾아 표시하시오. (단, 병치 구조로 동사가 여러 개인 경우는 번호를 매길 것)

087 Although paying an additional US$150 or so per extra day may seem like a lot when you're planning your trip, it will seem a relatively insignificant saving later on if you've gone to the expense and effort to start a trek and then need to come down without having reached the top.

정답

087 Although paying an additional $150 or so per extra day may seem like a lot when you're planning your trip, it(S) will seem(V) a relatively insignificant saving later on if you've gone to the expense and effort to start a trek and then need to come down without having reached the top.

37 to부정사를 목적어로 취하는 동사

다음의 동사는 to부정사를 목적어로 취한다.

want / would like 원하다, hope 희망하다 wish 바라다, expect 기대하다, decide / determine 결정하다, plan 계획하다, promise 약속하다, offer 제의하다, agree 동의하다, manage 그럭저럭 ~하다, tend ~하는 경향이 있다, pretend ~인 체하다, afford ~할 여유가 있다, refuse 거절하다, fail ~하지 못하다, hesitate 망설이다

ex I want going to the movies tonight. (×)

⇨ I want to go to the movies tonight. (○)

나는 오늘 밤에 영화를 보러 가고 싶다.

088 Because the government wishes to discourage people from traveling abroad and spending their money in other countries, the Minister of Finance decided to require Brazilian tourists to deposit $1,200 in a special account before leaving the country.

2009 지방직 9급

어휘 discourage 실망시키다, 낙담시키다 the Minister of Finance 재무장관 decide 결심하다 require 요구하다 deposit 예치하다, 적립하다 account 계좌

해석 왜냐하면 정부는 사람들이 다른 나라를 여행하고 다른 나라에서 소비하는 것을 못하기를 바라기 때문에, 그 재무장관은 브라질 관광객으로 하여금 그 나라를 떠나기 전에 특별 계좌에 1,200불을 예치하도록 요구하기로 결정했다.

089 However, many Protestant sects, such as the Pentecostals and Jehovah's Witnesses, refused to acknowledge the findings of modern science and wanted a return to what they thought were essentials of Christian belief, the Fundamentals. 2013 지방직 7급

어휘 Pretestant 신교의 sect 종파 refuse 거절하다 acknowledge 인정하다 essential 본질 Fundamental 근본주의

해석 그러나, 팬테코스트파와 여호와의 증인들과 같은 많은 신교도 종파들은 근대과학의 발견들을 인정하기를 거부했고, 그들의 생각에 기독교적 믿음의 본질인 근본주의로의 회귀를 원했다.

구문 Check-up

※ 다음 문장을 해석하여 문장의 주어(S)와 본동사(V)를 찾아 표시하시오.
(단, 병치 구조로 동사가 여러 개인 경우는 번호를 매길 것)

088 Because the government wishes to discourage people from traveling abroad and spending their money in other countries, the Minister of Finance decided to require Brazilian tourists to deposit $1,200 in a special account before leaving the country.

089 However, many Protestant sects, such as the Pentecostals and Jehovah's Witnesses, refused to acknowledge the findings of modern science and wanted a return to what they thought were essentials of Christian belief, the Fundamentals.

정답

088 Because the government wishes to discourage people from traveling abroad and spending their money in other countries, the Minister of Finance(S) decided(V) to require Brazilian tourists to deposit $ 1,200 in a special account before leaving the country.

089 However, many Protestant sects(S), such as the Pentecostals and Jehovah's Witnesses, refused(V_1) to acknowledge the findings of modern science and wanted(V_2) a return to what they thought were essentials of Christian belief, the Fundamentals.

38 동명사를 목적어로 취하는 동사

다음의 동사는 동명사를 목적어로 취한다.

enjoy 즐기다, **practice** 연습하다, **avoid / escape** 피하다, **mind** 꺼리다, **dislike** 싫어하다, **resent** 분개하다, **finish** 끝내다, **stop / quit** 멈추다, **give up** 포기하다, **deny** 부인하다, **miss** 놓치다, **delay / postpone / put off** 미루다, **admit** 인정하다, **allow / permit** 허락하다, **advise** 충고하다, **suggest** 제안하다, **consider** 고려하다, **imagine** 상상하다, **appreciate** 감사하다

ex) He enjoys to read detective novels. (×)
⇨ He enjoys reading detective novels. (○)
그는 탐정 소설 읽는 것을 즐긴다.

090 Some wine labels suggest opening the bottle and letting the wine "breathe" for a couple of hours before serving, while others recommend drinking it immediately. 2013 국회직 8급

어휘 label 라벨, 상표 suggest 제안하다 recommend 추천하다 immediately 즉시

해석 어떤 포도주 상표들은 와인을 제공하기 전에, 병을 열어서 와인이 두어 시간 동안 숨을 쉴 수 있도록 하는 것을 추천한다. 반면에 다른 회사들은 와인을 즉시 마실 것을 추천한다.

091 In individualistic cultures, it is easier to consider leaving one job and going to another because it is easier to separate jobs from the self. 2019 서울시 9급

어휘 individualistic 개인주의적인 consider 고려하다 separate 분리하다

해석 개인주의 문화에서는, 자기와 직업을 분리하는 것이 더 쉽기 때문에 한 직업을 버리고 다른 직업으로 가는 것을 고려하는 것이 더 쉽다.

구문 Check-up

※ 다음 문장을 해석하여 문장의 주어(S)와 본동사(V)를 찾아 표시하시오.
(단, 병치 구조로 동사가 여러 개인 경우는 번호를 매길 것)

090 Some wine labels suggest opening the bottle and letting the wine "breathe" for a couple of hours before serving, while others recommend drinking it immediately.

091 In individualistic cultures, it is easier to consider leaving one job and going to another because it is easier to separate jobs from the self.

정답

090 Some wine labels(S) suggest(V) opening the bottle and letting the wine "breathe" for a couple of hours before serving, while others recommend drinking it immediately.

091 In individualistic cultures, it is(V) easier to consider(S) leaving one job and going to another because it is easier to separate jobs from the self.

39 부정사 vs. 동명사 remember / forget / regret

1 remember / forget의 목적어로 to부정사는 미래, 동명사는 과거의 일을 나타낸다.

remember / forget + to V : ~할 것을 기억하다 / 잊다

remember / forget + ~ing : ~한 것을 기억하다 / 잊다

ex I remember/forgot to meet her tomorrow.
나는 내일 그녀를 만날 것을 기억한다 / 잊었다.

I remember/forgot meeting her before.
나는 전에 그녀를 만난 것을 기억한다 / 잊었다.

2 regret도 목적어로 to부정사는 미래, 동명사는 과거의 일을 나타낸다.

regret + to V : ~하게 되어 유감이다

regret + ~ing : ~한 것을 후회하다

ex I regret to say that I can't help you.
도와드릴 수 없다고 말씀드리게 되어 유감입니다.

I regret telling her what I thought.
내가 생각한 것을 그녀에게 말한 것을 후회한다.

092 I remember telling my eight-year-old son Brian, who was keenly interested in outer space, that astronomers had found a moon. 2011 서울시 9급

어휘 keenly 대단히, 예리하게 interested 관심이 있는 astronomer 천문학자
moon (행성 주위를 도는) 위성, 달

해석 나는 우주 공간에 매우 관심이 많은 여덟 살짜리 아들 Brian에게 천문학자들이 위성 하나를 발견했다고 이야기 했던 것을 기억한다.

093 Many people are so focused on sharing their thoughts, opinions, and ideas that they forget to think about how their message will be received, or whether it's a good idea to speak at all. 2016 기상직 9급

어휘 focused 집중을 하는 share 공유하다, 나누다 receive 받다

해석 많은 사람들은 그들의 생각, 의견 그리고 아이디어를 나누는데 너무 집중해서 그들의 메시지가 어떻게 받아들여질 것인지에 대해 혹은 말을 한다는 자체가 좋은 생각인지 아닌지에 대해 생각해야 하는 것을 망각한다.

094 Soon the Pope, realizing that people were seeking the book as a convincing argument in favor of Copernicanism, regretted having allowed its publication. 2008 지방직 7급

어휘 Pope 교황 realize 깨닫다 seek 추구하다 convincing 설득력 있는 argument 논쟁, 주장 in favor of ~를 찬성하는 publication 출판

해석 곧 교황은, 사람들이 코페르니쿠스의 이론을 지지하는 확실한 주장으로서 그 책을 찾고 있다는 것을 깨달았기 때문에, 그 책의 출판을 허락했던 것을 후회했다.

구문 Check-up

※ 다음 문장을 해석하여 문장의 주어(S)와 본동사(V)를 찾아 표시하시오.
(단, 병치 구조로 동사가 여러 개인 경우는 번호를 매길 것)

092 I remember telling my eight-year-old son Brian, who was keenly interested in outer space, that astronomers had found a moon.

093 Many people are so focused on sharing their thoughts, opinions, and ideas that they forget to think about how their message will be received, or whether it's a good idea to speak at all.

094 Soon the Pope, realizing that people were seeking the book as a convincing argument in favor of Copernicanism, regretted having allowed its publication.

정답

092 I(S) remember(V) telling my eight-year-old son Brian, who was keenly interested in outer space, that astronomers had found a moon.

093 Many people(S) are(V) so focused on sharing their thoughts, opinions, and ideas that they forget to think about how their message will be received, or whether it's a good idea to speak at all.

094 Soon the Pope(S), realizing that people were seeking the book as a convincing argument in favor of Copernicanism, regretted(V) having allowed its publication.

40 명사를 수식하는 분사

수식받는 명사와 진행 · 능동의 관계이면 현재분사를, 수동의 관계이면 과거분사를 쓴다.

분사 + 명사 : 분사가 단독으로 오는 경우 전치수식

명사 + 분사 : 분사가 목적어나 부사구 수반할 경우 후치수식

ex a sleeping baby (진행)
잠자고 있는 아기

fallen leaves (완료 – 자동사의 과거분사는 '완료'의 의미인 예외적인 경우에만 허용)
낙엽들

an exciting game (능동)
신나는 경기

a broken window (수동)
깨진 창문

The boy writing a letter is my friend. (진행)
편지를 쓰고 있는 소년이 내 친구이다.

Look at the mountain covered with snow. (수동)
눈으로 덮인 산을 보아라.

095 The United States is a country founded by people persecuted for their religious beliefs, and religious freedom is guaranteed by the Constitution. 2013 지방직 7급

어휘 found 설립하다, 건국하다 persecute 박해하다 religious 종교적인 guarantee 보장하다 Constitution 미국 헌법

해석 미국은 그들의 종교적 신념 때문에 박해받은 사람들에 의하여 세워진 나라이며, 종교의 자유는 헌법에 의하여 보장된다.

096 Berries growing on a bush are simply seed-carriers for the reproduction of the plant; they do not become "food" until they are identified as edible and taken off the bush.
2015 교육행정직 9급

어휘 bush 덤불 seed 씨앗, 종자 carrier 매개체 reproduction 번식 identify 확인하다, 식별하다 edible 식용의

해석 덤불에서 자라는 딸기는, 단지 그 식물의 번식을 위하여 씨앗을 나르는 매개체인 것이다. 덤불에서 채취되어 먹을 수 있다고 판명되기 전까지는, 그들은 "음식"이 되지 않는다.

097 The dream of a bureaucracy freed from interference from elected officials, which has been fancied by public administration theorists for over one hundred years, seems likely to remain just that. 2008 지방직 7급

어휘 bureaucracy 관료주의 free 자유롭게 하다 interference 간섭 elected 선출된 official 공무원 fancy 상상하다; 좋아하다 administration 행정, 집행 theorist 이론가 remain ~인 상태로 남다

해석 선출된 공무원들의 간섭으로부터 자유로운 관료사회에 대한 꿈은, 공공행정 이론가들이 100년이 넘도록 상상했던 바인데, 이는 그냥 그 상태 그대로 있을 것 같다.

구문 Check-up

※ 다음 문장을 해석하여 문장의 주어(S)와 본동사(V)를 찾아 표시하시오. (단, 병치 구조로 동사가 여러 개인 경우는 번호를 매길 것)

095 The United States is a country founded by people persecuted for their religious beliefs, and religious freedom is guaranteed by the Constitution.

096 Berries growing on a bush are simply seed-carriers for the reproduction of the plant ; they do not become “food” until they are identified as edible and taken off the bush.

097 The dream of a bureaucracy freed from interference from elected officials, which has been fancied by public administration theorists for over one hundred years, seems likely to remain just that.

정답

095 The United States(S_1) is(V_1) a country founded by people persecuted for their religious beliefs, and religious freedom(S_2) is(V_2) guaranteed by the Constitution.

096 Berries(S) growing on a bush are(V) simply seed-carriers for the reproduction of the plant; they do not become “food” until they are identified as edible and taken off the bush.

097 The dream(S) of a bureaucracy freed from interference from elected officials, which has been fancied by public administration theorists for over one hundred years, seems(V) likely to remain just that.

41 분사구문

분사구문은 부사절이나 등위절을 분사를 이용하여 부사구로 바꾼 것이다.

ex) Entering the room, I saw a strange sight. (시간)
= When I entered the room, ~
방에 들어갔을 때, 나는 이상한 광경을 보았다.

Having no money, I can't help you. (이유)
= Because I had no money, ~
돈이 없기 때문에, 너를 도울 수 없다.

Turning to the right, you will find the building. (조건)
= If you turn to the right, ~
오른쪽으로 돌면, 그 건물을 찾을 겁니다.

Admitting what you say, I still can't believe you. (양보)
= Though I admitted what you say, ~
네가 말하는 것을 인정해도, 아직 너를 믿을 수 없다.

Walking on tiptoe, I approached her. (동시동작)
= As I walked on tiptoe, ~
발끝으로 걸어서, 나는 그녀에게 다가갔다.

The train left Seoul at 6, arriving in Busan at 12. (연속동작)
= ~, and it arrived in Busan at 12.
기차가 6시에 서울을 떠나서, 12시에 부산에 도착했다.

098 Shortly after the accidental discovery, engineers at Raytheon went to work on Spencer's new idea, developing and refining it to be of practical use. 2016 법원직 9급

어휘 shortly after ~직후에 accidental 우연한 discovery 발견 engineer 기술자, 엔지니어 refine 정제하다, 개량하다 practical 실용적인

해석 뜻밖의 발견 직후에, Raytheon에 있는 엔지니어들은 Spencer의 새로운 아이디어를 돕기 위해 모였고 그것을 실용적으로 사용하기 위해 개발하고 개량했다.

099 Their swoosh logo is now one of the most recognizable images on the planet, rendering the actual name unnecessary. 2016 법원직 9급

어휘 swoosh 부메랑 모양의 logo 로고 recognizable 인식할 수 있는, 알아볼 수 있는 render ~하게 만들다

해석 그들의 부메랑 모양의 로고는 이제 전 세계적으로 가장 잘 알려진 것 중의 하나가 되었으며, 그들의 실제 이름을 불필요하게 만들었다.

100 These parasites and pathogens weaken bees' immune systems, making them even more susceptible to effects of poor nutrition from lack of flowers, particularly in countries with high agricultural intensity and pesticide use. 2016 법원직 9급

어휘 parasite 기생충 pathogen 병원균 immune system 면역체계
susceptible 영향 받기 쉬운, 취약한 effect 영향, 효과 nutrition 영양 agricultural 농업의
intensity 집중도, 집약도 pesticide 해충제, 살충제

해석 이런 기생 동식물과 병원균은 벌의 면역체계를 약화시켜서, 특히나 높은 농업 집약도와 해충제 사용을 가진 나라들에서, 그들을 꽃의 부족으로 인한 영양결핍의 영향에 훨씬 더 취약하게 만들었다.

101 The company that sought adjacencies becomes a second-place competitor, pouring an increasing amount of money into a capability that only supports a narrow piece of its business. 2016 국회직 8급

어휘 adjacency 인접 competitor 경쟁자 pour 쏟아 붓다 capability 능력
support 지지하다, 뒷받침하다

해석 인접영역들(adjacencies)을 추구했던 회사는 이류급의 경쟁자가 되고는, 점차 많은 양의 돈을 그 사업의 협소한 부분만을 뒷받침할 뿐인 능력에 쏟아붓게 된다.

102 Having spent most of his life on the farms in the country, he lived the life he wrote about. 2016 기상직 9급

해석 시골의 농장에서 그의 생의 대부분을 보냈으므로, 그는 그가 글로 쓴 삶을 실제로 살았다.

103 Many of these dictatorships were pro-capitalist, consistent with at least some U.S. ideological goals; thus the United States would form alliances with certain dictators, believing them to be the closest thing their respective nations had to a legitimate government and in any case much better than the alternative of a communist revolution in those nations. 2013 국회직 8급

어휘 dictatorship 독재 pro-capitalist 친 자본자주의자 ideological 이념적인 alliance 동맹, 연합
dictator 독재자 respective 각자의 alternative 대안 communist 공산주의자 revolution 혁명

해석 이러한 독재자들 가운데 많은 사람들은 적어도 미국의 이념적인 목표들 몇 가지와 일맥상통하는 친 자본주의자였다. 따라서 미국은 어떤 독재자들과 동맹을 맺곤 하였다. 이는 그 독재자들이 그나마 그들 각국이 가지고 있는 합법적인 정부에 가장 가까운 형태를 띠고 있다고 믿었기 때문이다. 그리고 어쨌든 그런 나라들에서 공산주의 혁명이라는 대안보다는 훨씬 더 낫기 때문이다.

104 Almost a century later, physicists have discovered that some unknown force is apparently pushing the universe apart, leading some scientists to conclude that Einstein's "cosmological constant" may in fact exist. 2014 서울시 9급

어휘 physicist 물리학자 unknown 알려지지 않은 apparently 분명히 push 밀다 universe 우주
conclude 결론짓다 cosmological constant 우주 상수 exist 존재하다

해석 거의 한 세기 뒤에, 물리학자들은 분명히 어떤 미지의 힘이 우주를 분리시키고 있음을 알아냈고, 이로 인해 일부 학자들은 아인슈타인의 "우주 상수"가 실제로 존재할지도 모른다는 결론을 내리게 되었다.

구문 Check-up

※ 다음 문장을 해석하여 문장의 주어(S)와 본동사(V)를 찾아 표시하시오.
(단, 병치 구조로 동사가 여러 개인 경우는 번호를 매길 것)

098 Shortly after the accidental discovery, engineers at Raytheon went to work on Spencer's new idea, developing and refining it to be of practical use.

099 Their swoosh logo is now one of the most recognizable images on the planet, rendering the actual name unnecessary.

100 These parasites and pathogens weaken bees' immune systems, making them even more susceptible to effects of poor nutrition from lack of flowers, particularly in countries with high agricultural intensity and pesticide use.

101 The company that sought adjacencies becomes a second-place competitor, pouring an increasing amount of money into a capability that only supports a narrow piece of its business.

102 Having spent most of his life on the farms in the country, he lived the life he wrote about.

103 Many of these dictatorships were pro-capitalist, consistent with at least some U.S. ideological goals; thus the United States would form alliances with certain dictators, believing them to be the closest thing their respective nations had to a legitimate government—and in any case much better than the alternative of a communist revolution in those nations.

104 Almost a century later, physicists have discovered that some unknown force is apparently pushing the universe apart, leading some scientists to conclude that Einstein's "cosmological constant" may in fact exist.

정답

098 Shortly after the accidental discovery, engineers(S) at Raytheon went(V) to work on Spencer's new idea, developing and refining it to be of practical use.

099 Their swoosh logo(S) is(V) now one of the most recognizable images on the planet, rendering the actual name unnecessary.

100 These parasites and pathogens(S) weaken(V) bees' immune systems, making them even more susceptible to effects of poor nutrition from lack of flowers, particularly in countries with high agricultural intensity and pesticide use.

101 The company(S) that sought adjacencies becomes(V) a second-place competitor, pouring an increasing amount of money into a capability that only supports a narrow piece of its business.

102 Having spent most of his life on the farms in the country, he(S) lived(V) the life he wrote about.

103 Many of these dictatorships(S) were(V) pro-capitalist, consistent with at least some U.S. ideological goals; thus the United States would form alliances with certain dictators, believing them to be the closest thing their respective nations had to a legitimate government — and in any case much better than the alternative of a communist revolution in those nations.

104 Almost a century later, physicists(S) have discovered(V) that some unknown force is apparently pushing the universe apart, leading some scientists to conclude that Einstein's cosmological constant"may in fact exist.

42 수동분사구문

1 과거분사 앞의 being이나 having been은 보통 생략한다.

단순수동 : (being) p.p

완료수동 : (having been) p.p

ex (Being) Seen from a distance, the stone looks like a human face.
멀리서 보면, 그 돌은 사람의 얼굴처럼 보인다.

(Having been) Written in haste, the book has many mistakes.
급하게 쓰였기 때문에, 그 책은 틀린 것이 많이 있다.

2 형용사 앞에서도 being을 생략할 수 있다.

ex (Being) Angry at my words, he made no reply.
내 말에 화가 나서, 그는 대답을 하지 않았다.

105 Admittedly Carlo had something to celebrate, having been informed by the Minister for War that Napoleone had been granted a scholarship and a place in the military school at Brienne as 'Royal Pupil' whose expenses would be paid by the King. 2016 사회복지직 9급

어휘 admittedly 틀림없이, 확실히 celebrate 축하하다 inform 알리다 the Minister of War 전쟁장관 grant 주다, 허용하다 scholarship 장학금; 학식 military school 군사학교 royal 왕의, 왕실의 expense 비용

해석 틀림없이 Carlo는 전쟁장관으로부터 Napoleone이 장학금을 수여받았고 국왕이 비용을 지급하는 Brienne 군사학교에 '왕실 장학생'으로 들어갈 수 있다는 정보를 받아 축하할 일이 있었다.

106 The annual awards, given by the Institute of Museum and Library Services in Washington, D. C., honor institutions for their collections and community involvement, and include a $10,000 award each. 2014 국가직 9급

어휘 annual 매년의 award 상, 상금 honor 영예를 주다, 존경하다 institution 기관 collection 수집 involvement 참여

해석 워싱턴의 the Institute of Museum and Library Services가 수여하는 그 연례상은 소장품과 지역 사회 참여에 대해 기관들에게 영예를 수여하며 1만 달러의 상금을 포함한다.

107 The European missionaries, planters, and administrators clung to its coastal lowlands, convinced that no one could live in the treacherous mountain range that ran in a solid line down the middle of the island. 2016 기상직 9급

어휘 missionary 전도사 planter 농장주 administrator 행정관 cling to 고수하다, 집착하다 coastal 해안의 lowland 저지대 convince 확신시키다 treacherous 험악한 mountain range 산맥, 산악지방 solid line 일직선

해석 유럽 선교사들, 농장주들, 그리고 행정관들은 누구도 섬의 중심부를 일직선으로 가로지르는 위험한 산악에서 살 수 없다고 확신해서 해안 저지대에서만 거주했다.

108 Backed by an army, an unscrupulous governor could easily take advantage of his power and enrich himself. 2016 국회직 8급

어휘 back 후원하다 unscrupulous 비양심적인 governor 주지사, 총독 take advantage of ~를 이용하다 enrich 부유하게 만들다

해석 군대에 의해서 후원을 받아서, 비양심적인 총독은 쉽사리 자신의 권력을 이용하여 부자가 될 수 있었다.

109 The new study, being published Monday in *The American Journal of Obstetrics and Gynecology*, finds that pregnant women who consume 200 milligrams or more of caffeine a day — the amount in 10 ounces of coffee or 25 ounces of tea — may double their risk of miscarriage. 2013 국가직 7급

어휘 publish 발표하다, 출판하다 pregnant 임신한 consume 소비하다, 먹다 caffeine 카페인 double 두 배로 늘리다 miscarriage 유산

해석 『미국 산부인과 저널』에 월요일에 실린 새로운 연구는, 하루에 200밀리그램 이상의 카페인을 섭취하는 – 이는 10온스의 커피나 25온스의 차에 들어 있는 양이다 – 임산부들은 유산의 위험이 두 배로 증가할 수 있음을 발견한다.

구문 Check-up

※ 다음 문장을 해석하여 문장의 주어(S)와 본동사(V)를 찾아 표시하시오.
(단, 병치 구조로 동사가 여러 개인 경우는 번호를 매길 것)

105 Admittedly Carlo had something to celebrate, having been informed by the Minister for War that Napoleone had been granted a scholarship and a place in the military school at Brienne as 'Royal Pupil' whose expenses would be paid by the King.

106 The annual awards, given by the Institute of Museum and Library Services in Washington, D. C., honor institutions for their collections and community involvement, and include a $10,000 award each.

107 The European missionaries, planters, and administrators clung to its coastal lowlands, convinced that no one could live in the treacherous mountain range that ran in a solid line down the middle of the island.

108 Backed by an army, an unscrupulous governor could easily take advantage of his power and enrich himself.

109 The new study, being published Monday in The American Journal of Obstetrics and Gynecology, finds that pregnant women who consume 200 milligrams or more of caffeine a day — the amount in 10 ounces of coffee or 25 ounces of tea — may double their risk of miscarriage.

정답

105 Admittedly Carlo(S) had(V) something to celebrate, having been informed by the Minister for War that Napoleone had been granted a scholarship and a place in the military school at Brienne as 'Royal Pupil' whose expenses would be paid by the King.

106 The annual awards(S), given by the Institute of Museum and Library Services in Washington, D. C., honor(V_1) institutions for their collections and community involvement, and include(V_2) a $10,000 award each.

107 The European missionaries, planters, and administrators(S) clung(V) to its coastal lowlands, convinced that no one could live in the treacherous mountain range that ran in a solid line down the middle of the island.

108 Backed by an army, an unscrupulous governor(S) could easily take(V_1) advantage of his power and enrich(V_2) himself.

109 The new study(S), being published Monday in The American Journal of Obstetrics and Gynecology, finds(V) that pregnant women who consume 200 milligrams or more of caffeine a day — the amount in 10 ounces of coffee or 25 ounces of tea — may double their risk of miscarriage.

43 접속사 + 분사구문

분사구문이 '시간 · 조건 · 양보'의 뜻을 나타내는 경우 분사 앞에 접속사가 생략되지 않고 남을 수 있다.

ex (While) swimming in the river, he was drowned.
강에서 수영하는 동안, 그는 익사했다.

(If) used wisely, leisure promotes health and happiness.
현명하게 사용되면, 레저는 건강과 행복을 증진한다.

(Though) born in Seoul, he lived in Busan.
서울에서 태어났지만, 그는 부산에서 살았다.

110 While testing a new vacuum tube known as a magnetron, he discovered that a candy bar in his pocket had melted. 2016 법원직 9급

어휘 test 실험하다 vacuum tube 진공관 magnetron 전자관 melt 녹다
해석 전자관으로 알려진 새로운 진공관을 테스트하는 동안, 그는 그의 호주머니에 있던 초코바가 녹았다는 사실을 발견했다.

111 When faced with an intruder, the Camponotus cylindricus ant of Borneo will grab onto the invader and squeeze itself until it explodes. 2016 서울시 9급

어휘 faced with ~와 맞선 intruder 침입자 grab 움켜쥐다 squeeze 압착하다, 쥐어짜다 explode 폭발하다
해석 침입자와 맞설 때, 보르네오의 Camponotus cylindricus 개미는 침입자에 달라붙어 자기의 몸이 터질 때까지 압착한다.

112 Human sewage can be a useful fertilizer, but when concentrated too highly it becomes a serious pollutant, menacing health and causing the depletion of oxygen in bodies of water. 2013 지방직 9급

어휘 sewage 오물, 하수 fertilizer 비료 concentrate 농축시키다 pollutant 오염물질 menace 위협하다 depletion 고갈
해석 인간의 오물은 쓸모 있는 비료가 될 수 있다. 그러나 너무나도 지나치게 농축되면 오물은 심각한 오염 물질이 되어, 건강을 위협하고 그리고 수중의 산소 고갈을 야기한다.

113 It seems to be a law of nature that any species will rapidly become extinct when confronted with a sudden change in environment or with a new foe whose ways it does not understand. 2012 국가직 7급

어휘 extinct 멸종한 species 종 confronted with ~과 직면한 foe 적

해석 환경의 급격한 변화를 직면하게 되거나 또는 그들이 이해하지 못하는 방법을 사용하는 적을 만나게 될 때 어떤 종이든지 빠르게 멸종하게 되는 것은 자연의 법칙인 것처럼 보인다.

구문 Check-up

※ 다음 문장을 해석하여 문장의 주어(S)와 본동사(V)를 찾아 표시하시오.
(단, 병치 구조로 동사가 여러 개인 경우는 번호를 매길 것)

110 While testing a new vacuum tube known as a magnetron, he discovered that a candy bar in his pocket had melted.

111 When faced with an intruder, the Camponotus cylindricus ant of Borneo will grab onto the invader and squeeze itself until it explodes.

112 Human sewage can be a useful fertilizer, but when concentrated too highly it becomes a serious pollutant, menacing health and causing the depletion of oxygen in bodies of water.

113 It seems to be a law of nature that any species will rapidly become extinct when confronted with a sudden change in environment or with a new foe whose ways it does not understand.

정답

110 While testing a new vacuum tube known as a magnetron, he(S) discovered(V) that a candy bar in his pocket had melted.

111 When faced with an intruder, the Camponotus cylindricus ant(S) of Borneo will grab(V_1) onto the invader and squeeze(V_2) itself until it explodes.

112 Human sewage(S_1) can be(V_1) a useful fertilizer, but when concentrated too highly it(S_2) becomes(V_2) a serious pollutant, menacing health and causing the depletion of oxygen in bodies of water.

113 It seems(V) to be a law of nature that any species will rapidly become extinct(S) when confronted with a sudden change in environment or with a new foe whose ways it does not understand.

44 독립분사구문

1 분사구문의 주어와 주절의 주어가 다른 독립분사구문

ex) Night coming on, we left for home.
밤이 다가와서 우리는 집으로 떠났다.

An eye bandaged, I could not write properly.
한쪽 눈이 붕대로 감겨서 나는 제대로 쓸 수가 없었다.

*인칭대명사는 독립분사구문의 의미상주어가 될 수 없다.

ex) It being my own decision, I didn't regret having parted from her. (×)

2 비인칭주어 it과 유도부사 there는 독립분사구문이 가능하다.

ex) It being a fine day, we went hiking.
날씨가 화창해서 우리는 하이킹을 갔다.

There being no bus service, we took a taxi.
버스 편이 없어서 우리는 택시를 탔다.

114 The human river can regulate its own velocity, its banks widening or narrowing to control the shifting tides. 2008 지방직 7급

어휘 regulate 조절하다; 규제하다　velocity 속도　bank 둑　control 통제하다, 조절하다
shifting 이동하는　tide 조류

해석 인체의 강은 변하는 조류를 조절하기 위하여 그 강둑이 넓어지거나 좁아지면서 자신의 속도를 조절할 수 있다.

115 Lavoisier stressed the importance of quantitative methods of investigation in chemistry, and in this connection, he introduced the principle of conservation of matter which stated that nothing was lost or gained during the course of a chemical reaction, the weight of the products equalling the weight of the starting materials. 2011 법원직 9급

어휘 stress 강조하다　quantitative 양적인　chemistry 화학　connection 관계, 연관
introduce 도입하다　conservation 보존　chemical 화학의　reaction 반응
equal 동등하다, 일치하다　material 물질, 재료

해석 Lavoisier는 화학에서 양적인 조사 방법들의 중요성을 강조했다. 그리고 이와 관련하여 그는 생성되는 물질의 무게가 처음의 본래 물질의 질량과 같기 때문에, 화학 반응이 일어나는 과정 동안에 질량은 변한이 없다고 언급한 질량 보존의 법칙을 소개하였다.

구문 Check-up

※ 다음 문장을 해석하여 문장의 주어(S)와 본동사(V)를 찾아 표시하시오.
(단, 병치 구조로 동사가 여러 개인 경우는 번호를 매길 것)

114 The human river can regulate its own velocity, its banks widening or narrowing to control the shifting tides.

115 Lavoisier stressed the importance of quantitative methods of investigation in chemistry, and in this connection, he introduced the principle of conservation of matter which stated that nothing was lost or gained during the course of a chemical reaction, the weight of the products equalling the weight of the starting materials.

정답

114 The human river(S) can regulate(V) its own velocity, its banks widening or narrowing to control the shifting tides.

115 Lavoisier(S_1) stressed(V_1) the importance of quantitative methods of investigation in chemistry, and in this connection, he(S_2) introduced(V_2) the principle of conservation of matter which stated that nothing was lost or gained during the course of a chemical reaction, the weight of the products equalling the weight of the starting materials.

45 with + 명사 + 분사

1 독립분사구문이 '이유'나 '동시동작'의 뜻일 때 with를 붙일 수 있다.

ex) With night coming on, we left for home.
밤이 다가와서, 우리는 집으로 떠났다.

She was listening to music with her eyes closed.
그녀는 눈을 감고 음악을 듣고 있었다.

2 being이 생략되어 분사 대신 형용사 · 전치사구 등이 올 수 있다.

ex) He is sleeping with his mouth (being) open.
그는 입을 벌리고 자고 있었다.

He was standing with his hands (being) in his pockets.
그는 주머니에 손을 넣고 서 있었다.

116 As you stand holding the umbrella perfectly straight, most of the raindrops fall off the edges down into the empty buckets, with some falling in between. 2012 법원직 9급

어휘 perfectly 완벽하게 raindrop 빗방울 bucket 양동이 in between 사이에

해석 당신이 우산을 완전히 똑바로 잡고 서 있기 때문에, 대부분의 빗방울들은 우산 가장자리에서 빈 양동이 안으로 떨어진다.

117 The number of Americans who owed more than their homes were worth was virtually nil when the real estate collapse began in mid-2006, but by the third quarter of 2009, an estimated 4.5 million homeowners reached the critical threshold, with their home's value dropping below 75 percent of the mortgage balance. 2012 지방직 9급

어휘 owe 빚을 지다 worth ~의 가치가 있는 virtually 실질적으로 nil 0 real estate 부동산 collapse 붕괴 estimated 추산된, 어림잡은 critical 중요한 threshold 문턱 mortgage 담보대출 balance 잔액, 잔고

해석 2006년 중반에 부동산 붕괴가 시작되었을 때 집의 가치보다 빚을 더 많이 진 미국인들의 숫자는 사실상 0이었다. 그러나 2009년 3 / 4분기에는 450만 명으로 추정되는 주택 소유주들이 담보 대출 잔고의 75퍼센트 아래로 그들의 집의 가치가 떨어지면서 위기의 문턱에 다다랐다.

구문 Check-up

※ 다음 문장을 해석하여 문장의 주어(S)와 본동사(V)를 찾아 표시하시오.
(단, 병치 구조로 동사가 여러 개인 경우는 번호를 매길 것)

116 As you stand holding the umbrella perfectly straight, most of the raindrops fall off the edges down into the empty buckets, with some falling in between.

117 The number of Americans who owed more than their homes were worth was virtually nil when the real estate collapse began in mid-2006, but by the third quarter of 2009, an estimated 4.5 million homeowners reached the critical threshold, with their home's value dropping below 75 percent of the mortgage balance.

정답

116 As you stand holding the umbrella perfectly straight, most of the raindrops(S) fall(V) off the edges down into the empty buckets, with some falling in between.

117 The number(S_1) of Americans who owed more than their homes were(V_1) worth was virtually nil when the real estate collapse began in mid-2006, but by the third quarter of 2009, an estimated 4.5 million homeowners(S_2) reached(V_2) the critical threshold, with their home's value dropping below 75 percent of the mortgage balance.

46 분사구문의 관용표현

분사구문의 관용표현으로는 다음과 같은 것들이 있다.

generally speaking 일반적으로 말하자면, broadly speaking 대체로 말하자면,
strictly speaking 엄격하게 말하자면, frankly speaking 솔직하게 말하자면,
briefly speaking 간단히 말하자면, judging from ~으로 판단하건대,
taking ~ into consideration ~을 고려하면, granting / granted (that) ~이라 할지라도,
talking[speaking] of ~으로 말하자면, seeing (that) ~이므로,
compared with [to] ~와 비교해서, weather permitting 날씨만 좋다면,
all things considered 만사를 고려하면

ex Generally speaking, men can run faster than women.
일반적으로 말하면, 남자가 여자보다 더 빨리 달릴 수 있다.

We'll go on a picnic, weather permitting.
날씨가 좋으면, 소풍을 갈 것이다.

118 Recognizing the biological status of this multitude requires a clear understanding of what constitutes a species, which is no easy task given that evolutionary biologists have yet to agree on a universally acceptable definition. 2020 국가직 9급

어휘 recognize 인식하다; 알아차리다 biological 생물학적인 status 지위, 신분 multitude 다수 require 요구하다 constitute 구성하다 species 종 evolutionary 진화론의 biologist 생물학자 have yet to do 아직 ~하지 못했다 universally 보편적으로 acceptable 수용 가능한, 받아들여질 수 있는 definition 정의

해석 이러한 많은 수의 생물학적 지위를 인식하는 것은 무엇이 종을 구성하는지에 대한 명확한 이해를 필요로 하는데, 그것은 진화 생물학자들이 아직 보편적으로 받아들여질 수 있는 정의에 합의하지 못했다는 것을 고려할 때 절대 쉬운 일이 아니다.

119 Generally speaking, people living in 2018 are pretty fortunate when you compare modern times to the full scale of human history. 2009 서울시 9급

어휘 generally speaking 일반적으로 말하자면 pretty 꽤, 상당히 fortunate 운 좋은 full scale 전체 규모

해석 일반적으로 말해서, 2018년에 사는 사람들은 현대사를 인류역사의 전체 규모와 비교했을 때 꽤 운이 좋다.

구문 Check-up

※ 다음 문장을 해석하여 문장의 주어(S)와 본동사(V)를 찾아 표시하시오.
(단, 병치 구조로 동사가 여러 개인 경우는 번호를 매길 것)

118 Recognizing the biological status of this multitude requires a clear understanding of what constitutes a species, which is no easy task given that evolutionary biologists have yet to agree on a universally acceptable definition.

119 Generally speaking, people living in 2018 are pretty fortunate when you compare modern times to the full scale of human history.

정답

118 Recognizing(S) the biological status of this multitude requires(V) a clear understanding of what constitutes a species, which is no easy task given that evolutionary biologists have yet to agree on a universally acceptable definition.

119 Generally speaking, people(S) living in 2018 are(V) pretty fortunate when you compare modern times to the full scale of human history.

CHAPTER

03 접속사와 기타 구문

47 등위접속사

1 단어 · 구 · 절을 대등하게 연결한다.

and 그리고, but / yet 그러나, or / nor 또는, so 그래서, for 왜냐하면 ~이니까

ex He heard an explosion and phoned the police.
그는 폭발 소리를 듣고 경찰에 전화를 했다.

It is a strange but / yet true story.
그것은 이상하지만 진실한 이야기이다.

Did you go there on foot or by bus?
거기에 걸어서 갔니 아니면 버스로 갔니?

I was tired, so I went to bed early.
나는 피곤했다. 그래서 일찍 잤다.

2 for는 부가적인 이유를 나타내며, 문두에 올 수 없다.

ex For I was tired, I went to bed early. (×)
⇨ I went to bed early, for I was tired. (○)
나는 일찍 잤다. 왜냐하면 피곤했기 때문이다.

120 Biologists used to think that the immune system was a separate, independent part of our body, but recently they have found that our brain can affect our immune system.

2015 지방직 7급

어휘 used to 한때 ~였다; ~하곤 했다 immune system 면역체계 separate 분리된, 별개의 independent 독립한 affect 영향을 주다

해석 면역체계는 우리 신체의 별도의, 독자적인 일부라고 생물학자들은 한때 생각했지만, 최근에 우리 뇌가 면역체계에 영향을 미칠 수 있다는 것을 그들은 알아냈다.

121 When a prisoner is released from the cave, he initially suffers from the sun's blinding brightness, yet as his eyes adjust he begins to see the truth. 2017 사회복지직 9급

어휘 release 석방하다 initially 처음에는 blinding 눈을 멀게 하는, 눈부신 adjust 적응하다

해석 한 명의 죄수가 동굴로부터 해방되었을 때, 그는 처음에는 태양의 강렬한 눈부심을 고통스럽게 경험한다. 그러나 그의 눈이 적응하면서 그는 진실을 보게 된다.

122 His life ended in tragedy, for although he conceived a perfect, clearly describable computer, and although the new insights about how electronics can leap or seemingly stop might have allowed him to construct it, the technology remained elusive. 2012 국가직 7급

어휘 end in ~로 끝나다 tragedy 비극 conceive 상상하다; 임신하다 describable 설명 가능한 insight 통찰력 electronics 전자공학 leap 도약하다, 비약적으로 발전하다 seemingly 겉보기에 construct 건설하다, 구축하다 elusive 잡히지 않는, 애매한

해석 그의 삶은 비극으로 끝났다. 왜냐하면 비록 그가 완벽하고, 명확하게 설명이 가능한 컴퓨터를 상상했을지라도, 그리고 비록 어떻게 전자공학이 도약할 수 있거나 또는 겉보기에 정지되어 있는지에 관한 새로운 통찰력이 그로 하여금 그것을 만들도록 했을지 모르지만, 그 기술은 달성하기 힘든 상태로 남아있었기 때문이다.

구문 Check-up

※ 다음 문장을 해석하여 문장의 주어(S)와 본동사(V)를 찾아 표시하시오.
(단, 병치 구조로 동사가 여러 개인 경우는 번호를 매길 것)

120 Biologists used to think that the immune system was a separate, independent part of our body, but recently they have found that our brain can affect our immune system.

121 When a prisoner is released from the cave, he initially suffers from the sun's blinding brightness, yet as his eyes adjust he begins to see the truth.

122 His life ended in tragedy, for although he conceived a perfect, clearly describable computer, and although the new insights about how electronics can leap or seemingly stop might have allowed him to construct it, the technology remained elusive.

정답

120 Biologists(S_1) used to think(V_1) that the immune system was a separate, independent part of our body, but recently they(S_2) have found(V_2) that our brain can affect our immune system.

121 When a prisoner is released from the cave, he(S_1) initially suffers(V_1) from the sun's blinding brightness, yet as his eyes adjust he(S_2) begins(V_2) to see the truth.

122 His life(S_1) ended(V_1) in tragedy, for although he conceived a perfect, clearly describable computer, and although the new insights about how electronics can leap or seemingly stop might have allowed him to construct it, the technology(S_2) remained(V_2) elusive.

48 either A or B / neither A nor B

1 either A or B : A와 B 둘 중 하나
neither A nor B : A와 B 둘 다 아닌

ex) He went either to London or to Paris.
그는 런던이나 파리로 갔다.

He can neither read nor write.
그는 읽을 줄도 쓸 줄도 모른다.

2 neither ~ nor는 셋 이상의 어구의 연결도 가능하다.

ex) She neither smiled, spoke, nor looked at me.
그녀는 나에게 미소를 짓지도, 말도 하지도, 보지도 않았다.

123 Animal species that seldom compete for food or shelter, either due to an abundance of resources or to a small population density, rarely exhibit aggressive tendencies. 2011 지방직 7급

어휘 compete 경쟁하다 shelter 피신처 abundance 풍부함 resources 자원 density 밀도 exhibit 보여주다, 전시하다 aggressive 공격적인; 적극적인 tendency 경향, 성향

해석 풍부한 자원 때문이든 또는 낮은 개체 밀도 때문이든, 식량이나 주거지를 위해 좀처럼 거의 경쟁을 하지 않는 동물종들은 공격적인 성향을 거의 드러내지 않는다.

124 NIH considers Healing Touch and other types of energy medicine among the most controversial of complementary and alternative medicine practices because neither the external energy fields nor their therapeutic effects have been demonstrated convincingly by any biophysical means. 2018 서울시 7급

어휘 controversial 논란이 많은 complementary 상호 보완적인 therapeutic 치료상의, 치료법의 demonstrate 입증하다, 보여주다 convincingly 설득력 있게, 확실하게

해석 NIH는 힐링 터치와 다른 유형의 에너지 의학을 보완 대체 의학 분야에서 가장 논란이 되는 분야 중 하나로 생각하는데, 그 이유는 외부 에너지 분야나 치료 효과가 생물 물리학적 수단에 의해 설득력 있게 입증되지 않았기 때문이다.

■ 구문 Check-up ■

※ 다음 문장을 해석하여 문장의 주어(S)와 본동사(V)를 찾아 표시하시오.
(단, 병치 구조로 동사가 여러 개인 경우는 번호를 매길 것)

123 Animal species that seldom compete for food or shelter, either due to an abundance of resources or to a small population density, rarely exhibit aggressive tendencies.

124 NIH considers Healing Touch and other types of energy medicine among the most controversial of complementary and alternative medicine practices because neither the external energy fields nor their therapeutic effects have been demonstrated convincingly by any biophysical means.

정답

123 Animal species(S) that seldom compete for food or shelter, either due to an abundance of resources or to a small population density, rarely exhibit(V) aggressive tendencies.

124 NIH(S) considers(V) Healing Touch and other types of energy medicine among the most controversial of complementary and alternative medicine practices because neither the external energy fields nor their therapeutic effects have been demonstrated convincingly by any biophysical means.

49 not only A but also B

1 not only[just] A but (also) B : A뿐만 아니라 B도

= not only[just] A but B as well

= B as well as A

ex He can speak not only English but (also) French.
= He can speak not only English but French as well.
= He can speak French as well as English.
그는 영어뿐만 아니라 불어도 할 줄 안다.

2 not only가 문두에 오면 '조동사 + 주어 + 동사'로 도치된다.

ex Not only did he hear it but he also saw it.
그는 그것을 들었을 뿐만 아니라 보기도 했다.

125 The impressionists, however, not only made sketches but also painted finished works in the open, which transformed their style by preserving the spontaneity of direct observation. 2015 서울시 7급

어휘 impressionist 인상파 화가 transform 변형하다 preserve 보존하다 spontaneity 자연스러움 observation 관찰

해석 그러나 인상파 화가들은 야외에서 스케치를 했을 뿐만 아니라 완성 작품까지 그렸다. 그것은 직접 관찰의 자연스러움을 지키는 것으로 그들의 스타일을 변형시켰다.

126 Just as people vary greatly in their outward physical makeup, they vary greatly in their inner wiring : wide individual differences exist in glandular activity and sensitivity of the autonomic nervous system — as well as in the activity of the brain centers concerned with emotion. 2007 국회직 8급

어휘 vary 변하다, 다양하다 outward 외형의 physical 신체적인 makeup 구성, 구조 wiring 배선 individual 개인적인 glandular 선(腺)의 sensitivity 민감성 autonomic 자율의 nervous system 신경계 concerned with ~과 관계된 emotion 감정

해석 마치 사람들이 자신들의 외형의 신체적인 체격 면에서 크게 다른 것처럼, 그것들은 자체의 내적인 배선(配線) 면에서 크게 다르다. 즉, 감정과 관련된 뇌의 중추의 활동은 물론이고 선(腺) 관련 활동이나 자율 신경계의 활동 면에서도 폭넓은 개인차가 존재한다.

127 For a computer to solve a problem, not only must the solution be very detailed, it must be written in a form the computer can understand. 2011 법원직 9급

어휘 solution 해결책 detailed 상세한, 세부적인 form 형식

해석 컴퓨터가 문제를 해결하게 하기 위해서는, 그 해결책이 매우 자세해야 할 뿐만 아니라, 그 컴퓨터가 이해할 수 있는 형태로 써져야 한다.

구문 Check-up

※ 다음 문장을 해석하여 문장의 주어(S)와 본동사(V)를 찾아 표시하시오.
(단, 병치 구조로 동사가 여러 개인 경우는 번호를 매길 것)

125 The impressionists, however, not only made sketches but also painted finished works in the open, which transformed their style but preserving the spontaneity of direct observation.

126 Just as people vary greatly in their outward physical makeup, they vary greatly in their inner wiring : wide individual differences exist in glandular activity and sensitivity of the autonomic nervous system — as well as in the activity of the brain centers concerned with emotion.

127 For a computer to solve a problem, not only must the solution be very detailed, it must be written in a form the computer can understand.

정답

125 The impressionists(S), however, not only made(V_1) sketches but also painted(V_2) finished works in the open, which transformed their style but preserving the spontaneity of direct observation.

126 Just as people vary greatly in their outward physical makeup, they(S) vary(V) greatly in their inner wiring : wide individual differences exist in glandular activity and sensitivity of the autonomic nervous system — as well as in the activity of the brain centers concerned with emotion.

127 For a computer to solve a problem, not only must the solution(S_1) be(V_1) very detailed, it(S_2) must be written(V_2) in a form the computer can understand.

50 not A but B

1 not A but B : A가 아니라 B

= B, not A

ex He is not a scholar but a poet.
= He is a poet, not a scholar.
그는 학자가 아니라 시인이다.

2 not because A but because B : A 때문이 아니라 B 때문에

ex I stayed at home not because I didn't like to go but because I was tired.
가고 싶지 않아서가 아니라 피곤해서 집에 있었다.

128 Love does not consist in gazing at each other, but in looking outward together in the same direction. 2016 사회복지직 9급

어휘 consist in ~에 있다 gaze 응시하다 outward 밖으로 direction 방향
해석 사랑은 서로를 응시하는 것에 있지 않고, 밖으로 같은 방향을 함께 바라보는 것에 있다.

129 If, then, that friend demands to know why I rose against Caesar, this is my answer: it's not that I loved Caesar less, but that I loved Rome more. 2015 법원직 9급

어휘 demand 요구하다 rise against ~에 대항하다, ~에 반란을 일으키다
해석 그런 다음 만약 그 친구가 왜 내가 Caesar에 대항하였는지를 알고자 한다면, 이것이 나의 대답이다: 내가 Caesar를 덜 사랑해서가 아니라, 로마를 더 사랑해서 였다고.

130 A skeptic might counter that it is caffeine, not flavor that made coffee into one of the world's most important commodities. 2011 법원직 9급

어휘 skeptic 회의론자 counter 반박하다 flavor 맛 commodity 상품

해석 회의적인 사람은 커피를 세계의 가장 중요한 상품들 중 하나로 만든 것은 맛이 아니라 카페인이라고 반박할지도 모른다.

131 Human beings have achieved preeminence among animals, not because of specialization, but because of adaptability. 2016 서울시 7급

어휘 achieve 성취하다 preeminence 탁월, 우월 specialization 전문화 adaptation 적응

해석 인간이 동물보다 우월해진 것은 전문화 때문이 아니라 적응 능력 때문이다.

132 People like Newton, Darwin, and Einstein stand out in the history of science not because they discovered a great many facts, but because their theories had such broad explanatory power. 2016 국회직 8급

어휘 stand out 탁월하다 explanatory 설명의

해석 뉴턴, 다윈, 그리고 아인슈타인과 같은 사람들은 그들이 많은 사실들을 발견했기 때문이 아니라 그들의 이론이 그토록 광범위한 설명적인 힘을 지니고 있었기 때문에 과학사에 있어서 두드러지는 것이다.

구문 Check-up

※ 다음 문장을 해석하여 문장의 주어(S)와 본동사(V)를 찾아 표시하시오. (단, 병치 구조로 동사가 여러 개인 경우는 번호를 매길 것)

128 Love does not consist in gazing at each other, but in looking outward together in the same direction.

129 If, then, that friend demands to know why I rose against Caesar, this is my answer: it's not that I loved Caesar less, but that I loved Rome more.

130 A skeptic might counter that it is caffeine, not flavor that made coffee into one of the world's most important commodities.

131 Human beings have achieved preeminence among animals, not because of specialization, but because of adaptability.

132 People like Newton, Darwin, and Einstein stand out in the history of science not because they discovered a great many facts, but because their theories had such broad explanatory power.

정답

128 Love(S) does not consist(V) in gazing at each other, but in looking outward together in the same direction.

129 If, then, that friend demands to know why I rose against Caesar, this(S) is(V) my answer: it's not that I loved Caesar less, but that I loved Rome more.

130 A skeptic(S) might counter(V) that it is caffeine, not flavor that made coffee into one of the world's most important commodities.

131 Human beings(S) have achieved(V) preeminence among animals, not because of specialization, but because of adaptability.

132 People(S) like Newton, Darwin, and Einstein stand out(V) in the history of science not because they discovered a great many facts, but because their theories had such broad explanatory power.

51 명사절 (1)

1 that은 ~라는 것의 의미로 that절 이하는 '사실'을 함축한다.

ex That she will pass the test is certain. (주어)

= It is certain that she will pass the test.

그녀가 시험에 합격할 것은 틀림없다.

I know (that) he is honest. (목적어)

나는 그가 정직하다는 것을 안다.

His only fault is that he has no fault. (보어)

그의 유일한 결점은 그가 결점이 없다는 것이다.

*접속사 that은 '사실'을 함축하기 때문에 'I don't know', 'I doubt' 등 뒤에 쓰이지 않는다.

ex I don't know that he is honest. (×)

*접속사 that은 추상명사 뒤에서 동격절을 이끌 수 있다.

ex The fact that he died surprised me. (동격)

그가 죽었다는 사실은 나를 놀라게 했다.

2 in과 except / but / save를 제외하고 전치사 뒤에는 that절이 올 수 없다.

ex Men differ from brutes in that they can think and speak.

인간은 생각을 하고 말을 한다는 점에서 짐승과 다르다.

This room is very good except that it is rather dark.
이 방은 좀 어둡다는 것을 제외하면 매우 좋다.

133 The researchers also found that teachers rarely identify poor working memory and often describe children with this problem as inattentive or less intelligent. 2016 국가직 9급

어휘 rarely 드물게 identify 확인하다 describe 묘사하다 inattentive 부주의한 intelligent 영리한
해석 연구자들은 또한 교사들이 (이러한) 떨어지는 단기 기억력의 문제를 거의 알아내지 못하며, 이러한 문제가 있는 아이들을 부주의하거나 지능이 낮다고 치부해 버리고 있음을 밝혀냈다.

134 Scientists estimate that there may be another 1 to 8 million undiscovered species of organisms living in and around reefs. 2016 법원직 9급

어휘 estimate 평가하다 species 종 organism 유기체 reef 산호초
해석 과학자들은 산호초와 그 주변에 살고 있는 또 다른 백만에서 팔백만 종에 이르는 미발견 유기체가 있을 것이라 추정한다.

135 Many scientists today feel that animals probably do have a limited form of consciousness, quite different from ours in that it lacks language and the capacity for propositional or symbolic thought. 2016 국가직 9급

어휘 consciousness 의식, 지각 lack 결핍되어 있다 capacity 수용능력 propositional 명제의 symbolic 상징의
해석 오늘날 많은 과학자들은 동물들은 아마도 제한된 형태의 지각능력을, 즉 언어와 명제적이거나 상징적인 사고에 대한 능력이 부재하다는 점에서 우리 인간의 것과는 다른 지각능력을 가지고 있다고 생각한다.

136 At any rate, they got the idea that if you imitated anything, you gained power over it. This idea was the beginning of the magic and also the beginning of the arts — music, poetry, painting, and drama. 2016 국회직 8급

어휘 imitate 모방하다 poetry 시
해석 여하튼, 여러분이 어떤 것을 모방한다면 여러분은 그것을 지배한다고 하는 생각을 그들은 가졌다. 이런 생각이 마술의 시작이었고 또한 음악, 시, 그림 및 드라마라고 하는 예술들의 시작이기도 했다.

137 Schwartz draws particular attention to Lane's assertion that Americans are paying for increased affluence and freedom with a substantial decrease in the quality and quantity of community. 2013 국회직 8급

어휘 draw attention to ~에 주목하다 particular 특별한 affluence 풍요 substantial 물질의; 상당한 decrease 감소 community 공동체
해석 Schwartz는 공동체의 질과 양에서 상당한 감소를 겪으면서 미국인들이 증가된 풍요로움과 자유에 대하여 대가를 지불하고 있다는 Lane의 주장에 특히 주목하고 있다.

138 Those exhibiting aggressive behavior seem to believe that the rights of others must be subservient to theirs. 2020 지방직 9급

어휘 exhibit 보이다, 전시하다 aggressive 공격적인; 적극적인 subservient 종속하는; 비굴한
해석 공격적인 행동을 보이는 사람들은 다른 사람들의 권리가 그들의 권리에 종속되어야 한다고 믿는 것 같다.

139 He noticed as they danced around him that there were holes at the tips of spears, and he realized this was the design feature he needed to solve his problem. 2019 서울시 9급

어휘 notice 주목하다, 발견하다 tip 끝; 조언; 팁 spear 창 realize 깨닫다 feature 특징
해석 그는 그들이 그의 주위에서 춤을 출 때 창끝에 구멍이 있다는 것을 알아차렸고, 그는 이것이 그의 문제를 해결하는 데 필요한 디자인적 특징이라는 것을 깨달았다.

140 Anthropologists believe wisdom teeth, or the third set of molars, were the evolutionary answer to our ancestor's early diet of coarse, rough food — like leaves, roots, nuts and meats — which required more chewing power and resulted in excessive wear of the teeth. 2016 법원직 9급

어휘 anthropologist 인류학자 wisdom teeth 사랑니 molar 어금니 evolutionary 진화상의
coarse 조잡한, 거친 rough 거친; 대강의 nut 견과 chew 씹다 result in ~를 초래하다
excessive 지나친 wear 마모
해석 인류학자들은 사랑니, 즉 세 번째 어금니가 우리 조상들이 옛날에 먹었던 나뭇잎, 뿌리, 나무 열매, 그리고 고기처럼 씹는 능력을 더 많이 필요로 하며 치아의 지나친 마모를 가져왔던 단단하고 거친 음식을 위한 진화상의 해결책이었다고 믿고 있다.

구문 Check-up

※ 다음 문장을 해석하여 문장의 주어(S)와 본동사(V)를 찾아 표시하시오.
(단, 병치 구조로 동사가 여러 개인 경우는 번호를 매길 것)

133 The researchers also found that teachers rarely identify poor working memory and often describe children with this problem as inattentive or less intelligent.

134 Scientists estimate that there may be another 1 to 8 million undiscovered species of organisms living in and around reefs.

135 Many scientists today feel that animals probably do have a limited form of consciousness, quite different from ours in that it lacks language and the capacity for propositional or symbolic thought.

136 At any rate, they got the idea that if you imitated anything, you gained power over it. This idea was the beginning of the magic and also the beginning of the arts — music, poetry, painting, and drama.

137 Schwartz draws particular attention to Lane's assertion that Americans are paying for increased affluence and freedom with a substantial decrease in the quality and quantity of community.

138 Those exhibiting aggressive behavior seem to believe that the rights of others must be subservient to theirs.

139 He noticed as they danced around him that there were holes at the tips of spears, and he realized this was the design feature he needed to solve his problem.

140 Anthropologists believe wisdom teeth, or the third set of molars, were the evolutionary answer to our ancestor's early diet of coarse, rough food — like leaves, roots, nuts and meats — which required more chewing power and resulted in excessive wear of the teeth.

정답

133 The researchers(S) also found(V) that teachers rarely identify poor working memory and often describe children with this problem as inattentive or less intelligent.

134 Scientists(S) estimate(V) that there may be another 1 to 8 million undiscovered species of organisms living in and around reefs.

135 Many scientists(S) today feel(V) that animals probably do have a limited form of consciousness, quite different from ours in that it lacks language and the capacity for propositional or symbolic thought.

136 At any rate, they(S) got(V) the idea that if you imitated anything, you gained power over it. This idea(S) was(V) the beginning of the magic and also the beginning of the arts — music, poetry, painting, and drama.

137 Schwartz(S) draws(V) particular attention to Lane's assertion that Americans are paying for increased affluence and freedom with a substantial decrease in the quality and quantity of community.

138 Those(S) exhibiting aggressive behavior seem(V) to believe that the rights of others must be subservient to theirs.

139 He(S_1) noticed(V_1) as they danced around him that there were holes at the tips of spears, and he(S_2) realized(V_2) this was the design feature he needed to solve his problem.

140 Anthropologists(S) believe(V) wisdom teeth, or the third set of molars, were the evolutionary answer to our ancestor's early diet of coarse, rough food - like leaves, roots, nuts and meats — which required more chewing power and resulted in excessive wear of the teeth.

52 명사절 (2)

1 whether / if ~인지 아닌지: whether와 if가 이끄는 명사절은 '불확실성'을 함축한다.

ex) Whether it will rain or not is not certain. (주어)
비가 올지 안 올지 확실하지 않다.

I don't know whether he will come to the party. (타동사의 목적어)
그가 파티에 올지 안 올지 모르겠다.

It depends on whether he loves her or not. (전치사의 목적어)
그것은 그가 그녀를 사랑하느냐 안 하느냐에 달려있다.

The question is whether he has enough money or not. (보어)
문제는 그가 충분한 돈이 있는가이다.

2 if는 타동사의 목적어인 경우에만 whether를 대신할 수 있는 것이 원칙이다.

ex) I don't know if he will come to the party.
나는 그가 파티에 올지를 알지 못한다.

141 The investigators were interested in whether the words that participants encountered in the first experiment would lead them to apply different schema and thus affect their evaluations of Donald. 2016 국회직 8급

어휘 investigator 연구자 participant 참여자 encounter 우연히 만나다 experiment 실험 apply 적용하다 schema 도식 affect 영향을 미치다 evaluation 평가

해석 연구자들은 참여자들이 첫 실험에서 만났던 단어들이 참여자들로 하여금 다른 도식을 적용하게 하고 그래서 Donald에 대한 그들의 평가들에 영향을 주는지 여부에 관심을 가졌다.

142 Some people think that the central dichotomy in life is 'whether you're positive or negative about the issues that interest or concern you'. 2018 국가직 9급

어휘 dichotomy 이분, 양분 interest 흥미를 일으키다 concern 관여시키다; 걱정시키다

해석 몇몇 사람들은 인생의 핵심적인 이분법은 '당신을 흥미 있게 하거나 걱정시키는 문제들에 대해서 당신이 긍정적인가, 아니면 부정적인가'에 관한 것이라고 생각한다.

143 Most police officers decide whether you're getting a ticket or a warning before they even approach your vehicle. 2011 국회직 9급

어휘 police officer 경찰관 warning 경고 vehicle 차량

해석 대부분의 경찰관들은, 심지어 그들이 당신의 차에 접근하기도 전에, 당신에게 벌금 티켓을 줄지 아니면 경고를 할지를 결정한다.

144 In 2007, former Federal Reserve Chair Alan Greenspan wondered if the euro would replace the dollar as the world's reserve currency — in other words, the benchmark that everyone uses in case of emergency — and even supermodel Gisele Bundchen reportedly insisted on being paid in euros. 2015 국가직 7급

어휘 euro 유로화 replace 대신하다 reserve currency 기축통화 benchmark 기준 emergency 응급, 위기 reportedly 보도에 따르면 insist 주장하다, 고집하다

해석 2007년에, 전 연방 준비 제도 이사회 의장 Alan Greenspan이 유로가 세계 기축통화로, 다시 말하면, 모든 사람들이 유사시에 기준으로서 사용하는 통화로서, 달러를 대체할지를 궁금해했다. 심지어 전하는 바에 따르면, 슈퍼모델 Gisele Bundchen은 유로로 급여를 받겠다고 주장을 했다고 한다.

구문 Check-up

※ 다음 문장을 해석하여 문장의 주어(S)와 본동사(V)를 찾아 표시하시오.
(단, 병치 구조로 동사가 여러 개인 경우는 번호를 매길 것)

141 The investigators were interested in whether the words that participants encountered in the first experiment would lead them to apply different schema and thus affect their evaluations of Donald.

142 Some people think that the central dichotomy in life is 'whether you're positive or negative about the issues that interest or concern you'.

143 Most police officers decide whether you're getting a ticket or a warning before they even approach your vehicle.

144 In 2007, former Federal Reserve Chair Alan Greenspan wondered if the euro would replace the dollar as the world's reserve currency — in other words, the benchmark that everyone uses in case of emergency — and even supermodel Gisele Bundchen reportedly insisted on being paid in euros.

정답

141 The investigators(S) were interested(V) in whether the words that participants encountered in the first experiment would lead them to apply different schema and thus affect their evaluations of Donald.

142 Some people(S) think(V) that the central dichotomy in life is whether you're positive or negative about the issues that interest or concern you.

143 Most police officers(S) decide(V) whether you're getting a ticket or a warning before they even approach your vehicle.

144 In 2007, former Federal Reserve Chair(S_1) Alan Greenspan wondered(V_1) if the euro would replace the dollar as the world's reserve currency — in other words, the benchmark that everyone uses in case of emergency — and even supermodel(S_2) Gisele Bundchen reportedly insisted(V_2) on being paid in euros.

53 간접의문문

1 의문사로 시작되어 문장 내에서 주어, 목적어, 보어 역할을 하는 명사절을 간접의문문이라고 하는데, 이 경우 의문사 뒤에는 '주어 + 동사'의 평서문의 어순이 온다.

ex) Do you know where is he? (×)

⇨ Do you know where he is? (○)

그가 어디에 있는지 아니?

2 주절에 'think, believe, suppose, guess, imagine' 등의 동사가 있는 의문문에서는 의문사가 문두로 간다.

ex) Do you think where he is? (×)

⇨ Where do you think he is? (○)

그가 어디에 있다고 생각하니?

145 That being the case, it's a good idea to consider what short-term goals we can accomplish that will eventually lead to accomplishing long-term goals. 2019 지방직 9급

어휘 consider 고려하다 short-term 단기적인 accomplish 성취하다 eventually 결국에는 lead to ~로 이어지다 long-term 장기적인

해석 그러한 경우라면, 우리가 결국 장기적인 목표 성취를 이끄는 어떤 단기적인 목표를 이룰 수 있을지를 생각해 보는 것이 좋다.

146 In nature's talent show we are simply a species of primate with our own act, a knack for communicating information about who did what to whom by modulating the sounds we make when we exhale. 2009 국회직 8급

어휘 talent 재능 species 종 primate 영장류 knack 솜씨, 기술 communicate 의사소통하다; 전달하다 modulate 조절하다 exhale 숨을 내쉬다

해석 자연의 재능쇼에서 우리는 우리 자신의 행동을 갖춘, 즉 우리가 숨을 내쉬면서 내는 소리를 조절함으로써 누가 누구에게 무엇을 했는지에 대한 정보를 교환하는 요령을 가진, 영장류의 한 종에 지나지 않는 것이다.

구문 Check-up

※ 다음 문장을 해석하여 문장의 주어(S)와 본동사(V)를 찾아 표시하시오.
(단, 병치 구조로 동사가 여러 개인 경우는 번호를 매길 것)

145 That being the case, it's a good idea to consider what short-term goals we can accomplish that will eventually lead to accomplishing long-term goals.

146 In nature's talent show we are simply a species of primate with our own act, a knack for communicating information about who did what to whom by modulating the sounds we make when we exhale.

정답

145 That being the case, it's(V) a good idea to consider(S) what short-term goals we can accomplish that will eventually lead to accomplishing long-term goals.

146 In nature's talent show we(S) are(V) simply a species of primate with our own act, a knack for communicating information about who did what to whom by modulating the sounds we make when we exhale.

54 시간부사절

1 시간부사절에는 다음과 같은 것들이 있다.

when ~할 때, **while** ~하는 동안, **as** ~할 때, ~하면서, ~함에 따라서, **before** ~하기 전에, **after** ~한 후에, **until / till** ~할 때 까지, **since** ~한 이래로, **as soon as** ~하자마자, **every time / each time** ~할 때마다

ex) I lived in Seoul when I was young.
나는 어렸을 때 서울에서 살았다.

Five years have passed since he died.
그가 죽은 지 5년이 흘렀다.

2 during은 while과 같은 의미이지만 전치사이므로 뒤에 절이 올 수 없다.

ex Make hay during the sun shines. (×)
⇨ Make hay while the sun shines. (○)
해가 비칠 때 건초를 말려라(기회를 놓치지 말라).

147 Our principle was to discuss every disagreement until it had been resolved to our mutual satisfaction. 2012 지방직 9급

어휘 principle 원칙, 원리 disagreement 불일치 resolved 해결하다; 결심하다 mutual 상호의 satisfaction 만족

해석 우리의 원칙은 그것이 우리 상호의 만족으로 해결이 될 때까지, 모든 의견 차이를 토론하는 것이었다.

148 They say that when animals are killed, they generate a lot of stress hormones, which affect humans who consume their meat. 2011 국회직 9급

어휘 generate 발생시키다 hormone 호르몬 affect 영향을 주다 consume 소비하다, 먹다

해석 그들은 동물이 죽임을 당할 때 동물은 많은 스트레스 호르몬을 생성하고, 이것들은 동물의 고기를 섭취하는 인간들에게 영향을 끼친다고 말한다.

구문 Check-up

※ 다음 문장을 해석하여 문장의 주어(S)와 본동사(V)를 찾아 표시하시오.
(단, 병치 구조로 동사가 여러 개인 경우는 번호를 매길 것)

147 Our principle was to discuss every disagreement until it had been resolved to our mutual satisfaction.

148 They say that when animals are killed, they generate a lot of stress hormones, which affect humans who consume their meat.

정답

147 Our principle(S) was(V) to discuss every disagreement until it had been resolved to our mutual satisfaction.

148 They(S) say(V) that when animals are killed, they generate a lot of stress hormones, which affect humans who consume their meat.

55 not A until B

1 not A until B : B하고 나서야 비로소 A하다

ex I didn't hear the news until I came to Korea.
나는 한국에 와서야 비로소 그 소식을 들었다.

2 It is ~ that : 강조구문으로 강조할 수 있다.

*not until이 문두에 오면 '조동사 + 주어 + 동사'로 도치된다.

ex It was not until I came to Korea that I heard the news.
= Not until I came to Korea did I hear the news.
한국에 오고 나서야 나는 그 소식을 들었다.

149 The person's reasons may be either strong or weak, but you will not know until you have asked the question and identified the reasons. 2016 경찰 1차

어휘 identify 확인하다
해석 그 사람의 근거는 강할 수도 약할 수도 있지만 당신이 그 질문을 해서 이유를 확인할 때 까지는 모를 것이다.

150 You'll never get a fair distribution of goods, or a satisfactory organization of human life, until you abolish private property altogether. 2014 지방직 9급

어휘 fair 공정한 distribution 분배 satisfactory 만족스러운 organization 조직 abolish 폐지하다 property 재산
해석 당신이 사유재산을 완전히 포기하기 전까지는 당신은 결코 재화의 공정한 분배나 인간적인 삶의 만족스러운 조직을 얻지 못할 것이다.

151 It wasn't until about 300 years ago that people began to use waterproof umbrellas in the rain. 2010 국가직 9급

어휘 waterproof 방수의 umbrella 우산
해석 약 300년 전에야 사람들은 비가 올 때 방수 우산을 사용하기 시작했던 것이다.

■ 구문 Check-up ■

※ 다음 문장을 해석하여 문장의 주어(S)와 본동사(V)를 찾아 표시하시오.
(단, 병치 구조로 동사가 여러 개인 경우는 번호를 매길 것)

149 The person's reasons may be either strong or weak, but you will not know until you have asked the question and identified the reasons.

150 You'll never get a fair distribution of goods, or a satisfactory organization of human life, until you abolish private property altogether.

151 It wasn't until about 300 years ago that people began to use waterproof umbrellas in the rain.

정답

149 The person's reasons(S_1) may be(V_1) either strong or weak, but you(S_2) will not know(V_2) until you have asked the question and identified the reasons.

150 You(S)'ll never get(V) a fair distribution of goods, or a satisfactory organization of human life, until you abolish private property altogether.

151 It wasn't until about 300 years ago that people(S) began(V) to use waterproof umbrellas in the rain.

56 이유부사절

1 because / since / as : ~때문에

ex He succeeded because he worked hard.
그는 열심히 일했기 때문에 성공했다.

2 now (that) : 이제는 ~하니까

ex Since / As I don't have much money, I can't buy it.
나는 돈이 많지 않기 때문에, 그것을 살 수 없다.

3 in that : ~라는 점에서

ex Now (that) you are retired, you can travel more.
이제는 퇴직했으니까, 여행을 더 많이 할 수 있겠네요.

152 But it may also be that high national emotions are permissible when a soccer team is playing precisely because they are impermissible at most other times. 2012 법원직 9급

어휘 emotion 감정 permissible 허용 가능한 precisely 정확히 impermissible 허용되지 않은

해석 그러나 그것은 또한 축구 경기가 있을 때 높은 국민적 감정들이 허용된다는 것 일수도 있다. 정확히 왜냐하면 높은 국민적 감정들이 대부분의 다른 경우에는 허용되지 않기 때문이다.

153 Carnegie was unusual in that he championed workers' rights and publicly supported trade unions. 2009 지방직 7급

어휘 unusual 흔하지 않은, 드문 champion 지지하다, 옹호하다 publicly 공개적으로
support 지지하다, 후원하다 trade union 노동조합

해석 카네기는 노동자의 권리를 옹호하고, 공공연하게 노동조합을 지원한 점에서 특별했다.

154 They attribute its differences from standard 'textbook' English to an inability of the children to distinguish between Apache and English, therefore mixing them up, since they are unable to speak either one. 2010 국회직 8급

어휘 attribute ~탓으로 돌리다 inability 무능력 distinguish 구별하다 mix up 혼동하다

해석 그들은 표준적인 교과서 영어와 그것의 차이들을 그 아이들이 아파치 말과 영어 사이를 구별할 능력이 없음의 탓으로 돌렸다. 그러므로 그들은 둘 중의 어느 것도 말할 수가 없기 때문에 그것들을 뒤섞게 되는 것이다.

구문 Check-up

※ 다음 문장을 해석하여 문장의 주어(S)와 본동사(V)를 찾아 표시하시오.
(단, 병치 구조로 동사가 여러 개인 경우는 번호를 매길 것)

152 But it may also be that high national emotions are permissible when a soccer team is playing precisely because they are impermissible at most other times.

153 Carnegie was unusual in that he championed workers' rights and publicly supported trade unions.

154 They attribute its differences from standard 'textbook' English to an inability of the children to distinguish between Apache and English, therefore mixing them up, since they are unable to speak either one.

정답

152 But it may also be(V) that high national emotions are permissible(S) when a soccer team is playing precisely because they are impermissible at most other times.

153 Carnegie(S) was(V) unusual in that he championed workers' rights and publicly supported trade unions.

154 They(S) attribute(V) its differences from standard textbook' English to an inability of the children to distinguish between Apache and English, therefore mixing them up, since they are unable to speak either one.

57 목적부사절

1 so that / in order that ~ may / can / will : ~하기 위하여

ex Mary works hard so that she may succeed.
= Mary works hard in order that she may succeed.
매리는 성공하기 위하여 열심히 일한다.

2 lest ~ (should) / for fear ~ should : ~하지 않기 위하여

ex Make haste lest you (should) be late.
늦지 않기 위하여 서둘러라.

155 On the other hand, the middle part of the web is flexible so that when an insect flies into it, it will stretch rather than break. 2009 국가직 7급

해석 반면에, 거미줄의 그물망 가운데 부분은 곤충이 거미줄 망으로 날아들 때, 그것이 끊어지기보다는 오히려 늘어날 수 있도록 하기 위해 신축성이 있다.

156 Reading and studying were more permissible for girls, but they, too, had to be careful not to get too intellectual, lest they acquire the stigma of being 'stuck up'. 2017 국가직 9급

어휘 permissible 허용될 수 있는　intellectual 똑똑한, 지적인　acquire 얻다　stigma 오명, 불명예　stuck up 건방진, 거만한

해석 책을 읽고 공부를 하는 것은 여자아이들에게 조금 더 허용되는 것이었지만, 그들도 역시 건방지다고 낙인찍히지 않기 위해 너무 똑똑해지지 않도록 주의를 기울여야만 했다.

구문 Check-up

※ 다음 문장을 해석하여 문장의 주어(S)와 본동사(V)를 찾아 표시하시오.
(단, 병치 구조로 동사가 여러 개인 경우는 번호를 매길 것)

155 On the other hand, the middle part of the web is flexible so that when an insect flies into it, it will stretch rather than break.

156 Reading and studying were more permissible for girls, but they, too, had to be careful not to get too intellectual, lest they acquire the stigma of being 'stuck up.'

정답

155 On the other hand, the middle part(S) of the web is(V) flexible so that when an insect flies into it, it will stretch rather than break.

156 Reading and studying(S_1) were(V_1) more permissible for girls, but they(S_2), too, had(V_2) to be careful not to get too intellectual, lest they acquire the stigma of being 'stuck up'.

58 결과부사절

1 so + (형용사 / 부사) + that : 매우 ~해서 (그 결과) …하다.

= such + a + 형용사 + 명사 + that

= so + 형용사 + a + 명사 + that

= such 불가산명사 / 가산명사복수형 + that

ex He worked so hard that he passed the exam.
그는 매우 열심히 공부해서 시험에 합격했다.

He is such a diligent man that everyone likes him.
그는 너무나 부지런한 사람이라 모든 사람이 그를 좋아한다.

2 such that = so great that : 너무나 심해서 …하다.

ex His anxiety was such that he lost his health.
= His anxiety was so great that he lost his health.
그의 걱정이 너무 커서 그는 건강을 잃었다.

157 The two cultures were so utterly disparate that she found it hard to adapt from one to the other. 2016 지방직 9급

어휘 culture 문화 utterly 완전히 disparate 상이한 adapt 적응하다
해석 두 문화는 완전히 이질적이어서 그녀는 한 쪽 문화에서 다른 쪽 문화로 적응하기가 어렵다는 것을 알았다.

158 A building or other object that is impregnable is so strong or solid that it cannot be broken or captured. 2015 서울시 7급

어휘 impregnable 난공불락의 solid 견고한, 튼실한; 만장일치의 capture 함락하다; 체포하다
해석 난공불락의 건물이나 다른 대상은 너무 강하거나 견고해서 침입을 당하거나 함락되지 않는다.

159 Moreover, the range of medical conditions is now so vast, and the doctor's time so limited, that several clinical centers have begun to introduce computer-assisted diagnostic systems. 2016 국회직 8급

어휘 moreover 더욱이, 게다가 range 범위 medical 의학의 vast 방대한, 거대한 limited 제한된 clinical 임상의, 치료상의 introduce 도입하다 computer-assisted 컴퓨터가 도와주는 diagnostic 진단의
해석 더욱이, 의학상의 질병들의 범위가 오늘날 너무나 방대하고, 또 의사들의 시간이 너무나 제한되어 있어서 여러 임상센터들은 컴퓨터의 지원을 받는 진단시스템들을 도입하기 시작했다.

160 Many people are so focused on sharing their thoughts, opinions, and ideas that they forget to think about how their message will be received, or whether it's a good idea to speak at all. 2016 기상직 9급

어휘 focused 집중한 share 나누다, 공유하다 forget to R ~해야 하는 것을 잊어버리다
해석 많은 사람들은 그들의 생각, 의견 그리고 아이디어를 나누는데 너무 집중해서 그들의 메시지가 어떻게 받아들여질 것인지에 대해 혹은 말을 한다는 자체가 좋은 생각인지 아닌지에 대해 생각하지 않게 된다.

161 Cookies allow a website to remember personal information such as a consumer's name, home address, email address, and phone number, so that these items do not have to be reentered. 2017 지방직 7급

어휘 cookie 인터넷 쿠키 item 항목, 품목 reenter 재입력하다
해석 쿠키는 판매자들이 고객의 이름, 집주소, 이메일 주소, 그리고 전화번호와 같은 웹사이트 방문자들에 관한 정보를 수집할 수 있게 해준다. 그래서 판매자들은 이 자료들을 광고와 기타 마케팅 목적으로 사용할 수 있다.

162 For a number of reasons, the problems and organization of science today are such that a scientist does not choose his problems; the problems force themselves upon the scientist. 2018 지방직 9급

어휘 organization 조직 force 강요하다
해석 많은 이유에서, 과학의 문제들과 구조는 너무나 심각해서 과학자가 그의 문제점들을 선택하는 것이 아니다; 문제점들 스스로가 과학자에게 강요되는 것이다.

구문 Check-up

※ 다음 문장을 해석하여 문장의 주어(S)와 본동사(V)를 찾아 표시하시오.
(단, 병치 구조로 동사가 여러 개인 경우는 번호를 매길 것)

157 The two cultures were so utterly disparate that she found it hard to adapt from one to the other.

158 A building or other object that is impregnable is so strong or solid that it cannot be broken or captured.

159 Moreover, the range of medical conditions is now so vast, and the doctor's time so limited, that several clinical centers have begun to introduce computer-assisted diagnostic systems.

160 Many people are so focused on sharing their thoughts, opinions, and ideas that they forget to think about how their message will be received, or whether it's a good idea to speak at all.

161 Cookies allow a website to remember personal information such as a consumer's name, home address, email address, and phone number, so that these items do not have to be reentered.

162 For a number of reasons, the problems and organization of science today are such that a scientist does not choose his problems; the problems force themselves upon the scientist.

정답

157 The two cultures(S) were(V) so utterly disparate that she found it hard to adapt from one to the other.

158 A building or other object(S) that is impregnable is(V) so strong or solid that it cannot be broken or captured.

159 Moreover, the range(S_1) of medical conditions is(V_1) now so vast, and the doctor's time(S_2) so limited, that several clinical centers have begun to introduce computer-assisted diagnostic systems.

160 Many people(S) are(V) so focused on sharing their thoughts, opinions, and ideas that they forget to think about how their message will be received, or whether it's a good idea to speak at all.

161 Cookies(S) allow(V) a website to remember personal information such as a consumer's name, home address, email address, and phone number, so that these items do not have to be reentered.

162 For a number of reasons, the problems and organization(S) of science today are(V) such that a scientist does not choose his problems; the problems force themselves upon the scientist.

59 조건부사절

1 if : ~하면

= suppose / supposing (that)

= providing / provided (that)

ex) If it rains, we'll stay at home.

= Suppose / Supposing (that) it rains, we'll stay at home.

= Providing / Provided (that) it rains, we'll stay at home.

비가 오면 집에 있겠다.

2 unless : ~하지 않으면

ex) Unless you work hard, you will fail.

열심히 일하지 않으면 실패할 것이다.

3 in case ~일 경우에; ~에 대비해서

ex Take an umbrella in case it rains.
비가 올 것에 대비해서 우산을 가져가라.

4 once : 일단 ~하면

ex Once you start, you can't stop on the way.
일단 시작하면, 도중에서 멈추면 안 된다.

163 If the players, the coaches, the announcers, and the crowd all sound like they're sitting midcourt, you may as well watch the game on television — you'll get just as much of a sense that you are "there". 2019 지방직 9급

어휘 may as well ~가 더 낫다 sound like ~처럼 들리다

해석 만약 선수들, 감독들, 아나운서들, 그리고 관중들이 모두 코트 중앙에 있는 것처럼 들린다면, 여러분은 텔레비전으로 경기를 보는 편이 나을 것이다. 여러분은 그저 그곳에 있다는 기분만 들 뿐이다.

164 The campaign to eliminate pollution will prove futile unless it has the understanding and full cooperation of the public. 2016 국가직 9급

해석 대중의 이해와 전적인 협조가 없다면, 환경오염을 제거하는 캠페인은 효과가 없음이 입증될 것이다.

구문 Check-up

※ 다음 문장을 해석하여 문장의 주어(S)와 본동사(V)를 찾아 표시하시오.
(단, 병치 구조로 동사가 여러 개인 경우는 번호를 매길 것)

163 If the players, the coaches, the announcers, and the crowd all sound like they're sitting midcourt, you may as well watch the game on television — you'll get just as much of a sense that you are "there".

164 The campaign to eliminate pollution will prove futile unless it has the understanding and full cooperation of the public.

정답

163 If the players, the coaches, the announcers, and the crowd all sound like they're sitting midcourt, you(S) may as well watch(V) the game on television — you'll get just as much of a sense that you are there".

164 The campaign(S) to eliminate pollution will prove(V) futile unless it has the understanding and full cooperation of the public.

60 양보부사절

1 though / although / even though / even if : ~이지만
while / whereas : ~이지만, ~인 반면에

ex Though / Although he is poor, he is happy.
= While / Whereas he is poor, he is happy.
그는 가난하지만 행복하다.

2 despite는 양보의 뜻을 나타내는 전치사이므로 뒤에 절이 올 수 없다.

ex Despite he was ill, he went to work. (×)
⇨ Though he was ill, he went to work. (○)
그는 아팠지만 출근했다.

165 This probably reflects the corals' ability to modify their environment and partially adjust to ocean acidification, whereas the dissolution of sands is a geochemical process that cannot adapt. 2020 지방직 9급

어휘 reflect 반영하다 coral 산호초 modify 조정하다; 변조하다 adapt 적응하다; 개작하다 acidification 산성화 dissolution 용해 geochemical 지구화학적인

해석 이것은 아마도 자신의 환경을 바꾸어서 바다의 산성화에 부분적으로 적응하는 산호초의 능력을 반영하는 반면에, 모래의 용해는 적응할 수 없는 지구화학적 과정이다.

166 But the problem with these sleep aids is that even though they induce drowsiness, they do not promote real sleep — deep, lasting, and refreshing. 2009 소방직 9급

어휘 sleep aid 수면제 induce 유도하다; 설득하다 drowsiness 졸림 promote 촉진하다, 증진하다 lasting 지속적인 refreshing 개운하게 하는

해석 그러나 이러한 수면제들이 가진 문제점은, 비록 그것들이 졸음을 유발하기는 하지만, 그들이 깊고, 지속적이고, 그리고 상쾌한 진정한 의미의 수면을 촉진하지는 않는다는 것이다.

■ 구문 Check-up ■

※ 다음 문장을 해석하여 문장의 주어(S)와 본동사(V)를 찾아 표시하시오.
(단, 병치 구조로 동사가 여러 개인 경우는 번호를 매길 것)

165 This probably reflects the corals' ability to modify their environment and partially adjust to ocean acidification, whereas the dissolution of sands is a geochemical process that cannot adapt.

166 But the problem with these sleep aids is that even though they induce drowsiness, they do not promote real sleep — deep, lasting, and refreshing.

정답

165 This(S) probably reflects(V) the corals' ability to modify their environment and partially adjust to ocean acidification, whereas the dissolution of sands is a geochemical process that cannot adapt.

166 But the problem(S) with these sleep aids is(V) that even though they induce drowsiness, they do not promote real sleep — deep, lasting, and refreshing.

61 주격 관계대명사

주격 관계대명사 뒤에는 주어 자리가 비어 있는 불완전한 절이 온다.

주격 관계대명사 + V

사람 + who / that

사물 + which / that

ex This is the man who lives next door to me.
= This is the man that lives next door to me.
이 분이 나의 옆집에 사는 남자이다.

The book which is on the desk is mine.
= The book that is on the desk is mine.
책상 위에 있는 그 책은 내 것이다.

*관계대명사 which는 앞문장의 일부분 또는 전체를 받을 수 있다.

ex He takes a regular exercise, which amazes me.
그는 주기적으로 운동을 하는데, 그것이 나를 놀랍게 한다.

167 There are people who through no fault of their own are deprived of some of the fundamental rights that all human beings are supposed to have. 2015 서울시 7급

어휘 fault 잘못, 실수 deprive 빼앗다 fundamental 근본적인 suppose 가정하다

해석 스스로는 아무 잘못이 없이도 모든 인간이 가지도록 되어 있는 근본적인 권리들 중 일부를 빼앗긴 사람들이 있다.

168 Flowers can be contaminated with insecticides that can kill bees directly or lead to chronic, debilitating effects on their health. 2016 법원직 9급

어휘 contaminate 오염시키다 insecticide 살충제 lead to ~로 이어지다 chronic 만성의 debilitate 쇠약하게 하다 effect 효과

해석 꽃들은 벌을 직접 죽이거나 그들의 건강에 만성적인, 쇠약하게 만드는 영향을 초래할 수 있는 살충제로 인해 오염될 수 있다.

169 It is likely that the vast majority of the crimes, which consist mainly of pick-pocketing and shop-lifting, are committed by outsiders. 2016 서울시 9급

어휘 vast 막대한 majority 다수 consist of ~로 이루어져 있다

해석 소매치기나 상점 절도가 대다수인 거의 대부분의 범죄들이 외부인들에 의한 소행이다.

170 The name England is derived from the Angles, one of the Germanic tribes which established monarchies in lowland Britain in the 5th century, after the final withdrawal of the Romans in 409. 2016 서울시 7급

어휘 tribe 부족, 종족 establish 세우다, 설립하다 monarchy 군주제 lowland 저지대 withdrawal 후퇴

해석 잉글랜드라는 이름은 로마인이 409년에 마지막으로 철수한 후인 5세기에 영국 저지대에서 군주제를 확립한 독일 부족 중 하나인 앵글로족에서 유래한 것이다.

171 They also had guides at these key sites, who would take people around and explain the relevance of the statues. 2016 국회직 8급

어휘 guide 안내자 take around 안내하다, 데리고 다니다 relevance 관련성, 적절성 statue 동상

해석 그것들은 또한 이런 중요한 지점들에 안내자들을 배치했는데, 그들은 사람들을 안내하면서 이 동상들의 관련성을 설명하고는 했다.

172 Simply put, its goal is to improve the quality of life for those who are dying. 2012 지방직 7급

어휘 put 표현하다, 말하다 quality 질

해석 간단히 말해서, 이것의 목표는 죽어가는 사람들의 삶의 질을 증대하는 것이다.

173 Those high schools which do teach languages other than English usually offer Spanish, French, Latin, or German to their students, in that order of frequency, depending upon the section of the country and the wealth of the individual school system. 2012 지방직 9급

어휘 other than ~이외의, ~과는 다른 frequency 빈도 section 지역, 부분

해석 영어 이외에 다른 언어를 가르치는 고등학교들은 대개 스페인어, 프랑스어, 라틴어, 또는 독일어를 그러한 빈도 순서로 학생들에게 제공하고 있다. 지역에 따라 그리고 개별 학교 시스템의 경제적 능력에 따라 학생들에게 제공한다.

174 Inge Sorensen of Denmark earned a bronze medal in the 200m breaststroke, which made her the youngest medallist in the history of the Olympic Games. 2018 서울시 7급

어휘 earn 얻다, 획득하다 bronze medal 동메달 breaststroke 평영

해석 덴마크의 Inge Sorensen은 200m 평영에서 동메달을 따서, 올림픽 역사상 가장 젊은 메달리스트가 되었다.

구문 Check-up

※ 다음 문장을 해석하여 문장의 주어(S)와 본동사(V)를 찾아 표시하시오.
(단, 병치 구조로 동사가 여러 개인 경우는 번호를 매길 것)

167 There are people who through no fault of their own are deprived of some of the fundamental rights that all human beings are supposed to have.

168 Flowers can be contaminated with insecticides that can kill bees directly or lead to chronic, debilitating effects on their health.

169 It is likely that the vast majority of the crimes, which consist mainly of pick-pocketing and shop-lifting, are committed by outsiders.

170 The name England is derived from the Angles, one of the Germanic tribes which established monarchies in lowland Britain in the 5th century, after the final withdrawal of the Romans in 409.

171 They also had guides at these key sites, who would take people around and explain the relevance of the statues.

172 Simply put, its goal is to improve the quality of life for those who are dying.

173 Those high schools which do teach languages other than English usually offer Spanish, French, Latin, or German to their students, in that order of frequency, depending upon the section of the country and the wealth of the individual school system.

174 Inge Sorensen of Denmark earned a bronze medal in the 200m breaststroke, which made her the youngest medallist in the history of the Olympic Games.

정답

167 There are(V) people(S) who through no fault of their own are deprived of some of the fundamental rights that all human beings are supposed to have.

168 Flowers(S) can be contaminated(V) with insecticides that can kill bees directly or lead to chronic, debilitating effects on their health.

169 It is(V) likely that the vast majority of the crimes, which consist mainly of pick-pocketing and shop-lifting, are committed by outsiders(S).

170 The name(S) England is(V) derived from the Angles, one of the Germanic tribes which established monarchies in lowland Britain in the 5th century, after the final withdrawal of the Romans in 09.

171 They(S) also had(V) guides at these key sites, who would take people around and explain the relevance of the statues.

172 Simply put, its goal(S) is(V) to improve the quality of life for those who are dying.

173 Those high schools(S) which do teach languages other than English usually offer(V) Spanish, French, Latin, or German to their students, in that order of frequency, depending upon the section of the country and the wealth of the individual school system.

174 Inge Sorensen(S) of Denmark earned(V) a bronze medal in the 200m breaststroke, which made her the youngest medallist in the history of the Olympic Games.

62 목적격 관계대명사

목적격 관계대명사 뒤에는 목적어 자리가 비어 있는 불완전한 절이 온다.

목적격 관계대명사 + S + V

사람 + whom / that + S + V

사물 + which / that + S + V

ex) This is the man whom I met yesterday.

= This is the man that I met yesterday.

이 분이 내가 어제 만난 남자이다.

The book which I bought yesterday is interesting.

= The book that I bought yesterday is interesting.

내가 어제 산 그 책은 재미있다.

175 In today's business climate, you've got to be clever enough to come up with ideas that others haven't thought of yet. 2013 서울시 9급

어휘 climate 기후; 환경 have got to R ~해야 한다 come up with ~를 고안하다, 제안하다

해석 오늘날의 사업 환경에서는, 다른 사람들이 아직까지 생각해내지 못한 아이디어를 고안해 낼 만큼 충분하게 영리해야 한다.

176 Under the profit system, however, such risks are dwarfed by the enormous financial windfall which the owners and media bosses are reaping from the record-breaking home run pace set by McGwire. 2013 국회직 8급

어휘 dwarf 작게 하다 enormous 거대한 windfall 불로소득 boss 사장 reap 수확하다, 얻다 record-breaking 기록을 경신하는, 신기록의 set 세우다

해석 그러나 이러한 이윤 구조하에서, 그러한 위험들은 McGwire에 의하여 달성되는 홈런 기록 경신 속도로부터 구단주들과 매체의 사장들이 얻고 있는 어마어마한 재정적인 횡재에 의하여 왜소해지고 있다.

177 The origin of new species, which the nineteenth-century English naturalist Charles Darwin once referred to as "the mystery of mysteries", is the natural process of speciation responsible for generating this remarkable diversity of living creatures with whom humans share the planet. 2020 국가직 9급

어휘 naturalist 동식물 연구가 refer to A as B A를 B라고 지칭하다 speciation 종 분화 generate 만들어내다 remarkable 놀랄 만한, 주목할 만한 diversity 다양성

해석 19세기 영국의 박물학자인 찰스 다윈이 "미스터리 중의 미스터리"라고 언급했던 새로운 종의 기원은 인간이 함께 지구를 공유하고 있는 생물체들의 이 놀라운 다양성을 이룩하는 것을 담당했던 자연적인 종 분화 과정이다.

178 Your interest in them will be considered good manners as long as you stay away from questions about three subjects that most American adults don't want to discuss — their age, weight, and income. 2018 지방직 7급

어휘 interest 관심사, 흥미; 이익; 이자 manners 예절 as long as ~인 한 income 수입

해석 당신이 대부분의 미국 성인들이 토론하고 싶지 않은 세 가지 주제, 즉 연령, 체중 및 소득에 관한 질문에서 벗어나는 한 자신들에 대한 당신의 관심은 훌륭한 매너로 간주된다.

구문 Check-up

※ 다음 문장을 해석하여 문장의 주어(S)와 본동사(V)를 찾아 표시하시오.
(단, 병치 구조로 동사가 여러 개인 경우는 번호를 매길 것)

175 In today's business climate, you've got to be clever enough to come up with ideas that others haven't thought of yet.

176 Under the profit system, however, such risks are dwarfed by the enormous financial windfall which the owners and media bosses are reaping from the record-breaking home run pace set by McGwire.

177 The origin of new species, which the nineteenth-century English naturalist Charles Darwin once referred to as "the mystery of mysteries", is the natural process of speciation responsible for generating this remarkable diversity of living creatures with whom humans share the planet.

178 Your interest in them will be considered good manners as long as you stay away from questions about three subjects that most American adults don't want to discuss — their age, weight, and income.

정답

175 In today's business climate, you(S)'ve got(V) to be clever enough to come up with ideas that others haven't thought of yet.

176 Under the profit system, however, such risks(S) are dwarfed(V) by the enormous financial windfall which the owners and media bosses are reaping from the record-breaking home run pace set by McGwire.

177 The origin(S) of new species, which the nineteenth-century English naturalist Charles Darwin once referred to as the "mystery of mysteries", is(V) the natural process of speciation responsible for generating this remarkable diversity of living creatures with whom humans share the planet.

178 Your interest(S) in them will be considered(V) good manners as long as you stay away from questions about three subjects that most American adults don't want to discuss — their age, weight, and income.

63 삽입절과 관계대명사의 격

관계대명사와 동사 사이에 'S + think, believe, know, say, be sure' 등의 삽입절이 있는 경우에는 주격 관계대명사를 써야 한다.

주격 관계대명사 + (S + V) + V

ex He is a boy whom I think is honest. (×)
⇨ He is a boy who I think is honest. (○)
= He is a boy. + I think he is honest.
그는 내가 생각하기에 정직한 소년이다.

cf He is a boy whom I think to be honest.

179 This pattern tends to repeat itself through time, allowing surfers to wait and take advantage of the sets of larger waves that they know will eventually arrive. 2017 서울시 7급

어휘 tend ~하는 경향이 있다 set 세트, 집합 take advantage of ~을 이용하다 eventually 결국, 마침내
해석 이 패턴은 시간을 거쳐 스스로 반복되는 경향이 있고, 이것은 서퍼가 결국 도착하리라고 그들이 알고 있는 큰 파도 세트를 기다렸다가 활용하는 것을 허용해준다.

180 Some experts suggest that one can start by making an inventory — a list of the things you enjoy doing, your talents and interests, and even new things that you think you might enjoy if you tried them. 2012 국가직 9급

어휘 suggest 제안하다; 시사하다, 암시하다 inventory 목록
해석 몇몇의 전문가들은 당신이 즐기는 것, 당신의 재능과 관심사, 심지어 당신이 생각하기에 시도해 본다면 즐길 수 있을 것 같은 새로운 것들의 목록을 만드는 것에 의하여, 당신은 시작할 수 있다고 말한다.

구문 Check-up

※ 다음 문장을 해석하여 문장의 주어(S)와 본동사(V)를 찾아 표시하시오.
(단, 병치 구조로 동사가 여러 개인 경우는 번호를 매길 것)

179 This pattern tends to repeat itself through time, allowing surfers to wait and take advantage of the sets of larger waves that they know will eventually arrive.

180 Some experts suggest that one can start by making an inventory — a list of the things you enjoy doing, your talents and interests, and even new things that you think you might enjoy if you tried them.

정답

179 This pattern(S) tends(V) to repeat itself through time, allowing surfers to wait and take advantage of the sets of larger waves that they know will eventually arrive.

180 Some experts(S) suggest(V) that one can start by making an inventory — a list of the things you enjoy doing, your talents and interests, and even new things that you think you might enjoy if you tried them.

64 소유격 관계대명사

1 소유격 관계대명사 뒤에는 반드시 명사가 오고, 그 명사는 관계사절의 주어나 목적어가 된다.

whose + 명사 + V

whose + 명사 + S + V

ex He is the boy whose father is a doctor.
그는 아버지가 의사인 소년이다.

2 선행사가 사물인 경우에는 which의 소유격으로 'whose 명사 / of which the 명사 / the 명사 of which'를 쓸 수 있다.

ex This is the word whose meaning I don't understand.
= This is the word the meaning of which I don't understand.
= This is the word of which the meaning I don't understand.

181 Umpires and other sports officials are the decision-makers and rulebook enforcers whose word is law on the field of play. 2016 법원직 9급

어휘 umpire 심판 decision-maker 의사 결정자 rulebook 규정집, 규칙서 enforcer 집행자

해석 심판과 다른 스포츠 관계자들은 그들의 말이 경기장에서 법인 의사결정자이며 규칙서의 집행자이다.

182 And wealth will tend to vary in inverse proportion to merit, since the rich will be totally useless greedy characters, while the poor will be simple, honest people whose daily work is profitable to the community. 2014 지방직 9급

어휘 vary 변화하다 inverse 역의, 거꾸로의 proportion 비례 merit 미덕 greedy 탐욕스러운 character 인격 profitable 이로운 community 공동체

해석 그리고 부는 미덕에 반비례하여 변화하는 경향이 있다. 왜냐하면 부자들은 완전히 쓸모없는 탐욕스러운 사람들인 반면에, 가난한 사람들은 그들의 매일의 노동이 사회에 이익이 되는 일을 하는 평범하고 정직한 사람들이기 때문이다.

183 A Caucasian territory whose inhabitants have resisted Russian rule almost since its beginnings in the late 18th century has been the center of the incessant political turmoil.

2013 지방직 9급

어휘 territory 영토, 지역 inhabitant 주민 resist 저항하다 incessant 끊임없는 turmoil 혼란, 격동

해석 주민들이 18세기 후반 초기부터 러시아의 통치에 저항을 해온 코카서스 지역은 끊임없는 정치적 혼란의 중심지였다.

구문 Check-up

※ 다음 문장을 해석하여 문장의 주어(S)와 본동사(V)를 찾아 표시하시오.
(단, 병치 구조로 동사가 여러 개인 경우는 번호를 매길 것)

181 Umpires and other sports officials are the decision-makers and rulebook enforcers whose word is law on the field of play.

182 And wealth will tend to vary in inverse proportion to merit, since the rich will be totally useless greedy characters, while the poor will be simple, honest people whose daily work is profitable to the community.

183 A Caucasian territory whose inhabitants have resisted Russian rule almost since its beginnings in the late 18th century has been the center of the incessant political turmoil.

정답

181 Umpires and other sports officials(S) are(V) the decision-makers and rulebook enforcers whose word is law on the field of play.

182 And wealth(S) will tend(V) to vary in inverse proportion to merit, since the rich will be totally useless greedy characters, while the poor will be simple, honest people whose daily work is profitable to the community.

183 A Caucasian territory(S) whose inhabitants have resisted Russian rule almost since its beginnings in the late 18th century has been(V) the center of the incessant political turmoil.

65 전치사의 목적격 관계대명사

1 관계대명사가 전치사의 목적어일 때, 전치사를 관계사절 끝이나 관계대명사 앞에 둘 수 있다. '전치사 + 관계대명사'의 앞과 뒤에는 완전한 절이 온다.

목적격 관계대명사 + S + V + 전치사
= 전치사 + 목적격 관계대명사 + S + V

ex This is the man whom I spoke of.
= This is the man of whom I spoke.
이 분이 내가 말한 그 사람이다.

This is the house which she lives in.
= This is the house in which she lives.
여기가 그녀가 사는 집이다.

2 관계대명사 that은 앞에 전치사를 쓸 수 없다.

ex This is the man of that I spoke. (×)
This is the house in that she lives. (×)

184 There is something at once sobering and absurd in the extent to which we are lifted by the attentions of others and sunk by their disregard. 2016 법원직 9급

어휘 sobering 정신 차리게 하는 absurd 불합리한 extent 정도 lift 고양시키다 attention 관심, 주의 disregard 무시

해석 우리가 다른 사람들의 관심에 의해 고양되고 그들의 무시에 의해 풀이 죽을 정도까지 즉시 정신 차리게 하고 어이없게 만드는 무엇인가가 있다.

185 Applause is a funny thing in which each person tries to give credit to the performers, but also tries to blend into the crowd; you don't want to clap before everyone else, or to go on after others have stopped. 2016 법원직 9급

어휘 applause 박수 credit 인정, 명예 performer 공연자 blend into 어울리다 clap 박수치다

해석 박수는 각 사람이 공연자들을 인정해주려고 노력하면서도 또한 관중들과 어우러지려고 노력하는 흥미로운 행위다. 당신은 다른 모든 사람들보다 먼저 박수 치거나 다른 사람들이 멈춘 이후에 계속 박수치기를 원하지 않는다.

186 Many businesses hire new workers through internships through which the companies offer full-time positions to a certain portion. 2016 서울시 7급

어휘 hire 고용하다 internship 인턴과정 full-time 정규직의 portion 몫, 부분

해석 많은 기업체들이 인턴과정을 통해 신입사원을 선발하고 있다. 이 과정을 통해 기업들은 인턴직의 일정 부분을 정규직으로 전환한다.

187 After completing the "perception" experiment, the participants moved on to the second study on "reading comprehension", in which they read the short paragraph about Donald and rated him on a number of trait scales. 2016 국회직 8급

어휘 complete 완성하다 perception 인식, 지각 experiment 실험 participant 참여자 comprehension 독해 paragraph 단락 rate 평가하다 trait 특성 scale 척도, 저울

해석 "인식" 실험을 마친 후에, 참여자들은 "독해력"에 대한 두 번째 연구로 이동했는데, 여기서 그들은 Donald에 대한 짧은 단락을 읽고는 여러 특징의 척도들(scales)에서 그를 평가했다.

188 I would encourage you to request a reference letter from those teachers with whom you have had the most opportunity to demonstrate those skills. 2016 경찰 1차

어휘 encourage 격려하다 request 요청하다 reference 추천서, 참고서 demonstrate 증명하다, 보여주다; 시위하다

해석 나는 여러분이 (추천서에서 요구하는) 그런 능력을 발휘할 가장 많은 기회를 가졌던 교사들에게 추천서를 요구하기를 권한다.

189 Goods for which the marginal costs are close to zero are inherently public goods and should be made publicly available. 2014 지방직 9급

어휘 marginal cost 한계비용(일정한 생산량이 한 단위 더 증가하는 데 따라 늘어나는 비용) inherently 본질적으로, 본래 available 이용 가능한

해석 한계비용이 0에 가까운 재화는 본질적으로 공공재이며, 대중이 공적으로(무료로) 이용할 수 있게 되어야 한다.

190 The rate at which the sands dissolve was strongly related to the acidity of the overlying seawater, and was ten times more sensitive than coral growth to ocean acidification. 2020 지방직 9급

어휘 rate 속도, 비율 dissolve 용해되다 acidity 산성 overlying 상층부의 coral 산호의 acidification 산성화

해석 모래가 용해되는 속도는 상층부 바닷물의 산성과 크게 연관이 있었고, 산호의 성장보다 바다의 산성화에 열 배 더 쉽게 영향을 받았다.

구문 Check-up

※ 다음 문장을 해석하여 문장의 주어(S)와 본동사(V)를 찾아 표시하시오.
(단, 병치 구조로 동사가 여러 개인 경우는 번호를 매길 것)

184 There is something at once sobering and absurd in the extent to which we are lifted by the attentions of others and sunk by their disregard.

185 Applause is a funny thing in which each person tries to give credit to the performers, but also tries to blend into the crowd; you don't want to clap before everyone else, or to go on after others have stopped.

186 Many businesses hire new workers through internships through which the companies offer full-time positions to a certain portion.

187 After completing the "perception" experiment, the participants moved on to the second study on "reading comprehension", in which they read the short paragraph about Donald and rated him on a number of trait scales.

188 I would encourage you to request a reference letter from those teachers with whom you have had the most opportunity to demonstrate those skills.

189 Goods for which the marginal costs are close to zero are inherently public goods and should be made publicly available.

190 The rate at which the sands dissolve was strongly related to the acidity of the overlying seawater, and was ten times more sensitive than coral growth to ocean acidification.

정답

184 There is(V) something(S) at once sobering and absurd in the extent to which we are lifted by the attentions of others and sunk by their disregard.

185 Applause(S) is(V) a funny thing in which each person tries to give credit to the performers, but also tries to blend into the crowd; you don't want to clap before everyone else, or to go on after others have stopped.

186 Many businesses(S) hire(V) new workers through internships through which the companies offer full-time positions to a certain portion.

187 After completing the "perception" experiment, the participants(S) moved(V) on to the second study on "reading comprehension", in which they read the short paragraph about Donald and rated him on a number of trait scales.

188 I(S) would encourage(V) you to request a reference letter from those teachers with whom you have had the most opportunity to demonstrate those skills.

189 Goods(S) for which the marginal costs are close to zero are(V_1) inherently public goods and should be made(V_2) publicly available.

190 The rate(S) at which the sands dissolve was strongly related(V_1) to the acidity of the overlying seawater, and was(V_2) ten times more sensitive than coral growth to ocean acidification.

66 부분사 + of + 목적격 관계대명사

1 'of + 목적격 관계대명사' 앞에 'all, any, none, both, either, neither, most, some, many, few, each, half, 수사' 등이 있는 경우 of는 '~중에서'의 뜻이다.

ex He has three daughters, all of whom are married.
그는 딸이 셋 있고, 그들 모두 결혼했다.

I bought many books, some of which I have already read.
나는 책을 많이 샀는데, 그중 일부는 이미 읽은 것이었다.

2 '수사, each' 등은 관계대명사 뒤에 올 수 있다.

ex I sent invitations to 80 people, of whom only 20 have replied.
80명에게 초대장을 보냈는데, 그중 20명만 답장을 보냈다.

191 To forestall this danger, they divided the population into castes, each of which was required to pursue a specific occupation or perform a specific role in society. 2017 기상직 9급

어휘 forestall 미연에 방지하다 divide 나누다 caste 카스트 제도 require 요구하다
pursue 추구하다; 추적하다 occupation 직업; 점령 specific 특정한, 구체적인

해석 이러한 위험을 방지하기 위해, 그들은 전체 주민을 카스트 제도로 나누었는데, 그것들 각각은 사회에서 특정한 직업에 종사하거나 특정한 역할을 수행하도록 요구되었다.

192 Continuing uprising against Russian / Soviet rule, the last of which was in 1934, caused the anger of Stalin. 2013 지방직 9급

어휘 uprising 폭동, 반란 cause 일으키다, 유발하다

해석 러시아 / 소비에트의 통치에 저항하는 지속적인 반란은, 그중의 마지막의 1934년에 있었는데, 스탈린의 분노를 샀다.

구문 Check-up

※ 다음 문장을 해석하여 문장의 주어(S)와 본동사(V)를 찾아 표시하시오.
(단, 병치 구조로 동사가 여러 개인 경우는 번호를 매길 것)

191 To forestall this danger, they divided the population into castes, each of which was required to pursue a specific occupation or perform a specific role in society.

192 Continuing uprising against Russian / Soviet rule, the last of which was in 1934, caused the anger of Stalin.

정답

191 To forestall this danger, they(S) divided(V) the population into castes, each of which was required to pursue a specific occupation or perform a specific role in society.

192 Continuing(S) uprising against Russian / Soviet rule, the last of which was in 193 , caused(V) the anger of Stalin.

67 관계대명사 what

관계대명사 what은 선행사를 포함하는 관계대명사로서 명사절이 된다. 그러므로 what이 이끄는 절은 문장 내에서 주어, 목적어, 보어 역할을 한다.

what : ~하는 것(= the thing that)

ex) What is beautiful is not always good. (주어)
아름다운 것이 항상 좋은 것은 아니다.

I don't believe what he said. (목적어)
나는 그가 말한 것을 믿지 않는다.

This is what I want. (보어)
이것이 내가 원하는 것이다.

193 What the mere exposure results show is that people develop a liking towards stimuli that are familiar. 2016 지방직 9급

어휘 exposure 노출 develop 발달시키다 stimuli 자극들 familiar 친숙한
해석 단순 접촉 효과의 결과가 보여주는 것은 사람들은 친숙한 자극들을 더 좋아한다는 것이다.

194 When the historian's vocation to pursue truth is combined with the reality that we can never produce a complete account of the past, we get what Hoffer calls "the historian's paradox". 2016 국회직 8급

어휘 historian 역사가 vocation 직업, 본업 paradox 역설
해석 진리를 추구하는 역사가의 소명이 우리가 결코 과거에 대한 완전한 설명을 만들어낼 수 없다고 하는 현실과 결합될 때, 우리는 Hoffer가 "역사가의 역설(paradox)"이라고 부르는 것을 얻게 된다.

195 The "denotation" of a word is what the word literally means. Blue, for instance, means "the color of the sky on a sunny day". 2016 법원직 9급

어휘 denotation 사전적인 의미, 뜻 literally 문자 그대로

해석 어느 단어의 "denotation"은 그 단어의 문자 그대로의 의미를 말한다. 예를 들어, "blue"는 "화창한 날의 하늘의 색깔"을 의미한다.

196 Much of what was drawn in prehistoric and early historical times has not survived, so what we find today may not be wholly representative of what was once there. 2016 법원직 9급

어휘 draw 그리다; 끌다; 매혹하다 prehistoric 선사시대의 survived 살아남다
representative 대표하는, 나타내는

해석 선사시대와 초기 역사시대에 그려진 많은 것들이 남아있지 않기 때문에, 오늘날 우리가 발견하는 것은 한때 존재했었던 것을 전적으로 대표하지 못할 수 있다.

197 What guides this thinking is a portfolio approach; wins and losses will both happen, but it's the overall portfolio of outcomes that matters most. 2018 국가직 9급

어휘 portfolio 서류가방; 장관직; 투자꾸러미 overall 종합적인 outcome 결과 matter 중요하다

해석 이러한 사고방식을 이끄는 것이 포트폴리오식 접근법이다; 이득과 손실은 모두 발생하지만, 가장 중요한 것은 결과의 전체적인 포트폴리오라는 것이다.

198 What we need to do is try not to eliminate these drawbacks, but to reasonably use their advantages. 2012 법원직 9급

어휘 eliminate 제거하다 drawback 결점, 흠 reasonably 합리적으로 advantage 장점, 이점

해석 우리가 해야 할 일은 이러한 결점들은 제거하려고 노력하는 것이 아니라, 그 장점들은 합리적으로 사용하려고 노력하는 것이다.

199 Clearly what they thought would happen resulted in the addition of a considerable amount of information to their sensations. 2015 지방직 9급

어휘 result in ~를 초래하다 addition 첨가 considerable 상당한 sensation 감각

해석 분명히 앞으로 일어날 것이라고 그들의 생각했던 것이 그들의 감각에 엄청난 양의 정보를 추가하는 결과를 초래하였다.

구문 Check-up

※ 다음 문장을 해석하여 문장의 주어(S)와 본동사(V)를 찾아 표시하시오.
(단, 병치 구조로 동사가 여러 개인 경우는 번호를 매길 것)

193 What the mere exposure results show is that people develop a liking towards stimuli that are familiar.

194 When the historian's vocation to pursue truth is combined with the reality that we can never produce a complete account of the past, we get what Hoffer calls "the historian's paradox".

195 The "denotation" of a word is what the word literally means. Blue, for instance, means "the color of the sky on a sunny day".

196 Much of what was drawn in prehistoric and early historical times has not survived, so what we find today may not be wholly representative of what was once there.

197 What guides this thinking is a portfolio approach; wins and losses will both happen, but it's the overall portfolio of outcomes that matters most.

198 What we need to do is try not to eliminate these drawbacks, but to reasonably use their advantages.

199 Clearly what they thought would happen resulted in the addition of a considerable amount of information to their sensations.

정답

193 What the mere exposure results show(S) is(V) that people develop a liking towards stimuli that are familiar.

194 When the historian's vocation to pursue truth is combined with the reality that we can never produce a complete account of the past, we(S) get(V) what Hoffer calls "the historian's paradox".

195 The "denotation"(S) of a word is(V) what the word literally means. Blue(S), for instance, means(V) "the color of the sky on a sunny day".

196 Much(S_1) of what was drawn in prehistoric and early historical times has not survived(V_1), so what we find today(S_2) may not be(V_2) wholly representative of what was once there.

197 What guides this thinking(S) is(V) a portfolio approach; wins and losses will both happen, but it's the overall portfolio of outcomes that matters most.

198 What we need to do(S) is(V) try not to eliminate these drawbacks, but to reasonably use their advantages.

199 Clearly what they thought would happen(S) resulted in(V) the addition of a considerable amount of information to their sensations.

68 what의 관용 표현

what의 관용 표현은 여러가지가 있다.

what + S + be : 지금의 / 과거의 주어

A is to B what C is to D : A와 B의 관계는 C와 D의 관계와 같다

what is called : 소위, 이른바(= what we / you / they call)

what is + 비교급 / 최상급 : 더욱 / 가장 ~한 것은

what is now + 장소 : 지금의 ~인 곳

ex I owe what I am to my father.
오늘의 나는 아버지의 덕이다.

Reading is to the mind what food is to the body.
독서와 정신의 관계는 음식과 육체의 관계와 같다.

He is what is called a bookworm.
그는 소위 책벌레이다.

Koguryo was a part of what is now Korea.
고구려는 지금의 한국의 일부였다.

200 What is worse, the anonymous users in cyberspace have gained chances to send impudent messages without having to take responsibility for their words. 2007 법원직 9급

어휘 what is worse 설상가상으로 anonymous 익명의 gain 얻다 impudent 염치없는, 뻔뻔한 responsibility 책임

해석 설상가상으로 사이버상의 익명의 사용자들이 그들의 말에 대한 책임을 지지 않고도 무례한 메시지를 보낼 기회를 갖게 되었다.

구문 Check-up

※ 다음 문장을 해석하여 문장의 주어(S)와 본동사(V)를 찾아 표시하시오.
(단, 병치 구조로 동사가 여러 개인 경우는 번호를 매길 것)

200 What is worse, the anonymous users in cyberspace have gained chances to send impudent messages without having to take responsibility for their words.

정답

200 What is worse, <u>the anonymous users(S)</u> in cyberspace <u>have gained(V)</u> chances to send impudent messages without having to take responsibility for their words.

69 관계대명사의 생략

1 목적격 관계대명사는 항상 생략할 수 있다.

ex This is the man (whom) I met yesterday.
이 분이 어제 내가 만난 남자이다.

2 주격 관계대명사는 생략할 수 없지만 '주격 관계대명사 + be동사'는 생략할 수 있다.

ex This is a book (which is) useful for children.
이것은 아이들에게 유용한 책이다.

This is a novel (which was) written by Hemingway.
이것은 헤밍웨이에 의해 쓰인 소설이다.

201 Historians have written the only asset he had when he died was the house he lived in, which was in Missouri. 2012 국가직 7급

어휘 historian 역사가 asset 자산, 재산
해석 역사가들은 그(Harry Truman 대통령)가 죽을 때 그가 가지고 있었던 유일한 재산은 Missouri에 있는 그가 살던 집이었다고 썼다.

202 Meanwhile, unlucky people tend to be tenser and too focused on certain tasks, which stops them from noticing opportunities they aren't explicitly looking for. 2016 법원직 9급

어휘 meanwhile 반면 tense 긴장한, 경직된 certain 어떤 stop A from ~ing A가 ~하는 것을 막다 notice 주목하다, 알아차리다 opportunity 기회 explicitly 분명하게 look for 찾다
해석 반면, 불운한 사람들은 더 경직되고 특정 업무에 너무 관심이 집중되어 있고, 그것은 그들이 분명하게 찾지 않고 있는 기회를 포착하는 것을 막는다.

203 The failure of the summit may be a blessing in disguise, because when it comes to dealing with climate change, the last thing we need right now is yet another empty agreement and yet more moral posturing. 2010 국가직 7급

어휘 failure 실패 summit 정상(회담) blessing 축복 disguise 변장, 위장 deal with 다루다 climate change 기후변화 empty 텅 빈, 공허한 agreement 합의 moral 도덕적인 posturing 보여주기, 가식
해석 정상 회담의 실패가 변장된 축복(전화위복)이 될지도 모른다. 왜냐하면 기후변화의 문제를 다루는 데에 있어서, 우리가 지금 당장 필요로 하지 않는 것이 또 다른 허울뿐인 협정과 더욱 심한 도덕적인 가식이기 때문이다.

204 It marked the beginning of the transformation of coffee from an obscure medicinal herb known only in the horn of Africa and southern Arabia to the most popular beverage in the world. 2011 법원직 9급

어휘 mark 표시하다, 나타내다 transformation 변화 obscure 이름 없는 medicinal herb 약초 horn 뿔 beverage 음료

해석 그것은 커피가 아프리카 북동부의 뿔 모양의 지역과 아라비아의 남쪽에서만 알려진 이름 없는 약초에서 세계에서 가장 인기 있는 음료로 탈바꿈한 것의 시작을 나타냈다.

구문 Check-up

※ 다음 문장을 해석하여 문장의 주어(S)와 본동사(V)를 찾아 표시하시오.
(단, 병치 구조로 동사가 여러 개인 경우는 번호를 매길 것)

201 Historians have written the only asset he had when he died was the house he lived in, which was in Missouri.

202 Meanwhile, unlucky people tend to be tenser and too focused on certain tasks, which stops them from noticing opportunities they aren't explicitly looking for.

203 The failure of the summit may be a blessing in disguise, because when it comes to dealing with climate change, the last thing we need right now is yet another empty agreement and yet more moral posturing.

204 It marked the beginning of the transformation of coffee from an obscure medicinal herb known only in the horn of Africa and southern Arabia to the most popular beverage in the world.

정답

201 Historians(S) have written(V) the only asset he had when he died was the house he lived in, which was in Missouri.

202 Meanwhile, unlucky people(S) tend(V) to be tenser and too focused on certain tasks, which stops them from noticing opportunities they aren't explicitly looking for.

203 The failure(S) of the summit may be(V) a blessing in disguise, because when it comes to dealing with climate change, the last thing we need right now is yet another empty agreement and yet more moral posturing.

204 It(S) marked(V) the beginning of the transformation of coffee from an obscure medicinal herb known only in the horn of Africa and southern Arabia to the most popular beverage in the world.

70 복합 관계대명사 (1)

1 선행사를 포함하여 <명사절>을 이끈다.

whoever : ~하는 사람은 누구든지(= anyone who)
whatever : ~하는 것은 무엇이든(= anything that)
whichever : ~하는 것은 어느 것이든(= any one that)

ex) Whoever says so is a liar.
그렇게 말하는 사람은 누구나 거짓말쟁이다.

Whatever he says is true.
그가 말하는 것은 무엇이든 진실하다.

I will give you whichever you choose.
네가 고르는 것은 어느 것이든 네게 주겠다.

2 복합 관계대명사의 격은 관계사절 내에서의 역할에 따라 결정된다.

ex) I'll give it to whoever wants it.
나는 그것을 원하는 사람은 누구에게나 주겠다.

I'll give it to whomever you like.
나는 그것을 네가 좋아하는 누구에게나 주겠다.

205 The supervisor was advised to give the assignment to whoever he believed had a strong sense of responsibility, and the courage of his conviction. 2009 서울시 9급

어휘 supervisor 감독관 advise 조언하다 assignment 과제 a sense of responsibility 책임감 courage 용기 conviction 확신

해석 그 관리자는 그가 믿기에 책임감이 강하고, 확신에 대한 용기가 있는 사람은 그 누구에게라도 그 과제를 맡기라고 충고를 받았다.

206 "Oh", she replied, "the President can just tell the Congress to take a vacation, and then he can go on and pass new laws or do whatever he wants". 2009 지방직 9급

어휘 reply 응답하다 president 대통령 congress 의회 vacation 휴가

해석 "아, 대통령은 그냥 의회에 휴가를 가라고 시킬 수 있어요. 그리고 그다음 그는 계속 진행하여 새 법을 통과시킬 수 있어요. 또는 그가 원하는 대로 무엇이든 할 수 있지요".라고 그녀가 대답했다.

■ 구문 Check-up ■

※ 다음 문장을 해석하여 문장의 주어(S)와 본동사(V)를 찾아 표시하시오.
(단, 병치 구조로 동사가 여러 개인 경우는 번호를 매길 것)

205 The supervisor was advised to give the assignment to whoever he believed had a strong sense of responsibility, and the courage of his conviction.

206 "Oh", she replied, "the President can just tell the Congress to take a vacation, and then he can go on and pass new laws or do whatever he wants".

정답

205 The supervisor(S) was advised(V) to give the assignment to whoever he believed had a strong sense of responsibility, and the courage of his conviction.

206 "Oh", she(S_1) replied(V_1), "the President can just tell the Congress to take a vacation, and then he(S_2) can go on and pass(V_2) new laws or do(V_2) whatever he wants".

71 복합 관계대명사 (2)

양보의 뜻을 갖는 '부사절'로도 쓰인다.

whoever : 누가 ~할지라도(= no matter who)
whatever : 무엇을 ~할지라도(= no matter what)
whichever : 어느 것을 ~할지라도(= no matter which)

ex Whoever says so, I don't believe it.
누가 그렇게 말할지라도, 나는 그것을 믿지 않는다.

Whatever he says, don't trust him.
그가 무슨 말을 할지라도, 그를 믿지 말라.

Whichever you choose, you will be satisfied.
어느 것을 고를지라도, 만족하실 겁니다.

207 Whatever the paintings meant, surely no one would have crawled to deep into these caves to paint had the pictures not had a special meaning. 2008 법원직 9급

어휘 crawl 기어가다 cave 동굴

해석 그 그림들이 무엇을 의미하든지 간에, 그 그림들이 특별한 의미가 없었더라면, 분명 어느 누구도 그 그림들을 그리기 위하여 이러한 동굴들 속으로 그렇게 깊이 들어가지 않았을 것이다.

208 No matter how satisfying our work is, it is a mistake to rely on a work as our only source of satisfaction. 2012 국가직 9급

어휘 satisfying 만족스러운 mistake 실수, 잘못 rely on 의존하다 source 출처, 원인

해석 우리의 일이 아무리 만족스럽다 할지라도, 우리의 유일한 만족의 원천으로 일에 의존하는 것은 실수이다.

209 No matter how upset you are, keep the feedback job-related and never criticize someone personally because of an inappropriate action. 2014 국가직 9급

어휘 upset 화가 난 feedback 반응 criticize 비판하다 personally 개인적으로 inappropriate 부적절한

해석 당신이 아무리 기분이 안 좋아도, 피드백을 항상 업무와 연관시키도록 하고, 누군가를 부적절한 행동 때문에 절대로 개인적으로 비난하지 마시오.

구문 Check-up

※ 다음 문장을 해석하여 문장의 주어(S)와 본동사(V)를 찾아 표시하시오. (단, 병치 구조로 동사가 여러 개인 경우는 번호를 매길 것)

207 Whatever the paintings meant, surely no one would have crawled to deep into these caves to paint had the pictures not had a special meaning.

208 No matter how satisfying our work is, it is a mistake to rely on a work as our only source of satisfaction.

209 No matter how upset you are, keep the feedback job-related and never criticize someone personally because of an inappropriate action.

정답

207 Whatever the paintings meant, surely no one(S) would have crawled(V) to deep into these caves to paint had the pictures not had a special meaning.

208 No matter how satisfying our work is, it is(V) a mistake to rely on a work(V) as our only source of satisfaction.

209 No matter how upset you are, keep(V_1) the feedback job-related and never criticize(V_2) someone personally because of an inappropriate action.

72 관계부사

1 관계부사는 부사를 대신하는 역할을 하므로 관계부사 뒤에는 완전한 절이 온다.

장소 + where

시간 + when

이유 + why

*관계부사 how는 the way how의 형식에서 the way나 how 중 하나가 생략되어야 한다.

ex This is the city where I was born.
여기가 내가 태어난 도시이다.

Now is the time when I need you most.
지금이 내가 너를 가장 필요한 때이다.

That's the reason why he was late.
그것이 그가 늦은 이유이다.

2 관계부사 where의 선행사로 'case, circumstance, instance, situation, point' 등의 비유적인 의미도 올 수 있다.

ex She got into a situation where she was forced to do so.
그녀는 그렇게 할 수 밖에 없는 상황에 처했다.

210 Casa Heiwa is an apartment building where people can learn some important life skills and how to cope with living in a new environment. 2016 서울시 9급

어휘 cope with 대처 / 대응하다 environment 환경

해석 카사 헤이와는 사람들이 몇 가지 삶의 중요한 능력들과 새로운 환경에 대처하는 방법을 배울 수 있는 아파트 건물이다.

211 Louis XIV needed a palace worthy of his greatness, so he decided to build a huge new house at Versailles, where a tiny hunting lodge stood. 2020 지방직 9급

어휘 worthy of ~ ~ 할 만한 가치가 있는, ~에 견줄만한 lodge 거처, 오두막
transform 바꾸다, 변신시키다

해석 루이 14세는 자신의 위대함에 견줄만한 궁전이 필요했고, 그래서 그는 베르사유에 거대한 새집을 짓기로 결정했는데, 그곳에는 아주 작은 사냥꾼 오두막이 있었다.

212 Children need to be taught that there are times when they will not be able to figure out the meaning from context clues. 2016 사회복지직 9급

어휘 be taught 배우다 figure out 알아내다, 이해하다 context 문맥, 맥락 clue 단서
해석 어린이들은 문맥의 실마리로부터 의미를 알아내지 못하는 때가 있다는 것을 배워야 할 필요가 있다.

213 On frigid winter days, when the wind and snow sweep down from Canada, the joggers wear heavy layers of clothes. 2011 국가직 9급

어휘 frigid 혹한의 sweep down 휩쓸고 내려오다 jogger 조깅하는 사람들 layer 겹, 층
해석 몹시 추운 겨울날, 그때는 바람과 눈이 캐나다로부터 휘몰아칠 때, 조깅하는 사람들은 두꺼운 층의 옷을 입는다.

214 Thousands of discarded computers from Western Europe and the U.S.A. arrive in the ports of West Africa every day, ending up in massive toxic dumps, where children burn and pull them apart to extract metals for cash. 2013 법원직 9급

어휘 discard 버리다 arrive 도착하다 port 항구 end up 결국 ~하다 massive 거대한 toxic 유해한, 유독한 dump 쓰레기 pull apart 분해하다 extract 추출하다 cash 현금
해석 서유럽과 미국에서 버려진 수천 대의 컴퓨터들은 매일 서아프리카의 항구에 도착하여, 결국 거대한 유독성 쓰레기 폐기장이 되는데, 그곳에서 아이들은 돈이 되는 금속을 골라내기 위하여 그것들을 태우고 분해한다.

구문 Check-up

※ 다음 문장을 해석하여 문장의 주어(S)와 본동사(V)를 찾아 표시하시오.
(단, 병치 구조로 동사가 여러 개인 경우는 번호를 매길 것)

210 Casa Heiwa is an apartment building where people can learn some important life skills and how to cope with living in a new environment.

211 Louis XIV needed a palace worthy of his greatness, so he decided to build a huge new house at Versailles, where a tiny hunting lodge stood.

212 Children need to be taught that there are times when they will not be able to figure out the meaning from context clues.

213 On frigid winter days, when the wind and snow sweep down from Canada, the joggers wear heavy layers of clothes.

214 Thousands of discarded computers from Western Europe and the U.S.A. arrive in the ports of West Africa every day, ending up in massive toxic dumps, where children burn and pull them apart to extract metals for cash.

정답

210 Casa Heiwa(S) is(V) an apartment building where people can learn some important life skills and how to cope with living in a new environment.

211 Louis XIV(S_1) needed(V_1) a palace worthy of his greatness, so he(S_2) decided(V_2) to build a huge new house at Versailles, where a tiny hunting lodge stood.

212 Children(S) need(V) to be taught that there are times when they will not be able to figure out the meaning from context clues.

213 On frigid winter days, when the wind and snow sweeo down from Canada, the joggers(S) wear(V) heavy layers of clothes.

214 Thousands of discarded computers(S) from Western Europe and the U.S.A. arrive(V) in the ports of West Africa every day, ending up in massive toxic dumps, where children burn and pull them apart to extract metals for cash.

73 a number of vs. an amount of

1 a (large / great / good) number of = many : 뒤에 가산명사의 복수형 an (large / great / good) amount of = much : 뒤에 불가산명사

ex) A number of books are displayed at the book fair.
많은 책들이 도서 박람회에서 전시되어 있다.

A great amount of water is needes.
많은 양의 물이 필요하다.

2 'the number of'는 '~의 수'라는 뜻으로 단수 취급한다.

ex) The number of books from the library is large.
그 도서관의 책의 수는 많다.

215 A number of students are studying very hard to get a job after their graduation. 2014 국가직 9급

어휘 graduation 졸업
해석 많은 학생들이 졸업 후 취직을 위해 열심히 공부한다.

216 The new research model has successfully demonstrated that the number of right whales has remained intact despite the worrisome, widening population gap between whale males and females. 2017 국가직 9급

어휘 right whale 참고래 intact 온전한, 완전한 worrisome 걱정되는, 귀찮은

해석 그 새로운 조사 모델은 고래 수컷과 암컷 사이의 개체 수 격차의 걱정스러운 확대에도 불구하고 참고래의 수가 온전한 상태로 남아 있다는 것을 성공적으로 입증하였다.

구문 Check-up

※ 다음 문장을 해석하여 문장의 주어(S)와 본동사(V)를 찾아 표시하시오.
(단, 병치 구조로 동사가 여러 개인 경우는 번호를 매길 것)

215 A number of students are studying very hard to get a job after their graduation.

216 The new research model has successfully demonstrated that the number of right whales has remained intact despite the worrisome, widening population gap between whale males and females.

정답

215 A number of students(S) are studying(V) very hard to get a job after their graduation.

216 The new research model(S) has successfully demonstrated(V) that the number of right whales has remained intact despite the worrisome, widening population gap between whale males and females.

74 that / those

1 두 가지를 비교하는 문장에서 반복되는 명사 뒤에 한정 수식어구가 있는 경우 단수명사는 that, 복수명사는 those로 받는다.

ex) The climate of Italy is similar to that of Korea.
= The climate of Italy is similar to the climate of Korea.
이탈리아의 기후는 한국의 기후와 비슷하다.

The ears of a rabbit are longer than those of a cat.
= The ears of a rabbit are longer than the ears of a cat.
토끼의 귀는 고양이의 귀보다 길다.

2 관계대명사의 선행사로 they, it은 쓸 수 없고, 복수는 those, 단수는 that으로 쓴다.

those who / which : ~하는 사람들 / 것들

that which : ~하는 것

ex They who were present were all pleased. (×)

⇨ Those who were present were all pleased. (○)

참석한 사람들은 모두 만족했다.

Say only it which is necessary. (×)

⇨ Say only that which is necessary. (○)

필요한 것만 말해라.

217 The adaptation of mammals to almost all possible modes of life parallels that of the reptiles in Mesozoic time. 2015 서울시 7급

어휘 adaptation 적응; 개작 mammal 포유류 mode of life 생활양식 parallel 유사한; 유사하다 reptile 파충류 Mesozoic 중생대의

해석 거의 모든 가능한 생활양식에 포유류가 적응하는 것은 중생대 파충류의 그것(적응)과 유사하다.

218 For its purpose any social regulation of mating and reproduction is as significant as our own, though it may be that of the Sea Dyaks, and have no possible historical relation to that of our civilization. 2010 국회직 8급

어휘 purpose 목적 regulation 규제 mating 짝짓기 reproduction 번식 significant 중요한 relation 관계 civilization 문명

해석 그것의 목적을 위하여 교미와 번식에 대한 그 어떠한 사회적인 규제도 비록 그것이 Sea Dyak족의 그것이고, 우리 문명의 그것과 가능한 역사적 관련이 없다고 할지라도 우리의 것만큼이나 중요하다.

219 Children are susceptible to the effects of television because their minds are growing, developing, and learning much faster than those of adults. I'd like to talk about some ways to make up with your families after an argument. 2016 경찰 1차

어휘 susceptible to~ ~에 민감한, 취약한 develop 발전하다 adult 성인 make up with~ ~와 화해하다

해석 아이들은 그들의 정신력이 성장하고 발달하고 성인들보다 더 빨리 학습하므로 텔레비전의 영향에 민감하다. 가족들과 말다툼 후에 화해할 수 있는 몇 가지 방법에 대해 이야기하겠다.

220 Those who do the right thing don't do it simply because of how they feel: the decision has to be based on reason, reason that tells you what your duty is, regardless of how you happen to feel. 2016 국가직 9급

어휘 decision 결정, 결심 be based on~ ~에 근거하다 duty 의무 regardless of~ ~에 상관없이 happen to R 우연히 ~하다

해석 올바른 일을 하는 사람은 단지 그들이 느끼는 감정 때문에 그 일을 하는 것이 아니다. 그 결정은 이성에 의거하며, 그 이성은 너에게 네가 어떠한 감정을 느끼는 것과는 상관없이 너의 의무가 무엇인지를 알려준다.

구문 Check-up

※ 다음 문장을 해석하여 문장의 주어(S)와 본동사(V)를 찾아 표시하시오.
(단, 병치 구조로 동사가 여러 개인 경우는 번호를 매길 것)

217 The adaptation of mammals to almost all possible modes of life parallels that of the reptiles in Mesozoic time.

218 For its purpose any social regulation of mating and reproduction is as significant as our own, though it may be that of the Sea Dyaks, and have no possible historical relation to that of our civilization.

219 Children are susceptible to the effects of television because their minds are growing, developing, and learning much faster than those of adults. I'd like to talk about some ways to make up with your families after an argument.

220 Those who do the right thing don't do it simply because of how they feel: the decision has to be based on reason, reason that tells you what your duty is, regardless of how you happen to feel.

정답

217 The adaptation(S) of mammals to almost all possible modes of life parallels(V) that of the reptiles in Mesozoic time.

218 For its purpose any social regulation(S) of mating and reproduction is(V) as significant as our own, though it may be that of the Sea Dyaks, and have no possible historical relation to that of our civilization.

219 Children(S) are(V) susceptible to the effects of television because their minds are growing, developing, and learning much faster than those of adults. I(S)'d like(V) to talk about some ways to make up with your families after an argument.

220 Those(S) who do the right thing don't do(V) it simply because of how they feel: the decision has to be based on reason, reason that tells you what your duty is, regardless of how you happen to feel.

75 원급 비교

1 as + 원급 + as~ : ~만큼 …하다

ex) She is as kind as her sister.
그녀는 언니만큼 친절하다.

2 부정문에서 앞의 as는 so가 대신 할 수 있다.

ex) She is not as / so kind as her sister.
그녀는 언니만큼 친절하지 않다.

3 긍정문에서 'so ~ as'는 쓸 수 없다.

ex) She is so kind as her sister. (×)

221 I walked on as briskly as the heat would let me until I reached the road which led to the village. 2017 지방직 7급

어휘 briskly 민첩하게, 빨리 lead to ~로 이어지다
해석 나는 더위가 허용하는 만큼 민첩하게 계속 걸어서, 마침내 그 마을로 이어지는 길에 도달하였다.

222 For example, trust in management — by far the biggest component of job satisfaction — is worth as much in your overall happiness as a very substantial raise. 2013 국가직 9급

어휘 trust 신뢰 management 관리, 경영 by far 단연코 component 요소 satisfaction 만족 worth 가치 있는 overall 전체적인, 전반적인 substantial 실질적인 raise 증가, 인상
해석 예를 들면, 경영진에 대한 신뢰는 — 이는 직무 만족에 있어서 단연코 가장 큰 요소인데 — 당신의 전반적인 행복에 있어서 아주 높은 임금 인상만큼이나 매우 가치가 있다.

구문 Check-up

※ 다음 문장을 해석하여 문장의 주어(S)와 본동사(V)를 찾아 표시하시오.
(단, 병치 구조로 동사가 여러 개인 경우는 번호를 매길 것)

221 I walked on as briskly as the heat would let me until I reached the road which led to the village.

222 For example, trust in management — by far the biggest component of job satisfaction — is worth as much in your overall happiness as a very substantial raise.

정답

221 I(S) walked(V) on as briskly as the heat would let me until I reached the road which led to the village.
222 For example, trust(S) in management — by far the biggest component of job satisfaction — is(V) worth as much in your overall happiness as a very substantial raise.

76 배수 비교

1 배수사 + as + 원급 + as~ : ~보다 몇 배 …한

= 배수사 + 비교급 + than(3배 이상일 때만 사용)
= 배수사 + the + 명사 + of

ex This is three times as long as that.
= This is three times longer than that.
= This is three times the length of that.
이것은 저것보다 3배나 길다.

2 twice(2배)는 비교급은 쓸 수 없고 'as ~ as'를 쓴다.

ex She has twice more money than you. (×)
⇨ She has twice as much money as you. (○)
그녀는 나보다 돈이 2배나 많다.

223 Their frequency and severity varies from person to person, but they strike women three times more often than men. 2009 법원직 9급

어휘 frequency 빈도 severity 심각함, 혹독함 vary 다르다 strike ~에게 발생하다 times ~배
해석 그것들(편두통)의 빈도와 혹독함은 사람마다 다르다. 하지만 그것들(편두통)은 남성들보다 여성들에게 세 배는 더 자주 발생한다.

■ 구문 Check-up ■

※ 다음 문장을 해석하여 문장의 주어(S)와 본동사(V)를 찾아 표시하시오.
(단, 병치 구조로 동사가 여러 개인 경우는 번호를 매길 것)

223 Their frequency and severity varies from person to person, but they strike women three times more often than men.

정답

223 Their frequency and severity(S_1) varies(V_1) from person to person, but they(S_2) strike(V_2) women three times more often than men.

77 원급을 이용한 관용 표현

1 not so much A as B : A라기 보다는 B이다.

= not A so much as B

= less A than B

= more B than A

= B rather than A

ex He is not so much a scholar as a writer.
= He is not a scholar so much as a writer.
= He is less a scholar than a writer.
= He is more a writer than a scholar.
= He is a writer rather than a scholar.
그는 학자라기보다는 작가이다.

2 not so much as + V : ~조차 못하다.

ex He cannot so much as write his own name.
그는 자신의 이름조차 쓰지 못한다.

224 "It's not so much what my husband says", a tearful wife tells me, "as the way he says it". 2008 지방직 9급

어휘 husband 남편 tearful 눈물 흘리는
해석 "문제는 제 남편이 말하는 내용보다는 그가 그것을 말하는 방식입니다".라고 한 울고 있는 부인이 나에게 말했다.

225 The important thing is not so much that every child should be taught, as that every child should be given the wish to learn. 2013 법원직 9급

어휘 be taught 배우다 wish 소망
해석 중요한 것은 모든 아이들이 배워야 한다는 것이라기 보다는 모든 아이들에게 배우고 싶은 소망이 주어져야 한다는 것이다.

226 Individuals captured office not so much on the strength of their political philosophy and policy as on the appeal of their personalities, charisma, and conquests. 2012 법원직 9급

어휘 individual 개인, 사람 capture 잡다 office 사무실; 공직 strength 힘, 장점 philosophy 철학 policy 정책 appeal 인기, 호소력 personality 성격, 인성
해석 개인들은 자신의 정치적인 철학과 정책에 힘을 입어서라기 보다는 자신의 성격, 카리스마, 그리고 정복에 호소하여 공직을 차지했다.

구문 Check-up

※ 다음 문장을 해석하여 문장의 주어(S)와 본동사(V)를 찾아 표시하시오.
(단, 병치 구조로 동사가 여러 개인 경우는 번호를 매길 것)

224 "It's not so much what my husband says", a tearful wife tells me, "as the way he says it".

225 The important thing is not so much that every child should be taught, as that every child should be given the wish to learn.

226 Individuals captured office not so much on the strength of their political philosophy and policy as on the appeal of their personalities, charisma, and conquests.

정답

224 "It's not so much what my husband says", "a tearful wife(S) tells(V) me, as the way he says it".

225 The important thing(S) is(V) not so much that every child should be taught, as that every child should be given the wish to learn.

226 Individuals(S) captured(V) office not so much on the strength of their political philosophy and policy as on the appeal of their personalities, charisma, and conquests.

78 비교급

1 비교급 + than~ : ~보다 더 …하다.

ex She studies harder than her brother.
그녀는 오빠보다 더 열심히 공부한다.

This is more interesting than that.
이것이 저것보다 재미있다.

2 동일한 대상의 두 가지 성질을 비교할 때는 음절에 관계없이 more를 쓴다. 이때의 more는 '오히려(rather)'의 뜻이다.

ex He is more clever than wise.
그는 현명하다기보다는 오히려 영리한 편이다.

227 The serum made from the crushed bodies of bees produced more adverse reactions than the injections of the venom did. 2013 국가직 9급

어휘 serum 혈청 crush 으깨다, 박살내다 adverse 반대의, 역의 injection 주사, 주입 venom 독
해석 수많은 으깬 벌의 몸통으로 만들어진 혈청은 독을 주사하는 것이 일으킨 것보다 더 많은 부작용을 낳았다.

228 For many viewers, the horrors they saw on television were more significant than the optimistic reports of impending victory issued by government officials and repeated in print accounts. 2008 법원직 9급

어휘 viewer 시청자 horror 공포 significant 중요한 optimistic 낙관적인 impending 임박한 issue 발행 / 발표하다 government official 정부관리 repeat 반복하다 account 설명, 보고
해석 많은 시청자들에게, 그들이 텔레비전에서 본 공포는 정부 공무원들에 의하여 공표되고 인쇄된 보고에서 반복된 임박한 승리의 낙관적인 보고들보다 더 의미심장했다.

229 Darwin knew far less about the various species he collected on the Beagle voyage than do experts in England at the time who classified these organisms for him. 2018 지방직 7급

어휘 various 다양한 species 종 collect 수집하다; 징수하다 voyage 항해 classify 분류하다 organism 유기체, 생물
해석 다윈은 그가 비글호 항해에서 수집한 다양한 종에 대해 그 당시 그를 위해 이 생물들을 분류한 영국의 전문가들보다 훨씬 덜 알고 있었다.

■ 구문 Check-up ■

※ 다음 문장을 해석하여 문장의 주어(S)와 본동사(V)를 찾아 표시하시오.
(단, 병치 구조로 동사가 여러 개인 경우는 번호를 매길 것)

227 The serum made from the crushed bodies of bees produced more adverse reactions than the injections of the venom did.

228 For many viewers, the horrors they saw on television were more significant than the optimistic reports of impending victory issued by government officials and repeated in print accounts.

229 Darwin knew far less about the various species he collected on the Beagle voyage than do experts in England at the time who classified these organisms for him.

정답

227 The serum(S) made from the crushed bodies of bees produced(V) more adverse reactions than the injections of the venom did.

228 For many viewers, the horrors(S) they saw on television were(V) more significant than the optimistic reports of impending victory issued by government officials and repeated in print accounts.

229 Darwin(S) knew(V) far less about the various species he collected on the Beagle voyage than do experts in England at the time who classified these organisms for him.

79 The + 비교급 ~, the + 비교급 ~

1 The + 비교급 + S + V, the + 비교급 + S + V : ~하면 할수록 더욱 더 …하다.

ex) The higher we go up, the colder the air becomes.
높이 올라갈수록, 공기는 더 차가워진다.

2 be동사가 생략되어 'the + 비교급' 뒤에 주어만 올 수도 있다.

ex) The thicker the clouds, the fiercer the storm.
= The thicker the clouds (are), the fiercer the storm (is).
구름이 짙으면 짙을수록, 폭풍우는 더 거세진다.

230 The more people there are in a conversation, the less well you know them, and the more status differences among them, the more a conversation is like public speaking or report-talk. 2015 서울시 7급

어휘 conversation 대화 status 지위, 위치 difference 차이 public 대중적인, 공적인, 공개적인

해석 대화에 더 많은 사람이 있을수록, 당신은 그들을 더 조금 알게 되고, 그들 사이의 상황의 차이가 더 많을수록, 대화는 공개 연설 또는 보고적 대화와 더 유사해진다.

231 Also, the more often a sea snake or other venomous animal is attacked, the more likely it is to get hurt — even if it can defend itself. 2016 법원직 9급

어휘 snake 뱀 venomous 독이 있는 attack 공격하다 likely 가능성 있는 get hurt 상처받다, 다치다 defend 방어하다

해석 또한, 바다뱀이나 다른 독을 가진 동물이 더 자주 공격을 받으면 받을수록, 비록 그것이 자신을 보호한다 해도, 그것이 다칠 가능성은 더욱 많아진다.

232 If you're sharing a living space with someone suffering from mild depression, you're at risk of becoming progressively more depressed the longer you live with them — you pick up their negative vibes. 2016 국회직 8급

어휘 share 공유하다 space 공간 suffer from ~로 인해 고통 받다 mild 약한, 온건한 depression 우울증 risk 위험 progressively 점진적으로, 점점 pick up 받아들이다 negative 부정적인

해석 만일 당신이 경미한 우울증을 앓고 있는 사람과 주거공간을 공유하고 있다면, 당신은 점차적으로 당신이 그들과 더 오래 함께 살수록 점차적으로 더 우울해지게 될 위험에 놓여서, 당신은 그들의 부정적인 기분(vibe)을 익히게 된다.

233 The more sophisticated an animal's brain, the greater the role that learning is likely to play in shaping its behavior, and the more variation we shall find between one individual and another. 2013 지방직 9급

어휘 sophisticated 정교한 role 역할 shape 형성하다, 만들다 behavior 행동 variation 변화, 변형 between ~사이에 individual 개인, 개체

해석 동물의 뇌가 정교하면 할수록, 행동을 형성하는 데에 학습이 기여할 역할은 더욱더 커지고, 그리고 한 개체와 다른 개체 사이에서 우리가 발견하게 될 차이는 점점 더 많아진다.

■ 구문 Check-up ■

※ 다음 문장을 해석하여 문장의 주어(S)와 본동사(V)를 찾아 표시하시오.
(단, 병치 구조로 동사가 여러 개인 경우는 번호를 매길 것)

230 The more people there are in a conversation, the less well you know them, and the more status differences among them, the more a conversation is like public speaking or report-talk.

231 Also, the more often a sea snake or other venomous animal is attacked, the more likely it is to get hurt — even if it can defend itself.

232 If you're sharing a living space with someone suffering from mild depression, you're at risk of becoming progressively more depressed the longer you live with them — you pick up their negative vibes.

233 The more sophisticated an animal's brain, the greater the role that learning is likely to play in shaping its behavior, and the more variation we shall find between one individual and another.

정답

230 The more people there are in a conversation, the less well <u>you(S_1)</u> <u>know(V_1)</u> them, and the more status differences among them, the more <u>a conversation(S_2)</u> <u>is(V_2)</u> like public speaking or report-talk.

231 Also, the more often a sea snake or other venomous animal is attacked, the more likely it <u>is(V)</u> <u>to get hurt(V)</u> — even if it can defend itself.

232 If you'are sharing a living space with someone suffering from mild depression, <u>you(S)'are(V)</u> at risk of becoming progressively more depressed the longer you live with them — you pick up their negative vibes.

233 The more sophisticated an animal's brain, the greater <u>the role(S_1)</u> that learning is likely to play in shaping its behavior, and the more variation <u>we(S_2)</u> <u>shall find(V_2)</u> between one individual and another.

80 no more ~ than / no less ~ than

1 A no more ~ than B…

= A not ~ any more than B… : A가 ~아닌 것은 B가 …아닌 것과 같다.

ex) A whale is no more a fish than a horse is.
= A whale is not a fish any more than a horse is.
고래가 물고기가 아닌 것은 말이 물고기가 아닌 것과 같다.

2 A no less ~ than B…: A가 ~인 것은 B가 …인 것과 같다.

ex) A whale is no less a mammal than a horse is.
고래가 포유동물인 것은 말이 포유동물인 것과 같다.

3 no less + 형용사 + than …
= as + 형용사 + as … : …만큼 ~한

ex) She is no less beautiful than her sister.
= She is as beautiful as her sister.
그녀는 언니만큼 예쁘다.

234 Language is no more a cultural invention than upright posture. 2009 국회직 8급

어휘 cultural 문화적인 invention 발명 upright 직립의 posture 자세
해석 언어는 직립 자세와 마찬가지로 문화적인 발명품이 아니다.

235 We are no more responsible for the evil thoughts which pass through our minds, than a scarecrow for the birds which fly over the seed plot he has to guard; the sole responsibility in each case is to prevent them from setting. 2009 국가직 9급

어휘 responsible 책임이 있는 evil 사악한 scarecrow 허수아비 seed 종자, 씨 plot (작은) 땅 guard 지키다 sole 유일한 responsibility 책임감 prevent A from ~ing A가 ~하는 것을 막다
해석 우리는 허수아비가 지켜야 하는 모판 위를 날아다니는 새에 대해서 책임이 없는 것처럼 우리 마음속을 지나는 나쁜 생각들에 대한 책임은 없다. 각각의 경우에서 책임은 그것들이 자리를 잡는 것을 막는 일에 있다.

구문 Check-up

※ 다음 문장을 해석하여 문장의 주어(S)와 본동사(V)를 찾아 표시하시오.
(단, 병치 구조로 동사가 여러 개인 경우는 번호를 매길 것)

234 Language is no more a cultural invention than upright posture.

235 We are no more responsible for the evil thoughts which pass through our minds, than a scarecrow for the birds which fly over the seed plot he has to guard; the sole responsibility in each case is to prevent them from setting.

정답

234 Language(S) is(V) no more a cultural invention than upright posture.

235 We(S) are(V) no more responsible for the evil thoughts which pass through our minds, than a scarecrow for the birds which fly over the seed plot he has to guard; the sole responsibility in each case is to prevent them from setting.

81 원급 · 비교급을 이용한 최상급 표현

1 부정주어 + so + 원급 + as …: 아무도 …만큼 ~하지 않다

= 부정주어 + 비교급 + than

ex No boy in his class is so tall as Tom.
= No boy in his class is taller than Tom.
그의 반의 어떤 애도 톰만큼 / 톰보다 키가 크지 않다.

2 비교급 + than any other + 단수명사: 그 누구보다 더 ~하다

= 비교급 + than any of the other + 복수명사
= 비교급 + than (all) the other + 복수명사
= 비교급 + than anyone / anything else

ex Tom is taller than any other boy in his class.
= Tom is taller than any of the other boys in his class.
= Tom is taller than (all) the other boys in his class.
= Tom is taller than anyone else in his class.
톰은 그의 반의 다른 어떤 아이보다 더 키가 크다.

236 Coral reefs support more species per unit area than any other marine environment, including about 4,000 species of fish, 800 species of hard corals and hundreds of other species. 2016 법원직 9급

어휘 coral reef 산호 species 종, 생물 per ~당 unit 단위 marine 바다의 environment 환경 include 포함하다

해석 산호초는 4천 종의 물고기, 8백 종의 단단한 산호 그리고 수백의 다른 종들을 포함해서 어떤 다른 해양환경보다 단위면적당 더 많은 종들을 부양한다.

237 The price of art attracts more public attention than any other commodity — except perhaps oil. 2010 법원직 9급

어휘 price 가격 attract 끌다, 끌어당기다 public attention 대중적인 관심 commodity 상품 except ~을 제외한

해석 예술 작품의 가격은 그 어떠한 다른 상품보다도 – 아마도 석유를 제외하고 – 더 대중의 관심을 끈다.

구문 Check-up

※ 다음 문장을 해석하여 문장의 주어(S)와 본동사(V)를 찾아 표시하시오.
(단, 병치 구조로 동사가 여러 개인 경우는 번호를 매길 것)

236 Coral reefs support more species per unit area than any other marine environment, including about 4,000 species of fish, 800 species of hard corals and hundreds of other species.

237 The price of art attracts more public attention than any other commodity — except perhaps oil.

정답

236 Coral reefs(S) support(V) more species per unit area than any other marine environment, including about ,000 species of fish, 800 species of hard corals and hundreds of other species.

237 The price(S) of art attracts(V) more public attention than any other commodity — except perhaps oil.

82 품사의 병치

1 명사 + 접속사 + 명사
형용사 + 접속사 + 형용사
부사(구) + 접속사 + 부사(구)

ex She has beauty and wealth.
그녀는 미모와 재력을 겸비했다.

These shoes are old but comfortable.
이 신발은 오래되었지만 편안하다.

He closed the door slowly and silently.
그는 문을 천천히 그리고 조용하게 닫았다.

2 부사구가 병치될 때 뒤의 전치사는 생략할 수 있다.

ex) We stayed mostly in Paris and (in) Rome.
우리는 주로 파리와 로마에 머물렀다.

238 Fifty years ago, bees lived healthy lives in our cities and rural areas because they had plenty of flowers to feed on, fewer insecticides contaminating their floral food and fewer exotic diseases and pests. 2016 법원직 9급

어휘 rural 시골의 plenty of~ 풍부한 feed on~ ~을 먹고 살다 insecticide 살충제 contaminate 오염시키다 floral 꽃의 exotic 이국적인, 외래의 pest 해충

해석 오십 년 전, 벌들은 그들이 먹고 살 많은 꽃들과 그들의 음식인 꽃을 오염시키는 더 적은 살충제와 더 적은 외래성 질병과 해충을 가졌었기 때문에 우리 도시와 시골에서 건강하게 살았었다.

239 The American withdrawal from the Philiippines and the decrease of the U.S. military because of the end of the Cold War and economic troubles at home are also partially reasonable for this power vacuum. 2013 국가직 7급

어휘 withdrawal from~ ~에서 철수, 도피 decrease 감소 military 군대의 trouble 문제 partially 부분적으로 reasonable 합리적인; 원인이 되는 vacuum 진공

해석 냉전의 종식과 미국 국내에서의 경제 침체 때문에, 필리핀에서의 미국 철수와 미군의 감소는 이러한 권력 공백에 부분적으로 책임이 있다.

구문 Check-up

※ 다음 문장을 해석하여 문장의 주어(S)와 본동사(V)를 찾아 표시하시오.
(단, 병치 구조로 동사가 여러 개인 경우는 번호를 매길 것)

238 Fifty years ago, bees lived healthy lives in our cities and rural areas because they had plenty of flowers to feed on, fewer insecticides contaminating their floral food and fewer exotic diseases and pests.

239 The American withdrawal from the Philiippines and the decrease of the U.S. military because of the end of the Cold War and economic troubles at home are also partially reasonable for this power vacuum.

정답

238 Fifty years ago, bees(S) lived(V) healthy lives in our cities and rural areas because they had plenty of flowers to feed on, fewer insecticides contaminating their floral food and fewer exotic diseases and pests.

239 The American withdrawal from the Philiippines and the decrease of the U.S. military because of the end of the Cold War and economic troubles at home(S) are(V) also partially reasonable for this power vacuum.

83 동사의 병치

1 동사 + 접속사 + 동사

ex) She raised her hand and asked a question.
그녀는 손을 들고 질문을 했다.

2 동일한 조동사가 반복될 때 뒤에 오는 조동사는 보통 생략한다.

ex) He will leave at eight and (will) arrive at nine.
그는 8시에 출발해서 9시에 도착할 것이다.

He is waving his arms and (is) shouting at us.
그는 양팔을 흔들고 우리에게 소리치고 있다.

Someone was killed or (was) injured.
누군가가 죽었거나 다쳤다.

240 Both diet and exercise can help you maintain a healthy weight, keep you feeling energized, and protect you from sickness. 2009 국가직 9급

어휘 exercise 운동 maintain 유지하다 weight 무게 protect 보호하다 sickness 질병
해석 식이 요법과 운동은 둘 다 당신이 건강한 몸무게를 유지하고, 열정을 느끼도록 유지하고, 당신을 질병으로부터 보호하는 데 도움을 준다.

241 And some of these agents, if taken over the course of months, may lead to dependency or stop working altogether. 2009 소방직 9급

어휘 agent 촉매제; 주체; 원인; 약 take 섭취하다 course 과정 lead to~ ~을 초래하다 dependency 의존 altogether 완전히
해석 그리고 이런 약들의 일부는, 몇 달에 걸쳐 복용을 하게 되면, 중독을 유발하거나 효과가 완전히 사라질 수 있다.

구문 Check-up

※ 다음 문장을 해석하여 문장의 주어(S)와 본동사(V)를 찾아 표시하시오.
(단, 병치 구조로 동사가 여러 개인 경우는 번호를 매길 것)

240 Both diet and exercise can help you maintain a healthy weight, keep you feeling energized, and protect you from sickness.

241 And some of these agents, if taken over the course of months, may lead to dependency or stop working altogether.

정답

240 Both diet and exercise(S) can help(V_1) you maintain a healthy weight, keep(V_2) you feeling energized, and protect(V_3) you from sickness.

241 And some of these agents(S), if taken over the course of months, may lead(V_1) to dependency or stop(V_2) working altogether.

84 준동사의 병치

1 부정사 + 접속사 + 부정사
동명사 + 접속사 + 동명사
분사 + 접속사 + 분사

ex To know and to teach are quite different things.
아는 것과 가르치는 것은 전혀 다른 것이다.

I enjoy reading novels or watching movies.
나는 소설을 읽거나 영화를 보는 것을 즐긴다.

Surprised and embarrassed, she burst into tears.
놀라고 당황해서 그녀는 울음을 터뜨렸다.

2 to부정사가 병치될 때 뒤의 to는 생략할 수 있다.

ex He wants to watch TV or (to) listen to music.
그는 TV를 보거나 음악을 듣고 싶어 한다.

242 Watching them grow from the experience and ultimately seeing them succeed because of your tuition and guidance is a feeling without comparison. 2016 사회복지직 9급

어휘 ultimately 궁극적으로 tuition 교육, 수업 guidance 지도 comparison 비교

해석 그들이 경험을 통해 성장하는 것을 보는 것과 마침내 그들이 당신의 교습과 지도로 인해 성공하는 것을 보는 것은 비교할 수 없는 (벅찬) 느낌이다.

243 When people are having a rough time, usually the first question we ask them is "How are you?" because we think it's a way to open up the conversation and to show that we care. 2016 기상직 9급

어휘 rough 거친 conversation 대화 care 배려하다, 신경 쓰다

해석 사람들이 힘든 시기를 겪고 있을 때, 우리가 묻는 첫 번째 질문은 대개 "어떻게 지내?"라는 말이다. 그 이유는 이것이 대화를 시작하게 하고 우리가 신경 쓰고 있다는 사실을 보여줄 수 있는 방법이라고 우리가 생각하기 때문이다.

244 You are constantly engaging with them on a personal level, inspiring them to strive to do the best they can and providing support when they run into problems. 2016 사회복지직 9급

어휘 constantly 끊임없이 engage with~ ~와 관계를 맺다 personal 개인적인
inspire 고무하다, 격려하다 strive to~ ~하려 애쓰다 provide 제공하다 run into~ ~에 부딪히다

해석 당신은 학생들에게 그들이 할 수 있는 최선을 다하도록 노력하라고 격려하고 그들이 문제에 직면했을 때 지원을 하면서, 당신은 지속적으로 개인적인 차원에서 그들과 관계를 맺는다.

245 Adrenaline travels all over the body doing things such as widening the eyes to be on the lookout for signs of danger, pumping the heart faster to keep blood and extra hormones flowing, and tensing the skeletal muscles so they are ready to lash out at or run from the threat. 2020 국가직 9급

어휘 lookout 경계 tense (근육 등을) 긴장시키다 skeletal muscles 골격근
lash out at 공격하다; 비난하다

해석 아드레날린은 온몸을 이동하면서 위험 징후들을 경계하기 위해 눈을 크게 뜨고, 혈액과 부수적인 호르몬들이 계속 흘러가도록 심장을 더 빠르게 펌프질하고, 그리고 골격근을 긴장시켜 위험에 맞서 공격하거나 위험으로부터 달아날 준비를 하는 것과 같은 일들을 한다.

246 The company should carry on internal brand building to help employees understand and be enthusiastic about the brand promise. 2013 지방직 7급

어휘 company 회사 carry on~ ~을 계속하다 internal 내적인 employee 직원
enthusiastic 열정적인 promise 약속; 가능성

해석 그 회사는 직원들이 브랜드 가능성을 이해하고 열의를 가지도록 하기 위하여 내부적인 브랜드 구축을 계속 해야 한다.

■ 구문 Check-up ■

※ 다음 문장을 해석하여 문장의 주어(S)와 본동사(V)를 찾아 표시하시오.
(단, 병치 구조로 동사가 여러 개인 경우는 번호를 매길 것)

242 Watching them grow from the experience and ultimately seeing them succeed because of your tuition and guidance is a feeling without comparison.

243 When people are having a rough time, usually the first question we ask them is "How are you?" because we think it's a way to open up the conversation and to show that we care.

244 You are constantly engaging with them on a personal level, inspiring them to strive to do the best they can and providing support when they run into problems.

245 Adrenaline travels all over the body doing things such as widening the eyes to be on the lookout for signs of danger, pumping the heart faster to keep blood and extra hormones flowing, and tensing the skeletal muscles so they are ready to lash out at or run from the threat.

246 The company should carry on internal brand building to help employees understand and be enthusiastic about the brand promise.

정답

242 Watching them grow from the experience and ultimately seeing them succeed because of your tuition and guidance(S) is(V) a feeling without comparison.

243 When people are having a rough time, usually the first question(S) we ask them is(V) How are you?" because we think it's a way to open up the conversation and to show that we care.

244 You(S) are constantly engaging(V) with them on a personal level, inspiring them to strive to do the best they can and providing support when they run into problems.

245 Adrenaline(S) travels(V) all over the body doing things such as widening the eyes to be on the lookout for signs of danger, pumping the heart faster to keep blood and extra hormones flowing, and tensing the skeletal muscles so they are ready to lash out at or run from the threat.

246 The company(S) should carry(V) on internal brand building to help employees understand and be enthusiastic about the brand promise.

85 절의 병치

1 절 + 접속사 + 절

ex) They went to the movies but I stayed at home.
그들은 영화를 보러 갔지만 나는 집에 있었다.

2 종속절이 병치될 때 뒤의 접속사는 생략하지 않는다.

ex) He knew that he was potentially an alcoholic, and he should drink no more. (×)
⇨ He knew that he was potentially an alcoholic, and that he should drink no more. (○)
그는 잠재적으로 알코올 중독자여서 더이상 술을 마시지 말아야 한다는 것을 알았다.

247 I have always taught my children that politeness, learning, and order are good things, and that something good is to be desired and developed for its own sake. 2016 법원직 9급

어휘 politeness 예절 order 질서, 정돈 desire 원하다 for its own sake 그 자체로

해석 나는 항상 아이들에게 공손함, 학습 그리고 정돈이 좋은 것이며 바람직한 것은 그것 자체 때문에 갈망되고 개발되어야 한다고 가르쳤다.

248 As an actor, director and teacher, he was destined to influence and inspire the many who worked with him and under him or who had the privilege of seeing him on the stage. 2016 국가직 9급

어휘 actor 배우 director 감독 be destined to R ~할 운명이다 influence 영향을 끼치다 inspire 영감을 주다, 고무하다 privilege 특권 stage 무대

해석 배우, 연출가, 교사로서 그와 함께 또는 밑에서 일하는 사람 또는 무대 위에 있는 그를 볼 수 있는 특권을 가졌던 사람들에게 그는 영향을 주고 고무시킬 운명이었다.

249 Confirmation that a severed head is a good match with an unidentified torso, and that a bent leg found on the Chatsworth Estate in Derbyshire actually belongs to a different body, sounds like the plot of a thriller, but this is the work of restorers preparing a star exhibit for a British Museum show on Sicily. 2016 국회직 8급

어휘 confirmation 확인, 확증 sever 절단하다, 자르다 match 어울리다 unidentified 신분 확인이 안 된, 정체를 모르는 torso 흉상 bent 휘어진 actually 실제로 belong to~ ~에 속하다 plot 음모; (작은) 땅 thriller 스릴러 restorer 복원전문가 exhibit 전시

해석 절단된 머리는 미확인 몸통과 좋은 조화를 이루고 있고 또 Derbyshire의 Chatsworth Estate에서 발견된 굽은 다리가 다른 신체에 속한다고 하는 확인은 스릴러물의 줄거리와 닮은 것처럼 생각되지만, 이것은 Sicily에서의 대영박물관 쇼를 위한 탁월한 하나의 전시물(a star exhibit)을 준비하고 있는 복원전문가들의 업무이다.

250 Among these distressed tribes there was developed a new type of scale — scales that were elongated into quill-like forms and that presently branched into the crude beginnings of feathers. 2016 국가직 9급

어휘 among ~중에서 distressed 고통 받는 tribe 부족 scale 비늘 elongate 늘리다 quill 깃털 form 형태 presently 바로, 즉시 branch into~ ~로 갈라지다 crude 조잡한, 뭉툭한 feather 깃털

해석 이러한 곤경에 처한 종족 사이에서, 새로운 형태의 비늘이 생겨나게 되었다 — 깃털과 같은 형태로 길어져 나와 곧 깃털의 뭉툭한 끝의 형태로 갈라져 나오는 형태의 비늘이다.

251 By all that I have ever read, I am convinced that it is very common indeed, that human nature is particularly prone to it, and that there are very few of us who do not cherish a feeling of self-complacency on the score of some quality or other, real or imaginary. 2013 법원직 9급

어휘 be convinced 확신하다 common 흔한 human nature 인간성 particularly 특히 be prone to~ ~하는 경향 / 성향이 있다 cherish 소중히 여기다 complacency 만족감 on the score of~ ~한 이유 때문에 quality 특징

해석 내가 여태껏 읽었던 모든 것에 의하여, 그것은 정말로 매우 흔하며, 인간의 본성은 특히 그러기 쉬우며, 그리고 실제로든지 상상으로든지, 이런저런 이유로 우리들 가운데에서 자만심을 품지 않은 사람은 거의 없다고 확신한다.

구문 Check-up

※ 다음 문장을 해석하여 문장의 주어(S)와 본동사(V)를 찾아 표시하시오.
(단, 병치 구조로 동사가 여러 개인 경우는 번호를 매길 것)

247 I have always taught my children that politeness, learning, and order are good things, and that something good is to be desired and developed for its own sake.

248 As an actor, director and teacher, he was destined to influence and inspire the many who worked with him and under him or who had the privilege of seeing him on the stage.

249 Confirmation that a severed head is a good match with an unidentified torso, and that a bent leg found on the Chatsworth Estate in Derbyshire actually belongs to a different body, sounds like the plot of a thriller, but this is the work of restorers preparing a star exhibit for a British Museum show on Sicily.

250 Among these distressed tribes there was developed a new type of scale — scales that were elongated into quill-like forms and that presently branched into the crude beginnings of feathers.

251 By all that I have ever read, I am convinced that it is very common indeed, that human nature is particularly prone to it, and that there are very few of us who do not cherish a feeling of self-complacency on the score of some quality or other, real or imaginary.

정답

247 I(S) have always taught(V) my children that politeness, learning, and order are good things, and that something good is to be desired and developed for its own sake.

248 As an actor, director and teacher, he(S) was(V) destined to influence and inspire the many who worked with him and under him or who had the privilege of seeing him on the stage.

249 Confirmation(S_1) that a severed head is a good match with an unidentified torso, and that a bent leg found on the Chatsworth Estate in Derbyshire actually belongs to a different body, sounds(V_1) like the plot of a thriller, but this(S_2) is(V_2) the work of restorers preparing a star exhibit for a British Museum show on Sicily.

250 Among these distressed tribes there was developed(V) a new type of scale(S) — scales that were elongated into quill-like forms and that presently branched into the crude beginnings of feathers.

251 By all that I have ever read, I(S) am convinced(V) that it is very common indeed, that human nature is particularly prone to it, and that there are very few of us who do not cherish a feeling of self-complacency on the score of some quality or other, real or imaginary.

86 부정부사(구) + 조동사 + 주어 + 동사

부정부사(구)가 문두에 오면 '조동사 + 주어 + 동사'로 도치된다.

never, little, hardly, scarcely, seldom, rarely, not only, not until, no sooner, no longer

ex Never will I forget your kindness.
= I will never forget your kindness.
결코 당신의 친절을 잊지 않겠습니다.

Little did I dream that I could see her again.
= I little dreamed that I could see her again.
그녀를 다시 보리라고는 꿈에도 생각하지 못했다.

Hardly had he seen me when he ran away.
= He had hardly seen me when he ran away.
그는 나를 보자마자 도망갔다.

252 Not only were residents' lives devastated by the tragedy, but emotional and other costs were also borne by families, friends, and fellow citizens throughout the country. 2013 국가직 7급

어휘 resident 주민 devastate 파괴하다 tragedy 비극 emotional 감정적인 cost 비용
be borne by ~ ~가 감당하다, 떠안다 fellow 동료 throughout ~의 도처에

해석 그 비극적인 참사에 의하여 주민들의 삶이 피폐해졌을 뿐만 아니라, 전국에 있는 가족들, 친구들 그리고 동료 시민들에 의하여 감정적인 그리고 다른 대가(희생)가 부담되었다.

253 When he left his hometown thirty years ago, little did he dream that he could never see it again. 2015 국가직 9급

어휘 hometown 고향

해석 30년 전 고향을 떠날 때, 그는 다시는 고향을 못 볼 거라고 꿈에도 생각하지 않았다.

254 No sooner had he finished one task than he was asked to do another one. 2017 지방직 7급

어휘 task 과제

해석 그는 하나의 일을 끝내자마자 다른 일을 하도록 요청을 받았다.

구문 Check-up

※ 다음 문장을 해석하여 문장의 주어(S)와 본동사(V)를 찾아 표시하시오.
(단, 병치 구조로 동사가 여러 개인 경우는 번호를 매길 것)

252 Not only were residents' lives devastated by the tragedy, but emotional and other costs were also borne by families, friends, and fellow citizens throughout the country.

253 When he left his hometown thirty years ago, little did he dream that he could never see it again.

254 No sooner had he finished one task than he was asked to do another one.

정답

252 Not only were(V_1) residents' lives(S_1) devastated(V_1) by the tragedy, but emotional and other costs(S_2) were also borne(V_2) by families, friends, and fellow citizens throughout the country.

253 When he left his hometown thirty years ago, little did(V) he(S) dream(V) that he could never see it again.

254 No sooner had(V) he(S) finished(V) one task than he was asked to do another one.

87 so / neither[nor] + 조동사 + 주어

1 앞 문장에 동의를 하며 다른 주어도 '역시' 그렇다는 내용을 전달할 때, 긍정문 뒤에는 so, 부정문 뒤에는 neither / nor를 쓰고 '조동사 + 주어'로 도치된다.

ex I like movies. – So do I.
나는 영화를 좋아해. – 나도 그래

I don't like movies. – Neither / Nor do I.
나는 영화를 좋아하지 않아. – 나도 그래.

2 so 뒤에 도치가 되지 않으면 '정말 그렇다'의 뜻이다.

ex You seem to like movies. – So I do.
당신은 영화를 좋아하는 것 같군요. – 정말 그래요.

255 Body type was useless as a predictor of how the men would fare in life. So was birth order or political affiliation. 2014 국가직 9급

어휘 useless 쓸모없는 predictor 예측지표 fare 지내다 birth order 태어난 순서 affiliation 연합, 소속

해석 신체 유형은 사람들이 사는 동안 어떻게 잘 살아갈 수 있을까에 대한 예측 지표로서 유용하지 못했다. 출생 순서나 정치적 소속 또한 마찬가지였다.

256 I never did anything by accident, nor did any of my inventions come by accident. 2016 사회복지직 9급

어휘 by accident 우연히 invention 발명품

해석 나는 어떤 일도 결코 우연히 하지 않았으며, 내 발명 중 어느 것도 우연히 이루어진 것은 없었다.

257 Unfortunately, the teacher-in-space program was indefinitely put on hold. So were NASA's plans to send musicians, journalists, and artists to space. 2013 국가직 9급

어휘 unfortunately 불행히도 space 우주 indefinitely 무기한 put on hold 연기하다 journalist 기자

해석 불행하게도, 선생님을 우주로 보내는 프로그램은 무한히 보류되었다. 음악가, 기자, 예술가들을 우주로 보내려는 NASA의 계획들도 역시 마찬가지였다.

구문 Check-up

※ 다음 문장을 해석하여 문장의 주어(S)와 본동사(V)를 찾아 표시하시오.
(단, 병치 구조로 동사가 여러 개인 경우는 번호를 매길 것)

255 Body type was useless as a predictor of how the men would fare in life. So was birth order or political affiliation.

256 I never did anything by accident, nor did any of my inventions come by accident.

257 Unfortunately, the teacher-in-space program was indefinitely put on hold. So were NASA's plans to send musicians, journalists, and artists to space.

정답

255 Body type(S) was(V) useless as a predictor of how the men would fare in life. So was(V) birth order or political affiliation(S).

256 I(S_1) never did(V_1) anything by accident, nor did(V_2) any of my inventions(S_2) come(V_2) by accident.

257 Unfortunately, the teacher-in-space program(S) was indefinitely put(V) on hold. So were(V) NASA's plans(S) to send musicians, journalists, and artists to space.

88 장소부사(구) + 동사 + 주어

1 장소부사(구)가 문두에 오고 동사가 자동사인 경우 동사와 주어가 조동사를 이용하지 않고 직접 도치된다.

ex On the hill does a church stand. (×)
⇨ On the hill stands a church. (○)
= A church stands on the hill.
언덕 위에 교회가 하나 있다.

Among his chief works are Hamlet and King Lear.
= Hamlet and King Lear are among his chief works.
그의 주요 작품 중에 햄릿과 리어왕이 있다.

2 주어가 대명사이면 도치가 일어나지 않는다.

ex Here comes he. (×)

⇨ Here he comes. (○)

여기 그가 온다.

258 In such foolish fears lie **the beginnings of the blighting of individuality, the thwarting of personality, the stealing of the wealth of one's capital for living joyously and well in a confused world.** 2016 서울시 7급

어휘 fear 두려움　blighting 파괴, 말살　individuality 개성　thwarting 전복, 파탄
personality 인성, 개성　stealing 절도　wealth 부, 재산　capital 자본　joyously 즐겁게
confused 혼란스러운

해석 그러한 어리석음의 근거는 개성의 상실, 성격의 파탄, 혼동의 세상에서 즐겁게 잘 살 수 있는 수단이 되는 개인의 부인 자본의 도난이 시작되었다는 것이다.

259 At the extreme end are **teenagers instant-messaging while they are talking on the cell phone, downloading music and doing homework.** 2016 사회복지직 9급

어휘 extreme 극단적인　instant 즉각적인

해석 그 최극단에는 통화, 음악 다운로드, 숙제 그리고 문자 전송을 동시에 하는 10대들이 있다.

260 Among her most prized possessions sold during the evening sale was **a 1961 bejeweled timepiece by Bulgari.** 2020 지방직 9급

어휘 prized 소중한　possession 소유물　bejeweled 보석이 박힌　timepiece 시계

해석 그 저녁 경매에서 팔린 그녀의 가장 소중한 소유물 중에는 Bulgari에서 1961년에 만든 보석으로 장식된 시계가 있었다.

구문 Check-up

※ 다음 문장을 해석하여 문장의 주어(S)와 본동사(V)를 찾아 표시하시오.
(단, 병치 구조로 동사가 여러 개인 경우는 번호를 매길 것)

258 In such foolish fears lie **the beginnings of the blighting of individuality, the thwarting of personality, the stealing of the wealth of one's capital for living joyously and well in a confused world.**

259 At the extreme end are **teenagers instant-messaging while they are talking on the cell phone, downloading music and doing homework.**

260 Among her most prized possessions sold during the evening sale was **a 1961 bejeweled timepiece by Bulgari.**

정답

258 In such foolish fears lie(V) the beginnings of the blighting of individuality, the thwarting of personality, the stealing of the wealth of one's capital for living joyously and well in a confused world(S).

259 At the extreme end are(V) teenagers(S) instant-messaging while they are talking on the cell phone, downloading music and doing homework.

260 Among her most prized possessions sold during the evening sale was(V) a 1961 bejeweled timepiece(S) by Bulgari.

89 보어 + be동사 + 주어

형용사나 분사보어가 강조를 위해 문두에 오면 be동사와 주어가 도치된다.

ex) Happy is the man who is content with his lot.
= The man who is content with his lot is happy.
자기의 운명에 만족하는 사람은 행복하다.

Standing by the door is a pretty girl.
= A pretty girl is standing by the door.
어떤 예쁜 여자애가 문 옆에 서 있다.

Forbidden in this building is smoking.
= Smoking is forbidden in this building.
이 건물에서는 흡연이 금지되어 있다.

261 Standing in front of you is a young man who needs help. 2016 국가직 9급

어휘 in front of~ ~의 앞에
해석 당신 앞에는 도움이 필요한 한 젊은이가 서 있다.

262 Happy are those who find joy and pleasure in helping others. 2011 지방직 7급

어휘 pleasure 기쁨
해석 남을 돕는 데서 기쁨과 즐거움을 찾는 사람들은 행복하다.

263 Of equal importance in wars of conquest were the germs that evolved in human societies with domestic animals. 2015 국가직 9급

어휘 equal 동등한 conquest 정복 germ 세균 evolve 진화하다 domestic 길들여진
해석 정복 전쟁에 있어서 그만큼이나 중요했던 것은 가축과 함께 있는 인간 사회 속에서 진화했던 세균들이었다.

■ 구문 Check-up ■

※ 다음 문장을 해석하여 문장의 주어(S)와 본동사(V)를 찾아 표시하시오.
(단, 병치 구조로 동사가 여러 개인 경우는 번호를 매길 것)

261 Standing in front of you is a young man who needs help.

262 Happy are those who find joy and pleasure in helping others.

263 Of equal importance in wars of conquest were the germs that evolved in human societies with domestic animals.

정답

261 Standing in front of you is(V) a young man(S) who needs help.
262 Happy are(V) those(S) who find joy and pleasure in helping others.
263 Of equal importance in wars of conquest were(V) the germs(S) that evolved in human societies with domestic animals.

90 as / than + 동사 + 주어

1 as, than 뒤에서 'be / 조동사 / 대동사 do'가 쓰인 경우 도치가 될 수 있다.

ex He traveled widely as did most of his friends.
= He traveled widely as most of his friends did.
그는 그의 대부분의 친구들이 그런 것처럼 널리 여행했다.

I spend more time reading books than does my brother.
= I spend more time reading books than my brother does.
나는 동생보다 독서하는 데 더 많은 시간을 보낸다.

2 주어가 대명사이면 도치되지 않는다.

ex They arrived earlier than did she. (×)
⇨ They arrived earlier than she did. (○)
그들은 그녀보다 일찍 도착했다.

264 Streets that are narrow, steep, or shaded, receive special attention, as do those streets scheduled for next-day trash collection. 2006 국가직 9급

어휘 narrow 좁은 steep 가파른 shade 그늘진, 어두운 attention 관심, 주목 trash 쓰레기

해석 좁거나, 가파르거나 또는 그늘진 길거리들은, 다음날 쓰레기 수거가 계획되어 있는 그러한 길거리들처럼 특별한 주목을 받는다.

구문 Check-up

※ 다음 문장을 해석하여 문장의 주어(S)와 본동사(V)를 찾아 표시하시오.
(단, 병치 구조로 동사가 여러 개인 경우는 번호를 매길 것)

264 Streets that are narrow, steep, or shaded, receive special attention, as do those streets scheduled for next-day trash collection.

정답

264 Streets(S) that are narrow, steep, or shaded, receive(V) special attention, as do those streets scheduled for next-day trash collection.

91 It is ~ that 강조구문

1 It is + 명사/부사(구) + that ~: ~한 것은 다름 아닌 …이다

ex) Columbus discovered America in 1492

콜럼버스가 1492년에 미국을 발견했다..

⇨ It was Columbus that discovered America in 1492. (주어 강조)

⇨ It was America that Columbus discovered in 1492. (목적어 강조)

⇨ It was in 1492 that Columbus discovered America. (부사구 강조)

2 강조어구가 '사람'일 경우는 that 대신에 who를, '사물'일 경우는 which를 쓸 수 있다.

ex) It was Columbus who discovered America in 1492.

1492년에 아메리카를 발견한 것은 콜럼버스였다.

It was America which Columbus discovered in 1492.

콜럼버스가 1492년에 발견한 것은 아메리카였다.

3 시간의 부사(구)를 강조할 때는 that 대신에 when으로 바꿀 수 없다.

ex It was in 1492 when Columbus discovered America. (×)

⇨ It was in 1492 that Columbus discovered America. (○)

콜럼버스가 아메리카를 발견한 것은 1492년이었다.

265 It was when I got support across the board politically, from Republicans as well as Democrats, that I knew I had done the right thing. 2016 서울시 9급

어휘 across the board 전반에 걸쳐 republican 공화당원 democrat 민주당원

해석 내가 민주당원뿐만 아니라 공화당원에게서도 폭넓은 정치적 지지를 받았을 때, 나는 내가 옳은 일을 했다는 것을 확신하게 되었다.

266 It was at the 1928 St. Moritz Winter Games that skeleton made its Olympic debut. 2016 기상직 9급

어휘 debut 데뷔, 첫 등장

해석 skeleton이 올림픽에 최초로 등장한 것은 1928년 St. Moritz 동계올림픽이었다.

267 In our time it is not only the law of the market which has its own life and rules over man, but also the development of science and technique. 2018 지방직 9급

어휘 rule over ~를 지배하다 development 발달 technique 기술

해석 우리의 시대에, 스스로의 생명력을 가지고 인간을 지배하는 것은 시장의 법칙뿐만이 아니라 과학과 기술의 발전도 마찬가지다.

268 Moreover, it is generally the young and active members of the population who tend to migrate, leaving the old people, the children, and the infirm to run the farms, which is hardly likely to improve the efficiency of the farms. 2013 서울시 9급

어휘 active 능동적인 migrate 이동하다 the infirm 병약자들 run the farms 농장을 운영하다 improve 개선하다 efficiency 효율성

해석 게다가, 노인들, 아이들 그리고 병약자들에게 농장을 운영하도록 남기고 도시로 이주하는 경향이 있는 것은 일반적으로 인구 중 젊고 활동적인 구성원들이다. 이로 인하여 농장은 효율성이 향상될 가능성이 거의 없다.

269 It was not until the mid-1950s that the term greenhouse effect was coupled with concern over climate change. 2008 지방직 7급

어휘 not until~ ~해서야, ~후에서야 term 용어 greenhouse effect 온실 효과 be coupled with~ ~와 결합되다 concern 우려 climate change 기후 변화

해석 온실 효과라는 용어가 기후 변화에 대한 우려와 결합된 것은 바로 1950년대 중반이 되어서였다.

■ 구문 Check-up ■

※ 다음 문장을 해석하여 문장의 주어(S)와 본동사(V)를 찾아 표시하시오.
(단, 병치 구조로 동사가 여러 개인 경우는 번호를 매길 것)

265 It was when I got support across the board politically, from Republicans as well as Democrats, that I knew I had done the right thing.

266 It was at the 1928 St. Moritz Winter Games that skeleton made its Olympic debut.

267 In our time it is not only the law of the market which has its own life and rules over man, but also the development of science and technique.

268 Moreover, it is generally the young and active members of the population who tend to migrate, leaving the old people, the children, and the infirm to run the farms, which is hardly likely to improve the efficiency of the farms.

269 It was not until the mid-1950s that the term greenhouse effect was coupled with concern over climate change.

정답

265 It was when I got support across the board politically, from Republicans as well as Democrats, that I(S) knew(V) I had done the right thing.

266 It was at the 1928 St. Moritz Winter Games that skeleton(S) made(V) its Olympic debut.

267 In our time it is not only the law of the market(S_1) which has(V_1) its own life and rules(V_2) over man, but also the development of science and technique(S_2).

268 Moreover, it is generally the young and active members of the population(S) who tend(V) to migrate, leaving the old people, the children, and the infirm to run the farms, which is hardly likely to improve the efficiency of the farms.

269 It was not until the mid-1950s that the term greenhouse effect(S) was coupled(V) with concern over climate change.

92 (As) + 형용사 / 명사 + As + S + V

(As) + 형용사 / 무관사 명사 + as + S + V: 비록 ~이지만

ex (As) young as he is, he has a lot of experiences
비록 그는 젊지만, 그는 많은 경험이 있다.

Boy as he is, he behaves himself like a woman.
비록 그는 소년이지만, 여자처럼 행동한다.

270 As admirable as setting goals and reaching them may be, **you can't get so focused on accomplishing your goals that you make the mistake of not enjoying where you are right now.** 2016 지방직 9급

어휘 admirable 존경, 경탄할 만한 set goal 목표를 정하다 reach 도달하다 focused on~ ~에 집중하는 accomplish 성취하다 mistake 실수, 잘못

해석 목표를 정하고 거기에 도달하는 것은 멋진 일이지만, 당신의 목표 도달에 너무 집중해서 현재 지금 있는 곳에서 즐기지 못하는 실수를 만들어서는 안 된다.

271 Intrigued as he was, **Spencer decided upon further experimentation.** 2016 법원직 9급

어휘 intrigued 흥미를 느끼는 decide upon~ ~을 결정, 선택하다 further 심화된, 추가적인 experimentation 실험

해석 그는 매우 흥미로웠지만, 추가적인 실험을 해 보기로 결정했다.

272 As incredible as it sounds, **there are some species of insects that will sacrifice themselves to protect their nests.** 2016 서울시 9급

어휘 incredible 믿을 수 없는 species 종, 생물 insect 곤충 sacrifice 희생하다 protect 보호하다

해석 믿을 수 없는 소리 같지만, 집을 지키기 위해 스스로를 희생하는 몇몇 곤충들이 있다.

구문 Check-up

※ 다음 문장을 해석하여 문장의 주어(S)와 본동사(V)를 찾아 표시하시오. (단, 병치 구조로 동사가 여러 개인 경우는 번호를 매길 것)

270 As admirable as setting goals and reaching them may be, **you can't get so focused on accomplishing your goals that you make the mistake of not enjoying where you are right now.**

271 Intrigued as he was, **Spencer decided upon further experimentation.**

272 As incredible as it sounds, **there are some species of insects that will sacrifice themselves to protect their nests.**

정답

270 As admirable as setting goals and reaching them may be, you(S) can't get(V) so focused on accomplishing your goals that you make the mistake of not enjoying where you are right now.

271 Intrigued as he was, Spencer(S) decided(V) upon further experimentation.

272 As incredible as it sounds, there are(V) some species(S) of insects that will sacrifice themselves to protect their nests.

문덕 영어
독해

PART

02

유형 독해

Chapter

01 독해 전략

01 문장 분석 부호 활용법

1 문장 성분에 대한 이해

모든 문장은 '주어'와 '동사'를 반드시 가지고 있어야 하며 문장 구조에 따라 다른 성분들로 구성될 수 있다.

(1) **주성분**: 주어(명사), 술어(동사), 목적어(명사), 보어(명사 또는 형용사)

(2) **수식어**: 형용사 수식어(명사 수식), 부사 수식어(동사, 형용사, 또는 다른 부사 수식)

ex) The student believes the truth firmly. (그 학생은 그 진리를 굳게 믿는다)

주어 / 동사 / 목적어 / 부사 수식어

2 문장 분석 기호의 단순화

기호 사용법

(1) **수식어구**(부사구, 부사절, 관계절 계속적 용법, 전명구, 분사구문, 동격의 명사구): ( )

(2) **후치 형용사구, 동격의 that절, 관계절 한정적 용법**: ↰( )

(3) **명사적 that절, 명사적 whether / if절, 의문사절, 관계대명사 what절**: [ ]

(4) **병치**: 밑줄로 번호 붙이기

ex) Though he is sometimes confronted with an unexpected barricade, the dauntless youth, a 30-year-old student, inspired by Tom's success, still believes firmly that he who does not give up his own dream will be given a hand from somewhere without fail, regain energy to revive the discouraged mind, and finally come by his cherished goal, if only he sticks it out with MD.

비록 그는 때때로 예기치 못한 장애물에 직면하고 있지만, 그 불굴의 청년은 이제 나이가 30이고 Tom의 성공에 영감을 받아서 아직도 굳게 믿고 있는 사실이 있으니 그것은 바로 자신만의 꿈을 포기하지 않는 사람은 반드시 어딘가로부터 도움을 받게 될 것이고 낙심한 마음을 다시 살려낼 에너지를 얻게 되어 마침내 소중히 품어온 목표를 얻게 된다는 것이다. 만약 그가 문덕과 함께 버티어 내기만 한다면 말이다.

02 문제 유형별 독해 전략

1 제목 / 주제 / 요지찾기 전략

- 주제(topic)나 요지(main idea)파악은 독해 문제 해결의 70%의 열쇠이다.
- 첫 문장과 두 번째 문장을 통해서 글의 ___(1)___(subject matter)를 먼저 찾고 주제를 탐색한다.
- 요지(main idea)는 주제를 문장으로 표현한 양식이다.
- 대부분의 글은 다음 세 가지의 유형의 주제나 요지를 드러내는 signal이 있다.

(1) **연결어 signal**: 이러한 연결어의 앞뒤에 주제문이 있다.

① **역접 연결어 ___(2)___의 문장이 주제문이다**: but, however, on the contrary, on the other hand

② 결론 표시 유도어 then, therefore, consequently, in sum, in fact, really, actually ___(3)___의 문장이 주제문이다.

③ for example와 같은 예시문 ___(4)___의 일반적(general)이고 포괄적인 진술이 주제문이다.

(2) **어휘 signal**: 이러한 표현이 들어 있는 문장이 주제문이다.

① I think, I believe처럼 자신의 생각을 표현하는 문장이 주제문이다.

② should, need to, necessary, important 등 ___(5)___을 드러내는 문장이 주제문이다.

③ no wonder(당연하게도), no doubt(명백히), in fact(사실상) 등은 주제문을 동반하는 경우가 있다.

④ '최상급/one of' 뒤에 key word가 나온다.

⑤ ___(6)___를 나타내는 시간부사들은 주제문이 될 가능성이 많다(구정보나 통속적 사실보다는 신정보나 예외적 사실이 주제문이다.).

⑥ 'It ___ that' 강조 구문/Not A but B/비교와 대조 구문에서 주제가 드러난다.

(3) **내용 signal**: 이러한 내용이 들어 있는 문장이 주제문이다.

① 전문가, 연구소, 통계자료 등의 인용이 나오면 주제문이다.

② '질문'과 '대답'에서는 ___(7)___이 주제문이다.

③ no wonder(당연하게도), no doubt(명백히), in fact(사실상) 등은 주제문을 동반하는 사실(fact)과 의견(opinion)에서는 ___(8)___이 주제문이다.

④ '사건'에 대해서는 '___(9)___'이 '문제'에 대해서는 '___(10)___'이 그리고 '주장'에 대해서는 '___(11)___'가 각각 주제문이다.

정답

(1) 소재 (2) 뒤 (3) 뒤 (4) 앞 (5) 당위성 (6) 현재 (7) 대답 (8) 의견 (9) 원인 (10) 해결책 (11) 논거

예제

다음 글의 주제로 가장 적절한 것은? 2019 국가직 9급

Imagine that two people are starting work at a law firm on the same day. One person has a very simple name. The other person has a very complex name. We've got pretty good evidence that over the course of their next 16 plus years of their career, the person with the simpler name will rise up the legal hierarchy more quickly. They will attain partnership more quickly in the middle parts of their career. And by about the eighth or ninth year after graduating from law school the people with simpler names are about seven to ten percent more likely to be partners — which is a striking effect. We try to eliminate all sorts of other alternative explanations. For example, we try to show that it's not about foreignness because foreign names tend to be harder to pronounce. But even if you look at just white males with Anglo-American names — so really the true in-group, you find that among those white males with Anglo names they are more likely to rise up if their names happen to be simpler. So simplicity is one key feature in names that determines various outcomes.

① the development of legal names
② the concept of attractive names
③ the benefit of simple names
④ the roots of foreign names

정답 ③

해설 이 글의 소재는 'name(이름)'이며 이름이 출세에 미치는 영향에 관하여 서술하고 있다. 주제문은 맨 마지막 문장인 'So simplicity is one key feature in names that determines various outcomes.'인데 결론 유도어 so가 주제를 드러내는 signal 역할을 하고 있다. 그러므로 정답은 단순한 이름이 이점이 있다는 ③이다.

어휘 **hierarchy** 계급, 계층; 지배층, 고위층 **partnership** 동반자 관계, 동업 **striking** 눈에 띄는, 두드러진 **alternative** 대체 가능한, 대안이 되는 **explanation** 해명, 이유; 설명 **rise up** 출세하다 **feature** 특징; 이목구비; 특집기사; 장편영화

해석 두 사람이 같은 날 로펌에서 일을 시작한다고 상상해 보라. 한 사람은 아주 간단한 이름을 가지고 있다. 다른 사람은 아주 복잡한 이름을 가지고 있다. 우리는 그들의 다음 16년 이상의 경력 동안 더 단순한 이름을 가진 사람이 더 빨리 법적인 직위 위에 오를 것이라는 꽤 충분한 증거를 가지고 있다. 그들은 자신들의 경력 중반부에 더 빨리 경영 변호사의 지위를 얻게 될 것이다. 그래서 로스쿨을 졸업한 지 8년 내지 9년쯤 되면 더 단순한 이름을 가진 사람들은 7에서 10프로 정도 더 경영 변호사가 될 가능성이 많으며 이것은 놀라운 효과이다. 우리는 다른 가능한 설명들을 없애려고 한다. 예를 들어 그것은 이국적임에 대한 것이 아닌 것은 이국적인 이름들은 발음하기가 더 어려워지는 경향이 있기 때문이다. 하지만 여러분이 영미인 이름을 가진 그러므로 진정으로 내집단인 백인 남성들일지라도, 여러분은 영미인 이름을 가진 백인 남성들 중에서, 만약 그들의 이름이 공교롭게도 더 단순하다면 그들이 출세할 가능성이 더 높다는 것을 알게 된다. 따라서 단순성은 다양한 결과를 결정하는 이름에 담겨있는 하나의 핵심적 특징이다.

① 법적인 이름의 발달
② 매력적인 이름의 개념
③ 단순한 이름의 이점
④ 외국 이름의 유래

2 내용 일치 문제 전략

(1) 내용 일치 문제 풀이 순서

① 일치와 불일치 중 어느 것을 묻는지 체크한다.

② 선택지의 ①과 ② 항목을 읽고 내용을 숙지한다.

③ 지문의 절반 정도를 읽어가며 선택지 ①②와 비교하며 정답을 찾는다.

④ (①②에 정답이 없는 경우) 선택지의 ③과 ④ 항목을 읽고 내용을 숙지한다.

⑤ 지문의 나머지 절반을 읽어가며 선택지 ③④와 비교하며 정답을 찾는다.

(2) 내용 일치 문제 풀기 유의 사항

① 반드시 선택지를 ___(1)___ 읽어야 한다.

② 선택지에 반복적으로 등장하는 단어가 주로 ___(2)___이다.

③ 선택지에서 특히 고유명사, 형용사, 숫자, 부정어, 비교급 표현 등에 표시한다.

④ 선택지에 'all, every, never, always, absolutely, the only' 등의 표현이 등장하면 본문에서 이러한 사항이 있었는지 반드시 확인해야 한다.

⑤ 선택지와 본문의 내용이 순서가 섞여 있는 경우는 우선 본문을 ___(3)___까지 빠르게 읽어나가면서 선택지 정답 여부를 체크한다.

⑥ 본문에 나온 사실에 초점을 맞추며 유추나 비약된 내용은 피해야 한다.

⑦ 본문의 내용을 유사한 표현으로 바꾸는 ___(4)___에 특히 유의한다(동의어나 반의어 활용, 구문변화 등).

⑧ 내용이 일치하는 것을 묻는 문제는 주로 ___(5)___이 정답이 확률이 대단히 높다. 내용의 불일치를 묻는 문제는 주로 글의 후반부 부분의 내용을 출제한다.

정답

(1) 먼저 (2) 핵심어(key word) (3) 중간 (4) paraphrasing (5) 주제문

예제

다음 글의 내용과 일치하지 않는 것은? 2020 국가직 9급

The Second Amendment of the U.S. Constitution states: "A well-regulated Militia, being necessary to the security of a free State, the right of the people to keep and bear Arms, shall not be infringed". Supreme Court rulings, citing this amendment, have upheld the right of states to regulate firearms. However, in a 2008 decision confirming an individual right to keep and bear arms, the court struck down Washington, D.C. laws that banned handguns and required those in the home to be locked or disassembled. A number of gun advocates consider ownership a birthright and an essential part of the nation's heritage. The United States, with less than 5 percent of the world's population, has about 35~50 percent of the world's civilian-owned guns, according to a 2007 report by the Switzerland-based Small Arms Survey. It ranks number one in firearms per capita. The United States also has the highest homicide-by-firearm rate among the world's most developed nations. But many gun-rights proponents say these statistics do not indicate a cause-and-effect relationship and note that the rates of gun homicide and other gun crimes in the United States have dropped since highs in the early 1990's.

① In 2008, the U.S. Supreme Court overturned Washington, D.C. laws banning handguns.
② Many gun advocates claim that owning guns is a natural-born right.
③ Among the most developed nations, the U.S. has the highest rate of gun homicides.
④ Gun crimes in the U.S. have steadily increased over the last three decades.

정답 ④

해설 마지막 문장에 나타나듯이 미국의 총기 관련 범죄는 1990년대 정점을 찍은 이후 감소세이므로 증가세라는 ④은 이 글의 내용과 일치하지 않는다. 또한 이 문제는 비록 주제 찾기 문제는 아니지만 그럼에도 불구하고 주제를 드러내는 강력한 signal인 역접 연결어 'but' 이하의 문장으로 내용 일치를 출제하고 있는 점에 유의하자. 이렇게 많은 내용 일치 문제 또한 주제 signal에 유의하면서 풀 필요가 있다.

① 세 번째 문장인 'However, in a 2008 decision confirming an individual right to keep and bear arms, the court struck down Washington, D.C. laws that banned handguns and required those in the home to be locked or disassembled.'에 권총을 금지하는 법안을 폐지했다는 내용이 나온다.

② 바로 아래 문장인 'A number of gun advocates consider ownership a birthright and an essential part of the nation's heritage'에 총기소유는 천부적 권리라는 내용이 드러난다.

③ A 마지막에서 위로 두 번째 문장인 'The United States also has the highest homicide-by-firearm rate among the world's most developed nations.'에 미국이 총기 살인 1위국임을 알 수 있다.

어휘 **well-regulated** 잘 규제된 **militia** 민병대 **security** 보안, 안보 **infringe** 침해하다 **cite** 인용하다 **uphold** 옹호하다, 지탱하다 **strike down** 폐지하다 **disassemble** 분해하다, 해체하다 **advocate** 옹호자, 지지자; 옹호하다, 지지하다 **birthright** 생득권, 타고난 권리 **heritage** 유산 **per capita** 1인당 **homicide** 살인 **proponent** 지지자, 제안자 **statistics** 통계학, 통계 자료 **indicate** 나타내다 **cause-and-effect relationship** 인과관계 **note** 언급하다, 지적하다

해석 미국 헌법 수정 제2조는 다음과 같다: "잘 규율된 민병대는 자유로운 주(洲)의 안보에 필수적이므로 무기를 소지할 수 있는 국민의 권리는 침해될 수 없다". 대법원의 판결은 이 헌법 수정조항을 인용하여 총기를 규제할 수 있는 주(洲)들의 권리를 옹호해왔다. 그러나 2008년의 무기를 소유하고 휴대할 수 있는 개인의 권리를 확인하는 결정에서 법원은 권총을 금지하고 권총을 가정에서 안전장치를 해 두거나 분해해 둘 것을 규정하는 워싱턴 D.C.의 법을 기각했다. 많은 총기의 약 35~50%를 보유하고 있는 지지자들은 소유권을 천부의 권리이며 이 국가 유산의 중요한 부분으로 여긴다. 스위스에 기반을 둔 Small Arms Survey(국제 무기조사기관)의 2007년 보고서에 따르면, 세계 인구의 5% 미만인 미국이 민간소유 총기의 약 35~50%를 가지고 있다. 미국은 1인당 총기에서 첫째를 차지한다. 미국은 또한 세계의 가장 발전된 국가들 중에서 가장 높은 총기에 의한 살인율을 가지고 있다. 그러나 많은 총기 소유권 지지자들은 이러한 통계들이 인과관계를 나타내지 않는다고 말하고 1990년대 초의 최고치를 찍은 이후로 총기 살인과 다른 총기 범죄의 비율이 계속해서 떨어지고 있다는 점을 지적한다.

① 2008년에 미국 연방 대법원은 권총을 금지하는 Washington D.C.의 법을 뒤집었다.

② 많은 총기 옹호자들은 총기의 소유는 천부의 권리라고 주장한다.

③ 선진국들 중에서 미국은 가장 높은 총기 살인율을 가지고 있다.

④ 미국에서 총기 관련 범죄는 최근 30년 넘게 꾸준하게 증가하고 있다.

3 빈칸 완성 문제 풀이 전략

(1) 빈칸 완성 문제란?

빈칸 완성 문제는 글의 논리적 흐름에 맞도록 적절한 단어나 내용을 빈칸에 채우는 '문장완성(sentence completion)형' 문제이다. 다른 문제에 비해 문장의 구조가 복잡하고 어휘의 수준이 높은 단어들이 주로 선택지로 등장하기 때문에 논리적 사고 능력과 함께 풍부한 어휘력을 필요로 하는 까다로운 문제형태이다.

(2) signal과 clue

signal(시그널, 신호)은 주어진 문장에 순접과 역접 중 어떤 논리관계가 들어있는지를 드러내는 접속사나 접속부사, 전치사 등을 가리킨다. Clue(단서)는 빈칸에 들어갈 내용을 짐작하게 하는 단어나 표현을 가리킨다.

ex) Because he was a brave soldier, he fought ________ during the battle.
signal(순접) clue
그는 용감한 병사였기 때문에 전투 중에 ________ 싸웠다.

(3) 전형적인 논리 문제 풀이 4단계

① △하기(signal 찾기)
먼저 △(순접, 역접의 signal)를 함으로써 두 가지 진술의 논리관계를 파악한다.

ex) 다음 문장들에서 순접이나 역접을 드러내는 signal을 찾아보자.

Because he was a brave soldier, he fought ________ during the battle.
△
Because he was a ________ soldier, he fought dauntlessly during the battle.
△
He was a brave soldier, and he fought ________ during the battle.
△
He was a ________ soldier, and fought dauntlessly during the battle.
△

② □하기(clue 찾기)
논리의 signal를 기준으로 빈칸이 있는 곳의 ______에 □(clue)가 있다.

1. △ □ , 빈칸
2. △ 빈칸 , □
3. □ △ 빈칸
4. 빈칸 △ □

ex 다음 문장들에서 머릿속으로 먼저 signal을 찾은 다음에 clue를 찾아보자.

> Because he was a brave soldier, he fought ________ during the battle.
> □
>
> Because he was a ________ soldier, he fought dauntlessly during the battle.
> □
>
> He was a brave soldier, and he fought ________ during the battle.
> □
>
> He was a ________ soldier, and he fought dauntlessly during the battle.
> □

③ □의 단순화(simplification)

확보된 위치의 clue가 긴 경우에는 그 내용을 간략하게 한국어로 요약하여 머릿속에 담는다.

참고 clue가 길지 않고 단순할 때는 통과하는 단계로서 빈칸 완성 문제가 어려워 보이는 가장 큰 이유가 바로 이 점에 있으며 파악한 단서가 긍정적인 내용(+)인지 부정적인(−) 내용인지로 가늠해보는 것도 역시 단순화에 해당한다.

ex 다음 주어진 문장에서 clue를 찾아보고 한글로 그 clue를 단순화해보자.

> Because he was a ______ soldier, the captain insisted on fighting it out along the line even if it took all the summer.
> 그는 ________ 병사였기 때문에 그 대위는 설사 여름 전체가 걸리더라도 계속 끝까지 싸울 것을 고집했다.
> ⇨ (용감하네!)
>
> Because he was a ________ soldier, the captain didn't hesitate to burn his boat.
> 그는 ________ 병사였기 때문에 그 대위는 배수진을 치는 것을 망설이지 않았다. ⇨ (용감하네!)
>
> Although the fighter was famous for his _______ nationwide. the latest incident in which he was involved a couple of weeks ago revealed the other side behind his gallant image. ⇨ (비겁하네!)
> 비록 그는 전국적으로 그의 ________로 유명했지만, 그가 몇 주전에 연루된 가장 최근의 사건은 그의 용감한 이미지 뒤에 있는 다른 면을 보여주었다.)

④ □를 빈칸에 적용하여 답 찾기

㉠ 순접: 단순화된 clue를 그대로 중얼거리며 빈칸을 채운다.

ex 다음 문장들의 빈칸에 들어갈 적절한 단어를 채우시오.

> Because he was a brave soldier, he fought ___①___ during the battle.
>
> Because he was a ___②___ soldier, he fought dauntlessly during the battle.
>
> He was a brave soldier; he fought ___③___ during the battle.

He was a ___④___ soldier; he fought dauntlessly during the battle.

Because he was a ___⑤___ soldier, the captain insisted on fighting it out along the line even if it took all the summer.
그는 ______ 군인이라서 그 대위는 설사 온 여름이 걸리더라도 끝까지 계속 싸우기를 주장했다.

Because he was a ___⑥___ soldier, the captain didn't hesitate to burn his boat. ⇨ (용감하네!)
그는 ______ 군인이라서, 그 대위는 배수진을 치는 것을 주저하지 않았다.

정답

① dauntlessly ② brave ③ dauntlessly ④ brave ⑤ brave ⑥ brave

ⓛ **역접**: clue나 단순화된 clue를 반대로 부정한 다음에 그것을 빈칸 부분과 함께 중얼거리며 빈칸을 채운다.

ex) 다음 문장에 빈칸에 들어갈 적절한 단어를 채우시오.

완성문장: Although he was a brave soldier, he got daunted by the enemy's raid.
(비록 그는 용감한 병사였지만 적의 급습에 겁을 먹었다.)

Although he was a brave soldier, he got ___①___ by the enemy's raid.
[1단계 signal 찾기: although(역접) ⇨ 2단계 clue 찾기: was a brave soldier(용감한 병사다) ⇨ (clue가 단순하므로 3단계 통과) ⇨ 4단계 정답 찾기: clue가 '용감한 병사다'인데 역접이므로 '용감한 병사가 아니다'로 부정한 후에 빈칸 부분에 함께 중얼거려 적용해보면 '용감한 병사가 아니므로 적의 급습에 겁을 먹게(daunted)되었다.'로 답을 유추해 낼 수 있다.]

Although he was a ___②___ soldier, he got daunted by the enemy's raid.
He was a brave soldier, but he got ___③___ by the enemy's raid.

He was a ___④___ soldier, but he got daunted by the enemy's raid.

Although the fighter was famous for his ___⑤___ nationwide. the latest incident in which he was involved a couple of weeks ago revealed the other side behind his gallant image.
비록 그 파이터는 전국적으로 그의 ________로 유명했지만, 그가 몇 주 전에 연루된 사건은 그의 용감한 이미지의 다른 면을 드러냈다.
[1단계 signal 찾기: although(역접) ⇨ 2단계 clue 찾기: revealed the other side behind his gallant image (그의 용감한 이미지 뒤의 다른 면을 보여주었다) ⇨ 3단계 clue 단순화: 비겁하다! ⇨ 4단계 정답 찾기: clue가 '비겁하다!'인데 signal이 역접이므로 '비겁한 병사가 아니다 / 용감한 병사다'로 부정한 후에 빈칸 부분에 함께 중얼거려 적용해보면 '전국적으로 용감함(bravery)으로 유명했다'로 답을 유추해 낼 수 있다.]

정답

① daunted ② brave ③ daunted ④ brave ⑤ bravery

(4) 순접과 역접의 signal들

순접 논리의 △Signal들

접속사	접속부사 or 부사	전치사
[그리고]	[그래서: 인과관계]	[~ 때문에]
And	Therefore	Because of
Or	Then	Due to
	Thus	Thanks to
[이유]	Hence	Owing to
Because	As a result	On account of
Since	Consequently	On the ground of
As	Accordingly	
In that / Now that / seeing that	So that	[~처럼, ~과 함께]
For	For that reason	Like
		According to
[시간과 조건]	[역시, 마찬가지로]	By
When	Also	With(~와 함께 / 부대상황)
As	Too	
After / Until	As well	[준동사들]
While(~하는 동안에)	Likewise	~ing/pp 분사구문
If와 대용어구	Moreover	to부정사
	Furthermore	동명사 구문
[관계사, 접속사]	Besides	(*to부정사/동명사는 내용에 따라
That, Who, Which, Where 등	In addition	역접 가능)
	In fact	
[문장 부호들]		
;(semicolon), :(colon)		
—(dash), ,(comma), .(period)		

순접의 상관어구 △Signal들

A와 B는 한 마음	너무나 A해서 B하다	술부가 주어와 보어의 순접을 유도하는 것들
A and B	so A that B (인과관계)	A is B
both A and B(역접 가능)	such A that B (인과관계)	A result in B
A and B alike(역접 가능)	such that	A lead to B
not only A but (also) B	(= so good / bad that)	A contribute to B
B as well as A(역접 가능)		A have an effect on B
(Just) as A, so B		A is a cause / the reason /
either A or B		the result of B

역접의 △Signal들

접속사	접속부사 or 부사	전치사
But	Nevertheless	Despite/ In spite of
Although	Nonetheless	Instead of(~하지 않고)
Though	On the other hand	Far from(결코 ~아닌)
Even Though	In / by contrast	Apart from(~는 제쳐두고)
(Even) if	Still	Except (for)
Even when	Actually	Without
While(~하는 반면에)	Ironically	Unlike
Unless	Paradoxically	Contrary to
Whereas	All the same(그래도, 역시)	regardless of(~과 상관없이)
Yet	However(그렇지만, 그러나)	After all(결국, ~에도 불구하고)
period	However(= no matter how) (아무리 ~해도)	Notwithstanding/ With all/ For all(~에도 불구하고)
	Even(~ 조차도)	

역접의 상관어구 △Signal들

A는 No, B는 Yes	A는 B와 두 마음	술부가 A와 B의 역접관계를 유도하는 것들
less A than B	whether A or B,	A is not B
more B than A	the former … A, the latter … B	A belie B
B rather than A	one … A~, the other … B	B is belied by A
would rather B than A	some A ~, others B ~	A disprove B
may as well B as A	range / shift from A to B	A contradict B
not A but B		
B, not A		
not so much A as B		
prefer B to A		

(5) 장문 빈칸 완성 전략

① '좁게' 풀려고 노력하라

㉠ '좁풀'은 장문 빈칸 완성 문제를 풀 때 무턱대고 처음부터 읽어 나가지 않고 '좁게 푸는' 것을 가리킨다.

㉡ blank가 포함된 문장으로 최대한 승부하라. 안 풀릴 때 앞뒤 문장으로 가는데 대부분 빈칸 이후의 문장에 clue가 있다.

㉢ 단 'however, therefore'와 같은 강한 연결사가 빈칸 앞쪽에 있을 때는 앞 문장을 본다.

㉣ 특별한 연결어가 없는 경우는 문장과 문장 사이는 '순접'의 논리가 유지됨을 기억하자.

ⓜ 빈칸에 해당하는 선택지는 아래의 방식처럼 문제를 풀어 clue에 대한 어느 정도의 이해가 된 이후에 읽어야 한다.

② 빈칸의 위치에 따른 문제 접근 전략

㉠ 빈칸이 첫 문장에 있을 때

ⓐ 첫 문장과 두 번째 문장으로 '좁풀'을 시도한다.

ⓑ 세 번째 문장 정도까지 읽어도 안 풀리면 맨 끝 문장으로 간다.

㉡ 빈칸이 중간에 있을 때

ⓐ 해당 문장과 그 다음 문장으로 '좁풀'을 시도한다.

ⓑ 강한 연결사가 빈칸이 포함된 문장에 들어있는 경우는 바로 앞 문장과의 관계로 푼다.

ⓒ 무슨 내용인지 전혀 감이 오지 않으면 맨 첫 문장으로 가서 글의 소재를 파악해 본다.

③ 빈칸이 끝 문장에 있을 때

㉠ 빈칸이 들어있는 문장과 바로 앞 문장으로 '좁풀'을 시도한다.

㉡ 거꾸로 세 번째 문장 정도까지 읽어도 안 풀리면 맨 첫 문장으로 간다.

㉢ 무슨 내용인지 전혀 감이 오지 않으면 맨 첫 문장으로 가서 소재를 파악해 본다.

예제

밑줄 친 부분에 들어갈 말로 가장 적절한 것은? 2020 지방직 9급

All of us inherit something: in some cases, it may be money, property or some object — a family heirloom such as a grandmother's wedding dress or a father's set of tools. But beyond that, all of us inherit something else, something ______________________, something we may not even be fully aware of. It may be a way of doing a daily task, or the way we solve a particular problem or decide a moral issue for ourselves. It may be a special way of keeping a holiday or a tradition to have a picnic on a certain date. It may be something important or central to our thinking, or something minor that we have long accepted quite casually.

① quite unrelated to our everyday life
② against our moral standards
③ much less concrete and tangible
④ of great monetary value

정답 ③

해설 빈칸이 포함된 문장의 맨 앞의 but은 역접의 signal이다. 그러므로 clue는 앞 문장에 있다. 앞 문장의 내용은 우리가 유형적인 것을 상속한다는 내용이므로 빈칸이 포함된 문장은 무형적인 것을 물려받기도 한다는 내용이 요구된다. 그러므로 정답은 무형적인 것과 유사한 '덜 구체적이고 유형적인'의 ③이다.

어휘 **inherit** 물려받다, 상속하다 **property** 재산; 성질, 속성 **heirloom** 가보 **beyond that** 그 이외에도 **be aware of** ~ 을 깨닫다, ~ 을 알다 **daily** 일상의, 매일의 **moral** 도덕적인 **certain** 특정한, 어떤; 확신하는 **minor** 사소한 **casually** 무심코, 우연히 **concrete** 구체적인 **tangible** 만져서 알 수 있는, 실재하는 **monetary** 금전적인

해석 우리 모두는 어떤 것을 물려받는다. 어떤 경우에는, 돈이나 재산 또는 어떤 물건, 예를 들어 할머니의 웨딩 드레스나 아버지의 공구 세트와 같은 가보가 될 수도 있다. 하지만, 그것 이외에 우리 모두는 다른 것, 훨씬 덜 구체적이고 유형적인 것, 심지어 완전히 인식할 수도 없는 것을 물려받는다. 그것은 일상적인 일을 하는 방식일 수도 있고, 우리가 특정 문제들을 해결하거나 스스로 도덕적인 문제를 결정하는 방식일 수도 있다. 그것은 휴일이나 특정한 날짜에 소풍을 가는 전통을 지키는 특별한 방식일 수도 있다. 그것은 우리 사고에 중요하거나 중심이 되는 어떤 것이거나, 우리가 오랫동안 아주 무심코 받아들여온 사소한 것일 수도 있다.

① 일상생활과는 전혀 무관한
② 우리의 도덕적 기준에 반하여
③ 덜 구체적이고 유형적인
④ 커다란 금전적 가치가 있는

4 순서 배열 문제 풀이 전략

(1) 순서 배열 문제란?

① 글의 전개 방식과 함께 논리적 관점에서 '일관성(coherence)'을 유지하도록 올바른 순서를 정하는 문제이다.

② 문장 삽입 문제와 마찬가지로 앞서 배운 빈칸 완성 문제의 논리성 파악 능력을 응용하여 풀어야 하는 유형의 문제이다.

③ 특별한 연결사가 없는 한 독해는 기본적으로 ___(1)___과 ___(2)___의 논리전개 방식을 취한다.

(2) 순서 배열의 두 가지 유형

① 먼저 주어진 문장이 제시되는 경우와 제시되는 않는 경우의 두 가지 형태로 출제된다.

② 주어진 문장이 제시되지 않는 경우가 좀 더 난이도가 높은 편이다.

(3) 순서 배열 문제 전략

주어진 문장이 있는 경우

1. 문장이 주어진 경우는 주어진 문장을 꼼꼼히 해석한다.
2. 주어진 문장이 글의 전개 방식의 측면에서 어떤 성격에 해당하는지 파악한다.
3. 주어진 문장은 대부분 글의 주제(topic)나 요지(main idea)가 드러나는 문장이다.
4. 주어진 문장의 성격에 비추어 바로 뒤에 나올 수 있는 문장을 추론한다. 특히 주어진 문장이 '일반적(general)' 진술인 경우에 뒤에 '구체적(particular)' 진술이 이어진다는 사실을 유념한다.
5. 문장 위치 문제의 3대 요소인 ___(3)___, ___(4)___, ___(5)___와 '연관지어' 이어질 문장들을 분석을 한다.
6. 제시된 문장들이 길 경우에는 순서상 앞서는 문장의 후반부와 뒤에 이어질 문장의 전반부의 관계에 특히 유의한다.
7. 이어질 문장들 중에서 위의 3대 요소를 활용하여 ___(6)___(decisive order)가 있는지 살핀다.

정답

(1) 순접 (2) 연역 (3) 연결사 (4) 관사 (5) 지시사 (6) 결정적 순서

주어진 문장이 없는 경우

1. 도입문은 보통 짧고 일반적 진술이 많다는 점에 유의한다.
2. '이야기(narration)'를 풀어나가는 전개 방식의 글인 경우에 도입문에는 시대나 배경 등이 제일 먼저 나온다는 사실에 유념한다.
3. 만약 사람의 이름이 나오는 경우에 이름 전체(full name)이 먼저 제시되고 나중에 last name(성)이나 인칭대명사로 이어진다는 사실에 유념한다(ex Donald Trump 〉 Trump).
4. 도입문이 결정이 되면 위의 문제 풀이 전략을 사용하여 문제를 푼다.

예제

주어진 문장 다음에 이어질 글의 순서로 가장 적절한 것은? 2019 국가직 9급

South Korea boasts of being the most wired nation on earth.

(A) This addiction has become a national issue in Korea in recent years, as users started dropping dead from exhaustion after playing online games for days on end. A growing number of students have skipped school to stay online, shockingly self-destructive behavior in this intensely competitive society.

(B) In fact, perhaps no other country has so fully embraced the Internet.

(C) But such ready access to the Web has come at a price as legions of obsessed users find that they cannot tear themselves away from their computer screens.

① (A) − (B) − (C) ② (A) − (C) − (B)

③ (B) − (A) − (C) ④ (B) − (C) − (A)

정답 ④

해설 주어진 문장은 한국이 지구상에서 가장 인터넷망이 잘 갖추어진 나라라는 일반적인 진술이다. (B)는 주어진 문장을 다른 나라와 비교하며 순접으로 연결하는 진술이므로 바로 뒤에 오는 것이 적절하다. (C)는 이러한 외관상 좋은 면의 부작용에 대하여 역접의 연결어인 but을 통하여 이어지고 있으므로 그 다음에 이어지기에 적절하다. 마지막으로 (A)에서 this addiction의 this는 지시사로서 (C)에서 '중독'이 처음 언급된 다음에 연결되는 것이 적절하며 그 내용은 (C)의 일반적 진술에 대한 구체적인 진술로서 (A)가 연결되고 있다. (C) − (A)는 '결정적 순서'이다.

어휘 **boast** 자랑하다 **wired** 컴퓨터 시스템에 연결된; 인터넷망을 갖춘 **addiction** 중독 **drop dead** 급사하다
exhaustion 탈진, 기진맥진; 고갈, 소진 **on end** 계속하여 **self-destructive** 자멸적인, 자기 파괴적인
intensely 몹시, 격하게; 열정적으로 **embrace** 안다, 포옹하다; 포괄하다, 수용하다
come at a price 대가가 따르다 **legions of** 다수의, 무수히 많은
obsessed ~에 사로잡힌, ~에 골몰하는 **tear away from** ~에서 떼어 놓다

해석 남한은 지구상에서 가장 인터넷 연결이 잘된 나라임을 자랑하고 있다.

(B) 사실상 아마도 어떤 다른 국가들도 인터넷을 충분하게 이용하지는 않을 것이다.

(C) 그러나 인터넷에의 그러한 빠른 접근은 이에 빠져있는 다수의 사용자들이 자신을 컴퓨터 화면으로부터 떼어놓을 수 없다는 것을 알게 됨에 따라 상당한 대가를 치르고 있다.

(A) 이러한 중독은 사용자들이 며칠간 계속하여 온라인 게임을 한 후, 피로로 인하여 급사하기 시작하면서 최근 한국에서 국가적 논점이 되고 있다. 더 많은 수의 학생들이 인터넷 접속을 유지하기 위해 수업을 빠지고 있는데, 이는 이러한 매우 경쟁적인 사회에서 매우 자기 파괴적인 행동이다.

5 문장 삽입 문제 풀이 전략

(1) 문장 삽입 문제란?

① 주어진 문장을 지문의 내용 전개상 가장 적절한 위치에 삽입하는 문제로서 앞서 배운 빈칸 문제의 논리성 파악 능력을 응용하여 풀어야 하는 유형의 문제이다.

② 특별한 연결사가 없는 한 독해는 기본적으로 순접과 연역의 논리전개 방식을 취한다는 점에 유의한다.

(2) 문장 삽입 문제 전략 10단계

① 주어진 문장의 정확한 의미를 해석하고 연결사나 대명사 등을 꼼꼼히 체크를 한다.

② 주어진 문장이 글의 전개 방식의 측면에서 어떤 성격에 해당하는지 파악한다. 특히 주어진 문장이 일반적(general) 진술인지 구체적(particular) 진술인지를 판단한다.

③ 주어진 문장의 성격에 비추어 앞뒤에 나올 수 있는 문장의 성격을 추론해본다.

④ 문장 위치 문제의 3대 요소인 '연결사, 관사, 지시사'와 '연관지어' 분석을 한다.

⑤ 주어진 문장의 맨 첫 머리에 강한 연결사가 있으면 삽입될 위치의 앞 문장과의 관계를 특히 고려한다. 이외에도 전후 논리 관계를 드러내는 단어나 어구가 있는지 살핀다.

⑥ 주어진 문장에 등위 상관접속사 표현이 있는 경우는 앞뒤 문장에서 나머지 요소를 찾아서 순서를 찾는다.

⑦ 주어진 문장 내에 지시대명사 this와 부정관사가 있으면 주로 적절한 삽입 위치의 뒷 문장과의 관계를 특히 고려한다.

⑧ 어려운 문제의 경우는 적절한 삽입 위치의 앞 문장보다는 뒷 문장과의 관계가 좀 더 결정적인 경우가 많다.

⑨ 문장을 삽입한 후에 앞 문장과 뒤 문장까지 연결지어 읽어가며 올바른 순서인지 확인을 한다.

예제

주어진 글이 들어갈 위치로 가장 적절한 것은? 2018 지방직 7급

These were incredibly valuable for Edith to understand the seemingly endless variations that resulted from chemical combinations occurring on a molecular level in the practice of ceramics.

Edith was filled with a consuming passion for what she was learning. She converted the basement laundry room below her Filbert Street flat into a ceramic studio. A large gas-fired kiln soon joined the treadle-powered pottery wheel. Getting it into the basement wasn't easy and required the help of several people. (①) They had to slowly lower the heavy furnace down one of the city's steepest streets with a rope before safely maneuvering it into the basement. (②) Edith placed a second, smaller kiln on her kitchen counter. (③) Here she ran a wide variety of clay and glaze tests. (④) In the process, she learned that the type of clay she used had a big impact on the aesthetic quality of her ware.

정답 ④

해설 주어진 글의 지시대명사 these는 문장 삽입 문제의 3대 signal '연관지' 중에서 '지'에 해당하는 가장 중요한 단서이다. ④ 바로 앞 문장에 tests가 복수이고, 이러한 여러 시험들이 Edith가 도자기 제조에 대해 좀 더 깊이 이해하게 하는 데 도움이 되었다는 점을 볼 때 ④가 가장 적절한 위치이다.

어휘 **valuable** 귀중한, 가치 있는 **seemingly** 겉보기에, 언뜻 보기에 **variation** 변이, 차이 **molecular** 분자의 **practice** 연습; 관습; 개업 **ceramics** 도자기 제조업, 요업 **consuming** 지치게 하는, 엄청난 **convert** 바꾸다, 전환하다 **basement** 지하실 **laundry** 세탁소 **flat** 아파트 **studio** 작업실, 스튜디오 **kiln** 가마 **treadle-powered** 페달로 작동되는 **pottery** 도자기 **furnace** 용광로 **steep** 가파른 **maneuver** 다루다, 조종하다 **clay** 점토 **glaze** 유약 **impact** 영향, 충격 **aesthetic** 미적인 **ware** 도자기

해석 Edith는 자신이 배우고 있는 것에 대한 엄청난 열정으로 가득 차 있었다. 그녀는 Filbert Street의 아파트 아래에 있는 지하실 세탁실을 도자기 작업실로 전환했다. 큰 가스 불가마가 곧 페달로 작동하는 도자기 바퀴에 합류했다. 지하실로 가져오는 것은 쉽지 않았고 몇몇 사람들의 도움이 필요했다. ① 그들은 지하실로 안전하게 옮기기 전에 로프를 이용하여 도시의 가장 가파른 거리 중 하나를 따라 아래로 천천히 내려야 했다. ② Edith는 주방 카운터에 두 번째 더 작은 가마를 놓았다. ③ 여기서 그녀는 다양한 점토와 유약 시험을 했다. ④ 이것들은 Edith가 도자기 제조 연습에서 분자 수준에서 발생하는 화학적 조합으로 인해 생기는 끝없는 변이를 이해하는 데 엄청난 가치가 있었다. 그 과정에서, 그녀는 그녀가 사용한 점토의 종류가 그녀의 도자기의 미적 품질에 큰 영향을 미친다는 것을 알게 되었다.

6 글의 흐름상 적절치 않은 문장 찾기 전략

(1) 첫 문장과 두 번째 문장을 읽어 가며 글의 소재(subject matter)를 반드시 확보하여 체크한다.

(2) 초반부에 글의 주제(topic)까지 드러나는 경우에는 반드시 체크한다.

(3) 대부분의 문제는 주어진 글의 소재와 적절치 않은 문장의 소재가 다른 경우가 많다.

(4) 난이도가 있는 문제는 글의 소재와 적절치 않은 문장의 소재는 같지만 주어진 글의 주제와 적절치 않은 문장의 내용이 어긋나는 경우의 문제이다.

예제

글의 흐름상 가장 어색한 문장은? 2020 지방직 9급

Philosophers have not been as concerned with anthropology as anthropologists have with philosophy. ① Few influential contemporary philosophers take anthropological studies into account in their work. ② Those who specialize in philosophy of social science may consider or analyze examples from anthropological research, but do this mostly to illustrate conceptual points or epistemological distinctions. ③ In fact, the great philosophers of our time often drew inspiration from other fields such as anthropology and psychology. ④ Philosophy students seldom study or show serious interest in anthropology. They may learn about experimental methods in science, but rarely about anthropological fieldwork.

정답 ③

해설 글의 주제문은 첫 번째 문장으로 철학자들이 인류학에 관심을 가지지 않는다는 내용의 글이다. ③은 철학자들이 다른 분야에서 영감을 받았다는 내용으로 글의 주제와 상반되기 때문에 흐름상 적절하지 않다.

어휘 philosopher 철학자 be concerned with ~에 관심이 있다 anthropology 인류학
influential 영향력이 있는 contemporary 현대의; 동시대의 take ~ into account ~를 고려하다
specialize ~을 전공하다 analyze 분석하다 illustrate 생생히 설명하다 conceptual 개념적인
epistemological 인식론적인 distinction 구별 criticize 비판하다 ethical 윤리적인 implication 암시
inspiration 영감; 격려 field 들판; 분야; 실전 배치하다

해석 철학자들은 인류학자들이 철학에 대해 가지고 있는 것만큼이나 인류학에 관심을 갖고 있지 않다. ① 영향력 있는 현대 철학자들은 자신들의 연구에 인류학적 연구를 거의 고려하지 않는다. ② 사회과학 철학을 전공하는 사람들이 인류학 연구의 사례들을 고려하고 분석할 수도 있지만, 대개 개념적 요점이나 인식론적 구별을 분명히 보여주기 위해서 이렇게 한다. ③ 사실상, 우리 시대의 위대한 철학자들은 인류학과 심리학과 같은 다른 분야에서 종종 영감을 끌어냈다. ④ 철학 연구가들은 좀처럼 인류학에 대해 연구하거나 진지한 관심을 보이지 않는다. 그들은 과학에서 실험적인 방법들에 대해 배울 수도 있지만, 인류학 현장 조사에 대해서는 거의 배우지 않는다.

Chapter

02 유형별 독해

01 주제 찾기

01 다음 글의 제목으로 가장 적절한 것은?

In the United States police officers wear identifiable uniforms when on duty. An officer at an accident scene who is wearing everyday clothes might find that crowds won't obey someone who claims to be a police officer but is without a uniform. The officer might have difficulty keeping onlookers at bay or redirecting traffic away from the scene. When the background assumption is not fulfilled, members of the public will not respond as respectfully as they would if the officer were in uniform, and the officer will have a hard time performing required duties.

① The importance of the uniform
② The police officer's required duty
③ The sequence of uniform identification
④ The public respect for the police officer

정답 ①

해설 글의 제목에는 반드시 key word가 포함되어야 하며 이 글의 key word는 uniform이다. 이 글은 경찰관들이 제복을 입어야 하는 이유, 즉 그 중요성에 관한 글이다.

어휘 **identifiable** 인식할 수 있는, 확인될 수 있는, 식별될 수 있는 **on duty** 근무 중인
accident scene 사고 현장 **onlooker** 방관자, 구경꾼
at bay (사냥감이) 궁지에 몰린, 더 이상 달아날 수 없게 된

해석 미국에서 경찰관은 근무를 할 때 식별할 수 있는 제복을 입는다. 평상복을 입고 사고 현장에 있는 경찰관은, 제복을 입지 않은 채 스스로를 경찰관이라고 주장하는 사람에게 대중들이 복종하지 않는다는 것을 발견한다. 아마도 (사복 차림의) 경찰관은 구경꾼들을 한쪽으로 몰아세우거나 사고 현장으로부터 교통의 흐름의 방향을 바꾸는 데 있어서 어려움을 겪게 될 것이다. 배경이 되는 가정이 충족되지 않을 때 (즉 경찰관이 경찰관답게 제복을 입고 있지 않을 때), 대중들은 경찰관이 제복을 입고 있을 때만큼 그렇게 고분고분 반응하지 않을 것이다. 그리고 경찰관은 자신에게 요구되는 의무를 수행하는데 있어서 어려움을 겪게 될 것이다.

① 제복의 중요성 ② 경찰관의 필수적인 의무
③ 제복 확인의 순서 ④ 경찰관에 대한 대중의 존경심

02 다음 글의 제목으로 가장 적절한 것을 고르시오.

Today, with the added pressures of global warming, overgrazing and unwise agricultural policies, China's desert is expanding at an alarming rate, devouring approximately one million acres of grassland annually. The Great Wall stands in its path. Shifting yellow sands may occasionally expose a long-buried section — as happened in Ningxia in 2002 — but for the most part, they do far more harm than good. Rising dunes swallow some part of the wall; fierce desert winds shear off its top and sides like a sandblaster. Meanwhile, along the flanks of the Helan Mountains, water, ironically enough, is the greatest threat. Flash floods run off denuded highlands, cutting holes in the wall's base and causing upper levels to teeter and collapse.

① Flash Floods Run in a Desert
② Yellow Sands Do Harm and Good
③ The Great Wall Is Being Threatened
④ Yellow Sands Swallow the Great Wall

정답 ③

해설 글 중반의 but은 제목을 드러내는 signal이다. 황사와 홍수로 인한 만리장성의 손상과 파괴에 대해 다루고 있다.

어휘 **overgraze** 지나치게 방목하다 **devour** 게걸스럽게 먹다 **approximately** 대략 **annually** 해마다 **the Great Wall** 만리장성 **shift** 이동하다 **expose** 노출시키다 **long-buried** 오랫동안 묻혀진 **section** 부분 **dune** 모래언덕 **shear off** 깎아 내다 **sandblaster** 모래분사기 **meanwhile** 한편 **flank** 옆구리 **ironically** 아이러니하게도, 모순되게 **flash flood** 돌발 홍수 **run off** 유출되다, 범람하다 **denude** 드러내다 **teether** 시소놀이를 하다, 위아래로 움직이다 **collapse** 붕괴하다

해석 오늘날, 지구 온난화, 과다한 방목, 현명하지 못한 농업정책으로 인해, 매년 대략 백만 에이커의 초지를 삼키면서, 중국 사막이 놀라운 속도로 확장되고 있다. 만리장성은 그 길에 놓여 있다. 2002년에 Ningxia에서 발생했던 것처럼, 이동하는 황사는 가끔 오랫동안 묻혀 있던 구역을 드러내 줄지도 모른다. 하지만 대개 그 모래들은 이득보다는 훨씬 더 많은 해를 가한다. 쌓이는 모래 언덕들이 그 성벽의 일부를 삼켜버린다. 격렬한 사막의 바람은 모래분사기처럼 성벽의 위와 측면을 깎아낸다. 한편, Helan 산맥의 옆구리를 따라서는 매우 아이러니컬하게도 물이 가장 큰 위협이다. 갑작스러운 홍수는 벌거벗겨진 고지대를 범람하여 성벽의 기저부에 구멍을 내고 상층부가 덜커덕거리고 무너지도록 만든다.

① 갑작스러운 홍수가 사막에 흐른다.
② 황사는 해와 도움을 준다.
③ 만리장성이 위협받고 있다.
④ 황사가 만리장성을 삼킨다.

03 다음 글의 요지로 가장 적절한 것은?

The white race divides itself upon economic grounds. The landowning whites look down on everyone else, mostly the working class Cajun whites. These poor whites serve the landowning whites by using violence to maintain the racial order. Despite their efforts, however, the landowning whites still detest and scorn them. In the black race, the Creole culture shuns all darker skin blacks. The Creoles are light skinned blacks who come from the original French colonists in Louisiana. When a Creole girl, Mary Agnes LeFarbre, goes to work on the Samson Plantation with common blacks, her family disowns her. Even though local whites consider the Creoles common blacks, the Creloes themselves refuse to mix with the general black population and act superior. The concept of racism within the black community itself suggests the ridiculousness in using skin color as a means of social division.

① The poor whites use violence for the rich whites.
② Class differences exist even inside the same race.
③ Humans erect boundaries to keep their fellows out.
④ Social frame of racial order constructs American identity.

정답 ②

해설 however는 주제를 드러내는 signal이다. 이 글을 통해서 우리는 같은 인종 사이에서도 경제력(백인)과 피부의 밝기(흑인)에 따라 구분과 차별이 이루어진다는 것을 알 수 있다.

어휘 Cajun 케이준(프랑스인 후손으로 프랑스이 고어의 한 형태인 케이준어를 사용하는 미국 루이시애나 사람)
shun 피하다　Creloe 크리올 사람(특히 서인도 제도에 사는, 유럽인과 흑인의 혼혈인)
disown 의절하다, 절연하다

해석 백인종은 경제적 이유에 근거해서 나누어진다. 토지를 소유하고 있는 백인들은 대부분이 노동계급인 케이준 백인들을 포함해서 다른 모든 사람들을 깔본다. 이들 가난한 백인들은 인종적인 질서를 유지하기 위해 폭력을 사용하는 것을 통해서 토지를 소유한 백인들에게 봉사한다. 그러나 이들의 노력에도 불구하고 토지를 소유한 백인들은 가난한 백인들을 혐오하고 경멸한다. 흑인종 중에서 크리올 문화는 피부색이 좀 더 검은 흑인들을 경원시한다. 크리올들은 최초의 프랑스 식민지인 루이지애나 출신으로 피부색이 밝은 흑인이다. 크리올 출신의 소녀인 Mary Agnes LeFarbre가 일반적인 흑인들과 함께 Samson Plantation(집단농장)에 일을 하기 위해 갈 때, 그녀의 가족들은 그녀와 의절한다. 비록 그 지역의 백인들은 크리올을 일반적인 흑인으로 여기지만 크리올들은 그들 자신이 일반적인 흑인 인구들과 뒤섞이는 것을 거절하고 그들보다 우월한 듯 행동한다. 흑인 공동체 안에서의 인종주의 개념은 그 자체로, 사회적 분할의 수단으로서 피부색을 사용하는 것의 어리석음을 나타내 보여준다.
① 가난한 백인들은 부유한 백인들에 대해 폭력을 사용한다.
② 계층 차이는 같은 인종 내에서도 존재한다.
③ 인간들은 그들의 동료들을 멀리하려고 경계를 세운다.
④ 인종 순위라는 사회적 프레임이 미국 사회의 정체성을 이룬다.

04 다음 글의 제목으로 가장 적절한 것은? 2017 국가직 9급

Drama is doing. Drama is being. Drama is such a normal thing. It is something that we all engage in every day when faced with difficult situations. You get up in the morning with a bad headache or an attack of depression, yet you face the day and cope with other people, pretending that nothing is wrong. You have an important meeting or an interview coming up, so you talk through the issues with yourself beforehand and decide how to present a confident, cheerful face, what to wear, what to do with your hands, and so on. You've spilt coffee over a colleague's papers, and immediately you prepare an elaborate excuse. Your partner has just run off with your best friend, yet you cannot avoid going in to teach a class of inquisitive students. Getting on with our day-to-day lives requires a series of civilized masks if we are to maintain our dignity and live in harmony with others.

① Dysfunctions of Drama
② Drama in Our Daily Lives
③ Drama as a Theatrical Art
④ Dramatic Changes in Emotions

정답 ②

해설 마지막 문장에 요지가 드러나고 있는데, 문장 내의 require는 '당위성'을 드러내는 signal이다. 우리가 다른 사람들과의 관계 속에서 살아가는 데는 고상한 가면 즉, 연기가 필요하다고 말하고 있다.

어휘 engage in ~에 참여하다 headache 두통 depression 우울증 face 직면하다 cope with 대처하다 pretend ~인 체하다 beforehand 미리 talk through ~에 대해 설명하다 present 제시하다 spill 쏟다 elaborate 정교한 run off 달아나다 inquisitive 캐묻는, 호기심 많은 get on with ~와 잘 지내다 day-to-day 일상적인 civilized 고상한, 문명화 된 dignity 위엄, 품격 dysfunction 역기능

해석 드라마는 행동이다. 드라마는 존재이다. 드라마는 아주 평범한 것이다. 드라마는 우리가 매일 어려운 상황을 직면할 때 참여하는 바로 그것이다. 당신이 아침에 일어났을 때 심각한 두통을 느끼거나 우울증이 발병했어도 당신은 그냥 받아들이고, 아무런 문제도 없는 척 다른 사람들을 대한다. 중요한 회의나 다가오는 인터뷰가 있으면 그 사안에 대해 스스로에게 미리 설명해보고, 자신감 넘치고 생기 있는 표정을 어떻게 보여줄지, 무엇을 입을지, 손으로는 무엇을 할 것인가 등을 결정한다. 동료의 서류에 커피를 쏟으면 당신은 즉시 정교한 변명을 준비한다. 당신의 애인이 당신의 가장 친한 친구와 달아난다 하더라도 당신은 호기심 많은 학생들 반에 수업을 들어가는 것을 피할 수는 없을 것이다. 우리가 우리의 품위를 유지하고, 다른 사람들과 조화롭게 살려면 일상적인 삶을 잘 꾸려나가는 데 일련의 고상한 가면이 필요한 것이다.

① 드라마의 역기능
② 우리 일상생활의 드라마
③ 공연 예술로서의 드라마
④ 감정의 극적인 변화

05 다음 글의 주제로 가장 적절한 것은?

In 1823 the American president James Monroe made a famous declaration to Congress, in which he warned Europe to keep its hands off North and South America. This warning became known as the Monroe Doctrine. At first most Latin Americans welcomed the Monroe Doctrine. But as time went on, they began to take a less positive view of the United States. In the late 1800s, American businessmen started making heavy investments in Latin America. Some Latin Americans thought these businessmen were trying to buy control of their countries. Then starting with the Spanish — American War of 1898, the United States began to get heavily involved in Latin American political affairs.

① the historical meaning of Monroe Doctrine
② the cause of Spanish — American War
③ the reclusive tendencies of Latin Americans
④ the change in the relationship between USA and Latin America in 1800s.

정답 ④

해설 at first, in the late 1800s, then과 같은 시간 부사들이 이 글이 서술 방식이 시간순에 의존함을 보여준다. 1823년 Monroe Doctrine을 선언한 이후 1898년 미국 — 스페인 전쟁이 일어날 때까지 미국과 라틴 아메리카의 관계가 어떻게 변했는지 보여주는 글이다. 따라서 이 글의 주제로 ④ '19세기 미국과 라틴 아메리카의 관계 변화'가 가장 적절하다.

어휘 **declaration** 선언, 발표 **affair** 사건, 일 **doctrine** 교리; 주의, 원칙 **investment** 투자
keep one's hands off 손대지 않다, 간섭하지 않다 **get involved in** ~에 연루되다

해석 1823년 미국 대통령 James Monroe는 국회에서 유럽이 북아메리카와 남아메리카에 간섭하지 않도록 경고하는 유명한 선언을 했다. 이 경고는 Monroe Doctrine(먼로주의)으로 알려지게 되었다. 처음에는 대부분의 라틴 아메리카 사람들이 먼로주의를 환영했다. 그러나 시간이 흐르면서, 그들은 미국을 덜 낙관적으로 보기 시작했다. 일부 라틴 아메리카 사람들은 이들 사업가들이 그들 나라의 통제권을 사려고 애쓰고 있다고 생각했다. 그리고 나서 1898년 미국 — 스페인 전쟁이 시작되면서, 미국은 라틴 아메리카의 정치적인 사건들에 깊이 관련되기 시작했다.
① 먼로 독트린의 역사적인 의미
② 스페인 — 미국전쟁의 원인
③ 라틴 아메리카인들의 은둔적인 성향
④ 미국과 라틴 아메리카 간의 관계의 변화

06 다음 글의 주제로 가장 적절한 것을 고르시오.

Prehistoric warfare is a topic that matters very much today, because it has the ability to tell us a great deal about the human condition and even the human future. The nature and extent of warfare deep in our tribal past can help throw light on whether human beings are a fundamentally warlike or peaceful species. If the human condition has always been bound by warfare, then a pessimism about the prospect of changing this and an investment in a heavily-armed nation would be the rational choice. But if human nature is ultimately peaceable, then it makes more sense to be optimistic, to believe all disputes can eventually be resolved nonviolently, and to work for an international order dedicated to negotiation and agreement.

① discovering human nature from primitive warfare
② the role of war in the development of civilization
③ peaceful approaches to resolving disputes
④ differences between modern war and prehistoric war

정답 ①

해설 첫 문장에 글의 주제가 드러나는 전형적인 양식의 글이다. 선사 시대 전쟁의 연구는 인류의 본성이 호전적인지 평화적인지를 밝히는 데 도움을 줄 것이라는 것이 이 글의 요지이므로 가장 적절한 주제는 ① '원시 전쟁을 통한 인간 본성의 발견'이다.

어휘 **warfare** 전쟁 **extent** 정도, 범위 **throw light on** ~을 밝히다 **fundamentally** 근본적으로 **bind** 묶다, 얽매다 **pessimism** 비관주의 **prospect** 전망, 기대 **armed** 무장한 **rational** 합리적인 **ultimately** 궁극적으로 **peaceable** 평화로운 **make sense** 이치에 맞다 **optimistic** 낙관적인 **dispute** 논쟁, 말다툼 **eventually** 결국 **resolve** 결심하다; 해결하다 **dedicate** 헌신하다, 바치다 **negotiation** 협상

해석 선사 시대의 전쟁은 오늘날 매우 중요한 하나의 주제인데, 그것은 인류의 상태나 심지어 인류의 미래에 대해 많은 것을 알려줄 가능성을 가지고 있기 때문이다. 과거 원시 부족에 깊숙이 자리 잡고 있는 전쟁의 본질이나 범위는 인간이 근본적으로 호전적인지 아니면 평화적인 종인지를 밝히는 데 도움을 줄 수 있다. 만약 인류의 상태가 항상 전쟁에서 벗어나지 못하는 것이었다면 이러한 상태를 바꾸는 전망에 대한 비관론과 과도하게 무장한 국가에 대한 투자는 합리적인 선택이 될 것이다. 그러나 인간의 본성이 궁극적으로 평화적이라면 낙관적으로 생각하고, 모든 분쟁이 결국 비폭력으로 해결될 수 있다고 믿고, 협상과 협의에 충실한 국제 질서를 만들기 위해 애쓰는 것이 더욱 타당하다.

① 원시 전쟁에서 인간의 본성을 발견
② 문명발달에 있어서의 전쟁의 역할
③ 논쟁을 해결하기위한 평화적인 접근법
④ 현대 전쟁과 원시 전쟁의 차이

07 다음 글의 주제로 가장 적절한 것을 고르시오.

Many people believe that they will be free of their anger if they express it, and that their tears will release their pain. This belief derives from a nineteenth-century understanding of emotions, and it is no truer than the flat earth. It sees the brain as a steam kettle in which negative feelings build up pressure. But no psychologist has ever succeeded in proving the unburdening effects of the supposed safety valves of tears and anger. On the contrary, over forty years ago, controlled studies showed that fits of anger are more likely to intensify anger, and that tears can drive us still deeper into depression. Our heads do not resemble steam kettles, and our brains involve a much more complicated system than can be accounted for by images taken from nineteenth-century technology.

① the misunderstanding of the effect of emotional expression
② the relationship between the brain structure and depression
③ the impact of 19th century's science on neuroscience
④ the variation of brain reaction based on emotion

정답 ①

해설 글의 중간에 but은 주제를 드러내는 signal이다. but을 기점으로 눈물과 감정 표출이 부정적인 감정 해소에 도움이 될 것이라는 19세기의 생각이 과학적으로 입증되지 못했으며 오히려 부정적인 영향을 미칠수 있다는 내용의 글이다.

어휘 **derive** 끌어내다 **kettle** 주전자 **unburdening** 짐을 덜어주는 **intensify** 강화하다
depression 침울; 불경기

해석 많은 사람들은 분노를 표현하면 분노로부터 자유로워질 것이며 눈물이 고통을 덜어줄 것이라고 믿고 있다. 이런 믿음은 감정에 대한 19세기의 이해에 그 기원이 있는데 이 믿음은 평평한 지구라는 생각처럼 사실이 아니다. 이 믿음에 따르면 뇌는 부정적인 감정이 압력을 키우는 증기 주전자로 간주된다. 하지만 어떤 심리학자도 지금까지 눈물과 분노의 안전밸브로 추정되는 것의 부담경감의 효과를 입증하는 데 성공하지 못했다. 오히려 40년이 넘는 동안의 통제된 연구의 결과에 따르면, 분노의 폭발이 분노를 강화시킬 가능성이 더 많으며 눈물이 우리를 훨씬 더 깊은 우울증으로 몰고 갈 수 있다고 한다. 우리의 머리는 증기 주전자를 닮지 않았으며 우리의 뇌는 19세기 과학기술이 이끌어낸 이미지에 의해 설명될 수 있는 것보다 훨씬 더 복잡한 시스템을 내포하고 있다.

① 감정 표출의 효과에 대한 오해
② 뇌의 구조와 우울증간의 관계
③ 19세기 과학의 신경과학에 대한 영향력
④ 감정에 기초한 뇌 반응의 차이

08 다음 글에 나타난 Johnbull의 심경으로 가장 적절한 것은? 2021 국가직 9급

In the blazing midday sun, the yellow egg-shaped rock stood out from a pile of recently unearthed gravel. Out of curiosity, sixteen-year-old miner Komba Johnbull picked it up and fingered its flat, pyramidal planes. Johnbull had never seen a diamond before, but he knew enough to understand that even a big find would be no larger than his thumbnail.
Still, the rock was unusual enough to merit a second opinion. Sheepishly, he brought it over to one of the more experienced miners working the muddy gash deep in the jungle. The pit boss's eyes widened when he saw the stone. "Put it in your pocket", he whispered. "Keep digging". The older miner warned that it could be dangerous if anyone thought they had found something big. So Johnbull kept shoveling gravel until nightfall, pausing occasionally to grip the heavy stone in his fist. Could it be?

① thrilled and excited
② painful and distressed
③ arrogant and convinced
④ detached and indifferent

정답 ①

해설 세 번째 문장의 still은 역접의 연결사로 주제와 심경을 드러내는 signal 역할을 할 수 있다. 뒤에 이어지는 내용이 이전에 경험하지 못한 다이아몬드라는 사실이므로 심경으로 적절한 것은 ①의 '신나고 흥분되는'이 적절하다.

어휘 **blazing** 타는 듯이 무더운 **midday** 한낮, 정오 **stand out** 두드러지다 **unearth** 파내다, 발굴하다
gravel 자갈 **curiosity** 호기심 **miner** 광부 **finger** 손으로 만지다 **plane** (평평한) 면
thumbnail 엄지손톱 **still** 하지만, 그러나 **merit** 가치, 이점, 장점; ~을 받을 만하다 **sheepishly** 소심하게
gash (깊이 베인) 상처, 움푹 패인 것 **pit** 갱, (광물) 채취장 **warn** 경고하다 **shovel** 삽으로 파다
nightfall 해 질 녘 **pause** 일시정지하다 **occasionally** 이따금 **grip** 잡다, 쥐다 **fist** 주먹
thrilled 신이 난, 황홀한 **distressed** 괴로운 **arrogant** 거만한 **detached** 무심한 **indifferent** 무관심한

해석 타는 듯이 더운 한낮의 태양에, 노란 달걀 모양의 바위가 최근에 발굴된 자갈 더미에서 눈에 띄었다. 호기심으로, 16살의 광부 콤바 존불은 그것을 집어 들고 그것의 납작하고 각뿔 모양의 면을 손가락으로 만졌다. 존불은 이전에 다이아몬드를 본 적이 없지만, 그는 심지어 큰 발견물이라 해도 그의 엄지손톱만큼 작을 것이라는 것을 충분히 알고 있었다. 그런데도, 그 돌은 다른 의견을 받을 만큼 충분히 특이했다. 소심하게, 그는 그것을 정글 깊숙한 곳에서 진흙 웅덩이를 파는 더 경험 많은 광부들 중 한 명에게 가지고 갔다. 탄갱의 우두머리의 눈은 돌을 봤을 때 커졌다. "그것을 주머니에 넣어라", 그가 속삭였다. "계속 캐라." 더 나이 많은 광부는 만약 누군가가 그들이 뭔가 큰 것을 찾았다고 생각한다면 위험할 수 있다고 경고했다. 그래서 존불은 해질 녘까지 계속해서 자갈을 퍼내고, 이따금 멈춰서 그의 주먹 속의 무거운 돌을 꽉 쥐었다. 그럴 수 있을까?
① 신나고 흥분되는
② 고통스럽고 괴로운
③ 오만하고 확신하는
④ 무심하고 무관심한

09 다음 글의 제목으로 가장 적절한 것을 고르시오.

"Mommy, why do I have to be nice to Johnny when he acts so mean to me?" As a parent you can probably answer this kind of question asked by your little one on a daily basis. Your child's social skills and how he or she relates to others are a reflection of the influence parents have on their children. As children mature, they begin to realize that the quality and endurance of their relationships depends largely on the type of social skills learned and refined during their early childhood years. Playtime is the perfect time to begin teaching your little children acceptable social skills and how to effectively relate to their playmates. Many of a child's social skills can be acquired by examples, but verbal reinforcement is also necessary.

① Teaching Children to Relate to Their Playmates
② Parents Should Organize Their Children's Schedules
③ Let Your Children Lead Their Friends
④ Innate Human Desire for Close Friendship

정답 ①

해설 글의 맨 마지막 부분에 제목이 드러나고 있다. 이 글처럼 narration(이야기하기)형의 글들은 주제나 요지가 글의 후반부에 드러난다는 점에 유의하자. 이 글은 어린 시절에 놀이를 통해서 아이들이 사교 기술을 습득할 수 있으며, 부모의 말을 통한 보강도 필요하다는 내용이다. 따라서, ① '아이들에게 그들의 놀이 친구들과 관계 맺는 것을 가르치기'가 제목으로 가장 적절하다.

어휘 **mean** 비열한 **on a daily basis** 매일 **reflection** 반영 **influence** 영향력 **mature** 성숙한 **endurance** 내구성, 지속성 **relationship** 관계 **depend on** ~에 의존하다 **social skill** 사교 기술 **refine** 세련되게 하다 **acceptable** 수용 가능한 **effectively** 효과적으로 **acquire** 습득하다 **verbal** 언어의, 말의 **reinforcement** 보강, 강화

해석 "엄마, 왜 나는 그가 나에게 비열하게 행동할 때에도 Johnny에게 친절해야 하나요?" 부모로서 당신은 아마도 당신의 어린 자녀로부터 매일 이런 종류의 질문에 대답할 수 있다. 당신 자녀의 사교 기술들과 그들이 다른 사람들과 관계를 맺는 방법은 부모들이 그들의 자녀들에게 미치는 영향력의 반영이다. 아이들은 성장하면서, 그들의 인간관계의 질과 지속성이 초기 어린 시절 동안에 배워지고 다듬어진 사교 기술의 형태에 대체로 달려 있다는 것을 깨닫기 시작한다. 놀이 시간은 당신의 어린 자녀들에게 수용 가능한 사교 기술들과 효과적으로 그들의 놀이 친구들과 관계를 맺는 방법을 가르치기 시작할 완벽한 때이다. 아이의 많은 사교 기술들은 본보기를 통해서 습득되어질 수 있지만, 말로 하는 보강도 필요하다.

① 아이들에게 그들의 놀이 친구들과 관계 맺는 것을 가르치기
② 부모들은 자신들의 아이들의 스케줄을 짜야한다.
③ 당신의 아이들이 친구들을 리드하게 하라.
④ 가까운 우정에 대한 선천적인 인간의 욕망

10 글의 주제로 가장 적절한 것은? 2018 지방직 7급

If you've been up with a crying infant all night, or can't seem to reason with your cranky toddler, we have bad news — it isn't all uphill from here. In fact, it may get a bit worse before it gets better, with the ultimate low-point being when your child enters middle school. New research from Arizona State University, published in the journal Developmental Psychology, proves what many parents have feared — and what many of us remember from our own childhoods — middle school is no fun for anyone. Researchers studied more than 2,200 educated mothers and their children — who ranged in age from infants to adults. Researchers studied the mothers' well-being, parenting, and feelings towards their children. They discovered that mothers of middle school children, between 12 and 14 years, were most stressed and depressed, while mothers of infants and adults had much better well-being.

① the relationship between stress levels and puberty
② the participation in community work by mothers of adolescents
③ the tough challenge of parenting middle schoolers
④ the rewarding experience of taking care of infants and toddlers

정답 ③

해설 마지막 문장에 요지가 드러나고 있으며 중학생을 둔 어머니들의 스트레스가 가장 심하다는 내용이다. ①은 사춘기와 스트레스 지수의 관계로서 어머니의 스트레스와 관련이 없다. 이 글은 양육을 하는 부모의 스트레스에 관한 글이다.

어휘 **cranky** 기이한; 짜증을 내는 **toddler** 영아, 유아 **uphill** 경사지; 오르막길 **well-being** 행복, 안녕, 복지

해석 밤새 우는 아기로 인해 깨어있거나 짜증내는 아이를 설득할 수 없는 것처럼 보일 경우라면, 우리는 나쁜 소식이 있다 — 지금부터 모두 오르막이 아니라는 것이다. 사실, 자녀가 중학교에 입학 할 때 최종적으로 저점이 될 것이며 더 나아지기 전에 조금 악화 될 수 있다. 발달 심리학 저널에 실린 Arizona State University의 새로운 연구는 많은 부모님이 두려워했던 것 — 우리 중 많은 사람들이 어린 시절부터 기억하고 있는 것 — 을 증명하는데 그것은 중학교는 누구에게도 재미가 없다는 것이다. 연구원들은 2,200명의 교육받은 어머니들과 유아에서 성인까지 다양한 연령대의 자녀들을 대상으로 연구했다. 연구원들은 어머니의 안녕, 육아, 자녀에 대한 감정을 연구했다. 그들은 12세에서 14세 사이의 중학교 어린이의 어머니가 가장 스트레스를 받고 우울한 반면 유아와 어른의 어머니는 건강이 훨씬 좋음을 발견했다.

① 스트레스 수준과 사춘기 사이의 관계
② 청소년 어머니들의 지역 사회 활동 참여
③ 중학생 양육의 힘든 과제
④ 영유아 보살핌의 보람있는 경험

11 다음 글의 요지로 가장 적절한 것은?

Greek mythology is largely made up of stories about gods and goddesses, but it must not be read as an account of the Greek religion. According to the most modern idea, a real myth has nothing to do with religion. It is an explanation of something in nature, how any and everything in nature came into existence: people, animals, trees or flowers, the stars, earthquakes, all that is and all that happens. Thunder and lightning, for instance, are caused when Zeus hurls his thunderbolt. Myths are early science, the result of peoplc's first trying to explain what they saw around them.

① Mythology is often very closely associated with religion.
② The most modern idea emphasizes the value of Greek myths.
③ Greek myths frequently mention natural phenomena in detail.
④ Greek myths are explanations of nature rather than religion.

정답 ④

해설 첫 문장의 but은 요지를 드러내는 signal이며 마지막 문장에도 요지가 드러난다. 이 글의 주제는 신화가 종교와 관련이 있는 것이 아니라 자연을 설명하는 일종의 과학과 관련이 있다는 것이다.

어휘 **mythology** 신화 **account** 진술, 설명; 계좌; 중요성; 이유 **come into existence** 존재하게 되다 **thunderbolt** 벼락, 번개

해석 그리스 신화는 주로 남신들과 여신들에 관한 이야기로 구성되어 있다. 그러나 그리스 신화는 그리스 종교의 이야기로 읽혀서는 안 된다. 가장 현대적인 사상에 따르면, 진정한 신화는 종교와 아무런 관련성도 가지고 있시 않다. 신화는 자연 속에 있는 어떤 것에 대한 설명이자 자연 속에 있는 어떤 것과 모든 것들이 어떻게 존재하게 되었는가에 대한 설명이다.: 사람들, 동물들, 나무들 혹은 꽃들, 별들, 지진들 등 존재하는 모든 것과 생겨난 모든 것에 대한 설명이다. 예를 들어 천둥과 번개는 제우스가 벼락을 던질 때 발생한다. 신화는 초기 과학이고 그들의 주변에서 본 것들을 설명하고자 하는 사람들의 최초 시도가 야기한 결과이다.
① 신화는 종종 종교와 매우 밀접하게 연관되어 있다.
② 가장 최근의 생각은 그리스 신화의 가치를 강조한다.
③ 그리스 신화는 주로 자연 현상을 상세히 언급한다.
④ 그리스 신화는 종교보다는 자연에 대한 설명이다.

12 다음 글의 제목으로 알맞은 것을 고르시오.

Communication took another giant leap forward when people began to write. Written language let people who could read and write share ideas with each other. Many ancient cultures came up with different ways to write. The Egyptians used hieroglyphs, or pictures. Each picture stood for a sound. People in Western Asia carved marks into clay They called these marks cuneiform. The Chinese and Japanese still use their ancient symbol systems. Every word has a unique symbol that must be memorized. In English, we use a 26-letter alphabet. We arrange these letters into patterns that make different words. Today, we write words in notes, reports, and e-mail messages.

① The differences of Written Language among Ancient Cultures
② The Development of Symbol Systems
③ The Various Types of Written Language
④ How did People Begin to Write?

정답 ③

해설 시대에 따라 변화해 오는 다양한 문자언어에 대해 시간순으로 서술한 글이다.

어휘 **leap** 도약 **come up with** 제시하다 **stand for** 상징하다, 나타내다; 지지하다 **carve** 새기다 **clay** 점토 **unique** 고유한 **arrange** 정리하다; 준비하다; 조정하다

해석 사람들이 문자를 쓰기 시작했을 때 의사소통은 또 한 번의 큰 도약을 했다. 글은 읽고 쓸 줄 아는 사람들이 서로서로 생각을 공유하도록 해주었다. 많은 고대 문화들이 글을 쓰는 다양한 방법을 생각해냈다. 이집트인들은 상형문자, 즉 그림을 이용했는데 각각의 그림은 소리를 나타냈다. 서아시아인들은 점토 속에 기호를 새겼다. 그들은 이 기호를 쐐기문자라고 불렀다. 중국 사람들과 일본 사람들은 아직도 고대의 시호체계를 이용하는데, 각각의 단어는 암기되어야만 하는 고유한 기호를 가지고 있다. 우리는 26자 알파벳을 사용한다. 우리는 문자들을 서로 다른 단어를 만드는 형태로 배열한다. 오늘날 우리는 메모, 보고서, 그리고 e메일 메시지에서 단어를 쓴다.

① 고대문화 속의 문자언어의 차이점들
② 상징체계의 발달
③ 문자언어의 다양한 형태
④ 사람들이 어떻게 쓰기 시작했는가?

13 다음 글의 제목으로 가장 적절한 것은?

When was the last time your family sat down together for a meal? Still trying to remember? Then it's been too long. Sure, everybody's life is hectic these days, but we all have to eat sometime. Try to make it a priority to eat together. Sitting around the table is a good way of communicating love or a strong liking. It gives your family members the opportunity to talk about their lives. It also gives you the chance to listen to your family members, to get connected, and to get a feel for how they'e really doing. Make sure you ask meaningful questions like: "Tell me about what you learned in your history class today?" Or, "What did you enjoy most about your work today?" After you ask the questions, be sure to listen! A face-to-face conversation during meals helps you build a strong bond with your family members and shows how you care for them.

① Help Children Develop a Good Eating Habit
② Economical Benefits of Eating Family Meals
③ Express Your Affection to Each Family Member
④ Family Meals: A Bonding Time for the Family

정답 ④

해설 명령문은 요지를 드러내는 중요한 signal이다. 가족이 함께 식사를 함으로써 유대감이 강화되는 이점을 설명하고 있으므로 글의 제목으로 ④의 '가족 간의 식사: 가족을 위한 결속의 시간'이 적절하다.

어휘 **meal** (아침, 점식, 저녁) 식사 **hectic** 매우 바쁜, 흥분한 **priority** 중요, 우선권 **meaningful** 의미 있는 **bond** 유대감

해석 당신 가족이 식사를 하려고 마지막으로 함께 앉았던 때가 언제였는가? 아직도 기억하려고 애쓰고 있는가? 그렇다면 그것은 너무 오래된 것이다. 확실히 모든 사람들의 생활은 요즈음 매우 바쁘지만 우리 모두는 언제든 식사를 해야 한다. 함께 식사하는 것을 우선순위로 만들도록 하라. 식탁에 둘러앉는 것은 사랑이나 무척 좋아한다는 것을 전달하는 좋은 방법이다. 그것은 당신의 가족 구성원들에게 그들의 생활에 대해 이야기할 기회를 준다. 그것은 또한 당신에게 당신의 가족 구성원들의 이야기를 경청하고 (그들과) 연결되며 그들이 정말로 어떻게 지내는지에 대한 느낌을 가질 기회를 준다. "오늘 역사 수업시간에 네가 무엇을 배웠는지 이야기해 줄래?" 또는 "오늘 네가 한 일 중 가장 즐거웠던 것이 무엇이었니?"와 같은 의미 있는 질문을 반드시 하도록 하라. 당신이 질문을 한 후에는 꼭 경청하도록 하라. 식사 중에 얼굴을 마주보고 하는 대화는 당신이 당신의 가족 구성원들과 강력한 유대를 형성하도록 도와주고 당신이 그들을 좋아한다는 것을 보여준다.
① 아이가 좋은 식습관을 기르도록 도와라.
② 가족이 함께 식사를 하는 것의 경제적 이점
③ 각 가족 구성원에게 당신의 애정을 표현하라.
④ 가족 간의 식사: 가족을 위한 결속의 시간

14 다음 글의 제목으로 가장 적절한 것은?

It started out to be a simple exploratory operation. Then, suddenly, the patient's heart stopped. Her brain waves started leveling off. The medical team immediately began emergency treatment to try to start the heart again. At last the chief surgeon announced that the patient had died. Minutes later, much to everyone's amazement, the "dead" patient came back to life. Her heart started, and her brain waves began to assume normal patterns. Later she told the doctors that she had been fully aware of everything that had happened while she was "dead". She believed that she came back to life because she wanted so badly to live longer. She said death was not frightening, but she wasn't ready to go yet. The experts admit that they have no satisfactory explanations for these death or near-death experiences. They admit that they do not fully understand life — and they do not fully understand death.

① Rehabilitation
② Death Penalty
③ Emergency Treatment
④ Mystery of Life and Death

정답 ④

해설 글의 맨 마지막에 제목이 드러나고 있다. 이 글과 같이 '실험'적인 내용이 담겨있는 글들은 반드시 주제가 글의 후반부에 드러난다는 점에 유의하자. 마지막 두 문장에 드러나듯이 전문가인 의사조차도 죽음과 삶의 의미를 온전히 이해할 수 없다는 것이다.

어휘 **exploratory operation** 진찰 수술, 검진을 위한 수술 **level off** 낮아지다 **chief surgeon** 수석 집도의 **assume** 가정하다; 취하다, 띠다; ~인 체하다 **near-death** 유사 죽음 **rehabilitation** 복귀, 재건; 교정 **mortality** 죽어야 할 운명 **immortality** 불멸

해석 이것은 간단한 검진을 위한 수술로 시작되었다. 그런 다음, 갑자기 환자의 심장이 멈췄다. 그녀의 뇌파는 낮아지기 시작했다. 의료 팀은 그녀의 심장을 다시 뛰게 하기 위해 즉시 응급치료를 시작했다. 마침내 수석 수술 집도의사는 환자가 사망했다고 선언했다. 몇 분이 지났을 때, 모두를 깜짝 놀라게 하면서, "죽은" 환자가 살아났다. 그녀의 심장은 뛰기 시작했고 그녀의 뇌파는 정상적인 패턴을 띠기 시작했다. 나중에 그녀는 그녀가 죽은 상태로 있는 동안 벌어진 모든 일들을 완벽하게 알고 있었다고 의사들에게 말했다. 그녀는 그녀가 더 오래 살기를 간절히 원했기 때문에 살아날 수 있었다고 믿었다. 그녀는 죽음이 두렵지는 않았지만 아직 죽을 때가 아니었다고 말했다. 전문가들은 이러한 죽음 혹은 유사 죽음 경험에 대해 만족스러운 설명을 내놓을 수 없다는 사실을 인정했다. 그들은 그들이 삶과 죽음을 완벽하게 이해할 수 없다는 사실을 인정했다.
① 교정
② 사형
③ 응급처치
④ 삶과 죽음의 신비

15 글의 제목으로 가장 옳은 것은? 2018 서울시 7급

When materials engineer Edgar Zanotto gave a talk at a glass technology conference, he might not have expected that he would spark a heated debate about the nature of vitreous materials. Despite humans having used glass for around 6000 years, it still seems to defy definition: glass is rigid and breaks like a crystalline solid, but it also flows like a liquid. While this movement is too slow to observe in typical window pane glass, some glasses flow quickly enough to allow measurements. The researchers argue that glass should be classed as a frozen liquid, because its structure is closer to that of its parent supercooled liquid than to the crystalline state. Glasses, like liquids, relax and deform under the action of gravity alone. Solids, on the other hand, deform only under external pressure.

① Glass can be transformed to crystal
② Glass has a variety of different uses
③ Glass should be redefined as a liquid
④ Glass technology has been remarkably developed

정답 ③

해설 글의 후반부의 'researchers argue that~'문장이 이 글의 요지문이라고 할 수 있으며 이렇게 전문가의 주장이나 인용에 해당하는 내용은 요지의 강력한 signal인 경우가 많다. 그 내용은 고체처럼 여겨지는 유리가 실제로는 액체로 정의가 되어 한다는 내용이다. 그러므로 정답은 ③이다.

어휘 **conference** 회의, 학회, 회담 **spark** 촉발시키다, 유발하다 **heated debate** 열띤 논의
vitreous 유리질의, 유리 같은 **defy definition** 정의가 불가능하다 **crystalline** 수정의, 맑은; 결정체의
pane (한 장의) 판유리, 창유리; 평면 **supercool** ~을 과냉하다 **deform** 기형으로 만들다

해석 Materials Engineer Edgar Zanotto가 유리 기술 회의에서 강연을 할 때, 그는 유리성 재료의 특성에 관한 열띤 논쟁을 일으킬 것으로 예상하지 못했을 것입니다. 인간이 약 6000년 동안 유리를 사용 했음에도 불구하고 유리는 여전히 정의를 할 수없는 것처럼 보입니다. 유리는 단단하고 결정성 고체처럼 부서지지만 액체처럼 흐르기도 합니다. 이 운동은 일반적인 창문 유리에서 관찰하기에는 너무 느리지만 어떤 유리들은 측정을 할 수 있을 정도로 빠르게 흐릅니다. 연구진은 유리가 결빙된 액체로 분류되어야 한다고 주장합니다. 왜냐하면 그 구조는 결정질 상태보다는 부모에 해당하는 과냉각 액체의 구조에 더 가깝기 때문입니다. 액체처럼 유리들은 중력만으로도 이완이 되기도 하고 변형됩니다. 반면에 고체는 외부 압력하에서만 변형됩니다.
① 유리는 결정으로 변환 될 수 있다.
② 유리는 다양한 용도로 사용된다.
③ 유리는 액체로 재정의 되어야 한다.
④ 유리 기술이 상당히 발달되었다.

16 다음 글의 제목으로 알맞은 것은?

The desire to eradicate malaria originated in the 1950s and 60s, when the disease was common in the United States and Europe. At that time, scientists initiated a major effort to rid the world of malaria, using the insecticide DDT. While the use of DDT in the 1960s did lead to a significant reduction in the incidence of malaria, scientists learned, within the following decade as the disease resurged, that mosquitoes could become resistant to DDT. This early effort to eliminate malaria from the world has since been considered as one of the biggest failures in the history of the fight against the disease.

① Symptoms and Signs of Malaria
② DDT — Temporary Measure for Malaria
③ Malaria: A Mosquito-borne Blood Disease
④ Contribution of Donors to Victory over Malaria

정답 ②

해설 글의 중반부에 전문가인 scientists를 통해서 글의 주요 내용이 드러나는바, DDT가 말라리아 박멸의 궁극적인 수단이 되지 못하였음을 말하고 있으므로 정답은 ②가 적절하다.

어휘 **eradicate** 박멸하다, 근절하다 **originate** 시작하다, 유래하다 **initiate** 창시하다, 개시하다
rid A of B A에게서 B를 제거하다 **insecticide** 살충제 **incidence** 발생, 발병률 **resurge** 다시 나타나다

해석 말라리아를 박멸하고자 하는 열망은 그 질병이 미국과 유럽에 널리 퍼졌던 1950년대와 60년대에 시작되었다. 그 당시 과학자들은 살충제 DDT를 사용하면서 전 세계에서 말라리아를 없애기 위한 주된 노력을 시작했다. DDT를 사용하던 1960년대에는 말라리아 발병률이 현저하게 떨어졌으나 그 뒤 10년 이내에 질병이 다시 창궐하면서 과학자들은 모기가 DDT에 내성이 생겼다는 것을 알게 되었다. 세상에서 말라리아를 없애고자 하는 이런 초기 노력은 질병에 대항한 싸움 중 역사상 가장 큰 실패 중 하나로 여겨지고 있다.
① 말라리아의 증상과 징후들
② DDT — 말라리아에 대한 일시적 대책
③ Malaria — 모기가 낳은 혈액 질환
④ 혈액 기증자들의 말라리아 정복에 대한 기여

17 다음 글에 나타난 화자의 심경으로 가장 적절한 것은? 2018 지방직 9급

My face turned white as a sheet. I looked at my watch. The tests would be almost over by now. I arrived at the testing center in an absolute panic. I tried to tell my story, but my sentences and descriptive gestures got so confused that I communicated nothing more than a very convincing version of a human tornado. In an effort to curb my distracting explanation, the proctor led me to an empty seat and put a test booklet in front of me. He looked doubtfully from me to the clock, and then he walked away. I tried desperately to make up for lost time, scrambling madly through analogies and sentence completions. "Fifteen minutes remain", the voice of doom declared from the front of the classroom. Algebraic equations, arithmetic calculations, geometric diagrams swam before my eyes. "Time! Pencils down, please".

① nervous and worried
② excited and cheerful
③ calm and determined
④ safe and relaxed

정답 ①

해설 이 글은 시험장에 늦게 도착한 상황의 초조하고 걱정스러운(nervous and worried) 심경을 구체적으로 서술하고 있다. 글의 초반부와 마지막을 통하여 충분히 I의 심경을 유추해 낼 수 있다.

어휘 **white as a sheet** 창백한, 핏기가 없는 **descriptive** 서술하는, 묘사하는 **convincing** 설득력 있는 **curb** 억제하다, 막다, 제한하다 **distracting** 마음을 심란케 하는 **booklet** 소책자 **desperately** 절망적으로; 필사적으로 **scramble** 서로 밀치다, 뒤죽박죽으로 만들다; 쟁탈하다 **arithmetic** 산수, 연산, 계산 **algebraic** 대수학의 **geometric** 기하학의 **determined** 단호한, 완강한

해석 나의 얼굴은 백지장처럼 하얗게 되었다. 나는 손목시계를 들여다보았다. 시험은 지금쯤 거의 끝났을 것이다. 나는 완전한 공황상태로 시험장에 도착했다. 나는 내 이야기를 하려고 했다. 그러나 내 문장들과 표현적인 몸짓들은 너무나 혼란스러워 나는 분명히 인간 회오리바람의 형식에 지나지 않는 것을 전달했을 뿐이다. 나의 산만한 설명을 막으려는 노력으로 시험 감독관은 나를 빈자리로 인도했고 시험지 책자를 내 앞에 놓았다. 그는 미심쩍게 나로부터 시계로 눈을 돌렸고, 걸어서 멀어져갔다. 나는 필사적으로 손실된 시간을 보충하려고 노력하였고, 미친 듯이 허둥지둥 유추 문제들과 문장완성 문제들을 풀어나갔다. "15분 남았습니다", 비운의 음성이 교실 앞에서 발표되었다. 대수 방정식, 산술 계산, 기하 도표들이 내 눈 앞을 헤엄쳐 갔다. "끝!, 연필 놓으세요".

① 초조하고 걱정스러운
② 흥분되고 흥겨운
③ 침착하고 단호한
④ 안전하고 편안한

18 다음 글의 제목으로 가장 적절한 것을 고르시오.

Next time you're in a restaurant, listen to the music; it's well known that loud music makes people more excited, so they eat more food and eat it faster than if soft classical music were playing. A restaurant that plays loud music may want its diners to eat quickly and leave to make room for more customers. Other businesses also try to affect our mood using music. Loud, fast music not only causes excitement, it can also make us feel happy and secure-with the result that we stay longer in the store and, with a bit of luck, buy more stuff. And some department stores and grocery stores play music with hidden message like "Stealing is dishonest". The hidden messages are thought to affect our behavior.

① Relationship Between Music and Food
② Hidden Power of Music on the Public
③ Effect of Music on Personality Types
④ Commercial Development of Music

정답 ②

해설 첫 문장에 명령형 signal인 'listen'이 나오는 것으로 보아 식당에서 음악이 중요한 역할을 한다는 것을 알 수 있다. '시끄러운 음악으로 식당 고객의 회전율을 높이기도 하고, 사람들이 더 많이 물건을 사도록 상점에 붙잡아 두거나, 숨겨진 메시지가 담긴 음악으로 사람들의 행동에 영향을 미칠 수도 있다, 즉 다시 말해 '음악에 숨겨진 힘이 있다'라는 내용이다.

어휘 diner 식사하는 사람 make room for ~을 위해 장소를 내주다 secure 안전한, 위험이 없는
with the result that 그 결과 ~하다 with a bit of luck 운수가 좋으면 stuff 물건
shoplifting 상점 절도

해석 다음에 식당에 가게 되면 음악을 들어보도록 해라. 시끄러운 음악이 사람들을 더 활기차게 해서, 부드러운 클래식 음악이 나올 때보다 사람들이 더 많은 음식을 더 빨리 먹는 것은 잘 알려진 사실이다. 요란한 음악을 트는 식당은 손님들이 빨리 음식을 먹고 추가 고객에게 자리를 내주고 나가기를 원할 것이다. 타 업계에서도 음악을 이용해서 우리 감정에 영향을 주려고 애를 쓴다. 시끄럽고 빠른 음악은 우리를 신나게 할 뿐만 아니라 우리가 행복하고 안전하다고 느끼도록 한다. 그리고 어떤 백화점과 식료품점에서는 '훔치는 것은 부도덕한 것이다'와 같이 숨겨진 메시지가 담긴 음악을 튼다. 이 숨겨진 메시지가 우리 행동에 영향을 준다.
① 음악과 음식의 관계
② 음악이 대중에 미치는 숨겨진 힘
③ 음악이 성격에 주는 영향
④ 음악의 상업적 발달

19 다음 글의 요지로 가장 적절한 것은? 2019 국가직 9급

When giving performance feedback, you should consider the recipient's past performance and your estimate of his or her future potential in designing its frequency, amount, and content. For high performers with potential for growth, feedback should be frequent enough to prod them into taking corrective action, but not so frequent that it is experienced as controlling and saps their initiative. For adequate performers who have settled into their jobs and have limited potential for advancement, very little feedback is needed because they have displayed reliable and steady behavior in the past, knowing their tasks and realizing what needs to be done. For poor performers — that is, people who will need to be removed from their jobs if their performance doesn't improve — feedback should be frequent and very specific, and the connection between acting on the feedback and negative sanctions such as being laid off or fired should be made explicit.

① Time your feedback well.
② Customize negative feedback.
③ Tailor feedback to the person.
④ Avoid goal-oriented feedback.

정답 ③

해설 이 글은 여러 번의 should의 사용으로 주제의 위치를 드러내고 있는 글로서 실적이나 성과에 대한 feedback을 줌에 있어서 사람에 따라 다른 기준으로 그 사람에게 적절한 피드백이 필요하다는 내용이다. 따라서 ③의 'tailor feedback to the person(피드백을 상대방에게 맞추라.)'는 내용이 이 글의 요지라고 할 수 있다.

어휘 **performance** 성능; 성과; 공연; 성적 **recipient** 수령인, 수취인 **potential** 가능성; 잠재력
content 콘텐츠, 내용물; 함유량; 목차 **prod** 찌르다; 재촉하다 **corrective** 교정하는, 바로잡는
sap 약화시키다 **initiative** 진취성, 자주성; 주도권 **adequate** 충분한, 적절한 **sanction** 제재; 허가, 인가
lay off 일시 해고하다 **explicit** 분명한, 명백한 **tailor** 맞추다, 조정하다 **goal-oriented** 목표 지향적인

해석 업무 피드백을 제공할 때, 당신은 피드백을 받는 사람의 과거 성과와 함께 빈도, 양 및 내용을 설계하는데 있어서의 그 혹은 그녀의 미래 잠재력에 대한 당신의 추정을 고려해야 한다. 성장가능성이 있는 높은 성과자의 경우, 피드백은 그들이 시정 조치를 취할 수 있을 정도로 자주 주어져야 한다. 그러나 너무 자주해서 그것이 통제로 받아들여지고 그들의 주도권을 약화시켜서는 안 된다. 자신의 직업에 정착하여 승진 가능성이 제한적인 적절한 수행자들에게 피드백은 거의 필요하지 않다. 왜냐하면 과거에 그들의 일을 알고 무엇을 해야 하는지 깨닫고 있으면서, 과거에 믿음직스럽고 착실한 행동을 보였기 때문이다. 형편없는 성과자들 — 성과가 개선되지 않으면 직장에서 퇴출되어야 할 사람들 — 에게 피드백은 자주 그리고 매우 구체적이어야 하며, 피드백에 대한 이행과 일시 해고 또는 해고와 같은 부정적인 제재 사이의 연관성이 명확해져야만 한다.

① 당신의 피드백의 시간을 잘 재라.
② 부정적인 피드백에 맞추라.
③ 피드백을 상대방에게 맞추라.
④ 목표지향적인 피드백을 피하다.

20 다음 글의 제목으로 가장 적절한 것은?

Paper is not only useful for preserving information. In its role as a wrapping material, paper also does a good job of hiding it. What would birthdays be like without this material, which performs the role of building excitement and anticipation better than all others? I have received presents wrapped in cloth, or hidden in a cupboard, but nothing has the magic of wrapping paper. A present really isn't a present unless it is wrapped in a paper. It is the paper that, by concealing and revealing an object, ritualizes the act of giving and receiving, turning that object into a gift. This is not just a cultural association. The material has fundamental properties that make it ideal for this role.

① Conflicting Views on Wrapping
② Various Useful Materials for Wrapping
③ Wrapping: An Old Custom We Should End
④ Paper: What Makes an Object a Present

정답 ④

해설 밑에서 두 번째 문장에 It is that 강조구문에서 전달하는 내용이 주제문이다. 물건을 선물로 바꾸는 힘은 바로 포장지에 있다는 주장이다.

어휘 **preserve** 보존하다 **wrap** 포장하다, 싸다 **anticipation** 기대 **cupboard** 찬장 **ritualize** 의례화하다 **association** 연관, 연상 **fundamental** 근본적인 **property** 성질, 속성; 재산 **ideal** 이상적인

해석 종이는 정보를 보존하는 것에만 유용한 것이 아니다. 포장 재료로서의 역할에서, 종이는 그것(정보)을 감추는 일 또한 잘한다. 다른 어떤 것들보다도 흥분과 기대를 만드는 역할을 더 잘 수행하는 이 재료가 없다면 생일이 어떻겠는가? 나는 천에 싸여져 있거나 찬장 속에 숨겨져 있던 선물들을 받아봤지만, 어떤 것도 포장지의 매력을 지니지는 않는다. 선물은 종이로 포장되어 있지 않다면 정말로 선물이 아니다. 어떤 물건을 감추거나 드러나게 하여 그 물건을 선물로 변화시키고 주고받는 행위를 의례화하는 것은 바로 종이이다. 이것은 단지 문화적으로만 연계된 것은 아니다. 그 재료는 이러한 역할을 위해 그것을 가장 이상적으로 만드는 근본적인 속성을 가지고 있다.

① 포장에 대한 상반된 견해
② 포장에 쓰는 다양한 유용한 재료들
③ 포장: 우리가 끝내야 할 구습
④ 포장지: 물건을 선물로 만드는 것

21 다음 글의 주제로 가장 적절한 것은?

There is an important difference between having an ideal and making a rule to live by. The ideal may be a perfect and flawless standard that one would be proud to attain. Such an ideal provides you with a guide, but it should not be a daily standard. Making the ideal into a rule is digging oneself a trap. If you constantly fall into the trap, you feel so bad about yourself that it becomes increasingly hard to keep going. The rule needs to be clear, and to direct you toward the ideal if that is what you want, but it also needs to be realistic, if it is not to undermine your self-esteem. That is why it makes more sense to do the best you can — rather than aim for perfection.

① difficulties of setting realistic goals
② why rules to live by need to be realistic
③ common characteristics of perfectionists
④ how self-esteem affects our relationships

정답 ②

해설 주장에 대한 논거가 제시되는 글의 전개 방식에서는 '논거'가 글의 주제이다. 마지막 두 문장에 논거가 드러나는데, 이상과 삶에서 지키며 살아갈 규칙 사이에는 차이가 존재하므로 그 규칙을 이상적이기보다는 현실적으로 만드는 것이 더 타당하다는 주제의 글이다.

어휘 **live by** ~를 믿고 따르며 살다 **flawless** 흠 없는, 결점 없는 **attain** 달성하다
undermine 손상을 주다, 약화시키다 **self-esteem** 자존감 **make sense** 이치에 맞다

해석 이상을 가지는 것과 지키며 살아갈 규칙을 만드는 것 사이에는 중요한 차이가 있다. 이상은 우리가 달성한다면 자랑스러울, 완벽하고 결점 없는 기준일 것이다. 이러한 이상은 당신에게 지침을 제공하지만 그것은 일상적 기준이 아니어야 한다. 이상을 (일상적인) 규칙으로 만드는 것은 자기 스스로에게 함정을 파는 것이다. 만약 당신이 지속적으로 그 함정에 빠진다면 당신은 스스로에게 너무 실망하여 계속 나아가기가 점점 어려워진다. 그 규칙은 명확해야 하고, 그러한 것이 당신이 원하는 것이라면 당신을 이상으로 향하도록 해야 하지만, 그것이 당신의 자부심을 약화시키지 않으려면 그것은 또한 현실적이어야 한다. 그것이 완벽함을 목표로 하기보다는 당신이 할 수 있는 최선을 하는 것이 더 타당한 이유이다.

① 현실적인 목표를 설정하는 것의 어려움
② 따라야 할 규칙은 왜 현실적이어야 하는가
③ 완벽주의자들의 공통된 특성들
④ 자존감이 우리의 관계들에 어떻게 영향을 미치는가

22 다음 글의 주제로 가장 적절한 것은? 2019 지방직 9급

As the digital revolution upends newsrooms across the country, here's my advice for all the reporters. I've been a reporter for more than 25 years, so I have lived through a half dozen technological life cycles. The most dramatic transformations have come in the last half dozen years. That means I am, with increasing frequency, making stuff up as I go along. Much of the time in the news business, we have no idea what we are doing. We show up in the morning and someone says, "Can you write a story about (pick one) tax policy/immigration/climate change?" When newspapers had once-a-day deadlines, we said a reporter would learn in the morning and teach at night — write a story that could inform tomorrow's readers on a topic the reporter knew nothing about 24 hours earlier. Now it is more like learning at the top of the hour and teaching at the bottom of the same hour. I'm also running a political podcast, for example, and during the presidential conventions, we should be able to use it to do real-time interviews anywhere. I am just increasingly working without a script.

① a reporter as a teacher
② a reporter and improvisation
③ technology in politics
④ fields of journalism and technology

정답 ②

해설 'I'와 같은 인칭대명사가 등장하여 다소 narration(이야기하기)형의 서술방식을 취하고 있는 이러한 전개 방식의 글들은, 후반부에 주제가 드러난다는 점에 유의하자. 글의 후반부에서 강조의 부사 'Now' 다음에 이어지고 마지막에 should를 통해 '당위성'을 드러내므로 주제문의 위치를 알 수 있다. 기술 발달과 함께 기자들이 대본을 더욱 빠른 시간 안에 기사를 써야하는 현실을 말하고 있다. 그래서 마지막 문장에 나타나듯이 심지어 대본없이 즉흥적으로 진행을 해야 하는 경우를 말하고 있다.

어휘 **upend** 뒤집다; 큰 영향을 미치다 **transformation** 변형 **make stuff up** 구색을 맞추다, 꿰맞추다 **deadline** 마감시한 **convention** 집회, 대회; 인습, 전통 **script** 대본

해석 디지털 혁명이 전국의 보도국을 완전히 뒤집어 놓고 있기에 여기 기자들에게 주는 나의 조언이 있다. 나는 25년 동안 기자였기 때문에, 여섯 번의 기술적 주기를 겪었다. 가장 극적인 변화들은 마지막의 6년간 찾아왔다. 이는 내가 지내면서 점점 더욱 구색을 맞춰가고 있음을 의미한다. 뉴스 업계에 있어 많은 시간 동안 우리는 우리가 하고 있는 것에 관해 모른다. 우리는 아침에 출근을 하고, 누군가는 "세금 정책이나 이민이나 기후 변화에 대해 하나 골라 기사를 써주실래요?"라고 말한다. 하루에 한 번씩 마감이 있었을 때, 우리는 기자는 아침에는 배우고 밤에는 가르치게 될 것이라고 말했다. 즉 그 기자가 24시간 전에는 알지 못했던 주제에 관해 내일의 독자들에게 알려주는 기사를 쓰는 것을 가리킨다. 이제는 이것은 마치 어느 시각이 시작할 때 배우고 해당 시각이 끝날 때 가르치는 것과 같다. 예를 들면 나는 또한 정치 팟캐스트를 운영 중인데 전국전당대회 중에 우리는 실시간 인터뷰를 위해서 어디에서든 그것을 이용할 수 있어야만 한다. 나는 점점 더 대본없이 일하고 있다.

① 교사로서의 기자
② 기자와 즉흥성
③ 정치학에서의 기술
④ 저널리즘과 기술의 분야들

23 다음 글의 제목으로 가장 적절한 것은?

Several studies have found that pet owners have lower blood pressure, a reduced risk of heart disease, and lower levels of stress. Pets can also be a plus in the workplace. A study found that in the course of workday, stress levels decreased for workers who brought in their dogs. The differences in perceived stress between days the dog was present and absent were significant. The employees as a whole had a higher job satisfaction than industry norms. Having a dog in the office had a positive effect on the general atmosphere, relieving stress and making everyone around happier. Pet presence may serve as a low-cost wellness solution readily available to many organizations.

① Why Your Pets Need Special Care
② Pets as Stressors in Organizations
③ Safer Choice: Let Dogs Stay at Home
④ Having Pets: Well-being in the Workplace

정답 ④

해설 첫 문장과 맨 끝 문장을 통해서 요지를 알 수 있다. 직장에서 애완동물과 함께 있는 것이 스트레스를 줄여주는 등의 이점이 있다는 내용의 글이다.

어휘 pet 애완동물　blood pressure 혈압　perceive 지각하다　significant 상당히 큰　norm 표준, 기준　positive 긍정적인　atmosphere 대기; 분위기　relieve 덜어주다　presence 존재　low-cost 저비용의　readily 쉽게

해석 몇몇 연구들은 애완동물 주인들이 더 낮은 혈압과 감소된 심장병 위험 그리고 더 낮은 수준의 스트레스를 가진다는 사실을 밝혀냈다. 애완동물들은 또한 직장에서도 이점이 될 수 있다. 한 연구 결과에 따르면 근무일 동안 자신들의 개를 데려온 직장인들에게 있어서 스트레스 수치가 더 낮아졌다. 개가 (직장에) 있는 날과 없는 날의 지각된 스트레스의 차이는 상당히 컸다. 그 직장인들은 전체적으로 업계 기준치보다 더 높은 직업 만족도를 가졌다. 사무실에 개를 데리고 있는 것은 전체적인 분위기에 긍정적인 영향을 미쳤고, 스트레스를 경감시켰으며 주변의 모든 사람들을 더 행복하게 했다. 애완동물의 존재가 많은 기관들이 쉽게 활용 가능한 저비용의 건강 대책으로써의 역할을 할 수 있다.

① 왜 당신의 애완동물은 특별한 보살핌이 필요한가
② 조직 내에서의 스트레스 유발자로서의 애완동물
③ 더 안전한 선택: 개들을 집에 머물게 하라
④ 애완동물과 함께 함: 직장 내에서의 웰빙

24 다음 글의 제목으로 가장 적절한 것은?

The uncertain economic conditions of recent years have caused union and management representatives to explore many ways of handling labor problems. Workers have always wanted to share in the profits when the company has good times. Now management representatives are saying, "Fine, We'll share the profits with you — if you'll share the losses with us". Workers are having to decide whether they are willing to take the chance of salary and benefit cuts in bad times. They are having to decide whether job security is more important than other benefits. In effect, they are having to decide whether they are willing and able to pay the cost of sharing.

① Labor Movement
② Economic Recession
③ The Price of Sharing
④ Management Strategy

정답 ③

해설 In effect는 요지를 드러내는 signal이다. 마지막 문장에 드러나듯이 이 글은 노조가 경영진과 이익은 물론이고 손실도 공유하는 데에는 대가와 희생이 필요하다는 글이다.

어휘 **union** 노조 **management representatives** 경영진 **benefit** 이익; 수당, 지급금; 자선
recession 경기 침체 **maximization** 극대화 **price** 대가; 가격, 요금

해석 최근 몇 년간의 불확실한 경제 환경은 노조와 경영자 대표들로 하여금 노동 문제들을 다루는 다양한 방법들을 찾도록 만들었다. 노동자들은 회사가 잘 나갈 때 이익을 공유하기를 늘 원해왔다. 이제 경영자 대표들은 말한다. "좋습니다. 만일 당신들이 우리와 손실도 공유한다면 우리도 당신들과 이익을 공유하겠습니다". 노동자들은 불경기에 그들의 임금과 복리후생이 줄어드는 것을 기꺼이 감수하는 것을 받아들일지 여부를 결정해야 한다. 그들은 일자리의 안전이 다른 혜택들보다 더 중요한지 여부를 결정해야 한다. 사실상, 그들은 그들이 (회사와 이익과 손실을) 공유하는 데 들어가는 비용을 지불할 의지와 능력이 있는지 여부를 결정해야 한다.
① 노동 운동
② 경제 불황
③ 나눔의 대가
④ 경영 전략

25 다음 글의 요지로 가장 적절한 것은? 2020 국가직 9급

Listening to somebody else's ideas is the one way to know whether the story you believe about the world — as well as about yourself and your place in it — remains intact. We all need to examine our beliefs, air them out and let them breathe. Hearing what other people have to say, especially about concepts we regard as foundational, is like opening a window in our minds and in our hearts. Speaking up is important. Yet to speak up without listening is like banging pots and pans together: even if it gets you attention, it's not going to get you respect. There are three prerequisites for conversation to be meaningful: 1. You have to know what you're talking about, meaning that you have an original point and are not echoing a worn-out, hand-me-down or pre-fab argument; 2. You respect the people with whom you're speaking and are authentically willing to treat them courteously even if you disagree with their positions; 3. You have to be both smart and informed enough to listen to what the opposition says while handling your own perspective on the topic with uninterrupted good humor and discernment.

① We should be more determined to persuade others.
② We need to listen and speak up in order to communicate well.
③ We are reluctant to change our beliefs about the world we see.
④ We hear only what we choose and attempt to ignore different opinions.

정답 ②

해설 중반의 Yet은 역접의 연결어로서 주제를 드러내는 signal이다. 이 글은 자신의 의견을 표현하는 것뿐만 아니라 상대방을 존중하고 듣는 자세가 필요하다는 내용의 글이다.

어휘 **intact** 온전한, 손상되지 않은 **examine** 점검하다, 조사하다 **concept** 개념 **foundational** 기초적인 **speak up** 목소리를 높이다, 터놓고 얘기하다 **bang** 두드리다 **prerequisite** 필요 / 전제 조건 **echo** 그대로 되풀이하다 **worn-out** 진부한, 낡은 **hand-me-down** 독창성이 없는, 전해 내려온 **prefab** 조립식 **authentically** 진실로, 진정으로 **courteously** 예의 바르게, 정중하게 **position** 입장, 태도

해석 다른 누군가의 생각을 듣는 것은, 당신 자신과 세상 안에 있는 당신의 위치에 대해서 뿐만 아니라 세상에 대해 당신이 믿는 이야기가 여전히 온전한 것인지를 알 수 있는 유일한 방법이다. 우리 모두는 우리의 믿음을 점검하고 그것들을 공개적으로 노출시키고 그것들이 호흡하도록 할 필요가 있다. 다른 사람들이, 특히 우리가 기본적이라고 여기는 개념에 대해 말해야 하는 것을 듣는 것은 우리 마음과 가슴속의 창문을 여는 것과 같다. 의견을 말하는 것은 중요하다. 그러나 듣지 않고 의견을 말하는 것은 냄비와 팬을 함께 세게 두드리는 것과 같다: 비록 그것이 당신에게 관심을 얻게 할지는 몰라도 당신에게 존경심을 가져다 주지는 못할 것이다. 대화가 유의미하게 하는 데 있어 세 가지 전제조건이 있다: 1. 당신이 무엇에 대해 말하고 있는지 알아야 하고, 이는 당신이 독창적인 견해를 가지며 진부하고 그저 독창성 없이 전해 내려온 미리 만들어 낸 주장을 그대로 되풀이하지 않는 것을 의미한다. 2. 당신은 당신이 이야기 하고 있는 사람들을 존중해야 하고 비록

당신이 그들의 입장에 동의하지 않더라도 진정으로 그들을 기꺼이 정중하게 대하려 해야 한다. 3. 당신은 중단 없이 좋은 유머와 분별력을 가지고 해당 주제에 대한 자신의 관점을 다루면서 상대방이 말하는 것을 들을 수 있을 만큼 똑똑하고 충분한 정보가 있어야 한다.
① 우리는 다른 사람들을 설득하는 데 좀 더 단호해져야 한다.
② 우리는 소통을 잘하기 위해서 듣고 의견을 말해야 할 필요가 있다.
③ 우리는 우리가 보는 세상에 대한 믿음을 바꾸길 꺼려한다.
④ 우리는 우리가 선택한 것만 듣고 다른 의견들을 무시하려고 시도한다.

26 글의 제목으로 가장 적절한 것은? 2019 서울시 9급

Economists say that production of an information good involves high fixed costs but low marginal costs. The cost of producing the first copy of an information good may be substantial, but the cost of producing (or reproducing) additional copies is negligible. This sort of cost structure has many important implications. For example, cost-based pricing just doesn't work: a 10 or 20 percent markup on unit cost makes no sense when unit cost is zero. You must price your information goods according to consumer value. not according to your production cost.

① Securing the Copyright
② Pricing the Information Goods
③ Information as Intellectual Property
④ The Cost of Technological Change

정답 ②

해설 문두에 전문가인 'Economists'가 있고 두 번째 문장부터 첫 문장을 부연설명하고 있으므로 첫 문장이 주제문이 된다. 따라서 ② '정보재의 가격 책정'이 제목으로 가장 적절하다.

어휘 marginal cost 한계비용 substantial 물질의, 실체의; 상당한 negligible 무시할 만한
implication 함축적 의미 markup 가격 인상 unit cost 제조 단가 copyright 저작권

해석 경제학자들은 정보재의 생산은 높은 고정비용과 낮은 한계비용을 수반한다고 말한다. 정보재화의 첫 번째 사본 제작비용은 상당할 수 있지만, 추가 사본을 제작(또는 복제)하는 비용은 크지 않을 수 있다. 이런 종류의 비용 구조는 많은 중요한 의미를 가지고 있다. 예를 들어, 비용 기반 가격이 작동하지 않는다. 단가가 0일 때 단가를 10~20% 인상하는 것은 말이 되지 않는다. 당신은 당신의 생산비가 아닌 소비자 가치에 따라 당신의 정보 상품의 가격을 책정해야 한다.
① 저작권을 확보하기
② 정보재의 가격 책정
③ 지적 재산으로서의 정보
④ 기술적 변화의 비용

27 다음 글의 주제로 알맞은 것은?

In 1979, when the party introduced the one-child policy, it believed that coercion was the only way to ensure that population growth did not become unsustainable. The party has since claimed that the policy has helped prevent 400 million births. In fact, there is little evidence to back this claim. China's birth rate had been falling rapidly since the early 1970s with the help of little more than education campaigns. The birth rate continued to fall under the new policy, but other countries have seen similar declines without resorting to cruelty and oppression. Their experience suggests that the more important factors behind China's lower birth rate were rising female participation in the workforce, improvements in education, later marriages and the rapidly increasing cost of education and housing. The main effect of the one-child policy was to foster egregious human-rights abuses against the minority who ignored it.

① female's role in China
② China's gender equality
③ censorship in China
④ family planning in China

정답 ④

해설 글의 초반부의 In fact는 주제를 드러내는 signal이다. 이 글은 중국의 강압적인 가족 계획 정책인 한 자녀 갖기 정책의 부정적인 면을 부각시키고 있다.

어휘 **coercion** 강압, 강제 **unsustainable** 지속할 수 없는 **back** 지지하다 **resort to** ~에 의지하다 **oppression** 억압, 박해 **workforce** 노동력 **egregious** 극악한; 터무니없는 **abuse** 유린, 학대; 남용

해석 1979년 (중국공산)당이 한 자녀 갖기 정책을 도입했을 때 공산당은 강압이 인구 증가를 지속가능하지 않게 확실히 하는 유일한 방법이라고 믿었다. 그 이후로 공산당은 한 자녀 갖기 정책이 4억 명의 아기들이 탄생하는 것을 막는 데 도움을 주었다고 주장했다. 사실을 말하자면, 이러한 주장을 지지해줄 수 있는 증거는 거의 없다. 중국의 출산율은 1970년대 초 이후 교육 캠페인에 불과한 것의 도움을 받아가며 급격하게 하락했다. 새로운 정책(한 자녀 갖기 정책) 아래서 출산율은 지속적으로 떨어졌다. 그러나 다른 나라들은 (한 자녀 갖기 정책 같은) 잔인함과 억압에 의존하지 않고서도 유사한 출생율의 감소를 목격했다. 그 나라들의 경험은 중국의 낮은 출산율 뒤에 있는 중요한 요소들이, 일터에서의 여성 참여의 증가, 교육의 향상, 만혼, 그리고 빠르게 증가하는 교육비용과 주택비용 등이라는 사실을 나타내 보여주고 있다. 한 자녀 갖기 정책의 주된 효과는 한 자녀 갖기 정책을 무시하는 소수의 인민들을 대상으로 한 악명 높은 인권 유린을 조장하는 것이었다.

① 중국 내에서의 여성의 역할
② 중국의 성 평등
③ 중국 내에서의 검열
④ 중국의 가족 계획

28 다음 글의 요지로 적절한 것은?

Ever wonder why you can buy frozen pizza that stays "fresh" for five-plus months? Thank the military, which has outsize influence on the contents of our modern-day grocery carts. For decades, it has worked to perfect meals that are ready for combat — meaning they don't go bad even in extreme conditions. That has yielded many civilian-friendly advancements that trickle down to companies like Nabisco and General Mills — everything from preservatives that stop bread from going stale to the reconstituted meat in, say, the McDonald's McRib. During WWII, the military even worked with the United States Department of Agriculture to pioneer a method for "dehydrating" cheese. It's now used to make one of America's most popular snack foods, the Cheeto.

① Military necessity encouraged food-technological invention.
② The U.S. military spoiled the way Americans eat.
③ Foreign food companies infiltrated American diet.
④ Major food companies maintain their strong influence through lobbying.

정답 ①

해설 첫 문장이 질문으로 시작하고 있으며 그 해답에 해당하는 두 번째 문장에서 주제를 엿볼 수 있다. 이 글은 군대가 현대 식품산업에 한 기여를 다루고 있다.

어휘 **outsize** 대형의 **yield** 생산하다, 산출하다 **civilian-friendly** 민간 친화적인 **trickle down** 흘러내리다 **reconstituted meat** 가공육 **preservative** 방부제 **stale** 상한; 딱딱해진

해석 왜 당신이 5개월 이상 동안 "신선한" 상태로 있는 냉동피자를 사는지에 대해서 의문을 가져본 적이 있는가? 우리의 현대적인 식료품 카트에 담긴 내용물에 대해 엄청난 영향력을 행사한 군대에 감사하라. 수 십 년 동안 군대는 전투를 위해 준비된 음식을 완벽하게 하기 위해서 일해 왔다 — 그것이 의미하는 바는 음식들이 심지어 극단적인 조건에서도 상하지 않는다는 것이다. 군대의 이러한 노력은 Nabisco and General Mills 같은 회사들로 흘러 내려가는 많은 민간 친화적인 기술의 진보를 이루어냈는데, 이러한 식품기술의 진보는 빵이 상하는 것을 막는 방부제에서부터 예를 들어 McDonald's McRib의 가공육에 이르는 모든 것을 아우르고 있다. 세계 제2차 대전 동안 군대는 치즈를 "탈수화"하는 방법을 개척하기 위해 심지어 미 농무부와 함께 일하기도 했다. 이때 나온 방법은 현재 미국에서 가장 인기 있는 스낵들 가운데 하나인 Cheeto를 만드는데 사용되고 있다.

① 군대의 필요성이 식품 기술의 발명을 북돋았다.
② 미국 군대는 미국인의 식습관을 망쳤다.
③ 외국 음식회사가 미국의 식단에 침입했다.
④ 대기업 식품 회사들은 로비를 통해 강한 영향력을 유지한다.

29 다음 글의 제목으로 가장 적절한 것은?

A few years ago, a university professor tried a little experiment. He sent Christmas cards to a sample of perfect strangers. Although he expected some reaction, the response he received was amazing — holiday cards addressed to him came pouring back from the people how had never met nor heard of him. The great majority of those who returned a card never inquired into the identity of the unknown professor. They received his holiday greeting card and they automatically sent one in return. While small in scope, this study nicely shows the action of one of the most potent of the weapons of influence around us, which suggests that we should try to repay, in kind, what another person has provided us. If a woman does us a favor, we should do her one in return; if a man sends us a birthday present, we should remember his birthday with a gift of our own; and if a couple invites us to a party, we should be sure to invite them to one of ours.

① A Rule for Reciprocation
② The Knots Kindness Can Tie
③ Interactions That Require Ingenuity
④ Folding Big Ideas Down into Small Gifts

정답 ①

해설 마지막 문장에 반복적으로 사용되는 should는 주제를 드러내는 signal이다. 사람이 무엇인가를 받으면 그에 대해 보답하기 마련이라는 것이 이 글의 전언이다.

어휘 reaction 반응　pour back 쇄도해 오다　identity 정체성, 신분　in return 보답으로
potent 강력한, 강한　reciprocation 교환, 보답, 사례　ingenuity 영리함, 독창성

해석 몇 년 전, 한 대학 교수가 작은 실험을 시도했다. 그는 완전히 낯선 사람들을 표본으로 연하장을 보냈다. 그는 비록 어느 정도의 반응을 기대했지만, 그가 받은 반응은 놀라운 것이었다. — 그의 주소가 적힌 연하장들이 그가 만나본 적도 없고 들어 본적도 없는 사람들로부터 쇄도했다. 답장 카드를 보내준 사람들의 대다수는 알려지지 않은 교수의 신원에 대해서 절대로 묻지 않았다. 그들은 (교수의) 연하장을 받았고 그에 대한 보답으로서 자동적으로 답장 카드를 보냈던 것이다. 그 범위가 좁았음에도 불구하고 이 연구는 우리 주변에 가장 강력한 영향력을 미치는 무기들 중의 하나가 작용하고 있음을 잘 보여주고 있는데, 그것은 우리가 다른 사람이 우리에게 제공한 것과 같은 종류의 것을 일종의 보답으로서 다른 사람에게 제공한다는 것이다. 만일 한 여성이 우리에게 호의를 베푼다면 우리는 보답으로 유사한 호의를 그녀에 베푼다. 만일 한 남자가 우리에게 생일 선물을 보내준다면 우리는 우리 자신이 준비한 선물로 그의 생일을 기억해야 한다. 만일 한 부부가 우리를 그들의 파티에 초대한다면 우리는 틀림없이 그들을 우리의 파티에 초대할 것이다.
① 답례에 대한 규칙
② 친절이 묶어내는 인연
③ 독창성을 요구하는 상호교류
④ 작은 선물 속에 큰 생각을 접어 넣기

30 다음 글의 제목으로 가장 적합한 것을 고르시오.

Android is based on open source technology, which was at its inception not as refined as paid technologies from Apple and Microsoft. However, over the past two decades, open source software technology has become equally as sophisticated as conventional development technologies. This is evident in Internet 2.0, as the majority of the consumer electronics manufacturers have chosen Linux and Java over the Windows and Macintosh operating systems. Therefore, Android developers can develop not only for smartphones, but also for new and emerging consumer electronic devices that are network-compatible and thus available to connect to the Android Market. This translates into more sales onto more devices in more areas of the customer's life, and thus more incentive to develop for Android over closed and PC operating systems. In addition to being free for commercial use, Android has one of the largest, wealthiest, and most innovative companies in modern-day computing behind it: Google. Finally, and most importantly, it's much easier to get your Android applications published than those for other platforms that are similar to Android. We've all heard the horror stories regarding major development companies waiting months, and sometimes years, for their apps to be approved for the app marketplace. These problems are nearly nonexistent on the open source Android platform.

① How to Succeed in the Android Market
② How Can Android Benefit Us?
③ Role of Google in Developing Android
④ Potential of Open Source Technology

정답 ②

해설 글의 초중반부에 나오는 therefore는 요지를 드러내는 signal이다. 이 글은 안드로이드의 이점에 대해서 기술하고 있다.

어휘 **inception** 처음, 시작　**refined** 정제[정련]된; 세련된, 우아한
sophisticated 세련된; 속 때 묻은; 복잡한, 정교한　**conventional** 인습적인, 전통적인
consumer electronics 가전제품　**compatible** 양립할 수 있는; 호환이 가능한　**innovative** 혁신적인

해석 안드로이드는 공개 소스 기술에 기반한 것으로서, 그 초기 단계만 해도 애플과 마이크로소프트의 유료기술만큼 정교하지 않았다. 그러나 지난 20년 동안, 공개 소스 소프트웨어 기술은 기존의 개발된 기술만큼 정교해져왔다. 대부분의 가전제품 생산업체들이 윈도우나 매킨토시의 운영체계를 대신해서 리눅스와 자바의 운영체계를 선택하는 데서 알 수 있듯이 제2세대 인터넷에서 이러한 현상이 분명해지고 있다. 그러므로 안드로이드 개발자들은 스마트폰뿐만 아니라 네트워크 간의 호환이 가능하고 안드로이드 마켓과 접속도 가능한, 새롭

게 등장하는 가전제품장비들 또한 개발할 수 있게 되었다. 이러한 현상은 소비자의 삶의 영역에서 더 많은 제품들에 대한 더 많은 판매를 의미하고, 더 나아가 폐쇄적인 PC운영체계를 넘어서는 안드로이드 운영체계의 개발에 대한 더 많은 동기부여를 의미한다. 그 상업적 활용이 무료라는 것 이외에도, 안드로이드는 현대 컴퓨터 영역에서 가장 크고, 가장 부유하고, 가장 혁신적인 기업인 구글을 그 배경으로 삼고 있다. 마지막으로, 가장 중요한 것은, 안드로이드와 유사한 다른 플랫폼을 위한 앱을 출시하는 것보다 안드로이드 앱을 출시하는 것이 훨씬 더 쉽다는 점이다. 우리 모두는 주요 앱 개발자들이 자신들이 개발한 앱을 승인받기 위해서 몇 달씩, 때로는 몇 년씩 기다린다는 것과 관련된 끔직한 이야기를 들어왔다. 이런 종류의 문제들은 공개 소스인 안드로이드 플랫폼에서는 거의 존재하지 않는다.

① 안드로이드 시장에서 성공하는 법
② 안드로이드는 우리에게 어떤 이득을 줄 수 있는가?
③ 안드로이드를 개발하는데 있어서의 구글의 역할
④ 오픈 소스 기술의 잠재력

02 내용 일치

01 다음 글의 내용과 일치하는 것은? 2015 국가직 9급

The WAIS-R is made up of eleven subtests, or scales. The subtests of the WAIS-R are arranged by the type of ability or skill being tested. The subtests are organized into two categories. Six subtests define the verbal scale, and five subtests constitute a performance scale. We can compute three scores: a verbal score, a performance score, and a total (or full-scale) score. The total score can be taken as an approximation of general intellectual ability. To administer the WAIS-R, you present each of the eleven subtests to your subject. The items within each subtest are arranged in order of difficulty. You start with relatively easy items, and then you progress to more difficult ones. You stop administering any one subtest when your subject fails a specified number of items in a row. You alternate between verbal and performance subtests. The whole process takes up to an hour and a half.

① The WAIS-R has eleven subtests, each of which has two main parts.
② Several subtests with higher scores among the eleven ones should be presented.
③ The items of each subtest in the WAIS-R begin from easy and continue on to more difficult ones.
④ Subjects take all of the verbal subtests first and then all of the performance subtests.

정답 ③

해설 아래에서 세 번째 문장인 'You start with relatively easy items, and then you progress to more difficult ones.'처럼 비교적 쉬운 항목에서 시작하여 좀 더 어려운 항목으로 시험이 진행된다고 하였으므로 내용과 일치한다.

① 본문에서 11개의 하부검사 각각이 두 개의 부분을 가지는 것이 아니라, 11개가 두 개로 분류된다는 의미이므로 옳지 않다.

② 본문에서 더 높은 점수를 가진 몇 개의 세부검사가 제출되어야 하는 것이 아니라, 11개 각각을 제시한다고 하였으므로 옳지 않다.

④ 본문에서 모든 언어성 검사를 치르고 그 다음에 동작성 검사를 치르게 되는 것이 아니라 언어성과 동작성 하부검사를 번갈아 한다고 했으므로 옳지 않다.

어휘 **be made up of** ~로 구성되다 **subtest** 하위검사, 보조시험 **arrange** 마련하다, 처리하다 **verbal** 언어(말)의 **approximation** 근사치 **administer** 관리하다, 운영하다 **specify** 명시하다 **alternate** 번갈아 하는, 교대하는

해석 WAIS-R(Wide Area Information Servers, 광역정보서버 R)은 11개의 하위검사 혹은 단계들로 구성되어 있다. WAIS-R의 하위검사는 검증되는 능력이나 기술의 유형에 의해 배열된다. 이 하위검사는 두 가지 범주로 구성되어 있다. 여섯 개의 하부검사는 언어성 검사를 규정하고 다섯 개의 하부 검사는 동작성 검사를 구성한다. 우리는 세 가지의 점수를 계산할 수 있는데 이는 언어성 점수, 동작성 점수, 합산 (또는 전면적인) 점수이다. 전체점수는 일반적 지적 능력의 근사치이다. WAIS-R을 실행하기 위해서는 11개 각각의 하부검사 항목들을 당신의 실험 대상에 제공한다. 각 하부검사 항목들은 난이도 순서로 배열된다. 당신은 비교적 쉬운 문항부터 시작하여 더 어려운 것들로 진행하게 된다. 당신은 당신의 실험 대상이 연속적으로 특정한 수의 항목을 실패할 때 어떠한 하부검사도 실행을 중단하게 된다. 당신은 언어성과 동작성 하부검사를 번갈아 사용하게 된다. 이 모든 과정은 대략 한 시간 반 정도 걸린다.

① WAIS-R은 11개의 하위검사들이 있으며, 각각 2개의 주요 부문들로 이루어져있다.

② 11개 중 높은 점수를 기록한 몇몇의 하위 검사들이 제출되어야 한다.

③ WAIS-R의 각각의 하위 검사들의 항목은 쉬운 것에서 시작해 더 어려운 것으로 진행된다.

④ 대상자들은 우선 모든 언어성 검사를 치르고 그 다음에 동작성 검사를 치르게 된다.

02 다음 글의 내용과 일치하는 것을 고르시오.

I never knew President Roosevelt as well as I did some of the other world leaders, but in the few conferences I had with him I was impressed, not only by his inspirational qualities, but by his amazing grasp of the whole complex war effort. He could discuss strategy on equal terms with his generals and admirals. His knowledge of the geography of the war theaters was so encyclopedic that the most obscure places in faraway countries were always accurately sited on his mental map. President Roosevelt possessed personality, surely, but as the nation's leader in a global conflict, he also did his homework thoroughly.

① President Roosevelt had an amazing knowledge of the geography, but this was not instrumental in discussing strategy.
② President Roosevelt's knowledge of the geography was as detailed as that of the cartographers.
③ President Roosevelt had the capability to do his homework as the nation's leader.
④ President Roosevelt was not so much a politician as a general.

정답 ③

해설 마지막 문장에 루스벨트가 지도자로서의 자신의 과제를 잘 이행하였다는 내용이 나온다.

어휘 **amazing** 놀라운 **grasp** 잡다; 파악하다 **strategy** 전략 **geography** 지리(학) **obscure** 불분명한; 숨기다 **global** 지구의, 세계의 **inspirational** 영감의, 고무적인 **threat** 위협 **encyclopedic** 백과사전적인, 해박한 **thoroughly** 철저하게 **cartographer** 지도 제작자

해석 나는 다른 세계 지도자들 몇몇을 아는 만큼 루즈벨트 대통령을 알지 못했다. 그러나 나는 그와 나누었던 몇 번의 대화에서 그의 고무적인 자질에 의해서 뿐만 아니라 그 복잡한 전체의 전쟁성과를 놀랍게 파악하고 있는 것에 감명 받았다. 그는 육군장군이나 해군장군들과 동등한 관계에서 전략을 토론할 수 있었다. 전쟁 무대의 지리적 위치에 대한 그의 지식은 매우 해박한 것이어서 먼 나라의 가장 불분명한 장소들도 그의 머릿속 지도에 정확히 위치되어 있었다. 루즈벨트 대통령은 확실히 개성을 소유하고 있었지만 세계의 갈등 속에 처한 국가의 지도자로서 그는 또한 그의 과제를 철저하게 이행했던 것이다.

① 루즈벨트 대통령은 지리학에 대한 놀라운 지식을 가지고 있었으나 이것이 전략을 논의하는데 도움이 되지는 않았다.
② 루즈벨트 대통령의 지리에 대한 지식은 지도제작자들 만큼이나 상세했다.
③ 루즈벨트 대통령은 국가의 지도자로서 국내 문제를 해결할 능력을 가지고 있었다.
④ 루즈벨트 대통령은 정치가라기보다는 장군이었다.

03 다음 글의 내용과 일치하지 않는 것은?

A company has a great product and naturally wants consumers to think of it as the best they can buy. So the marketing team rolls out an advertising campaign showing why the product is superior to the competition in terms of features and price, and is rewarded with robust sales. Instead of being able to bask in that success, however, the company starts to hear a lot of complaints and get a lot of returns. Clearly, the strategy backfired. But why? It turns out that comparative ads and "Ours is the best!" product positioning activate something known as the maximizing mind-set, which leads people to regard anything that's less than perfect as a waste of money. Our research has found that although some people are "maximizers" by nature, and others tend to be content with "good enough", those attitude aren't fixed. The maximizing mind-set can be induced by situations that encourage people to make comparisons and to look for the very best. When marketing messages inadvertently induce it, the results may be post-purchase regret and brand switching at the slightest hint of disappointed.

① Comparative ads do not always pay off.
② Maximizers tend to entice other people to make comparisons.
③ The maximizing mind-set is contingent upon situations.
④ Consumers with a maximizing mind-set are inclined to seek after the very best.

정답 ②

해설 최고 지향자들(최고 지향 심리를 가진 소비자들)이 제품을 비교하도록 다른 사람들을 유혹한다는 내용은 본문에 언급되지 않으며 글의 후반에 최고 지향자들이 아니라 비교하도록 하는 상황이 최고 지향자적인 마음자세를 만든다고 되어 있다.

어휘 robust 강한, 확고한　rolls out (신형 비행기의) 첫 공개·전시
bask in 일광욕을 하다; (관심·칭찬 등을) 누리다　backfire 실패하다 기대에 어긋나다
comparative ads 비교 광고　adversity 역경, 불운　recoil 후퇴하다, 위축되다
flounder 버둥거리다, 허둥대다, 실패하다　gratification 만족, 기쁨　entice 유혹하다

해석 회사는 멋진 제품을 가지고 있고 소비자들이 당연히 그 제품을 그들이 살 수 있는 최고의 것으로 생각해 주길 원한다. 그래서 회사의 마케팅팀은 특징과 가격이란 관점에서 왜 이 제품이 경쟁 제품보다 더 우위에 있는지를 보여주는 광고를 제작하며, 강력한 판매 증가로 보상받고자 한다. 그러나 그러한 성공을 누리는 대신, 회사는 많은 불만사항들을 듣게 되고 많은 환불에 직면하게 된다. 전략은 명백히 실패했다. 그러나 왜 실패했을까? 비교 광고와 "우리 것이 최고다".라는 제품의 포지셔닝은, 최고 지향 심리로 알려져 있는 것을 활성화시키는데, 그것(최고 지향 심리)은 사람들로 하여금 완벽하지 않은 어떤 것을 구입하는 것을 돈의 낭비라고 여기도록 만든다. 우리 연구는, 비록 일부 사람들이 천성적으로 '최고 지향자'이고 다른 사람들은 '충분히 좋은 것'에 만족하지만 이러한 태도들이 고정되지 않았다는 것을 발견했다. 최고 지향 심리는 사람들이 (제품들

을) 비교하고 가장 좋은 것만을 추구하는 상황에 의해서 촉발될 수 있다. 마케팅 메시지가 의도와 무관하게 이러한 상황을 촉발시킬 때, 그 결과는 구입 후의 후회나 약간의 실망에도 브랜드 스위칭(브랜드를 교체하는 것)일지도 모른다.
① 비교 광고가 항상 이익이 되는 것은 아니다.
② 최고 지향자들은 제품을 비교하도록 다른 사람들을 유혹한다.
③ 최고 지향 마음 자세는 상황에 달려있다.
④ 최고 지향 마음 자세를 갖는 소비자들은 진짜 최고만을 쫓으려한다.

04 다음 글의 내용과 일치하는 것은?

The computers of decades ago could run numerical models of the weather no more than three days ahead before their predictions became pure fiction. Today better data, more detailed atmospheric models and immensely faster computers have pushed the range of reliable forecasts to nearly six days on average.
Though better predictions are saving many lives and a lot of money, each extension in range of prediction comes at a higher price. For the weather is intrinsically chaotic, so that a tiny inaccuracy in the initial data can easily snowball into a huge error which renders long-term prediction hopeless.

① Computers have increased our near-term predictive power for weather.
② It is believed that weather can be predicted with precision very soon.
③ Computers have made long-term weather forecasting a purefiction.
④ It is highly unlikely that a small change in weather data causes a sizable difference in prediction.

정답 ①
해설 두 번째 문장에 컴퓨터 발달이 단기적인 기상 예측 능력의 향상을 가져왔다고 언급되어 있다.
어휘 numerical 수의, 숫자의 prediction 예측 immensely 막대하게 extension 확대 range 범위 intrinsically 본래 chaotic 혼돈스러운 render ~하게 만들다; 제공하다
해석 수 십 년 전의 컴퓨터들의 계산능력으로는 날씨를 사실적으로 예측할 수 있는 최대한도가 3일에 불과하였다. 오늘날, 더 나은 정보와 더 정교한 기상 모델 그리고 대단히 빠른 컴퓨터들이 신뢰할 수 있는 기상 예보의 한계를 평균 6일 정도로 늘렸다. 더 나은 예측이 더 많은 생명을 구하고 더 많은 돈을 절약시켜 주기는 하지만 한계를 늘리는 것에는 그보다 더 많은 돈이 든다. 날씨가 본질적으로 혼돈스럽기 때문에 초기의 아주 작은 부정확성도 눈덩이처럼 불어나 장기간의 예측을 절망적으로 만드는 거대한 오류가 될 수 있다.
① 컴퓨터 발달이 단기적인 기상 예측 능력의 향상을 가져왔다.
② 날씨는 조만간 정확하게 예측될 수 있다고 믿어진다.
③ 컴퓨터들은 장기적인 기상 예측을 순전히 허구로 만들었다.
④ 기상 데이터의 작은 변화가 예측에 있어서 상당한 차이를 일으킬 수 있다는 것은 매우 가능성이 낮다.

05 다음 글의 내용과 가장 일치하는 것은?

For years, the motor industry lived by the mantra, "bigger is better". The number of liters that a car's pistons displaced within its engine's cylinders was a matter of pride for its owner. This was because displacement equaled power, and power equaled — well, whatever it was that the owner wanted to show off beyond the mere ability to travel from A to B. Times change, though, and technology moves on. Power is no less in demand than it was, but as the clamor for fuel economy rises, raw displacement, which sucks fuel from a tank like an enthusiastic child with a straw and a bottle of pop, is going out of fashion. Instead, a new mantra is taking over. This is, "small is beautiful". What tickles today's motor heads, therefore, is not so much how many liters an engine displaces as how much horsepower it can extract from a given volume. For, even as they get more powerful, car motors are shrinking.

① Fuel economy has usurped power in the motor industry as a point of pride.
② Internal-combustion engines are getting smaller and more efficient.
③ Motor heads now care more about engine displacement than volume.
④ Smaller cars put beauty before power.

정답 ②

해설 자동차의 엔진이 크기는 작아지면서 마력은 더욱더 강력해지고 있다는 마지막 문장의 내용으로부터 정답을 추론할 수 있다.

어휘 mantra 기도, 주문 displace 배기량을 가지다; 쫓아내다, 대신하다 show off 자랑하다
fuel economy 엔진의 연비 pop 탄산수 tickle 자극하다; 간질이다 horsepower 마력
usurp 빼앗다, 강탈하다

해석 오랜 세월 동안, 자동차 업계는 "클수록 더 좋다"라는 주문(마법)에 기대 살아왔다. 자동차의 엔진에 있는 실린더들 안에서 자동차의 피스톤이 바꿔놓는 배기량의 수치는 자동차 소유자들에게 자부심의 문제였다. 이것은 배기량이 힘과 동등한 것이고, 이 힘은 단지 A지역에서 B지역으로 이동하는 능력을 넘어서 자동차의 소유자가 자동차에 대해서 뽐내고 싶어 하는 그 무엇과 동일한 것이다. 그럼에도 불구하고 시대는 변하고 기술은 앞으로 나간다. 힘에 대한 수요는 과거에 그랬던 것처럼 여전히 존재하지만, 연비에 대한 요청이 증가함에 따라, 열정적인 아이가 빨대로 병에 들어 있는 탄산수를 빨아 마시는 것처럼 연료탱크에서 연료를 빨아내 버리는 순수한 배기량은 이제 인기가 시들해지고 있다. 그 대신 새로운 주문이 등장해 주도권을 잡아가고 있다. 그 새로운 주문은 "작은 것이 아름답다"이다. 그러므로 오늘날의 자동차 업계 수뇌부의 관심을 사로잡고 있는 것은 엔진이 얼마나 많은 배기량을 내보낼 수 있느냐가 아니라, (엔진이) 주어진 부피에서 얼마나 많은 마력을 뽑아 낼 수 있는가이다. 왜냐하면, 더욱더 강력해지는 가운데 자동차의 엔진이 점점 더 작아지고 있기 때문이다.

① 연비 효율은 자존심의 요점인 자동차 산업에서의 힘(마력)을 강탈했다.
② 내연기관 엔진들은 더더욱 작아지고 효율적이게 되고 있다.
③ 자동차 산업의 수뇌부들은 이제 엔진의 부피보다는 엔진 출력에 더 관심이 많다.
④ 더 작은 차들이 힘보다 아름다움을 우선시한다.

06 다음 글의 내용과 일치하지 않는 것은? 2015 지방직 7급

Saccharin, the oldest artificial sweetener, was accidentally discovered in 1879 by researcher Constantine Fahlberg, who was working at Johns Hopkins University in the laboratory of professor Ira Remsen. Fahlberg's discovery came after he forgot to wash his hands before lunch. He had spilled a chemical on his hands and it, in turn, caused the bread he ate to taste unusually sweet. In 1880, the two scientists jointly published the discovery, but in 1884, Fahlberg obtained a patent and began mass-producing saccharin without Remsen. The use of saccharin did not become widespread until World War I when sugar supply was limited. Its popularity increased during the 1960s and 1970s with the manufacture of Sweet'N Low and diet soft drinks.

① The discovery of saccharin by Fahlberg was unplanned and unintentional.
② Fahlberg published the discovery of saccharin with Remsen, but received a patent without him.
③ Saccharin replaced previously used artificial sweeteners thanks to its mass production.
④ Sugar shortages during World War I made the use of saccharin widespread.

정답 ③

해설 이 글의 첫 문장에 사카린이 가장 오래된 인공 감미료라는 언급과 생산이 증가했다는 언급이 있다. 그리고 사카린의 발견이 의도하지 않은 우연에 의한 것이라는 일화도 소개되었다. 그러나 사카린이 기존에 사용되었던 인공 감미류를 대체했다는 언급은 명확히 언급된바가 없다. 그러므로 정답은 ③이다.

어휘 **saccharin** 사카린 **artificial** 인공의 **sweetener** 감미료(설탕 대신에 쓰는 것) **spill** 흘리다, 쏟다 **patent** 특허, 특허권; 명백한 **popularity** 인기 **unplanned** 미리 계획하지 않은 **unintentional** 뜻하지 않은, 무심코 한

해석 가장 오래된 인공 감미료인 사카린은 Johns Hopkins 대학의 Ira Remsen 교수 연구실에서 작업했던 Constantine Fahlberg 연구원에 의해 1879년에 우연히 발견되었다. Fahlberg의 발견은 그가 점심 식사 전에 손을 씻는 것을 잊은 다음에 나왔다. 그는 자신의 손에 어떤 화학물질을 쏟았었다. 그리고 그것이, 결과적으로, 그가 먹는 빵을 비정상적으로 단맛이 나게 했다. 1880년 두 과학자는 함께 이 발견을 발표했다. 그러나 1884년 Fahlberg는 Remsen 없이 특허권을 획득하여 사카린을 대량 생산하기 시작했다. 사카린의 사용은 설탕의 공급이 제한되었던 때인 제1차 세계 대전 전까지는 널리 퍼지지 않았다. 그것의 인기는 1960년대와 70년대에 Sweet N Low의 생산과 다이어트 청량음료와 함께 증가했다.

① Fahlberg에 의한 사카린의 발견은 계획되고 의도된 것은 아니었다.
② Fahlberg는 Remsen과 함께 사카린의 발견을 발표했지만 Remsen 없이 특허권을 받았다.
③ 사카린은 대량 생산 덕분에 기존에 사용되었던 인공 감미료를 대체했다.
④ 제1차 세계 대전 기간 중의 설탕 부족은 사카린 사용의 증가를 이끌었다.

07 다음 중 Claudius에 관한 내용과 일치하는 것은?

Claudius, a Roman emperor, was at first glance an unlikely choice, and was not viewed as suitable by the Roman elites. He was already fifty, had no administrative or military career, and suffered from physical defects such as weak legs and a lolling head. His mother had hated him and the rest of his family had not considered him Princeps material. Still, he was not without merits. Augustus had seen he was smart, and had spent late nights talking to him over drinks. Claudius was also an historian. He had written about Carthage, and he had also produced a forty-one-volume history of Augustus. Thus, he knew all about the Empire, its history, and how to administrate it.

① He was favored by the Roman elites.
② His deformities made him bureaucratic.
③ His mother was proud of his intelligence.
④ He was considered too old to be an emperor.

정답 ④

해설 내용 일치 문제에서 숫자와 관련된 표현은 원래 빈출되는 사항임을 유의하자. 두 번째 문장에서 '이미' 오십 세라는 표현을 볼 때 나이가 많음을 부정적으로 묘사하고 있는 것을 알 수 있다. 그러므로 정답은 ④이다.

어휘 administrative 행정의 defect 결점, 단점 loll 축 늘어지다
Princeps 주요한 것; (로마 제국의) 원수, 족장; 초판[본(本)] deformity 기형
administrate 관리하다, 통치하다

해석 로마의 황제인 Claudius는 언뜻 보기에 있을 법하지 않은 선택이었고 로마의 엘리트들에 의해서 (황제 역할을 하기에) 적합하다고 여겨지지 않았다. 그는 이미 나이가 50이었고 행정적인 경력이나 군사적인 경력도 가지고 있지 않았으며 약한 다리와 축 늘어진 머리 같은 신체적인 결점들로 인해 고통 받고 있었다. 그의 어머니는 그를 미워했고 나머지 그의 가족들은 그를 로마의 황제가 될 재목으로 여기지 않았다. 그럼에도 불구하고 여전히 그에게 장점이 없는 것은 아니었다. (그 당시 로마의 황제인) Augustus는 그를 현명하다고 여겼고 그와 함께 밤늦도록 술을 마시며 시간을 보내곤 했다. Claudius는 또한 역사학자였다. 그는 Carthage에 관한 글을 썼고 또한 41권으로 된 Augustus에 관한 역사서도 만들어 냈다. 이와 같이 그는 로마 제국, 로마의 역사, 그리고 로마를 어떻게 통치해야 하는지에 대해서 잘 알고 있었다.

참고 로마는 조선을 포함한 동아시아 왕국들과 달리 왕위를 자식에게 물려주지 않고 유력한 귀족이나 왕족들 가운데서 유능한 인물에게 물려주었다. 이것이 이른바, 선양 제도다.

① 그는 로마 엘리트들의 총애를 받았다.
② 그의 기형은 그를 관료적으로 만들었다.
③ 그의 어머니는 그가 영리함을 자랑스러워했다.
④ 그는 황제가 되기에는 너무 늙었다고 여겨졌다.

08 글의 내용과 일치하지 않는 것은? 2016 국가직 7급

Can you imagine anyone choosing to live without money in our consumer society? Well, that's exactly what Franz Schmidt has been doing since he quit his job as a psychotherapist and gave away all his possessions. This 75-year-old father of three and grandfather of four has chosen to live a simple life without the pressure to buy and own. Schmidt has thought about possession and value since he was a young boy. Schmidt and his family had to leave all their possessions during World War Ⅱ to flee from the Russian forces in Memel. They could not take anything with them, and this made a great impression on him. Schmidt knew what it was like to be penniless and he learned from experience that possessions are not what give a person value. Schmidt moved to Heidelberg, a major city in Germany, with his wife and three children in the nineties, and was so shocked by the homelessness of the poor in the neighborhood that he decided to open a swap shop called Share. Members of this group swap things and skills without money. What amazed Schmidt was not only how people's needs could be met, but also how much the participants benefited from the social aspect of their contact. This experience deeply moved not only Schmidt, but other people as well.

① He used to work in the mental health care field.
② He and his family left Memel very poor during World War Ⅱ.
③ He moved to Heidelberg in Germany with his family.
④ He opened a swap shop where people could buy items at low prices.

정답 ④

해설 ④의 "그는 중고품 (교환) 가게를 열었고 거기에서 사람들이 물건들을 저렴한 가격으로 샀다"는 내용은 본문의 "이 그룹의 멤버들은 돈 없이(돈을 사용하지 않고) 물건들과 기술들을 교환한다".라는 부분과 일치하지 않으므로 정답은 ④이다.

어휘 **consumer society** 소비 사회 **psychotherapist** 정신(심리) 요법 의사
give something away ~을 선물로 주다, 기부하다 **in the nineties** 90년대에
homelessness 집 없음; 노숙자임 **swap shop** 중고품 (교환) 가게

해석 당신은 우리의 소비 사회에서 어떤 사람이 돈 없이 사는 것을 선택한다는 것을 상상할 수 있는가? Franz Schmidt가 심리치료사로서의 직업을 그만두고 그리고 그의 모든 재산들을 기부한 이후로부터 계속 해오는 일이 바로 그것이다. 이 75세의 세 자녀를 둔 아버지이자 네 명의 손자 손녀를 둔 할아버지는 물건을 사고 그리고 소유하는 즐거움 없이 단순한 삶을 살기로 결심했다. Schmidt는 그가 어렸을 때 이후로 소유와 가치에 대하여 계속 생각해오고 있다. Schmidt와 그의 가족은 제2차 세계 대전 동안에 Memel에서 러시아 군대로부터 도망을 가기 위하여 그들의 재산들을 남겨두어야 했다. 그들을 그 어떤 것도 그들과 함께 가지고 올 수 없었고 그리고 이것이 그에게 큰 인상을 남겼다. Schmidt는 무일푼이라는 것이 어떤 상태라는 것을 알았

고 그리고 한 인간에게 가치를 주는 것이 재산들이 아니라는 것을 경험으로부터 배웠다. Schmidt는 90년대에 그의 부인과 세 명의 아이들과 함께 독일의 주요도시인 Heidelberg로 이사를 갔고 그리고 그의 이웃의 가난한 사람들이 집 없이 노숙을 하는 것에 너무나도 쇼크를 먹어서 그 결과 Share라고 불리는 중고품 (교환) 가게를 열기로 결심했다. 이 그룹의 멤버들은 돈 없이 물건들과 기술들을 교환한다. Schmidt를 놀라게 했던 것은 어떻게 사람들의 필요(욕구)들이 충족되는가 뿐만 아니라, 그들의 접촉이라는 사회적인 측면으로부터 그 참여자들이 얼마나 많이 혜택을 받는가였다. 이 경험은 Schmidt뿐만 아니라 게다가 다른 사람들을 매우 감동시켰다.

① 그는 정신 건강 치료 분야에서 한때 일을 했다.
② 그와 그의 가족은 제2차 세계 대전 Memel을 매우 가난한 상태로 떠났다.
③ 그는 독일의 하이델베르크로 가족과 함께 이사를 갔다.
④ 그는 중고품 교환 가게를 열었고 거기에서 사람들이 물건들을 저렴한 가격으로 샀다.

PART 02

09 다음 글을 읽고 내용과 일치하는 것을 고르시오.

The rush of companies on to the Internet has turned into crush of businesses trying to get noticed. Those who fail are quickly trampled underfoot. Marketing is what differentiates the winners from the losers, and advertising is therefore by far the biggest item in the budget of new-media companies. The rule of thumb is that 70% of the budget of an Internet company goes in marketing.

① New-media companies have cut down their advertising cost.
② New-media companies have to spend a large amount of money making themselves known.
③ The Internet has offered the companies an efficient way of marketing.
④ Getting on to the Internet has resulted in increasing the profit of the companies.

정답 ②

해설 마지막 문장에 언급 된 것처럼 인터넷 회사들은 많은 예산을 광고에 투자한다.

어휘 rush 돌진, 쇄도 crush 으깨지다; 쇄도하다; 쇄도; 반함 trample 짓밟다 underfoot 발밑에, 짓밟아서, differentiate from ~을 구분하다 budget 예산 rule of thumb 경험의 법칙, 어림짐작

해석 인터넷으로의 회사들의 쇄도는 회사를 돋보이게 하려 노력하는 업체들의 쇄도로 변했다. 그것에 실패한 회사들은 빠르게 마구 짓밟혀 사라졌다. 마케팅은 승자와 패자를 구분하는 것이며, 그러므로 광고는 새로운 미디어 회사들의 예산에 아주 가장 큰 항목이다. 어림짐작으로 인터넷 회사의 예산 중 70%가 마케팅에 들어간다.

① 뉴미디어 회사들은 그들의 광고 비용을 줄였다.
② 뉴미디어 회사들을 자신들을 알리기 위해서 많은 양의 돈을 써야 한다.
③ 인터넷은 그 회사들에게 효율적인 마케팅 방법을 제공했다.
④ 인터넷에 나타나는 것은 그 회사들이 주목을 받게 하는 것을 보장한다.

10 다음 글에서 Tuva에 관한 내용과 일치하지 않는 것은?

Nestled along the northern border of Mongolia, Tuva is easy to miss. There are no direct flights from Moscow; the only ways in are turbo-prop planes from nearby Siberian cities or a long drive through the surrounding mountains. Most of the region's 308,000 people are native Tuvans, a Turkic people some of whom still practise a traditional nomadic lifestyle. Shamanism and Buddhism remain more widespread than Orthodox Christianity, Russia's dominant religion. As Oksana Tyulyush, artistic director of the Tuvan National Orchestra, quips, "God is a long way up and Moscow is a long way away". Russians typically know little of the region, which lived under Mongol or Chinese rule for most of its history. Between 1921 and 1944 Tuvans enjoyed a brief run of de jure independence as Tannu Tuva, or the Tuvan People's Republic, which delighted philatelists by issuing a series of oddly shaped stamps. After the end of the second world war, the Soviet Union moved in, making Tuvan an official protectorate at the request of local authorities. For most outsiders, Tuva is best known for its music: khoomei , or throat singing, a trance-inducing drone created when one singer hits several notes simultaneously. Khoomei is inspired by nature, as performers seek to channel the waters, winds and beasts of their surroundings. In Tuva harking back to tradition has helped fill the void left after the Soviet collapse.

① It is surrounded by mountains.
② It used to be ruled by China and Mongolia.
③ It once was an independent country.
④ It was invaded by Russia after the second world war.

정답 ④

해설 글의 중후반부에 따르면, 투바는 2차 대전 후, 투바인들의 요청에 의해서 소련의 보호국이 되었다.

어휘 **nestle** 자리 잡고 있다, 편안하게 드러누워 있다 **turbo-prop plane** 터보프롭 엔진이 달린 비행기
quip 빈정대다, 조롱하다, 놀리다 **de jure** 법에 따른 **philatelist** 우표 수집가 **protectorate** 보호국
hark back (과거에 있었던 일을) 기억하다(들먹이다) **drone** 수벌; 윙윙거림, 단조로운 소리
hit a note 건반을 치다 **void** 틈, 공백, 공허

해석 몽고의 북쪽 국경을 따라 자리 잡고 있는 투바는 관심에서 놓치기가 쉽다. 모스크바에서 투바까지 가는 직항로는 없다. 그곳까지 가는 유일한 방법은 부근 시베리아에 있는 도시들로부터 터보프롭 엔진이 달린 비행기(낡은 구형 비행기)를 타거나 혹은 주변을 둘러싸고 있는 산맥들을 통과해 장거리 운전을 하는 것이다. 308,000명인 이 지역에 살고 있는 주민들 대다수는 토착민인 투바인들 인데, 이들 투바인들 가운데 일부는 여전히 전통적인 유목민 생활방식에 따라 살아가고 있다. 이 지역에서는 러시아의 지배적인 종교인 러시아 정교보다 샤머니즘과 불교가 더 널리 퍼져있다. 투바 국립 오케스트라의 예술 감독인 Oksana Tyulyush는 "기독교적인 신은 너무나 먼 하늘 높은 곳에 있고 모스크바는 먼 곳에 떨어져 있습니다"라고, 빈정거린다. 러시아인들은 일반적으로, 그 역사의 대부분 기간을 몽고와 중국의 지배 아래서 살아온 이 지역에 대해서 아는 것이 별로 없다. 1921년부터 1944년에 이르는 기간 동안 투바인들은 투바인민공화국으로서 법에 따른 짧은 독립을 누렸다. 이 짧은 독립 기간 동안 투바인민공화국은 기묘한 모양의 우표들을 발행했는데 이 우표

들은 우표수집가들에게 기쁨을 주었다. 제2차 세계 대전이 끝나고 나서, 소련이 이 지역에 들어왔고 지역 당국의 요청에 따라 투바 지역을 공식적인 보호국으로 만들었다. 대부분의 외부인들에게, 투바는 'khoomei(흐미)', 즉 목노래로 유명한데, 흐미는 한 가수가 여러 개의 건반을 동시에 칠 때 무아지경으로 인도하는 윙윙대는 소리를 만들어낸다. khoomei(흐미)는 자연에 의해서 영감을 받는데, 흐미를 부르는 사람들은 그들 주변에 있는 강, 바람, 그리고 짐승들과의 소통을 추구하기 때문이다. 투바에서 과거의 전통을 기억하는 것이 소련이 붕괴한 난 후 남겨진 공백을 메우는데 도움을 주고 있다.

① 그것은 산으로 둘러싸여 있다.
② 그것은 한때 중국과 몽고에 의해 지배를 받았다.
③ 그것은 한때는 독립 국가였다.
④ 그것은 제2차 세계 대전 이후에 러시아의 침략을 받았다.

11 글의 내용과 일치하지 않는 것은?

Most students' visual problems are correctable by glasses or other types of corrective lenses. Vision loss is considered a disability only if it is not correctable. It is estimated that approximately 1 out of every 1,000 children has a visual disability. Individuals with such disabilities are usually referred to as blind or visually impaired. It is a misconception to assume that individuals who are legally blind have no sight. More than 80 percent of students who are legally blind can read large or regular-print books. This implies that many students with vision loss can be taught by means of a modification of usual teaching materials. Classroom teachers should be aware of the signs that indicate that a child is having a vision problem.

① A majority of legally blind students can participate in class with the help of corrective lenses.
② Educators should pay more attention to children with a vision problem in class.
③ Students with vision loss can be taught by modifying class materials.
④ Not every student with vision loss suffers a visual disability.

정답 ①

해설 밑에서 두 번째 문장에 나온 대로 법률적으로 시각 장애 학생들은 교정 렌즈가 아니라 교재의 수정을 통하여 수업을 들을 수 있지만 수정 렌즈를 통하여 교정되는 것은 아니다.

어휘 correctable 교정가능한, 수정할 수 있는　corrective 교정하는　approximately 대략, 약
disability 장애, 불구　refer to A as B A를 B로 지칭하다　impair 손상하다　misconception 오해, 착각
regular-print 보통 글씨 인쇄　modification 조정, 변경

해석 대부분의 학생들의 시력 문제는 안경이나 다른 종류의 수정 렌즈로 교정할 수 있다. 시력 손실은 시정 불가능한 경우에만 장애로 간주된다. 1,000명의 어린이 중 약 1명이 시각 장애가 있는 것으로 추산된다. 그러한 장애를 가진 사람들은 일반적으로 맹인 또는 시각 장애가 있는 것으로 지칭된다. 법적으로 맹인인 사람은 시력이 아예 없다고 가정하는 것은 오해이다. 법적으로 시각 장애가 있는 학생의 80% 이상이 큰 글씨 또는 보통 사이즈로 인쇄된 도서를 읽을 수 있다. 이는 시각 장애가 있는 많은 학생들을 일반적인 교재를 수정하여 가르칠 수 있음을 의미한다. 학급의 교사들은 아이가 시력 문제가 있음을 나타내는 신호를 인식하고 있어야 한다.
① 법률적으로 시각 장애 학생의 대부분은 교정 렌즈를 사용하여 수업에 참여할 수 있다.
② 교육자는 시력 문제가 있는 어린이들에게 더욱 주의를 기울여야 한다.
③ 시력을 잃은 학생들은 수업 자료를 수정하여 가르칠 수 있다.
④ 시력 손실을 가진 모든 학생이 시각 장애가 있는 것은 아니다.

12 다음 글의 내용과 일치하는 것을 고르시오.

Mr. Makari's highly engaging story begins with Rene Descartes. Ever since Greek philosophy had merged with Christianity, the soul had been regarded as the "unifying link between nature, man and God", Mr. Makari writes. By the 17th century, however, Christendom was in crisis, and many found it hard to reconcile the notion of an incorporeal soul with a mechanical world that was increasingly understood as made up of matter. Descartes tried to satisfy the demand of skeptical naturalists by narrowing the concept of the soul to a "thing that thinks", yet that was separate from the body. The French philosopher thus breathed new life into the Christian belief in an immortal soul. At the other end of the gamut stood Thomas Hobbes, who thought there was no such thing as "immaterial substance". In his view the soul, rather than being rational and Godlike, was "material, prone to illness and errors". The disparate views on the nature of the "thing that thinks" were to have monumental implications. And they were to demonstrate the importance of Mr. Makari's narrative as more than just an intellectual exercise. After Hobbes concluded that men were controlled by animal feelings that inevitably produced conflict, his proposed solution was to hand over power to an absolute monarch.

① European philosophy became increasingly religious in the seventeenth century.
② Mr. Makari charts the rise of modern secular philosophy.
③ Hobbes advocated modern forms of demagoguery based on humans' tendency to "illness and errors".
④ Descartes emphasized the insignificance of the mechanical world.

정답 ②

해설 데카르트와 홉스는 각각 관념론과 유물론을 대표하는 철학자로서 근대철학의 문을 열어젖힌 선구자들이다. 첫 문장에 언급된 대로 마카리는 바로 이들의 출현에 대해 차례로 언급하고 있는 것이다.

어휘 engaging 매력 있는 incorporeal 무형의; 영적인 naturalist 자연주의자; 박물학자 immortal 불멸의 substance 물질; 본질, 실체 disparate 다른, 이종의 implication 함축, 암시; 연루 extrapolate 외삽법에 의해 추정하다 immaculate 흠 없는 absolute monarch 절대군주 diaspora 집단 이주 bulwark 성채, 보루 gamut 전음계(全音階); 전 범위, 전반

해석 마카리의 호감을 불러일으키는 이야기는 르네 데카르트와 더불어 시작된다. 그리스 철학이 기독교와 하나로 뒤섞여 든 이래, 영혼은 "자연, 인간, 그리고 신을 통합시켜주는 연결고리라고 여겨져 왔다".라고 마카리는 쓰고 있다. 그러나 17세기에 기독교는 위기에 처해있었고, 많은 사람들은 형체가 없는 영혼이라는 개념을 물질로 이루어진 것으로 점점 더 이해되고 있던 기계적인 세계와의 화해가 어렵다는 사실을 발견했다. 데카르트는 영혼의 개념을 신체로부터 분리된 "사유하는 존재"라고 좁힘으로써 회의적인 자연철학자들(박물학자들)의 요구를 만족시키고자 했다. 이와 같이 프랑스의 철학자인 데카르트는 불멸의 영혼에 대한 기독교적인 믿음에 새로운 생명을 불어넣어 주었다. 당대 철학을 전체적인 관점에서 보았을 때, 데카르트와 대비되는 정반대쪽 극단에는 홉스가 서있었는데, 그는 비물질적인 존재 같은 것은 없다고 생각했다. 그의 견해에 따르면, 영혼

은, 이성적인 존재 그리고 신과 같은 존재라기보다는, 질병에도 걸리고 오류도 저지르는 경향을 가지고 있는 물질이었다. 사유하는 존재의 본성에 관한 이와 같은 상이한 견해들은 (철학사적으로) 기념비적인 의미를 가지고 있다. 그리고 이러한 상이한 견해들은 마카리가 제기한 담론이 단지 하나의 지적 운동 이상의 것으로서의 중요성을 가지고 있음을 증명해 보여주었다. 인간이 필연적으로 갈등을 만들어 내고야 마는 동물적 감정에 의해 지배받는 존재라고 결론을 내리고 난 후, 홉스가 제시한 결론은 권력을 절대군주에게 넘겨주는 것이었다.

① 유럽 철학은 17세기에 점점 종교적이 되었다.
② Makari씨는 현대 세속 철학의 출현을 차례대로 설명하고 있다.
③ 홉스는 인간의 "병에 걸리고 실수를 하는" 경향에 기초하여 선동의 현대적인 양식을 옹호했다.
④ 데카르트는 기계적인 세상의 무의미함을 강조했다.

13 다음 글의 내용과 일치하는 것은? 2017 국가직 9급

Taste buds got their name from the nineteenth-century German scientists Georg Meissner and Rudolf Wagner, who discovered mounds made up of taste cells that overlap like petals. Taste buds wear out every week to ten days, and we replace them, although not as frequently over the age of forty-five: our palates really do become jaded as we get older. It takes a more intense taste to produce the same level of sensation, and children have the keenest sense of taste. A baby's mouth has many more taste buds than an adult's, with some even dotting the cheeks. Children adore sweets partly because the tips of their tongues, more sensitive to sugar, haven't yet been blunted by trying to eat hot soup before it cools.

① Taste buds were invented in the nineteenth century.
② Replacement of taste buds does not slow down with age.
③ Children have more sensitive palates than adults.
④ The sense of taste declines by eating cold soup.

정답 ③

해설 중간 부분에 아이들은 어른들보다 더 많은 미뢰를 가지고 있다고 언급되어 있다.

어휘 **taste bud** 미뢰, 미각세포 **name** 명명하다 **mound** 더미, 무더기 **cell** 세포 **overlap** 겹쳐지다 **petal** 꽃잎 **wear out** 낡아지다 **replace** 대체하다 **frequently** 자주 **palate** 입천장 **jade** 닳게 하다, 지치게 하다 **intense** 강렬한 **sensation** 감각 **dot** 점을 찍다, 흩어져 있다 **adore** 좋아하다 **sensitive** 민감한 **blunt** 무딘, 둔한; 둔하게 하다

해석 미뢰(味雷)는 꽃잎처럼 겹쳐진 미각 세포들로 구성된 더미를 발견했던 19세기의 독일의 과학자인 게오르그 메스너와 루돌프 와그너에 의해 이름을 얻게 되었다. 미뢰는 일주일에서 10일마다 닳아버리며, 비록 45세가 넘어가면 그렇게 자주는 아니더라도 이들을 매번 다른 것으로 바꾸게 된다. 즉, 우리의 미각은 정말로 우리가 나이가 들어감에 따라 약해지는 것이다. 같은 수준의 감각을 만들기 위해서는 더욱 강렬한 맛이 필요해진다. 아이의 입은 어른의 미뢰보다 더 많은 미뢰를 가지고 있으며, 몇몇은 심지어 뺨에도 산재해 있다. 아이들은 단 것을 좋아하는데, 그 부분적인 이유는 설탕에 더 민감한 그들의 혀끝이 식기도 전에 뜨거운 스프를 먹으려는 시도에 의해 아직 감각이 둔해지지 않았기 때문이다.
① 미뢰는 19세기에 발명되었다. ② 미뢰의 대체물(재생산된 미뢰)은 나이와 함께 둔화되지 않는다.
③ 아이들은 어른들보다 더욱 민감한 미각을 가지고 있다. ④ 미각은 차가운 스프를 먹으면서 기능이 저하된다.

14 다음 글의 내용으로 미루어 일치하지 않는 것은?

In vitro fertilization does not contribute to developmental delays up to age 3, according to a new study. As many couples who use IVF to have children are older, for example, other factors can affect fetal development. The study showed that developmental delays were not more prevalent among children conceived through IVF. The new study also said children conceived through IVF were not at greater risk with full-blown developmental disabilities such as learning disabilities, speech or language disorders, or autism. The researchers found no significant difference between IVF and non-treatment groups of children with developmental delays — 13 percent of children conceived with IVF had a delay, while 18 percent of those not conceived with treatment had a delay.

① IVF is not one of the factors in neonatal developmental delays.
② The IVF industry has been disrupted by parental perturbations.
③ IVF is not more precarious than other factors for fetal development.
④ The age of parents can be germane to the health of their child.

정답 ②

해설 체외수정을 통해 태어난 아이들이 그렇지 않은 아이들과 별반 다르지 않다는 단서로부터 정답을 추론할 수 있다. 즉 체외수정을 시행하는 업체들이 부모들의 동요로 붕괴되었다는 언급은 없다.

어휘 **in vitro fertilization** 체외수정 **developmental delay** 발육지연 **autism** 자폐 **fetal** 태아의
prevalent 널리 행해지는, 유행하는 **conceive** 임신하다; 상상하다, 생각하다 **full-blown** 만개한, 활짝 핀
perturbation 마음의 동요, 불안의 원인 **precarious** 위험한; 불안정한
germane 밀접한 관계가 있는, 적절한

해석 새로운 연구에 따르면 체외수정은 3세까지의 발육지연의 원인이 아니다. 예를 들어, 체외수정을 통해 아이를 갖는 부부들은 나이가 많은 편이기 때문에, 다른 요인들이 태아의 발육에 영향을 줄 수 있다. 연구는 발육지연이 인공수정을 통해 임신된 아이들 사이에서 더 널리 펴져 있지 않다는 것을 보여주었다. 새로운 연구 또한 체외수정을 통해 임신된 아이들이 학습장애, 언어장애, 그리고 자폐증 등과 같은 상당히 진행된 발달장애에 걸릴 위험이 더 크지 않다는 사실에 대해서 말했다. 연구자들은 발육지연에 관해서 체외수정을 통해 태어난 아이들과 그러한 시술을 받지 않고 태어난 아이들 사이에 별다른 차이가 없다는 것을 발견했다 — 체외수정을 통해 태어난 아이들의 13%가 발육지연 증세를 보인 반면, 체외수정 시술 없이 태어난 아이들 가운데는 18%가 발육지연증상을 보였다.
① 체외수정은 신생아의 발육지연의 요인 중의 하나가 아니다.
② 체외수정 산업은 부모들의 동요로 붕괴되었다.
③ 체외수정은 배아의 발달에 대한 다른 요인들보다 더 위험한 것은 아니다.
④ 부모들의 나이는 그들의 아이들의 건강과 관계가 있을 수 있다.

15 다음 글의 내용과 일치하지 않는 것을 고르시오. 2019 지방직 9급

In the nineteenth century, the most respected health and medical experts all insisted that diseases were caused by "miasma", a fancy term for bad air. Western society's system of health was based on this assumption: to prevent diseases, windows were kept open or closed, depending on whether there was more miasma inside or outside the room; it was believed that doctors could not pass along disease because gentlemen did not inhabit quarters with bad air. Then the idea of germs came along. One day, everyone believed that bad air makes you sick. Then, almost overnight, people started realizing there were invisible things called microbes and bacteria that were the real cause of diseases. This new view of disease brought sweeping changes to medicine, as surgeons adopted antiseptics and scientists invented vaccines and antibiotics. But, just as momentously, the idea of germs gave ordinary people the power to influence their own lives. Now, if you wanted to stay healthy, you could wash your hands, boil your water, cook your food thoroughly, and clean cuts and scrapes with iodine.

① In the nineteenth century, opening windows was irrelevant to the density of miasma.
② In the nineteenth century, it was believed that gentlemen did not live in places with bad air.
③ Vaccines were invented after people realized that microbes and bacteria were the real cause of diseases.
④ Cleaning cuts and scrapes could help people to stay healthy.

정답 ①

해설 두 번째 문장에서 miasma가 방의 안과 바깥 중 어디에 더 많은지에 따라 문을 열거나 닫는다는 언급을 보아 miasma밀도와 무관하다는 말은 위 글의 내용과 일치하지 않는다.

어휘 **pass along** 전달하다 **antiseptic** 소독약, 방부제 **based on** ~에 기반한, ~에 기초한
prevent 예방하다 **depending on** ~에 따라 **inhabit** 살다 **germ** 세균, 병균, 병원균, 미생물
invisible 눈에 보이지 않는 **microbe** 세균, 미생물 **vaccine** 백신 **antibiotic** 항생제
momentously 중대하게 **irrelevant** 관련 없는 **cuts** 베인 상처 **scrapes** 긁힌 상처 **iodine** 요오드

해석 19세기에 가장 존경받는 건강과 의학 전문가들 모두 질병은 나쁜 공기에 대한 공상적인 용어인 "miasma"에 의해 유발된다고 주장했다. 서구 사회의 건강에 대한 체계는 이 가정에 기초했다. 병을 막기 위해서 방 안이나 바깥 중 어디에 더 많은 miasma가 있느냐에 따라서 창문은 열리거나 닫혔다. 신사들은 나쁜 공기가 있는 방에 거주하지 않기 때문에 의사들은 병을 전하지 않는다고 믿었다. 그 다음에는 세균이라는 생각이 따라왔다. 한때는, 모든 사람들은 나쁜 공기가 당신을 아프게 한다고 믿었다. 그러다 거의 하룻밤 사이에 사람들은 병의 진정한 원인인 세균과 박테리아라고 불리는 보이지 않는 것들이 있다는 것을 깨닫기 시작했다. 이 새로운 병에 대한 견해는 의사들이 소독약을 채택하고 과학자들이 백신과 항생제를 발명하면서 약에 대한 전면적 변화를 가져왔다. 그러나 그만큼 중요하게 병원균이라는 개념은 일반 사람들에게도 자신들의 삶에 영향을 미치는 능력을 주었다. 이제 건강을 유지하기를 원한다면, 손을 씻거나, 물을 끓이거나, 음식을 철저하게 조리하거나 베인 상처와 긁힌 상처를 요오드 용액으로 소독할 수 있었던 것이다.

① 19세기에, 창문은 여는 것은 miasma의 밀도와는 무관했었다.
② 19세기에, 귀족은 나쁜 공기가 있는 장소에서는 살지 않는다고 믿었다.
③ 백신은 사람들이 병원균과 박테리아가 병의 진정한 원인이라는 것을 깨달은 후에 발명되었다.
④ 베인 상처와 긁힌 상처를 소독하는 것은 사람들이 건강을 유지하는 데 도움을 줄 수 있을 것이다.

16 다음 내용과 일치하지 않는 것은?

After a 13 year tedious tug-of-war, the bill on the U.S. style law school system has finally passed. But the public dispute has not ended yet, with many people raising issues over the law school enrollment quota. The writer argues that as long as the government limits the number of first-year law school students, the reform is not much different from the traditional bar exam because it leads only to serve the interest of practicing lawyers and grant privilege of selective universities. In order to expand the legal service to people in every corner of the country, the government should not impose a quota on law school entrants. At the same time, to realize the spirit of the reform, the government should push for the development of an exclusive curriculum so that law schools can differentiate themselves from the existing undergraduate program. This debate that started 13 years ago with a goal "to improve the legal service for the entire population" has finally borne fruit. The lengthy delay was largely due to the entanglement of interests put forth by lawyers and scholars. After more than a decade of remaining on the agenda, the new system is at last endorsed, which is worthy of a hearty welcome.

① The dispute concerning law school is still going on.
② The present bill on law school is restricting the number of enrollments.
③ Law school is expected to remedy the evils of the traditional bar exam.
④ Law school finally began recruiting students after 13-year-long controversy.

정답 ③

해설 필자는 세 번째 문장을 통해서 정부가 law school의 입학 정원을 제안하는 한 기존 사법 시험과 크게 다를 것이 없을 거라고 했으므로, ③ 'law school 제도가 현 사법 시험의 폐단을 해소할 것이라고 기대된다.'는 본문의 내용과 일치하지 않는다.

어휘 **tedious** 지루한 **tug of war** 줄다리기 **bill** 법안 **dispute** 논쟁 **enrollment** 등록; 징집 **quota** 입학 정원 **reform** 개혁 **grant** 주다 **privilege** 특권 **selective** 선택적인 **impose** 부과하다 **exclusive** 독점적인 **differentiate** 차별화하다, 구별하다 **undergraduate** 학부생 **lengthy** 너무 긴, 장황한 **entanglement** 얽힘 **agenda** 일정, 의제 **endorse** 승인하다, 지지하다

해석 13년간의 지루한 줄다리기 끝에, 미국 스타일의 로스쿨 체제에 대한 법안이 마침내 통과되었다. 그러나 많은 사람들이 입학 정원 제한에 대해 문제를 제기하고 있는 상황 속에서 대중적인 논쟁은 아직 끝나지 않았다. 필자는 정부가 로스쿨의 신입생 입학 정원을 제한하는 한 로스쿨 제도는 오로지 개업 변호사의 이익에 복무

하고 선별적인 대학에 특권을 부여하는 것이기 때문에 이 개혁은 전통적인 사법 시험과 그다지 다를 것이 없을 것이라고 생각한다. 모든 계층의 국민들에게 법률 서비스를 확대하기 위해서 정부를 로스쿨 신입생에 대한 정원을 제한해서는 안된다. 동시에, 이 개혁의 정신을 실현하기 위해서 정부는 로스쿨이 기존의 학부 과정의 프로그램과는 차별화될 수 있도록 특화된 교육 과정 계발을 독려해야 한다. 13년 전에 "모든 국민을 위한 법률 서비스 개선을 위하여"라는 목적을 가지고 시작된 이 논쟁은 마침내 결실을 맺게 되었다. 이 긴 지연은 변호사와 학자들에 의해서 제기된 이해의 상충에서 비롯되었다. 의제로서 10년 이상을 머물러 있은 후에 이 새로운 체제는 승인을 받았고, 그것은 열렬한 환영을 받을 만한 가치가 있다.
① 로스쿨에 관한 논쟁은 아직도 진행 중이다.
② 로스쿨에 대한 현재의 법안은 등록 인원을 제한하고 있다.
③ 로스쿨은 전통적인 변호사 시험의 폐단을 시정할 것으로 예상된다.
④ 로스쿨은 13년간의 논쟁 후에 드디어 신입생을 모집하기 시작했다.

03 빈칸 완성

01 빈 칸에 들어갈 가장 알맞은 것을 고르시오.

Perhaps the language is a reason why: you cannot learn Chinese unless you spend years memorizing thousands of characters needed to achieve literacy, unless you copy, single-mindedly, unquestioningly. Some linguists and cultural historians believe so much mental energy and brain space is taken up by __________ learning of the language, that little is left over for innovative thinking.

① gramma ② culture
③ rote ④ history

정답 ③

해설 빈칸은 so ~ that 구문이 쓰인 문장으로 순접의 구조이다. 뒤에 혁신적인 사고를 위한 공간이 남아있지 않다는 언급이 나오므로 앞에는 혁신과는 반대되는 내용을 찾으면 된다.

어휘 **single-minded** 한결같은; 외고집의 **rote learning** 암기 위주 학습 **innovative** 혁신적인

해석 아마도 언어가 이유일 것이다. 그것은 만약 당신이 읽고 쓸 수 있는 능력을 성취하는 데 필요한 수천 개의 문자를 기억하는 데 여러 해를 보내지 않거나, 성실하고 무조건적으로 옮겨 적지 않는다면 당신은 중국어를 배울 수 없다. 몇몇 언어학자들과 문화 사학자들은 언어를 암기 위주의 학습을 하는 데 너무 많은 정신력과 뇌용량이 차지하기 때문에 혁신적인 사고를 위한 공간이 거의 남아있지 않다고 믿고 있다.
① 문법
② 문화
③ 암기
④ 역사

02 밑줄 친 부분에 들어갈 말로 가장 적절한 것은? 2020 지방직 9급

All of us inherit something: in some cases, it may be money, property or some object — a family heirloom such as a grandmother's wedding dress or a father's set of tools. But beyond that, all of us inherit something else, something ______________________, something we may not even be fully aware of. It may be a way of doing a daily task, or the way we solve a particular problem or decide a moral issue for ourselves. It may be a special way of keeping a holiday or a tradition to have a picnic on a certain date. It may be something important or central to our thinking, or something minor that we have long accepted quite casually.

① quite unrelated to our everyday life ② against our moral standards
③ much less concrete and tangible ④ of great monetary value

정답 ③

해설 빈칸이 포함된 문장의 맨 앞의 but은 역접의 signal이다. 그러므로 단서는 앞 문장에 있다. 앞 문장의 내용은 우리가 유형적인 것을 상속한다는 내용이므로 빈칸이 포함된 문장은 무형적인 것을 물려받기도 한다는 내용이 요구된다. 그러므로 정답은 ③이다.

어휘 **inherit** 물려받다, 상속하다 **property** 재산; 성질, 속성 **heirloom** 가보 **beyond that** 그 이외에도
be aware of ~을 깨닫다, ~을 알다 **daily** 일상의, 매일의 **moral** 도덕적인
certain 특정한, 어떤; 확신하는 **minor** 사소한 **casually** 무심코, 우연히 **concrete** 구체적인
tangible 만져서 알 수 있는, 실재하는 **monetary** 금전적인

해석 우리 모두는 어떤 것을 물려받는다. 어떤 경우에는, 돈이나 재산 또는 어떤 물건, 예를 들어 할머니의 웨딩드레스나 아버지의 공구 세트와 같은 가보가 될 수도 있다. 하지만, 그것 이외에 우리 모두는 다른 것, 훨씬 덜 구체적이고 유형적인 것, 심지어 완전히 인식할 수도 없는 것을 물려받는다. 그것은 일상적인 일을 하는 방식일 수도 있고, 우리가 특정 문제들을 해결하거나 스스로 도덕적인 문제를 결정하는 방식일 수도 있다. 그것은 휴일이나 특정한 날짜에 소풍을 가는 전통을 지키는 특별한 방식일 수도 있다. 그것은 우리 사고에 중요하거나 중심이 되는 어떤 것이거나, 우리가 오랫동안 아주 무심코 받아들인 사소한 것일 수도 있다.
① 일상생활과는 전혀 무관한
② 우리의 도덕적 기준에 반하여
③ 덜 구체적이고 유형적인
④ 커다란 금전적 가치가 있는

03 다음 글의 빈칸에 들어갈 말로 가장 적절한 것은?

Some elementary school teachers in the U.S. might be thinking "Recess is free time for the students" or "Why should I care about recess?" In reality, recess has become more important than ever. Since physical education at the elementary level has seen a decline in recent years, recess has in fact become __________ for children to participate in physical activity in school. With this in mind, what should happen during recess is that students have a chance to participate in physical activity in a setting that is helpful for learning. What actually occurs is that students are left to engage in unorganized activities during this 'free time'. As a matter of fact, recess is much more than free time. Recess should be viewed as an opportunity for students not only to engage in physical activity, but also to build their character and develop social interaction skills. Therefore, the classroom teachers must realize that recess is an important part of the school day.

① the class sign
② mind control
③ the main outlet
④ a health problem

정답 ③

해설 쉬는 시간이 체육 시간을 대신할 수 있는 부분이라고 말하고 있다. 다른 보기들은 문맥상 거리가 멀다.

어휘 a class sign 수업 관련 표지/게시 mind control 지성 통제(cf mental concentration 정신집중)

해석 미국의 일부 초등학교 선생님들은 "쉬는 시간은 학생들을 위한 자유 시간이다" 또는 "왜 내가 쉬는 시간까지 신경 써야 돼?"라고 생각할지도 모른다. 현실적으로 쉬는 시간은 이전보다 더 중요해졌다. 최근 초등학교에서 체육 시간이 감소하고 있기 때문에 쉬는 시간은 사실 아이들이 학교에서 신체적인 활동을 할 수 있는 중요한 돌파구가 되었다. 이런 상황을 염두에 둔다면, 학생들은 쉬는 시간에 학습에 도움이 되는 환경 속에서 신체 활동을 하는 기회를 가져야 할 것이다. 실제로 일어나고 있는 것은 학생들이 이 '자유 시간'에 계획성 없는 활동을 하게 되는 것이다.
사실 쉬는 시간은 자유 시간 그 이상이다. 쉬는 시간은 학생들이 신체 활동에 참여할 뿐 아니라 그들의 인성을 쌓고 사회적인 상호작용 기술을 개발할 수 있는 기회로 여겨져야 한다. 그러므로 학교 선생님들은 쉬는 시간이 학교 일과의 중요한 부분이라는 것을 깨달아야한다.
① 수업 신호
② 마인드 컨트롤
③ 돌파구
④ 건강 문제

04 글의 흐름상 빈칸에 들어갈 단어로 가장 옳지 않은 것은? 2018 서울시 9급

Following his father's imprisonment, Charles Dickens was forced to leave school to work at a boot-blacking factory alongside the River Thames. At the run-down, rodent-ridden factory, Dickens earned six shillings a week labeling pots of "blacking", a substance used to clean fireplaces. It was the best he could do to help support his family. Looking back on the experience, Dickens saw it as the moment he said goodbye to his youthful innocence, stating that he wondered "how he could be so easily cast away at such a young age". He felt ________by the adults who were supposed to take care of him.

① abandoned
② betrayed
③ buttressed
④ disregarded

정답 ③

해설 빈칸이 포함된 문장과 빈칸 앞 문장은 순접의 관계이다. 그러므로 앞 문장의 그렇게 어린 나이에 너무나 쉽게 버림을 받았다는 것에 놀랐다는 내용이 단서이다. 따라서 빈칸에는 어른들에 의해 버림받은 것과 부정적인 내용이 적절한데 buttress(지지하다)는 적절치 않다.

어휘 **imprisonment** 투옥, 감금, 구속 **boot-black** 구두닦이 **run-down** 황폐한; 쇠퇴한
rodent-ridden 쥐가 들끓는 **pot** 단지, 항아리, 솥 **substance** 물질, 실체; 본질, 핵심
fireplace 벽난로, 난로 **look back on** 되돌아보다 **innocence** 결백, 무죄; 천진 **cast away** 버리다
betray 배신하다; 누설하다 **buttress** 지지하다 **disregard** 무시하다, 묵살하다

해석 그의 아버지가 감옥에 간 후, 찰스디킨스는 템스강을 따라 위치한 구두 닦기 공장에서 일하기 위해 학교를 떠날 수밖에 없었다. 황폐하고 쥐가 들끓던 공장에서, 디킨스는 벽난로를 닦는 데 사용되는 물질인 구두약통에 라벨링을 하면서 일주일에 6실링을 벌었다. 그것이 그의 가족을 부양하기 위해 그가 할 수 있는 최선이었다. 그의 경험을 되돌아보면서, 디킨스는 그때를 그가 그의 젊은 날의 순수함에 작별인사를 보내던 순간으로 보았다. 또한 그가 말하길 "그렇게 어린 나이에 어떻게 그렇게 쉽게 버림을 받았을까"라며 의아해했었다고 한다. 그는 그를 돌보아야 하는 어른들로부터 버려진/배신받은/무시받는 느낌을 받았다.
① 버려진
② 배신받은
③ 지지를 받는
④ 무시받는

05 다음의 밑줄 친 곳에 알맞은 연결사는?

Psychologists tell us that to be happy we need a mixture of enjoyable leisure time and satisfying work. I doubt that my great-grandmother, who raised 14 children and took in laundry, had much of either. She did have a network of close friends and family, and maybe this is what fulfilled her. If she was happy with what she had, perhaps it was because she didn't expect life to be very different. We, __________, with so many choices and such pressure to succeed in every area, have turned happiness into one more thing we "must have". We're so self-conscious about our "right" to is that it's making us miserarble. So we chase it and equate it with wealth and success, without moticing that the people who have those things aren't necessarily happier.

① for example
② on the other hand
③ in addition
④ in short

정답 ②

해설 빈칸 앞에는 현실에 만족하는 그녀의 모습이 나오고 빈칸 뒤에는 미래의 성공에 행복을 느끼는 우리의 모습이 나오므로 상반관계이다.

어휘 laundry 세탁소　network 방송망　self-conscious 자의식이 강한, 수줍어하는
mixture 혼합, 혼합물, 감정의 교착　chase 뒤쫓다, ~을 추구하다, 찾아내다, (사냥감을) 사냥하다

해석 심리학자들은 우리가 행복하기 위해서는 즐길 수 있는 여가 시간과 만족하는 일의 혼합이 필요하다고 우리에게 이야기한다. 14명의 아이를 키우고 세탁소에서 일하셨던 나의 증조모는 두 가지 모두 많이 가지고 계셨는지 나는 궁금하다. 그녀는 가까운 친구와 가족들과의 연락망을 가지고 계셨으며, 아마도 이것이 그녀를 실현시킨 것일 것이다. 만약 그녀가 그녀의 재산으로 행복했다면, 그것은 아마도 그녀가 인생이 다양해지는 것을 기대하지 않았기 때문이었을 것이다. 반면에 매우 많은 선택과 모든 영역에서 성공에 대한 압력을 지닌 우리는 우리가 "지녀야 하는 것"의 더 많은 것들 안에 행복을 추가시켜왔다. 우리는 우리를 비참하게 만들 것에 대한 권리에 대해서 매우 이기적이다. 그래서 우리는 그것을 쫓아내고 그러한 것들이 반드시 더 행복한 것이 아니라는 사람들을 고려하지 않고 부와 성공과 그것을 동등하다고 생각한다.

① 예를 들어
② 반면에
③ 게다가
④ 요약하면

06 밑줄 친 (A), (B)에 들어갈 말로 가장 적절한 것은? 2020 국가직 9급

Advocates of homeschooling believe that children learn better when they are in a secure, loving environment. Many psychologists see the home as the most natural learning environment, and originally the home was the classroom, long before schools were established. Parents who homeschool argue that they can monitor their children's education and give them the attention that is lacking in a traditional school setting. Students can also pick and choose what to study and when to study, thus enabling them to learn at their own pace. ___(A)___, critics of homeschooling say that children who are not in the classroom miss out on learning important social skills because they have little interaction with their peers. Several studies, though, have shown that the home-educated children appear to do just as well in terms of social and emotional development as other students, having spent more time in the comfort and security of their home, with guidance from parents who care about their welfare. ___(B)___, many critics of homeschooling have raised concerns about the ability of parents to teach their kids effectively.

	(A)	(B)
①	Therefore	Nevertheless
②	In contrast	In spite of this
③	Therefore	Contrary to that
④	In contrast	Furthermore

정답 ②

해설 (A) 앞에서는 홈스쿨링을 지지하는 사람들의 입장이 설명되고 있고, 뒤에는 홈스쿨링을 비판하는 비평가들의 입장이 나오고 있으므로 빈칸 (A)에는 역접의 연결어인 In contrast가 가장 적절하다.
빈칸 (B)의 앞에는 홈스쿨링의 긍정적인 측면을 서술하고 다시 빈칸 (B) 뒤에서 홈스쿨링에 대한 우려가 나오고 있으므로 빈칸 (B)에는 역시 역접의 연결어인 In spite of this가 오는 것이 가장 적절하다. 그러므로 ②가 가장 적절하다.

어휘 **advocate** 옹호자, 지지자 **psychologist** 심리학자 **originally** 원래, 본래 **establish** 설립하다
homeschool 홈스쿨링하다 **monitor** 감시하다 **is lacking in** ~이 부족하다 **pace** 속도
miss out on ~을 놓치다 **interaction** 상호작용 **peer** 또래 **in terms of** ~의 측면에서
guidance 지도, 안내 **welfare** 행복, 안녕 **raise** 제기하다; 올리다; 모금하다; 기르다

해석 홈스쿨링을 지지하는 사람들은 아이들이 안전하고 자신들이 사랑하는 환경에 있을 때 더 잘 배운다고 믿는다. 많은 심리학자들은 집을 가장 자연적인 학습 환경으로 보고 있으며, 원래 집은 학교가 설립되기 훨씬 전부터 교실이었다. 홈스쿨링을 하는 학부모들은 자녀의 교육을 관찰할 수 있고 전통적인 학교 환경에서는 부족한 관심을 줄 수 있다고 주장한다. 학생들은 또한 무엇을 공부할지, 언제 공부할지를 고르고 선택할 수 있고 그리하여 그들 자신만의 속도로 학습할 수 있다. (A) 대조적으로 홈스쿨링에 대한 비평가들은 교실에

있지 않은 아이들은 또래와의 상호작용이 거의 없기 때문에 중요한 사회적 기술을 배우는 것을 놓친다고 말한다. 하지만, 몇몇 연구들은 가정에서 교육받은 아이들도 다른 학생들만큼 사회적이고 정서적인 발달에 있어서 잘하는 것 같이 보이고, 그들의 행복에 신경을 쓰는 부모들의 지도와 함께 그들은 가정의 편안함과 안전 속에서 더 많은 시간을 보낸다는 것을 보여주었다. (B) 이런 점에도 불구하고, 홈스쿨링에 대한 많은 비평가들이 자신의 아이들을 효과적으로 가르칠 수 있는 부모들의 능력에 대해 우려를 제기해왔다.

① (A) 그러므로 (B) 그럼에도 불구하고 ② (A) 대조적으로 (B) 이런 점에도 불구하고
③ (A) 그러므로 (B) 대조적으로 ④ (A) 대조적으로 (B) 게다가

07 다음 지문의 빈칸에 가장 적절한 보기를 고르시오.

We live in an age of opportunity: If you've got ambition, drive, and smarts, you can rise to the top of your chosen profession — regardless of where you started out. But with this opportunity comes responsibility. Companies today aren't managing their knowledge workers' careers. Rather, we must each be our own chief executive officer. Simply put, it's up to you to keep yourself engaged and productive during a work life. To do all of these things well, you'll need to ____________________. What are your most valuable strengths and most dangerous weakness? Equally important, how do you learn and work with others? What are your most deeply held values? The implication is clear: Only when you operate from a combination of your strengths and self-knowledge can you achieve true — and lasting — excellence.

① follow your company's philosophy
② make substantial profits for the company
③ cultivate a deep understanding of yourself
④ stay on good terms with your co-workers

정답 ③

해설 자신의 강점과 자신에 대한 이해를 조합하여 탁월함을 이룰 수 있다는 내용을 통해 자기 자신에 대한 깊은 이해를 기를 필요가 있다는 빈칸의 내용을 추론할 수 있다.

어휘 implication 함축, 암시, 시사 self-knowledge 자기이해

해석 우리는 기회의 시대에 살고 있다. 만일 당신이 야망, 추진력, 그리고 지성을 가지고 있다면 당신이 어디에서 시작을 했든지 상관없이 당신은 당신이 선택한 직업에서 최고까지 오를 수 있다. 하지만 이런 기회와 함께 책임이 따라온다. 요즘 회사들은 그들의 지식 노동자들의 경력을 관리하지 않는다. 오히려 우리는 각자가 우리 자신의 최고 경영자가 되어야 한다. 간단히 말하자면, 직장 생활을 하는 동안에 우리 자신을 계속적으로 몰두하고 생산적이게 하는 것은 당신에게 달려 있다. 이 모든 것들을 잘하기 위해서는 당신은 자기 자신에 대한 깊은 이해를 기를 필요가 있다. 당신의 가장 가치 있는 강점과 가장 위험한 약점은 무엇인가? 똑같이 중요하게, 당신은 어떻게 배우고 다른 사람들과 함께 일하는가? 당신이 가장 깊이 간직하는 가치는 무엇인가? 시사하는 바는 분명하다. 당신이 당신의 강점과 자기 이해의 조합으로부터 일을 할 때에만 당신은 진정한 그리고 지속되는 탁월함을 이루어낼 수 있다.

① 당신의 회사의 철학을 따르다 ② 회사에 실질적인 이윤을 만들어내다
③ 자기 자신에 대한 깊은 이해를 기르다. ④ 당신의 동료와 좋은 관계를 유지하다

08 밑줄 친 부분에 들어갈 말로 가장 적절한 것을 고르시오. 2021 국가직 9급

Excellence is the absolute prerequisite in fine dining because the prices charged are necessarily high. An operator may do everything possible to make the restaurant efficient, but the guests still expect careful, personal service: food prepared to order by highly skilled chefs and delivered by expert servers. Because this service is, quite literally, manual labor, only marginal improvements in productivity are possible. For example, a cook, server, or bartender can move only so much faster before she or he reaches the limits of human performance. Thus, only moderate savings are possible through improved efficiency, which makes an escalation of prices ______________. (It is an axiom of economics that as prices rise, consumers become more discriminating.) Thus, the clientele of the fine-dining restaurant expects, demands, and is willing to pay for excellence.

① ludicrous ② inevitable
③ preposterous ④ inconceivable

정답 ②

해설 빈칸이 포함된 문장과 이어지는 다음 문장은 순접의 관계이며 thus는 순접의 연결어이다. 그러므로 단서는 마지막 문장에 있는데, 그 내용은 고객들이 우수함에 대하여 기꺼이 돈을 지불하려 한다는 내용이다. 또한 빈칸이 포함된 문장 내에서도 작업의 능률 또한 절약은 조금밖에 안된다는 내용을 볼 때 빈칸에는 고급레스토랑들의 가격 상승은 불가피하는 내용이 적당하다.

어휘 prerequisite 전제 조건 fine dining 고급식당 charge 요금을 부과하다 operator 운영자
efficient 효율적인 lliterally 문자 그대로 lmanual labor 육제 노동 lmarginal 가장자리의; 미미한, 빈약한
lmoderate 적당한, 절제있는 lescalation 상승 laxiom 공리, 자명한 이치
ldiscriminating 안목 있는, 분별력이 있는 lclientele 고객들 ludicrous 우스꽝스러운, 어처구니없는
linevitable 불가피한 lpreposterous 터무니없는 linconceivable 상상할 수 없는

해석 탁월함은 고급 레스토랑의 절대적인 전제 조건인데, 왜냐하면 부가된 가격이 필연적으로 높기 때문이다. 운영자는 레스토랑을 효율적으로 만들기 위해서 할 수 있는 모든 것을 하겠지만, 손님들은 신중한 손님 접대를 여전히 기대한다: 음식은 대단히 숙련된 주방장에 의해 (손님들이) 주문하도록 준비되고 능숙한 서빙하는 사람에 의해 전달되기 때문이다. 그야말로, 이 서비스는 육체노동이기 때문에, 오직 적당량의 생산성 향상만이 가능하다. 예를 들어, 요리사, 서빙하는 사람, 또는 바텐더는 인간 수행력의 한계에 도달하기 전에 고작 조금밖에 더 빨리 움직이지 못한다. 따라서, 향상된 효율성을 통해서는 겨우 약간의 절약만이 가능한데, 이는 가격의 증가를 불가피하게 만든다. (가격이 오르면 소비자들의 안목이 더 좋아지는 것은 경제학의 핵심 원리이다.) 따라서, 고급 레스토랑의 고객은 탁월함을 기대하고 요구하며 그리고 기꺼이 값을 지불하려고 한다.
① 우스꽝스러운
② 불가피한
③ 터무니없는
④ 상상할 수 없는

09 글의 흐름으로 보아 빈칸에 알맞은 말을 고르시오.

Tom Willard was ambitious for his son. He had always thought of himself as a successful man, __________ nothing he had ever done had turned out successful. However, when he was out of sight of the New Willard House and had no fear of coming upon his wife, he swaggered and began to dramatize himself as one of the chief men of the town. He wanted his son to succeed.

① when ② for ③ because ④ although

정답 ④

해설 빈칸 앞은 성공적인 내용이 나오고 빈칸 뒤는 실패의 내용이 나오고 있으므로 역접의 연결어가 필요하다.

어휘 turn out 결국 ~임이 판정되다 out of sight 보이지 않는 (곳에), 멀리 떨어진
swagger 뽐내며 걷다, 활보하다 dramatize 극화(각색)하다, 과장하다

해석 탐 윌라드는 그의 아들에게 큰 희망을 품고 있었다. 비록 그가 행한 어떤 것도 성공해 본 적은 없었지만, 그는 늘 스스로를 성공한 사람이라고 생각해 왔다. 그러나 그는 집에서 멀리 떨어진 곳에 있어 그의 아내와 마주칠 두려움이 없을 때는 으스대며 걸었고, 자신을 읍내에서 중요한 사람중의 하나인 것처럼 과장하기 시작했다. 그는 그의 아들이 성공하길 원했다.

① 그때 ② 왜냐하면 ③ 왜냐하면 ④ 비록

10 밑줄 친 (A), (B)에 들어갈 말로 가장 적절한 것은? 2018 지방직 9급

Does terrorism ever work? 9/11 was an enormous tactical success for al Qaeda, partly because it involved attacks that took place in the media capital of the world and the actual capital of the United States, ___(A)___ ensuring the widest possible coverage of the event. If terrorism is a form of theater where you want a lot of people watching, no event in human history was likely ever seen by a larger global audience than the 9/11 attacks. At the time, there was much discussion about how 9/11 was like the attack on Pearl Harbor. They were indeed similar since they were both surprise attacks that drew America into significant wars. But they were also similar in another sense. Pearl Harbor was a great tactical success for Imperial Japan, but it led to a great strategic failure: Within four years of Pearl Harbor the Japanese empire lay in ruins, utterly defeated. ___(B)___, 9/11 was a great tactical success for al Qaeda, but it also turned out to be a great strategic failure for Osama bin Laden.

	(A)	(B)
①	thereby	Similarly
②	while	Therefore
③	while	Fortunately
④	thereby	On the contrary

정답 ①

해설 (A) 빈칸 앞의 내용은 9/11 테러가 미국의 실질적 수도이자 세계 미디어의 중심인 뉴욕에서 발생하였다는 내용이다. 빈칸 뒤의 내용은 9/11 테러의 폭넓은 보도를 보장하였다는 내용이므로 순접이면서 인과관계적인 내용을 연결하는 thereby가 적절하다.

(B) 빈칸 앞의 내용은 일본의 진주만 공습은 일본의 패망으로 결말지어졌다는 내용이다. 빈칸 뒤의 내용은 알카에다의 테러가 성공처럼 보였지만 결국 알카에다 빈 라덴에게는 실패로 판명이 났다는 내용이므로 순접이면서 다른 예를 제시하는 similarly가 적절하다.

어휘 **enormous** 막대한, 거대 **tactical** 작전의, 전술의 **partly** 부분적으로 **take place in** ~에서 열리다, 일어나다 **ensure** 보장하다, 확보하다 **coverage** 보도, 방송; 보상 **significant** 중요한, 의미 있는; 눈에 띄는 **strategic** 전략상 중요한, 전략적인 **thereby** 그렇게 함으로써, 그것 때문에

해석 테러리즘은 제대로 작동할까? 9/11 공격은 알카에다에게는 엄청난 전술적인 성공이었다. 부분적인 이유는 이것이 세계의 언론의 중심지이며 미국의 실질적인 수도에서 일어난 공격을 포함했고, (A) 그것으로 인해 이 사건의 가능한 한 가장 폭넓은 방송 보도를 확보했기 때문이다. 만약 테러리즘이 많은 사람들이 시청하기를 당신이 원하는 극장의 한 형태라면 인간 역사에서 9/11 공격보다 더 많은 전 세계 시청자들에 의해 시청된 사건은 없을 것이다. 그 당시 9/11 공격이 진주만 공격과 어떻게 같은 것인지에 대해 많은 토론이 있었다. 그것들은 모두 미국을 중요한 전쟁으로 끌어들인 기습공격이었기 때문에 그것들은 정말로 유사했다. 그러나 그것들은 또한 다른 의미에서 유사했다. 진주만 공격은 제국주의 일본의 전술적인 대성공이었다. 그러나 이 공격은 전략적인 실패로 이어졌다: 진주만 공격 이후 4년 만에 일본 제국은 완전히 패배한 채, 폐허상태가 되었다. (B) 마찬가지로 유사하게, 9/11 공격은 알카에다의 전술적인 대성공이었다. 그러나 이 또한 오사마 빈 라덴에게는 전략적인 커다란 실패로 판명 되었다.

① (A) 그것으로 인해 (B) 마찬가지로
② (A) 반면에 (B) 따라서
③ (A) 반면에 (B) 다행히도
④ (A) 그것으로 인해 (B) 반대로

11 빈칸에 들어갈 가장 알맞은 것은?

I would like to express my concern at the growing number of lottery games in this country. ______________________. First, the people who run the lotteries are taking substantial amounts of money away from people, many of whom are old and can least afford to lose it. The elderly couple down the street from me, for example, spent over $20 on lottery tickets last week, and they have only their meager social security checks to support them. Second, while I do not object to gambling in principle, I feel that this particular kind, where no skill is required on the part of the player, is especially offensive to the intellect. Finally, the places where lottery tickets are sold often attract undesirable people to otherwise quiet neighborhoods. In conclusion, I wish to express my opinion that lottery games of all types should be abolished.

① I am addicted to lottery games myself.
② I want to suggest some ways to win a bet.
③ There are many steps to play lottery games.
④ There are several reasons why I object to this kind of gambling.

정답 ④

해설 빈칸 뒤에는 필자가 복권추첨에 반대하는 이유가 뒤따르고 있다.

어휘 lottery 복권 substantial 상당한 can afford to do ~할 여유가 있다 meager 불충분한, 부족한 social security 사회 보장 in principle 원칙적으로 offensive 불쾌한 intellect 지성 win a bet 내기에서 이기다.

해석 우리나라에서 점점 복권이 늘어나는 것에 대해 우려를 표명하고 싶다. 왜 내가 이러한 종류의 도박에 반대하는지 몇몇 이유가 있다. 먼저, 복권 사업자들은 사람들로부터 상당한 양의 돈을 긁어가는데 그중 상당 부분은 늙어서 복권에 돈을 낭비할 여력이 없는 사람들이다. 예를 들어 아랫마을의 늙은 부부는 저번 주에 20달러가 넘는 돈을 복권을 사는 데 썼는데 그들은 정부 보조금에 의존하여 살고 있는 사람들이다. 둘째로, 내가 비록 도박 그 자체에는 반대하지 않기는 해도, 아무런 기술이 필요 없는 종류의 도박은 지성에는 불쾌감을 준다고 느낀다. 끝으로, 복권을 파는 곳은 이따금 거기 복권 가게가 없었더라면 복권을 사지 않았을 사람들을 유인하게 된다. 결론적으로 내 생각을 말하자면, 모든 종류의 복권은 금지되어야 한다.

① 내 자신이 복권 게임에 중독이 되어 있다.
② 나는 내기에 이기는 몇 가지 방법을 제안하고 싶다.
③ 복권 게임을 하기 위한 많은 단계가 있다.
④ 왜 내가 이러한 종류의 도박에 반대하는지 몇몇 이유가 있다.

12 빈 칸에 들어갈 가장 알맞은 것을 고르시오.

To become a kinder, more loving individual requires action. Yet, ironically, there is nothing specific you have to do, no prescription to follow. Rather, most genuine acts of kindness and generosity seem __________; they stem from a type of thinking in which service and giving have been integrated into the person's thought process.

① indecisive ② natural
③ coarse ④ sophisticated

정답 ②

해설 빈칸 뒤의 세미콜론은 순접의 연결사로서 뒤의 내용이 남에게 봉사하고 무엇인가 주는 행위가 생각 속에 통합된다는 언급으로 보아 친절과 관대함이 자연스럽다는 내용이 적절하다.

어휘 prescription 처방 genuine 진짜인 generosity 관대함 integrate 통합하다

해석 좀 더 친절하고 애정 어린 사람이 되는 것은 실천을 요구한다. 하지만, 아이러니하게도 당신이 해야 할 특별한 것이나 따라야 할 규범은 존재하지 않는다. 오히려, 가장 진심에서 우러난 친절과 관대함의 행위는 자연스러워 보이고, 그것은 봉사와 베풂이 개인이 생각하는 과정에 통합되어진 일종의 사고방식에서 우러나온다.

① 우유부단한 ② 자연스러운
③ 조잡한 ④ 세련된

13 다음 밑줄 친 곳에 가장 적절한 것을 고르시오.

It used to be fashionable for women to have very small waists. They often wore tight clothes around their middles to make them thinner. A woman with a very thin waist was said to be "wasp-waisted" because her body looked like the body of a wasp. The wasp is an insect with ____________________.

① a very thin middle ② a large body and small head
③ tight clothes around its middle ④ six thin and long legs.

정답 ①
해설 바로 앞 문장에 허리가 가는데 "말벌허리"로 불린다고 되어있다.
어휘 used to ~하곤 했다; 한 때 ~였다 wasp 말벌
해석 여성들에게 아주 가는 허리가 유행이었던 적이 있다. 그들은 허리를 더 가늘게 하기 위해서 허리 부분에 꽉 끼는 옷을 입기도 했다. 아주 가는 허리를 가진 여성을 몸이 마치 말벌의 몸처럼 보인다고 하여 "말벌허리"라고 부르기도 했다. 말벌은 가는 허리를 가진 곤충이다.
① 매우 가는 허리 ② 커다란 몸통과 작은 머리
③ 허리주변의 꽉 끼는 옷 ④ 여섯 개의 가늘고 긴 다리

14 다음 밑줄 친 곳에 가장 적절한 것을 고르시오.

The thermal pollution entering the water supply comes from electric power generation as well as other industrial processes. Heat changes water by reducing the oxygen content. This, of course, negatively affects marine life. Despite this, it may be that the advantages of thermal pollution outweigh the disadvantages. ________________, warm temperatures are helpful in the development of fish eggs.

① For instance ② In contrast ③ As a result ④ In the same way

정답 ①
해설 빈칸 앞에는 열 공해의 단점보다 장점이 많다는 일반적 언급이 나오고 뒤에 구체적인 물고기 알 발육에 대한 도움의 사례가 나오므로 예시의 연결어가 적당하다.
어휘 thermal pollution 열 공해, 열 오염 water supply 상수시설, 급수시설 marine life 해양 생태 outweigh (중요성이)~보다 뛰어나다 development 발달, 성장, 발육
해석 상수시설로 흘러드는 열 공해는 발전소뿐만 아니라 다른 산업과정으로부터도 나온다. 열은 산소함량을 줄임으로써 물을 변화시킨다. 이것은 수중 생태에 부정적인 영향을 미친다. 이러함에도 불구하고, 열 공해의 장점들이 단점들보다 더 클 수도 있다. 예를 들어, 따뜻한 온도가 물고기 알의 발육에 도움이 된다.
① 예를 들어 ② 대조적으로 ③ 결과적으로 ④ 같은 방법으로

15 다음 밑줄 친 곳에 가장 적절한 것을 고르시오.

Many people are superstitious about black cats, Friday the thirteenth, walking under ladders. But few people have ever heard about a strange superstition regarding eggs. It seems that many years ago, in the northern part of Germany, people believed that you could beautify your complexion by simply making the sign of a cross in front of your face with an egg. ________________________.
It had to be the first egg laid by a chicken that had been hatched during the spring and that had laid its first egg shortly before Christmas of the same year.

① But there were not much money enough to buy any egg
② But it couldn't be just any egg
③ And it might have been every egg around you
④ But eggs were very uncommon food in those days

정답 ②

해설 빈칸 바로 뒷 문장에 반드시 봄에 부화한 닭이 낳은 첫 번째 계란이어야 한다는 제약조건을 제시하고 있으므로 아무 계란이나 다 되는 것은 아니라는 내용이 적절하다.
a chicken 뒤의 that절과 and that절은 a chicken을 선행사로 하는 이중한정의 관계절이다.

어휘 **superstitious** 미신에 사로잡힌 **complexion** 안색, 용모, 얼굴의 윤기
make a sign of a cross 성호를 긋다

해석 많은 사람들은 검은 고양이에 대해서, 13일의 금요일에 대해서, 사다리 밑을 걷는 것에 대해서 미신을 갖고 있다. 그러나 계란에 관한 이상한 미신에 대해서 들어본 사람은 거의 없을 것이다. 그것은 오래 전에 독일의 북부지방에서 사람들이 계란 하나를 들고 얼굴 앞에서 단지 십자를 긋기만 해도 얼굴의 용모를 아름답게 할 수 있다고 믿었던 것 같다. 그러나 그것은 아무 계란이어서는 안 되었다. 그것은 봄에 부화한 닭이 그해 크리스마스 직전에 처음으로 낳은 바로 그 계란이어야만 했다.
① 그러나 계란을 살 충분히 많은 돈이 없었다.
② 그러나 그것은 아무 계란이어서는 안 되었다.
③ 그리고 그것은 당신 주변의 모든 계란이었을 지도 모른다.
④ 그러나 계란은 그 당시에는 흔치 않은 음식이어다.

16 글의 흐름상 빈칸에 들어갈 표현으로 가장 옳은 것은? 2018 서울시 7급

In the event of an emergency, local emergency officials may order you to evacuate your premises. In some cases, they may instruct you to shut off the water, gas, and electricity. If you have access to radio or television, listen to newscasts to keep informed and follow whatever the officials order. In other cases, a designated person within your business should be responsible for making the decision to ____________________. Protecting the health and safety of everyone in the facility should be the first priority.

① clear away the debris
② protect the facility and property
③ develop an emergency action plan
④ evacuate or shut down operations

정답 ④

해설 ④ 빈칸이 포함된 문장과 다음 문장은 순접의 관계이다. 그러므로 단서는 다음 문장이며 그 내용은 모든 이의 건강과 안전이 최우선이라는 내용이다. 이 내용과 가장 호응이 되는 것은 사람들을 대피시키거나 영업장의 가동을 폐쇄하는 내용이 될 것이다.

어휘 **evacuate** 대피시키다; 떠나다, 피난하다 **premises** 부지; 구내, 가택 **instruct** 지시하다, 가르치다 **shut off** 멈추다, 차단하다 **have access to** ~에게 접근할 수 있다 **designated** 지정된, 할당된 **facility** 시설, 기관; 재능, 솜씨 **priority** 우선 사항; 우선, 우선권 **clear away** ~을 치우다 **debris** 잔해, 파편 **property** 재산, 부동산; 속성, 특성

해석 긴급 사태가 발생하면 지역 응급 공무원이 귀하에게 사유지에서 대피하라는 명령을 내릴 수 있습니다. 어떤 경우에는 물, 가스 및 전기를 차단하도록 지시할 수 있습니다. 라디오나 텔레비전에 접속할 수 있는 경우에는 정보를 받도록 뉴스 보도를 듣고 공무원이 명령한 대로 따르십시오. 다른 경우에는 귀하의 사업장 내 지정된 사람이 대피를 하거나 작업을 중단하는 결정을 내릴 책임이 있습니다. 시설 내 모든 사람의 건강과 안전을 보호하는 것이 가장 중요한 임무가 되어야 합니다.
① 파편을 치우다
② 시설 및 재산을 보호하다
③ 비상 행동 계획 수립하다
④ 대피하거나 작업을 중단하다

17 다음 글의 결론으로 밑줄 친 곳에 가장 적절한 것을 고르시오.

I agree with the need for racial and ethnic groups to want to strengthen their communities through intraracial marriage, especially when the group finds itself in the minority in a society. However, I believe that love is love and it is a person's right to date and choose whomever he or she wants regardless of ethnicity. Interracial relationships ______________________.

① should be strictly banned in today's society
② should be encouraged just like intraracial relationships
③ are rarely found in advanced countries
④ are likely to hurt the independence of each race

정답 ②

해설 빈칸 앞의 문장에서 인종에 상관없이 사랑하고 결혼할 권리를 강조하고 있으므로 마지막 문장은 인종 간의 국제결혼에 대한 찬성적인 입장이 진술되어야 한다.

어휘 ethic 민족적인 strengthen 강화하다 interracial 민족 간의 minority 소수 regardless of ~에 상관없다

해석 인종집단들(racial and ethnic groups)은 특히 자신들이 사회 속의 소수집단일 때는 종족 내부 구성원 간의 혼인(intra-racial marriage)에 의하여 그들의 공동체를 공고히 할 필요성에 공감한다. 그러나 사랑은 사랑이다. 따라서 인종관계에 관계없이 자신이 데이트하고 사랑할 대상을 자유롭게 선택할 수 있는 것 또한 개인의 중요한 권리라고 믿어진다. 인종 상호 간의 관계(interracial relationship)도 종족 내부 간의 관계 못지않게 권장되어야 한다.
① 오늘날의 사회에서는 엄격히 금지되어야 한다.
② 종족 내부 간의 관계 못지않게 권장되어야 한다.
③ 선진국들에게는 좀처럼 발견되지 않는다.
④ 각 인종의 독립을 훼손할 것 같다.

18 빈칸에 들어갈 말은?

Lichen are one of the few kinds of life that can survive in the mountains of Antarctica. These tiny plants live in small holes in the rocks. Outside, the extreme cold and strong winds do not allow any life at all. Inside the holes, these lichen manage to find enough water and warmth to keep alive. However, much of the time they are frozen. This fact means that the lichen function very, very slowly, and live a very long time. Scientists believe that a lichen may remain alive for thousands of years. If this is true, the lichen may ______________________.

① die in cold and strong winds
② be among the oldest forms of life on earth
③ not survive in the mountains of Antarctica
④ be one of the newest form of life on earth

정답 ②

해설 빈칸 앞의 문장에 이끼가 수천 년동안 살아있다는 언급과 순접관계로 빈칸 문장을 완성하면 된다.

어휘 **lichen** 이끼 **survive** 살아남다, 잔존하다, 남아있다 **Antarctica** 남극 대륙(cf **the Arctic** 북극)
tiny 작은, 조그마한 **manage to find** 그럭저럭(가까스로) 찾아내다 **keep alive** 살아있는 상태로 유지하다
frozen 얼어붙은, 극한의, 냉랭한, 냉혹한 **freeze**의 과거분사형 **function** 기능을 하다, 작용하다
remain alive 살아있는 상태로 유지하다 **thousands of** 수천 년의(막연한 다수는 복수형으로 나타냄)
cf **two thousand** 이천(구체적인 수는 단수형으로 나타냄)

해석 이끼는 남극의 산지 속에서 살아남을 수 있는 몇 가지 종류의 생명체 가운데 하나이다. 이들 작은 식물들은 바위 속 작은 구멍 속에서 산다. 밖에는 극한의 추위와 강한 바람들이 어떤 생명체로 전혀 살아갈 수 있게 허용해 주질 않는다. 구멍의 안에서 이 이끼들은 생명을 유지하기에는 충분한 물과 따뜻함을 그럭저럭 찾아낸다. 그러나, 시간의 대부분 그들은 얼어 있는 상태이다. 이 사실은 이끼가 매우 매우 느리게 기능을 한다는 것이며, 그래서 매우 오랜 시간 동안을 살아간다는 것을 의미한다. 과학자들은 이끼는 수 천년의 기간을 살아남을 수 있다고 믿는다. 이것이 사실이라면, 이끼는 지구상 생물체 가운데 가장 오래된 형태에 속할 수 있을 것이다.
① 차갑고 강한 바람에는 죽는다
② 지구상 샘물체 가운데 가장 오래된 형태에 속한다
③ 남극대륙의 산에서는 생존할 수 없다
④ 지구상의 새로운 생명의 형태이다

19 빈칸에 들어갈 말은?

Today there are various kinds of motorcycles. Street-bikes are mostly for riding in cities. Touring bikes are fast motorcycles designed for long highway trips. Trail bikes are for riding through fields and climbing hills.
Thus each of these kinds has its own __________. Small cycles are more like bicycles. Mopeds resemble bikes with motors attached. Motor scooters are bicycles with small wheels and little power. The one thing that all these cycles have in common is that they are all self-propelled, two-wheeled vehicles.

① beauty
② purpose
③ settlement
④ elevation

정답 ②

해설 빈칸 문장 앞에 thus란 연결사는 앞 문장과의 순접관계를 드러내며 앞 문장에 bike의 종류와 서로 다른 용도를 언급하고 있으므로 bike들이 각각의 purpose가 다르다는 내용이 적당하다.

어휘 **street-bike** 거리용 오토바이 **mostly** 주로, 대부분 **touring-bike** 여행용 오토바이
highway-trips 고속도로용 오토바이 **trai-bike** 험로용 오토바이 **moped** 발동기가 달린 자전거
motor-scooter 모터 스쿠터 **self-propelled** 스스로의 힘으로 추진되어지는
two-wheeled 두개의 바퀴를 가진 **vehicle** 운송수단, 탈 것

해석 오늘날에는 다양한 motorcycle이 있다. street-bike(거리용 오토바이)는 주로 도시에서 타고 다니기 위한 것이며, touring-bike(여행용 오토바이)는 장기간의 고속도로 여행들을 위해 도안되어진 속도가 빠른 motor cycle이다. trail-bike(험로용 오토바이)는 들판을 뚫고 다니거나 언덕을 오르도록 도안되어진 것이다. 그러므로 이들 각 종류들은 나름대로의 목적을 가지고 있다. 작은 cycle은 오히려 bicycle처럼 생겼다. 발동기가 달린 자전거는 모터를 가진 오토바이와 닮았다. 모터 스쿠터는 작은 바퀴에 힘이 적은 bicycle이다. 이들 cycle들의 공통된 한 가지는 그들 모두 스스로의 추진력을 갖고 있는, 두 개의 바퀴를 가진 운송수단이라는 것이다.

① 미
② 목적
③ 해결책
④ 고양, 상승

20 밑줄 친 (A), (B)에 들어갈 말로 가장 적절한 것은? 2019 지방직 7급

When the white people first explored the American West, they found Native Americans living in every part of the region, many of them on the Great Plains. White people saw the Plains Indians as ____(A)____, but in fact each tribe had its own complex culture and social structure. They didn't believe that land should be owned by individuals or families, but should belong to all people. They believed that human beings were indivisible from all the other elements of the natural world: animals, birds, soil, air, mountains, water, and the sun. In the early days of migration, relations between the pioneers and Native Americans were generally ____(B)____. Trade was common, and sometimes fur traders married and integrated into Indian society. The travelers gave Native Americans blankets, beads, and mirrors in exchange for food. They also sold them guns and ammunition. In the 1840s, attacks on wagons were rare and the Plains Indians generally regarded these first white travelers with amusement.

	(A)	(B)
①	traitors	harmonious
②	savages	friendly
③	merchants	hostile
④	barbarians	indifferent

정답 ②

해설 (A) 빈칸 뒤의 but은 역접의 signal이다. 뒤에 이어지는 내용은 인디언 부족이 자신만의 복잡한 문화와 사회구조를 갖추고 있었다는 내용이므로 빈칸에는 이와 반대적인 '야만인'이 적절하다.
(B) 빈칸이 포함된 문장과 다음 문장은 순접의 관계이다. 다음 문장의 내용은 서로 교역이 이루어지고 심지어 결혼을 통해 인디언 사회로 통합되어 들어갔다는 내용이므로 빈칸에는 '우호적인'이 적절하다.

어휘 explore 탐험하다 region 지역 Great Plain 대평원 tribe 부족 complex 복잡한
belong to ~에 속하다 indivisible 불가분의, 분리시킬 수 없는 element 요소 migration 이주
pioneer 개척자, 선구자 fur 모피 integrate 통합시키다 blanket 담요 bead 구슬
ammunition 탄약 wagon 마차 rare 드문, 희귀한 traitor 반역자 savage 미개인, 야만인
merchant 상인 hostile 적대적인 barbarian 야만인 indifferent 무관심한

해석 백인들이 처음 미 서부를 탐험했을 때, 그들은 그 지역의 모든 부분에서 원주민들이 살고 있는 것을 발견했는데 그들 중 많은 사람들은 대 평원에서 살고 있었다. 백인들은 대평원 원주민들을 미개인들로 여겼지만, 사실, 각 부족은 자신만의 복잡한 문화와 사회구조를 가지고 있었다. 그들은 땅이 개인이나 가족에 의해 소유되어야 한다고 생각하지 않았고, 모든 사람들에게 속해야 한다고 믿었다. 그들은 인간들은 자연 세계의 다른 요소들인 동물, 새, 땅, 공기, 산, 물, 그리고 태양으로부터 불가분하다고 믿었다. 이주 초기에, 개척자들과 원주민들 간의 관계는 대체로 우호적이었다. 무역은 흔했고, 때때로 모피 무역인들은 결혼해서 원주민 사회

로 통합되었다. 여행자들은 원주민들에게 담요, 염주, 그리고 거울을 음식과 교환했다. 그들은 또한 그들에게 총과 탄약을 팔았다. 1840년대에는, 마차에 대한 공격은 드물었고 대평원 원주민들은 일반적으로 이 첫 백인 여행자들을 흥미롭게 여겼다.

① (A) 반역자 (B) 조화로운
② (A) 야만인 (B) 우호적인
③ (A) 상인 (B) 적대적인
④ (A) 야만인 (B) 무관심한

21 빈 칸에 들어갈 가장 알맞은 것을 고르시오.

I don't want to be anything but what I am, and that is a human being. I really like being human. And that means forgetting; it means bumping into walls; it means going into wrong rooms; it means getting out at the wrong stop from elevator. The door opens, and I walk out and discover I am on the sixth floor instead of the third, and I say, "Oh!" And then I think, "You sweet old thing, you did it again!" You meet a boy in your neighborhood and say, "Hi, Tom, long time no see. I haven't seen you for a year". Then he says, "A year? It's been three years!" You know what being human means. It means "______________________".

① making mistakes
② realizing who one is
③ fulfilling one's dream
④ meeting people often

정답 ①

해설 빈칸 앞에 서술된 내용은 소년을 3년 만에 만나고서 1년 만에 만났다고 인사를 건네는 모습이다. 따라서 인간은 망각과 실수를 되풀이한다는 내용이 적절하다.

어휘 bump into 부딪히다

해석 나는 지금의 나 이외의 것이고 싶지 않으며 그것이 인간이다. 나는 인간적인 것을 정말로 좋아한다. 그리고 그것은 망각을 의미하며 그것은 벽에 부딪히는 것을 의미한다. 그것은 잘못된 방들에 들어가는 것을 의미하고 그것은 엘리베이터에서 잘못된 층에 내리는 것을 의미한다. 문이 열리고 나는 걸어나온 후 내가 3층 대신에 6층에 있다는 것을 발견하고서 "오!"라고 말을 한다. 그리고 나는 "너 사랑스러운 오랜 것이여 그 일을 또 하였구나!"라고 말한다. 당신은 이웃의 한 소년을 만나고서는 "안녕 탐, 오랜만이야. 일 년 동안 못 보았구나".라고 말한다. 그러면 그는 "일년이요? 삼년이에요".라고 말한다. 인간적이라는 것이 무엇을 의미하는지 알지 않는가. 그것은 <u>실수를 하는</u> 것이다.

① 실수를 하는
② 자신이 누구인지를 깨닫는
③ 자신의 꿈을 성취하는
④ 사람들을 종종 만나는

22 빈 칸에 들어갈 가장 알맞은 것을 고르시오.

Although memory function is difficult to understand and analyze, memory loss is something that many people experience and worry about as they age. In the past, scientists believed that age-related memory loss was associated with the total number of brain cells. The theory was that the brain contained a finite number of neurons and no more brain cells were made. However, more recent research suggests that this may not be so and that ______________________________ may take place throughout a lifetime. Also, the research suggests that the power to retrieve information can be influenced by food and sleep. Vitamin E, for example, is able to break down some chemicals that are thought to damage brain cells.

① the memory loss of old people
② changing positions of the brain cells
③ chemical reactions in the brain cells
④ the manufacturing of new brain cells

정답 ④

해설 빈칸이 포함된 문장의 첫머리에 강한 역접의 연결사 however가 있으므로 앞문장의 내용과 역접으로 채우면 된다. 앞의 문장이 뇌세포의 개수가 미리 한정이 되어 있다는 주장이므로 뒤에는 뇌세포가 새로이 만들어질 수 있다는 내용이 나오면 된다.

어휘 **analyze** 분석하다 **associate** 연관시키다; 교류하다 **age** 노화되다 **finite** 유한한, 한정된 **neuron** 뉴런, 신경단위 **take place** 발생하다 **retrieve** 되찾다; 보상하다 **break down** 파괴하다

해석 비록 기억의 기능이 이해하고 분석하기 어렵기는 하지만 기억의 상실은 사람들이 나이가 들어가면서 경험하고 걱정하는 것이다. 과거에는 과학자들은 나이와 연관된 기억력의 상실은 뇌세포의 총 개수와 관계가 있다고 믿었다. 그 이론은 뇌는 한정된 수의 뉴런을 포함하고 있으면 더 이상의 뇌세포는 만들어지지 않는다는 것이었다. 그러나 좀더 최근의 연구는 이것은 그렇지 않으며 새로운 뇌세포의 제조는 평생동안 발생할 수 있다고 시사한다. 또한 그 연구는 정보를 다시 찾아내는 힘은 음식과 잠에 의해 영향을 받는다는 것을 시사한다. 예를 들어 비타민 E는 뇌세포에 해를 줄 수 있는 어떤 화학물질들을 파괴할 수 있다.

① 나이든 사람들의 기억력 상실
② 뇌 세포들의 바뀌는 위치
③ 뇌세포 내에서의 화학 반응
④ 새로운 뇌세포의 제조

23 빈 칸에 들어갈 가장 알맞은 것을 고르시오.

Legend has it that the ancient Greek artist Zeuxis painted in such a realistic style that birds would flock to his canvas, thinking that the grapes pictured on it were real. Not all of the artists in Athens admired Zeuxis's talent, though. One day, a young painter challenged Zeuxis to paint something else realistic. Zeuxis took the challenge, and chose a boy as his subject. This time Zeuxis had the boy pose holding a bunch of grapes, and began to paint. He triumphantly declared his success when the birds again rushed to his picture, but the young artist claimed that Zeuxis had failed. He pointed out that if the boy had been painted realistically enough, ______________________.

① the birds would have eaten the grapes
② Zeuxis would not have been challenged yet
③ the birds would have been afraid to approach
④ Zeuxis would have been awarded big presents

정답 ③

해설 빈칸 문장 앞에 Zeuxis가 실패했다는 주장이 나오므로 뭔가 실패하는 내용이 이어져야 한다. 새들이 포도에 몰려든 것은 사실이므로 Zeuxis의 그림 속 소년이 사실적이지 않다는 주장이 타당하다고 할 수 있다.

어휘 **realistic** 사실적인 **flock** 몰려들다 **canvas** 화포 **subject** 소재, 대상 **triumphant** 승리감에 휩싸여 **declare** 선언하다 **claim** 주장하다

해석 전설이 말하기를 고대의 그리스 화가인 Zeuxis는 너무나 사실적으로 그림을 그려서 새들이 그려진 포도가 진짜라고 생각하고는 화포로 날아들었다고 한다. 그렇지만 아테네의 모든 예술가들이 Zeuxis를 존경했던 것은 아니다. 어느 날, 어느 젊은 화가가 다른 사실적인 어떤 것을 그리는 것을 Zeuxis에게 도전을 했다. Zeuxis는 그 도전을 받아 들였고 대상으로 한 소년을 선택했다. 이번에는 Zeuxis는 그 소년이 포도 한송이를 잡고있도록 하고 나서 그림을 그리기 시작했다. 그는 새들이 다시 그의 그림에 몰려들었을 때 의기양양하게 그의 성공을 선언했지만 그 젊은 화가는 Zeuxis가 실패했다고 주장했다. 그는 그 소년이 충분히 사실적으로 그려졌더라면 새들이 접근하기를 두려워했을 것이라는 점을 지적했다.

① 새들이 포도를 먹었을 것이다
② Zeuxis는 아직 도전을 받지 않았을 것이다
③ 새들이 접근하기를 두려워했을 것이다
④ Zeuxis는 큰 선물을 받았을 것이다

24 밑줄 친 부분에 들어갈 말로 가장 적절한 것은? 2017 지방직 7급

The intrinsic value of the biosphere is not rejected but is integrated with a recognition that man makes up part of the universe and cannot exist without conservation of the biosphere and the ecosystems which comprise it. In this perspective all sectors of the environment have a value not only in their short-term utility to humans, as the earlier exclusively anthropocentric approach would have it, but also as indispensable elements of an interrelated system which must be protected to ensure human survival. While this ultimate aim of human survival remains anthropocentric, humans are not viewed as apart from or above the natural universe, but as an interlinked and interdependent part of it. It follows that because all parts of the natural web are linked, they ______________________.

① must each be protected and conserved
② cannot exist without human survival
③ support the exclusively anthropocentric view
④ may be devoid of the intrinsic value

정답 ①

해설 빈칸이 포함된 문장과 바로 앞 문장은 순접으로 연결되어 있다. 앞 문장의 내용은 인간의 생존이 인간중심적이라 할지라도 인간의 자연과 밀접히 연관되어 있으며 상호 의존하는 관계라고 되어 있다. 그러므로 자연의 모든 요소는 보호받고 보존되어야 한다는 결론이 빈칸에 나와야 한다.

어휘 intrinsic 본질적인, 고유한 biosphere 생물권 reject 거절하다 integrated 통합된 recognition 인식 make up 구성하다 conservation 보호, 보존 ecosystem 생태계 comprise 구성하다, 포함하다 perspective 전망, 견해; 원근법 sector 부문 utility 유용성 exclusively 독점적으로, 배타적으로 anthropocentric 인간 중심의 indispensable 필수불가결한 interlinked 서로 연결된 interdependent 상호 의존하는 It follows that ~라는 결론이 나온다 be devoid of ~가 없다

해석 생물권의 본질적인 가치는 거부될 수 없고, 인간이 세상의 한 부분을 구성하며 생물권과 생물권으로 구성된 생태계를 보호하지 않고서는 존재할 수 없다는 인식과 함께 연결되어 있다. 이런 관점에서 환경의 모든 부문들은, 예전의 독점적인 인간 중심적 접근법이 그러했던 것 같이, 인간에게 주는 그들의 단기적인 유용성에 있어서 가치가 있을 뿐만 아니라, 인간의 생존을 확보하기 위해 보호되어야 할 상호 관련된 필요불가결한 요소들로서도 가치가 있다. 인간의 생존이라는 이러한 궁극적 목적이 인간 중심적인 것으로 남기는 하지만, 인간은 자연적인 세상을 떠나서 또는 그 위에서 보아서는 안 되며, 세상과 상호 연결되고 상호 의존하는 부분으로 보아야 한다. 그러므로 다음과 같은 결론이 가능한데, 자연이라는 그물망의 모든 구성요소들은 연결되어 있기 때문에, 그 모든 부분들은 서로 보호되고 보존되어야 한다.

① 서로 보호되고 보존되어야 한다
② 인간의 생존 없이는 존재할 수 없다
③ 독점적으로 인간 중심적 견해를 지지해야 한다
④ 본질적인 가치가 없을지도 모른다

25 다음 글의 (A)와 (B)에 들어갈 말로 가장 적절한 것을 고르시오.

Orlando, which was a quiet farming town a little more than thirty years ago, has more people passing through it today than any other place in the state of Florida. The reason, of course, is Walt Disney World, Universal Studios, Sea World and a host of other theme attractions. These theme parks pull more than twenty-five million people a year to what was until fairly recently an empty area of land. Few of these people visit the actual city of Orlando. ___(A)___, they prefer to stay in one of the motels and hotels fifteen miles to the south along highway 19. Despite enormous expansion over the last decade, the city itself remains free of the commercialism. ___(B)___, the city itself has not been able to escape the traffic congestion and other problems associated with the visit of so many millions of tourists as well as the thousands of people who work in the tourist industry. Without a doubt, tourism has certainly changed life for the residents of Orlando and the surrounding area.

	(A)	(B)
①	Despite	Therefore
②	In other words	In addition
③	Instead	However
④	That is	In short

정답 ③

해설 첫 번째 빈칸의 앞은 사람들이 올랜도라는 실제 도시를 방문하지는 않는다는 내용이며 뒤의 내용은 주변의 모텔이나 호텔에 숙박한다는 내용이므로 Instead(대신에)가 적절하다. 두 번째 빈칸에서 앞은 상업주의에 찌들지 않은 도시의 내용이 나오고 뒤는 교통혼잡이 있는 도시의 내용이 나오므로 상반된 내용이므로 역접의 연결사가 필요하다.

어휘 theme attraction 테마 유원지 commercialism 상업주의 congestion 혼잡

해석 30년 전 조용한 농촌마을이었던 올랜도는 오늘날 플로리다주의 어떤 지역보다도 더 많은 사람들의 왕래가 있다. 물론 그 이유는 월트디즈니월드 유니버설 스튜디오, 씨월드 그리고 많은 다른 테마가 있는 볼거리들 때문이다. 아주 최근까지 만해도 아무것도 없었던 곳에 이러한 테마 공원이 지금은 1년에 2500만 명이상의 관광객들을 끌어들인다. 그러나 올랜도 시를 실제 방문하는 사람들은 19번 고속도로를 따라 남쪽으로 15마일 떨어진 모텔이나 호텔에 머무르는 것을 더 좋아한다. 지난 10년 넘게 엄청난 발전을 했음에도 불구하고 그 도시 자체는 상업주의가 없는 도시로 남아있다. 그렇지만 교통 혼잡, 관광산업에 종사하는 수 천 명의 사람들과 수백만 명의 관광객들의 방문으로 인한 문제를 피할 수는 없다. 확실히 관광산업은 올랜도와 그 주변지역 사람들의 삶을 바꿔 놓았다.

① (A) ~에도 불구하고 (B) 따라서　② (A) 다시 말해서 (B) 게다가
③ (A) 대신에 (B) 그러나　④ (A) 즉 (B) 요컨대

04 순서 배열

01 주어진 문장 다음에 이어질 글의 순서로 가장 적절한 것은? 2018 지방직 9급

Devices that monitor and track your health are becoming more popular among all age populations.

(A) For example, falls are a leading cause of death for adults 65 and older. Fall alerts are a popular gerotechnology that has been around for many years but have now improved.
(B) However, for seniors aging in place, especially those without a caretaker in the home, these technologies can be lifesaving.
(C) This simple technology can automatically alert 911 or a close family member the moment a senior has fallen.

※ gerotechnology 노인을 위한 양로 기술

① (B) − (C) − (A)
② (B) − (A) − (C)
③ (C) − (A) − (B)
④ (C) − (B) − (A)

정답 ②

해설 주어진 문장은 건강을 체크하는 의료기기들이 모든 연령대에 인기가 있다는 내용이다. (B)는 however라는 연결어를 통해서 특히 주위의 보살핌을 받을 수 없는 노인들의 경우에는 이러한 기술이 특별히 중요하고 생명을 구할 수 있다는 내용이므로 (B)가 바로 이어지는 것이 적절하다. (A)는 (B)의 일반적 진술에 대한 구체적인 예이므로 그 다음에 (A)가 이어지는 것이 적절하며 마지막으로 (C)의 this simple technology의 this를 볼 때 (A) 다음에 (C)가 좀더 구체적인 기능의 묘사로서 이어지는 것이 적절하다. 그러므로 정답은 ②이다.

어휘 monitor 감시하다, 조사하다, 관찰하다　track 추적하다　fall 낙상, 넘어짐, 떨어짐; 폭포
gerotechnology 노인 양로 기술　alert 경계 태세; 경계경보　caretaker 관리인; 다른 사람을 돌보는 사람
lifesaving 구명의, 구명용의

해석 당신의 건강을 모니터하고 추적하는 장치들은 점점 더 모든 연령대의 사람들에게 인기를 얻고 있다.
(B) 하지만 지역사회에서 계속 거주하는 노인들 중 특히 가정 내에 돌보는 사람들이 없는 경우 이러한 기술들은 생명을 구할 수도 있다.
(A) 예를 들어, 낙상은 65세 이상 성인들에게 있어 사망의 주된 원인이다. 낙상 경보는 수년 동안 있어 왔던 대중적인 노인 양로 기술이지만 지금은 개선되었다.
(C) 이 단순한 기술은 노인이 넘어지는 순간, 자동으로 911나 가까운 가족 구성원에게 경보를 울려준다.

02 글의 문맥에 가장 어울리는 순서대로 배열한 것은?

(A) So, climate is a long view of weather.
(B) On the other land, climate refers to the typical weather patterns of an area over many years.
(C) Weather refers to the temperature and amount of rain, wind, sun, and snow during a specific time.
(D) Although weather and climate are closely related, climate is different from weather.
(E) Most people probably spend more time thinking about weather than about climate.

① (D) − (E) − (B) − (C) − (A)
② (E) − (D) − (C) − (B) − (A)
③ (B) − (C) − (A) − (E) − (D)
④ (C) − (D) − (E) − (A) − (B)

정답 ②

해설 주어진 문장이 제시되지 않은 경우 도입문을 파악하는 것이 가장 중요한데 (E)의 'Most people~'에서 엿볼 수 있듯이 통속적이고 일반적 개념이 처음에 나올 가능성이 많다는 데 유의하자. 그러므로 (E)가 도입문일 가능성이 높은 것이다. (B)에서 '기후'를 장기간에 걸친 날씨의 패턴으로 묘사를 했고 (C)는 날씨를 '특정한' 시간대의 현상들로 설명을 하고 있으며 연결어 'on the other hand(반면에)'가 (C) 앞에 있는 것으로 보아 '(B) – (C)'는 '결정적인 순서(decisive order)'이다. 이렇게 '결정적인 순서'가 발견될 때는 그것과 무관한 문장들을 지워나가며 문제를 풀면 보다 효율적이고 빨리 문제를 풀수가 있다.

어휘 refer to ~를 가리키다; 참조하다 typical 전형적인 specific 특정한

해석 (E) 아마도 대부분의 사람들은 기후보다는 날씨에 대해 생각하면서 더 많은 시간을 보낸다.
(D) 비록 날씨와 기후가 밀접하게 관련되어 있지만, 기후는 날씨와 다르다.
(C) 날씨는 특정한 시간에 걸친 온도와 비의 양, 바람, 태양 그리고 눈을 말한다.
(B) 반면에, 기후란 한 지역의 수년에 걸친 기상의 전형적인 날씨의 유형들을 말한다.
(A) 그래서, 기후는 날씨를 장기적으로 관찰한 것이다.

03 글의 문맥에 가장 어울리는 순서대로 배열한 것은?

(A) Here is a good way.
(B) Your list might include being head of a fund-raising campaign or acting a juicy role in the senior play.
(C) Before you try to find a job opening, you have to answer the hardest question of your working life: "What do I want to do?"
(D) Sit down with a piece of paper and don't get up till you have listed all the things you are proud to have accomplished.

① (A) − (C) − (B) − (D)
② (A) − (D) − (B) − (C)
③ (C) − (D) − (B) − (A)
④ (C) − (A) − (D) − (B)

정답 ④

해설 이 글은 질문을 던지고 그 대답을 통해 글을 전개해 가는 방식을 취하고 있다. (A)는 (C)에 대한 대답으로서 (C) − (A)가 '결정적 순서'이며, (A)는 대단히 일반적인 진술로서 그 뒤에 예시가 따라 나오게 되므로 앞쪽에 위치해야 한다.

어휘 fund-raising 기금 모으기 juicy 즙이 많은, 재미있는 accomplish 성취하다

해석 (C) 네가 일자리를 찾으려 하기 전에, 너는 너의 직업 생활에 관한 가장 어려운 질문에 답해야 한다: "나는 무엇을 하기를 원하는가?"
(A) 여기 좋은 방법이 하나 있다.
(D) 종이 한 장을 가지고 앉아라. 그리고 네가 성취했었기에 자랑스러워하는 모든 것들의 목록을 작성할 때까지 일어나지 말라.
(B) 너의 목록은 기금 조성 운동의 지휘자이었던 것, 혹은 4학년 연극에서 맡았던 재미있는 역할을 했던 것을 포함할 수도 있다.

04 글의 문맥에 가장 어울리는 순서대로 배열한 것은? 2018 서울시 9급

(A) Today, however, trees are being cut down far more rapidly. Each year, about 2 million acres of forests are cut down. That is more than equal to the area of the whole of Great Britain.

(B) There is not enough wood in these countries to satisfy the demand. Wood companies, therefore, have begun taking wood from the forests of Asia, Africa, South America, and even Siberia.

(C) While there are important reasons for cutting down trees, there are also dangerous consequences for life on earth. A major cause of the present destruction is the worldwide demand for wood. In industrialized countries, people are using more and more wood for paper.

(D) There is nothing new about people cutting down trees. In ancient times, Greece, Italy, and Great Britain were covered with forests. Over the centuries those forests were gradually cut back. Until now almost nothing is left.

① (A) – (B) – (C) – (D)
② (D) – (A) – (B) – (C)
③ (B) – (A) – (C) – (D)
④ (D) – (A) – (C) – (B)

정답 ④

해설 주어진 문장이 없으므로 도입문의 결정이 필요한데, 벌목에 대한 '구정보'에 해당하는 (D)가 도입문으로서 매우 가능성이 높다. 이는 과거의 사례에서 현재로 서술해 가는 전형적인 패턴인 것이다. 또한 (A)의 연결어인 however를 볼 때 (A)가 맨 앞에 오는 ①은 잘못된 것이다. (B)의 these countries라는 언급을 통해 (C) – (B)가 '결정적 순서(decisive order)'임을 알 수가 있다. 따라서 (D)가 과거의 벌목에 관한 내용이므로 도입문이 되기에 가장 적절하다. ④의 (D) – (A) – (C) – (B)가 올바른 순서이다.

어휘 **acre** 에이커 **consequence** 결과; 중요성 **destruction** 파괴, 파멸; 말살 **industrialized** 산업화된

해석 (D) 벌목은 그다지 새로울 만한 일은 아니다. 고대에는 그리스, 이탈리아, 영국이 숲으로 덮여있었으나, 수세기에 걸쳐 그러한 숲들은 점차 벌목되었다. 지금에 이르러 어떤 숲도 거의 남아 있지 않다.

(A) 하지만 오늘날 나무들은 훨씬 더 빠르게 벌목되고 있다. 매년 약 2백만 에이커 가량의 숲이 벌목되며, 그 면적은 영국 전체의 영토 면적과 맞먹는 것 이상이다.

(C) 벌목을 하는 중요한 이유들이 있긴 하나, 이에 따라 지구 생명체들에게 가해지는 위험한 결과들 또한 존재한다. 현재 이러한 파괴의 주원인은 나무에 대한 전 세계적 수요이다. 산업화된 나라에서 사람들은 종이를 사용하기 위해 점점 더 많은 나무를 사용하고 있는 중이다.

(B) 이러한 나라들에는 그 수요를 충족시킬 만한 충분한 목재가 존재하지 않는다. 그러므로 목재 회사들은 아시아, 아프리카, 남아메리카, 심지어 시베리아의 숲에서까지 목재들을 가져오기 시작했다.

05 다음 문장들을 논리적인 글이 되도록 배열하시오.

(A) In march 1979 Wertheimer and physicist Ed Leeper, Ph. D., published this ominous finding in the American Journal of Epidemiology, one of the foremost epidemiological journals in the world.
(B) In addition, appliances tend to be used sporadically and therefore do not constitute source of chronic or continues, magnetic field exposure.
(C) They pointed out, however, that unlike the magnetic fields given off by power lines, the fields from most household appliances fall off sharply with distance from the appliance.
(D) Their article noted that certain household appliances-hair dryers, toasters, and electric drills-can also produce strong magnetic fields.
(E) They wrote that power lines "are taken for granted and generally assumed to be harmless", but that assumption had "never been adequately tested".

① (A) − (E) − (C) − (D) − (B)
② (E) − (D) − (C) − (B) − (A)
③ (C) − (A) − (D) − (B) − (E)
④ (B) − (C) − (A) − (E) − (D)

정답 ①

해설 (A)가 도입문인 것을 찾아내는 것이 가장 중요하다. 그리고 (B) 안의 in addition를 보아, (D)는 (B)보다는 앞에 있어야 한다.

어휘 sporadically 산발적으로　ominous 불길한　epidemiology 유행병학

해석 (A) 1979년 3월 Wertheimer와 물리학자인 Ed Leeper 박사는 세계에서 가장 뛰어난 유행병학 잡지 중의 하나인 American Journal of epidemiology에 다음과 같은 불길한 내용을 실었다.
(E) 그들은 전선은 당연히 무해한 것으로 추정되지만 그러한 추정은 적절하게 점검된 적이 없다고 썼다.
(C) 그러나 그들은 전선에서 발산되는 자기장과는 달리 가전제품의 자기장은 가전제품과의 거리가 떨어질수록 급격히 감소한다는 것을 지적했다.
(D) 그들의 기고문은 헤어드라이어, 토스트, 전기드릴 등의 어떤 가전제품도 강력한 자기장을 발산할 수 있다고 언급했다.
(B) 게다가 가전제품들은 산발적으로 사용되는 경향이 있고 그래서 만성적이고 계속적인 자기장 노출의 원인이 되는 것은 아니다.

06 다음 글의 순서로 가장 적절한 것은?

(A) Such chains tend to intertwine in a disorderly fashion when part of a solid.

(B) Polymers are long, chainlike molecules; each link in the chain is either an identical chemical unit (as in the case of polyethylene) or one of a small set of such units (as in the case of nylon, which has two sorts of link).

(C) Strength, however, requires order.

(D) To make a strong material the individual molecules should, as far as possible, be stretched out in parallel with one another, thus forming an elongated crystal, and the crystals should then be similarly aligned in a fiber as that fiber is being drawn.

① (D) − (A) − (C) − (B)
② (D) − (C) − (A) − (B)
③ (B) − (C) − (D) − (A)
④ (B) − (A) − (C) − (D)

정답 ④

해설 이 글의 소재는 polymer(중합체)이기 때문에, 중합체에 대한 정의로서의 일반적인 설명이 도입문으로 제시되어야 한다. (A)의 'such chains'의 such는 '지시사'적인 기능도 하고 있으므로 순서 배열의 3대 sign(A)l인 '연관지'의 '지'에 해당한다. 그러므로 (B) – (A)가 '결정적인 순서'이다. 또한 (C)가 (D)에 대한 '일반적인 설명'이며 (D)가 '구체적인 설명'이라는 점에서 (C) – (D)도 역시 '결정적인 순서'이다. 이렇게 모든 항목의 순서를 완벽하게 잡으려하기 보다는 어떤 두 가지의 '결정적인 순서'를 발견하려는 노력이 대단히 중요함을 알 수 있다.

어휘 **polymer** 중합체(**重合體**), 중합물, 이량체(**異量體**) **intertwine** 서로 얽히게 하다, 한데 얽히다, 한데 꼬이다
in a disorderly fashion 무질서한 방식으로 **elongate** 길게 하다
align 일직선으로 배열하다; 곧바르게 하다

해석 (B) 중합체는 길고 체인같이 생긴 분자다; 체인 속에 있는 각각의 링크는 (폴리에틸렌의 경우처럼) 동일한 화학적 단위이거나 (두 종류의 링크를 가지고 있는 나일론의 경우처럼) 그와 같은 단위들의 작은 하나의 세트다.
(A) 고체의 일부로 존재할 경우, 이러한 체인들은 무질서한 방식으로 뒤섞이는 경향이 있다.
(C) 그러나 힘은 질서를 요구한다.
(D) 강한 물질을 만들기 위해서 개별적인 분자는 가능한 최대치로 서로가 서로에 대해 평행이 된 상태에서 팽팽하게 잡아 늘어져야 하고, 이를 통해 잡아 늘여진 결정을 형성해야 하는데, 섬유를 잡아 늘일 때 섬유 안에 있는 결정도 유사하게 정렬되어야만 한다.

07 다음 주어진 문장에 이어질 순서로 가장 적절한 것은?

In the early 1900s, a course of study at the London School of Hygiene and Tropical Medicine might have meant traveling to a hut in Italy for several months to study the causes of malaria.

(A) Today, medical academics say that in an interconnected world, the study of such illnesses has become more complex. Researchers have realized that factors outside biology contribute to patient's well-being. Addressing public health goes beyond microbes and pathogens, they say, to factors like socioeconomic status and politics.

(B) Or it might have included sailing to the West Indies to help a team of researchers investigate something called filariasis, a pathogen that seemed to be spread by mosquitoes. It could even have meant heading to Africa to help combat outbreaks of bubonic plague or dysentery.

(C) "The colonial legacy gave rise to schools of tropical medicine", explained Dr. Peter Piot, who has been the director of the school since 2010. "Belgium, Germany, France, Portugal — all colonial powers had them". Such schools' main purpose, according to Dr. Piot, was to study sicknesses endemic to overseas territories before the diseases reached the European countries' shores, usually carried by sailors returning home.

① (A) − (C) − (B) ② (B) − (A) − (C)
③ (B) − (C) − (A) ④ (C) − (A) − (B)

정답 ③

해설 주어진 단락은 위생 열대 의과대학의 교육과정이 만들어진 예를 들고 있다. 이 단락 다음에는 또 다른 예가 나오는 것이 자연스럽다. 그리고 '공공의 건강을 다룬다는 것은, 미생물과 병원균을 넘어서 사회경제적 지위와 정치와 같은 요인까지 포괄하고 있는 것이라고, 그들은 말한다.'라는 과거와 대비하여 현재에 관한 언급인 (A)가 결론 부분임을 추론할 수 있다.

어휘 **hygiene** 위생; 건강법, 위생법 **hut** 오두막 **filariasis** 필라리아 **pathogen** 병원균(病原菌), 병원체 **outbreak** 발발, 돌발; 격증, 급증; 폭동, 소요 **bubonic plague** 림프절 페스트, 흑사병 **dysentery** 이질; 설사 **colonial** 식민지의 **give rise to** 야기 시키다 **endemic** 원산지의, 지방의, 고유의 **address** 다루다, 처리하다 **territory** 영토; 지방, 구역

해석 1900년대 초, 런던 위생 열대 의과대학의 교육과정은 말라리아의 원인을 연구하기 위해 몇 개월 동안 이탈리아에 있는 한 임시막사로 여행 가는 것을 의미했을지도 모른다.

(B) 그게 아니라면, 그 교육과정은, 모기에 의해서 확산되는 것처럼 보이는 병원균 필라리아증이라고 불리는 어떤 것을 조사하는 연구팀을 돕기 위해서 배를 타고 서인도제도로 항해하는 것을 포함하고 있었을지도 모른다. 또 그것은 흑사병이나 이질의 발병과 맞서 싸우는 것을 돕기 위해 아프리카로 향하는 것을 의미할 수 있었다.

(C) "식민지의 유산은 열대 의과대학을 탄생시켰습니다. 벨기에, 독일, 프랑스, 포르투갈 같은 식민 열강들은 모두 열대 의과대학을 가지고 있습니다".라고 2010년부터 런던 위생 열대 의과대학장을 맡아온 피터 피오트(Peter Piot) 박사가 말했다. 피오트 박사에 따르면, 이와 같은 위생 열대 의과대학의 주된 목적은 해외영토의 풍토병들이 유럽국가에 유입되기 전에 그 풍토병을 연구하는 것인데, 이 풍토병들은 대개 귀국하는 선원들을 통해서 들어온다.

(A) 오늘날, 의대 교수들은 상호 연결된 세상에서 그러한 질병연구가 더 복잡해졌다고 말한다. 연구자들은 생물학 외부에 있는 요인들이 환자의 행복에 기여한다는 것을 깨닫고 있다. 공공의 건강을 다룬다는 것은, 미생물과 병원균을 넘어서 사회경제적 지위와 정치와 같은 요인까지 포괄하고 있는 것이라고, 그들은 말한다.

08 주어진 문장에 이어질 글의 순서로 가장 알맞은 것은?

The stage of prewriting includes any activity you do in order to start writing the composition. It may include freely discussing the topic in a group, making a list, or drawing a diagram or chart.

(A) The selections are intended both to model effective argument writing, as well as to cause the reader to agree or disagree.

(B) Your opinions, elicited by the selections, should form the basis for your own argument writing.

(C) It may also include reading about the topic. Each chapter in this book includes a selection from a major newspaper or magazine on a controversial topic.

① (A) – (B) – (C)　② (B) – (A) – (C)
③ (C) – (A) – (B)　④ (B) – (C) – (A)

정답 ③

해설 윗글은 (C) 글쓰기 전 단계 활동으로써의 인용문 발췌 – (A) 인용문의 목적 – (B) 인용문에 의한 글의 틀 형성의 논리적 구조를 갖추고 있다. (C)의 also를 볼 때 주어진 문장에 바로 이어질 필요가 있으며 (C)의 a selection이 (A), (B) 안의 the selections보다 앞서야 한다.

어휘 **in a group** 무리를 지어, 떼지어　**drawing a diagram or chart** 도식이나 도표를 그리다
selection 선발, 선택(= choice) 여기서는 발췌된 인용문을 의미한다　**be intended to** ~할 의도(목적)이다
elicit 이끌어 내다, 분명히 하다(= extract)　**controversial** 논쟁(상)의, 토론하는, 토론의 여지가 있는

해석 미리 글쓰기를 준비하는 단계에는 작문을 쓰기 시작하기 위해서 하는 모든 활동이 포함된다. 그것은 전체 주제에 관한 자유로운 의견개진, 항목작성, 도식이나 도표를 그리는 것도 포함될 수 있다.

(C) 그것은 또한 주제에 관한 독서도 포함할 수 있다. 이 책의 각 장은 토론의 주제에 관해 주요 신문이나 잡지에서 발췌된 인용문을 포함한다.

(A) 그 인용문들은 효율적으로 주장하고자 하는 글의 틀을 형성하기 위해서 뿐만 아니라 독자들로 하여금 (글에 대해) 찬성 혹은 반대의견을 갖도록 하는 것이다.

(B) 그 인용문들에 의해서 도출된 당신의 의견은 자신이 주장하고자 하는 글의 기초를 형성하게 된다.

09 다음 글의 흐름에 맞는 적절한 순서는?

How can a fake medicine help someone to get better? Sensory experience and thoughts can affect the brain, and the brain can affect other systems, including the hormonal and immune systems.

(A) Some experts believe that placebos, or fake medicines, simply cause a psychological response.
(B) Therefore, a person's optimism and hopefulness may be important to his physical recovery from an injury or sickness.
(C) However, H. K. Beecher found in a revolutionary 1955 study that 32% of patients responded medically to a placebo.
(D) In other words, taking them only enhances your sense of well-being.
(E) Subsequent studies support this finding with specific and measurable results.

① (A) − (B) − (C) − (D) − (E)　② (A) − (B) − (C) − (E) − (D)
③ (B) − (C) − (D) − (E) − (A)　④ (B) − (A) − (D) − (C) − (E)

정답 ④

해설 위 글이 위약의 효과에 대한 두 가지 상반된 견해를 순차적으로 제시하고 있다는 단서로부터 정답을 추론할 수 있다. In other words라는 순접의 연결사를 볼 때 A – D는 '결정적 순서'임을 알 수 있다.

어휘 **fake** 가짜의　**hormonal** 호르몬의
placebo 플라시보, (유효 성분이 없는 심리 효과 · 신약 테스트 등을 위한) 위약(僞藥)

해석 어떻게 위약이 누군가를 나아지게 하는 데 있어 도움을 주는 것일까? 감각 경험과 생각들은 뇌에 영향을 미칠 수 있다. 그리고 뇌는 호르몬 체계와 면역 체계 등을 포함해서 다른 신체 체계에 영향을 미칠 수 있다.
(B) 그러므로 한 사람이 가지고 있는 낙관주의와 희망은 부상이나 질병으로부터 그가 신체적으로 회복하는 데 있어서 중요할 수도 있다.
(A) 일부 전문가들은 플라시보 혹은 위약이 단순히 심리적 반응을 야기시키는 것이라고 믿고 있다.
(D) 달리 말해, 위약을 복용하는 것은 단지 몸이 나아졌다는 느낌을 높여줄 뿐이라는 것이다.
(C) 그러나 비처(H. k. Beecher)는 1955년에 행해진 혁명적인 연구를 통해서 환자들 가운데 32%가 위약에 대해서 의학적으로 반응했다는 사실을 발견했다.
(E) 이어진 연구들은 구체적이고 측정할 수 있는 결과들을 통해 이 발견을 지지하고 있다.

10 다음 글의 순서로 문맥상 의미가 가장 잘 통할 수 있도록 나열한 것을 고르시오. 2016 국회직 9급

(A) A little more investigative work led the officer to the boy's accomplice: another boy about 100 yards beyond the radar trap with a sign reading "TIPS" and a bucket at his feet full of change.

(B) One day, however, the officer was amazed when everyone was under the speed limit, so he investigated and found the problem.

(C) A 10-year-old boy was standing on the side of the road with a huge hand painted sign which said "Radar Trap Ahead".

(D) A police officer found a perfect hiding place for watching for speeding motorists.

① (B) − (C) − (A) − (D)
② (B) − (D) − (A) − (C)
③ (C) − (A) − (B) − (D)
④ (D) − (B) − (C) − (A)
⑤ (D) − (C) − (B) − (A)

정답 ④

해설 부정관사 (A)로 시작하기 때문에 전체 사건의 도입문으로 (D)가 가장 적절하다. the office가 등장하는 (A)나 (B)는 '결정적 순서'에 의하여 반드시 (D)의 뒤쪽에 위치해야 한다. 그러므로 ①②③은 모두 정답이 아니다. 또한 (C)는 (B)에서 언급한 문제점의 구체적인 내용이므로 (B) – (C) 또한 '결정적 순서'이다.

어휘 investigative 조사의, 수사의　accomplice 공범(자)　tip 팁, 사례금; 조언, 경고
change 변화, 전환; 거스름돈, 동전　radar trap 속도위반 탐지 장치　hiding place 은신처; 은폐 장소
speeding 속도위반　motorist 운전자

해석 (D) 한 경찰관이 속도위반 운전자를 감시할 완벽한 은신처를 발견했다.
(B) 그러나, 어느 날 그 경찰은 모든 사람들이 제한 속도 이하였을 때 놀라서, 그는 조사했고 문제점을 찾아냈다.
(C) 한 10살짜리 소년이 "앞에 속도위반 탐지 장치"라고 적혀있는 커다란 손칠 표지를 들고 도로 한편에 서 있었다.
(A) 추가 조사는 그 경찰관을 그 소년의 공범에게 인도했는데, 속도위반 탐지 장치를 100야드 지나서 "사례금"이라고 적혀있는 표지를 들고 그의 발 앞에 동전이 가득한 양동이를 가진 또 다른 소년이었다.

11 다음 주어진 글에 이어질 순서로 가장 적절한 것은?

The Smithonian Institution was established with funds from James Smithon (1765-1829), a British scientist who left his estate to the United States to fund the Institution. He believed that it was "an establishment for the increase and diffusion of knowledge".

(A) Why, then, would Smithon decide to give the entirety of his estate to a country that was foreign to him?
(B) Others attribute his philanthropy to ideals inspired by such organizations as the Royal Institution.
(C) Some speculate it was because Smithon was denied his father's legacy.
(D) Smithon traveled a lot during his life, but never once set foot on American soil.

① (B) − (C) − (A) − (D)　　② (B) − (D) − (A) − (C)
③ (C) − (B) − (D) − (A)　　④ (D) − (A) − (C) − (B)

정답 ④

해설 스미슨(Smithon)에 대한 이야기가 먼저 나오고, (A)의 why로 시작되는 질문의 답이 이어지도록 (C) 그의 기부행위의 동기에 대한 추론이 이어짐이 옳다. some과 others로 이어지는 (C)－(B)는 '결정적 순서'이다.

어휘 **institution** 협회　**estate** 재산; 사유지　**establishment** 기관; (공공)시설　**diffusion** 보급　**set foot on** ~에 발을 딛다　**legacy** 유산　**philanthropy** 박애, 자선; 자선사업　**bereavement** 여읨, 사별　**bestowal** 증여, 수여; 처치; 저장

해석 스미소니언(Smithonian) 협회는 영국의 과학자 제임스 스미슨(James Smithon, 1765-1829)이 기부한 돈으로 설립되었다. 그는 스미소니언 협회에 기금을 기부하기 위해 그의 재산을 미국에 남겼다. 그는 스미소니언 협회가 '지식을 증진하고 보급하기 위한 기관'이라고 믿었다.

(D) 스미슨(Smithon)은 살아있는 동안 여행을 많이 다녔음에도 불구하고 단 한 번도 미국 땅을 밟아본 적이 없었다.

(A) 그런데, 왜 스미슨(Smithon)은 그의 전 재산을 그에게 낯선 나라에 기부하기로 결심했을까?

(C) 그 이유와 관련해서, 일부에서는 Smithon이 그의 아버지의 유산을 물려받지 못하게 되었기 때문이라고 추측하고 있다.

(B) 다른 사람들은 그의 박애정신과 영국왕립과학연구소와 같은 기관에서 영감을 받은 이상 때문이라고 여긴다.

12 주어진 글 다음에 이어질 글의 순서로 가장 적절한 것은?

To be sure, human language stands out from the decidedly restricted vocalizations of monkeys and apes. Moreover, it exhibits a degree of sophistication that far exceeds any other form of animal communication.

(A) That said, many species, while falling far short of human language, do nevertheless exhibit impressively complex communication systems in natural settings.
(B) And they can be taught far more complex systems in artificial contexts, as when raised alongside humans.
(C) Even our closest primate cousins seem incapable of acquiring anything more than a rudimentary communicative system, even after intensive training over several years. The complexity that is language is surely a species-specific trait.

① (A) − (B) − (C)　　② (B) − (C) − (A)
③ (C) − (A) − (B)　　④ (C) − (B) − (A)

정답 ③

해설 주어진 문장에서는 인간의 언어가 다른 동물들의 의사소통 체계와 비교하여 눈에 띄게 탁월하다는 내용이다. 이러한 내용의 구체적인 예시라고 할 수 있는 (C)가 이어져 영장류들도 초보적인 의사소통 이상은 불가능하다는 내용이 이어지는 것이 적절하다. (A) 내의 nevertheless는 역접의 연결어이므로 반대로 인상적인 의사소통 체계를 보여준다는 (A)가 이어지는 것이 타당하다. 그러므로 (C) − (A)는 '결정적 순서'이다. 마지막으로 (B)에서 인공적인 환경에서는 더욱 정교한 의사소통체계도 가능하다는 내용이 이어지는 것이 적절하다.

어휘 **to be sure** 확실히　**stand out** 눈에 띄다　**decidedly** 분명히, 확실히　**restricted** 제한된
vocalization 발성(법)　**ape** 유인원　**exhibit** 드러내다, 보여주다　**sophistication** 정교함, 세련됨
exceed 능가하다, 초월하다　**That said** 그렇긴 해도　**fall short of** ~에 못 미치다, ~에 부족하다
impressively 인상적으로　**complex** 정교한, 복잡한　**artificial** 인위적인, 인공적인
context 상황, 문맥, 맥락　**alongside** ~와 함께　**primate** 영장류　**incapable of** ~할 수 없는
acquire 습득하다, 얻다　**rudimentary** 기본적인, 초보적인　**intensive** 집중적인
species-specific 종 고유의　**trait**특성

해석 확실히, 인간의 언어는 원숭이나 영장류들의 명백히 제한된 발성과는 구별된다. 게다가 이는 동물들의 의사소통 중 어떠한 형식을 훨씬 초월하는 어느 정도의 정교함을 보여준다.
(C) 심지어 우리와 가장 가까운 영장류 사촌들조차도 심지어 몇 년 이상의 집중적인 훈련을 거친 이후에도 기초적인 의사소통 체계 이상의 것은 어떤 것도 획득하지 못하는 것처럼 보인다. 언어라는 복잡함은 분명 종의 고유한 특성이다.
(A) 그렇다지만, 인간의 언어에는 훨씬 못 미치기는 하지만, 그럼에도 불구하고 많은 종들이 자연환경에서는 인상적으로 정교한 의사소통 체계를 보여준다.
(B) 그리고 인간과 함께 길러지는 때와 같이 인공적 상황에서는 이들은 훨씬 더 복잡한 체계를 배울 수 있다.

13 다음 주어진 글에 이어질 순서로 가장 적절한 것은?

Lightening has been a mystery since early times. People living in ancient civilizations believed angry gods threw lightening bolts from the sky. Nobody understood that lightening resulted from electricity until Benjamin Franklin flew a kite with a key dangling from the string, and it was struck by lightening. In modern times, it is known that lightening has a very scientific cause.

(A) When that negative charge is too great for the air to hold it back, it is combined with a positive charge from the Earth, forming a channel of electricity that flows between the two points.

(B) Once the charges "converge", a fifty thousand degree current superheats the air around the channel, leading to an explosion of sound known as thunder.

(C) Typically, within a storm cloud, friction from water and ice-laden clouds creates a negative charge at the bottom of the cloud.

(D) This positive charge remains hidden as it moves towards the ground until it meets the charge rising from the ground.

① (C) − (D) − (B) − (A)　　② (A) − (B) − (C) − (D)
③ (B) − (C) − (D) − (A)　　④ (C) − (A) − (D) − (B)

정답 ④

해설 이 글이 번개의 발생과정을 순서에 따라 기술하고 있다는 단서로부터 정답을 추론할 수 있다. 번개의 발생현상의 도입문을 나타내는 부사로 typically가 단서가 될 수 있으므로 주어진 문장 바로 뒤에는 (C)가 가장 적절하다. 또한 순서 배열의 signal 역할을 하는 정관사와 부정관사를 볼 때 (C)안의 'a negative charge'와 (A) 안의 'that negative charge'를 통해 (C) − (A)는 '결정적 순서'임을 알 수 있다. 마찬가지로 (A) 후반부의 'a positive charge'와 (D) 안의 'this positive charge'도 역시 '결정적 순서'에 대한 강력한 힌트를 주고 있다.

어휘 **lightning** 번개　**string** 줄　**friction** 마찰　**negative** 음전기의　**charge** 전하　**positive** 양전기의　**current** 전류　**superheat** 가열시키다　**thunder** 천둥

해석 번개는 고대 이래로 미스터리였다. 고대 문명에서 살던 사람들은 분노한 신이 하늘에서 번개를 던졌다고 믿었다. 벤저민 프랭클린(Benjamin Franklin)이 열쇠가 줄에 매달려있는 연을 날려, 연이 번개를 맞았을 때까지 그 누구도 번개가 전기 때문이라는 사실을 이해하지 못했다. 근대에 이르러서야, 번개가 매우 과학적인 이유를 가지고 있다는 사실이 알려지게 된다.

(C) 일반적으로, 먹구름 안에서, 물과 얼음이 가득 들어 찬 구름으로부터 생기는 마찰로 인해 구름 하단에서 음전하가 발생하게 된다.

(A) 음전하가, 대기가 막을 수 없을 정도로 거대해질 경우, 음전하는 대지에 있는 양전하와 결합하게 되어 구름과 대지에 있는 두 지점 사이를 오가는 전기 통로가 생긴다.

(D) 이때 양전하는 음전하가 땅으로 이동할 때 숨어 있게 되고, 결국 음전하는 대지에서 올라오는 양전하와 만나게 된다.

(B) 음전하와 양전하가 만나게 되면, 5만도에 달하는 전류가 전기 통로 주변의 대기를 급속히 가열시켜, 천둥이라고 알려진 소리의 폭발을 야기시킨다.

14 주어진 문장 다음에 이어질 글의 순서로 가장 적절한 것은? 2017 기상직 9급

A direct strike of a major hurricane on New Orleans had long been every weather forecaster's worst nightmare. The city presented a perfect set of circumstances that might contribute to the death and destruction there. On the one hand there was its geography.

(A) On the other hand there was its culture. New Orleans does many things well, but there are two things that it proudly refuses to do. New Orleans does not move quickly, and New Orleans does not place much faith in authority.

(B) If it did those things, it would have been much better prepared to deal with Katrina, since those are the exact two things you need to do when a hurricane threatens to strike.

(C) New Orleans does not border the Gulf of Mexico as much as sink into it. Much of the population lived below sea level and was counting on protection from an outmoded system of levees and a set of natural barriers that had literally been washing away to sea.

① (B) − (A) − (C)　② (A) − (B) − (C)

③ (C) − (A) − (B)　④ (B) − (C) − (A)

정답 ③

해설 주어진 문장의 끝에 지리에 관한 언급이 있으므로 지리에 관한 내용인 (C)가 바로 이어지는 것이 적절하다. (A)에 two things를 통해 뉴올리언스인들이 하지 않는 두 가지를 처음 소개하고 (B)에서 those things로 받는 것으로 보아 (A) – (B)는 '결정적 순서'이다. 그러므로 정답은 ③이다.

어휘 **nightmare** 악몽　**geography** 지리　**authority** 권위; 당국　**sink** 가라앉다　**sea level** 해수면　**outmoded** 구식의, 낡은　**levee** 제방　**barrier** 장벽　**literally** 문자 그대로

해석 뉴올리언스에서 발생한 주요 허리케인의 직접적인 강타는 오랫동안 모든 기상 예보관의 최악의 악몽이었습니다. 이 도시는 그 곳에서 죽음과 파괴를 가져올 완벽한 상황을 제시했습니다. 한편으로는 그 지형문제였습니다.

(C) 뉴올리언스는 멕시코 만과 접해 있다기 보다는 아래로 가라앉아 있습니다. 인구의 상당 부분은 해수면 아래서 살았으며, 시대에 뒤쳐진 제방 시스템과 문자 그대로 바다로 씻겨 내린 일련의 자연적 장벽으로부터의 보호에 의존하고 있었습니다.

(A) 다른 한편엔 그 문화가 있었습니다. 뉴올리언스는 많은 일을 잘하지만, 자랑스럽게 거부하는 두 가지 일이 있습니다. 뉴올리언스는 빨리 움직이지 않으며 뉴올리언스는 정부 당국에 대해 많은 믿음을 두지 않습니다.

(B) 그것이 그러한 일을 했다면 카트리나를 다룰 준비가 훨씬 더 쉬웠을 것입니다. 그것들은 허리케인이 강타하려 위협할 때 당신이 해야 할 정확한 두 가지이기 때문입니다.

15 주어진 문장에 이어질 글의 순서로 가장 알맞은 것은?

Women, on the average, live longer. In general they can expect to live six or seven years more than men.

(A) Today young women are smoking more and working in more positions of responsibility than they used to. These changes will not help women's health. If they are not careful, they will have the same life expectancy as men.
(B) One biological factor that helps women live longer is the difference in hormones between men and women. Female hormones protect the body by helping it to defend itself against various infections.
(C) The cultural context can also affect life expectancy. Previously women smoked less and worked in less stressful environments than men. Both cigarettes and stress have proven to cause many health problems and to shorten lives.

① (B) – (C) – (A) ② (B) – (A) – (C)
③ (A) – (C) – (B) ④ (C) – (B) – (A)

정답 ①

해설 주어진 문장은 여성의 평균수명이 길다는 일반적 진술이며 (B)가 그 원인에 대하여 진술하고 있다. (C) 또한 그 원인에 대해 다른 분석을 제시하고 있는데 also가 있으므로 (B) – (C)가 '결정적 순서'이다.

어휘 life expectancy 기대 수명, 예상 수명 factor 요인 hormone 호르몬 context 환경
stressful 스트레스가 쌓이는

해석 여자들은 평균적으로 더 오래산다. 일반적으로 그들은 남자들보다 6, 7년을 더 살 것이라고 예상된다.
(B) 여성들을 더 오래 살도록 돕는 하나의 생물학적 요인은 남녀 간의 호르몬의 차이이다. 여성의 호르몬들은 다양한 감염으로부터 스스로를 보호하도록 도와줌으로써 신체를 보호해준다.
(C) 문화적인 환경 또한 수명에 영향을 미친다. 이전에는 여성들은 담배를 덜 피우고 남자들보다 덜 스트레스가 쌓이는 환경에서 일을 했다. 담배와 스트레스는 많은 건강문제를 일으키고 수명을 단축시킨다고 판명되었다.
(A) 오늘날 젊은 여성들은 담배를 더욱 많이 피우고 예전보다는 더욱 책임감이 있는 위치에서 일을 하고 있다. 이러한 변화들은 여성들의 건강에 도움을 주지 않을 것이다. 그들이 주의를 하지 않는다면 남성들과 같은 수명을 갖게 될 것이다.

16 주어진 문장에 이어질 글의 순서로 가장 알맞은 것은?

The brain is the most complex organ in the human body. It produces our every thought, action, memory, feeling, and experience of the world. This jellylike mass of tissue contains neurons.

(A) It is in these changing connections that memories are stored, habits learned, and personalities shaped, by reinforcing certain patterns of brain activity and losing others.
(B) Our brain forms millions of new connections through the synapses for every second of our lives. The pattern and strength are constantly changing.
(C) These neurons connect to each other with great complexity. Each one can make contact with thousands or even tens of thousands of others, by means of tiny structures called synapses.

① (B) − (A) − (C)　　② (B) − (C) − (A)
③ (A) − (C) − (B)　　④ (C) − (B) − (A)

정답 ④

해설 주어진 문장은 뇌의 구성요소인 neuron을 소개하고 있다. (C)에서 these neuron과 같이 지시사를 포함하고 있으므로 (C)가 바로 뒤에 이어질 문장이다. (C)의 맨 마지막에 synapsis를 소개하고 있고 (B)에서 the synapses로 정관사를 포함하고 있으므로 (C) – (B)는 '결정적 순서'이다.

어휘 jellylike 젤리같은　tissue 조직　neuron 뉴런, 신경단위　connection 연계, 연결, 연결망
reinforce 강화하다　synapsis 시냅시스, 연접

해석 뇌는 인체에서 가장 복잡한 기관이다. 그것은 우리의 일상적인 생각, 행동, 기억, 감정, 그리고 세상의 경험을 생산해 낸다. 이 젤리 같은 조직 덩어리는 뉴런을 포함한다.
(C) 이 뉴런들은 대단히 복잡하게 서로서로 연결이 되어 있다. 각각은 수천 개 혹은 심지어 수만 개의 다른 뉴런들과 시냅스라고 불리우는 작은 구조를 통하여 접촉할 수 있다.
(B) 우리의 뇌는 우리 생애의 매 순간마다 시냅시스를 통하여 수백만 가지의 연결망을 만들어 낸다. 그 모양과 힘은 항상 변화를 하고 있다.
(A) 어떤 형태의 뇌활동을 강화하고 다른 것들은 버리는 것을 이용하여 기억이 저장이 되고 습관이 습득이 되고 또한 성격이 형성되는 곳은 이 변화하는 연결망이다.

05 문장 삽입, 제거

01 다음 내용이 들어가기에 가장 적절한 곳은?

Despite its apparent emptiness, Australia's outback has always been full of food for those who know where to look.

(①) It's a lesson you can learn first-hand during a stay at Lombadina, an indigenous community. The accommodation may be simple, just a collection of cabins surrounded by flowering shrubs. (②) However, the bush tucker is first rate. For an unforgettable feast, head to the nearby mangroves for a mud crab hunt. (③) Wading through knee-deep water, you will be given a hooked metal rod to thrust into the mangrove roots where the mud crabs like to hide. Finding a crab is not easy; even more challenging is trying to drag it out. The mud crabs are huge, and in no great hurry to emerge from their homes. (④) Fortunately your hosts have had plenty of practice, and will ensure you have enough to feed the group.

정답 ①

해설 주어진 지문 전체가 호주 원주민의 전통음식에 대한 일반적 설명이며 아래의 첫 문장의 대명사 it이라는 단서로부터 주어진 문장이 문두에 와야 함을 추론할 수 있다.

어휘 apparent 외견상의; 분명한 first-hand 직접적으로 indigenous 토착의, 고유의 shrub 관목(灌木) bush tucker 부시 터커(호주 원주민의 전통음식) feast 축연, 잔치 mangrove 맹그로브나무(열대나무) wade 걸어서 건너다 thrust 밀어 넣다 challenging 도전적인, 힘든

해석 ① 외견상은 텅 비어있는 것으로 보이지만, 호주의 오지는, 어디에서 음식을 찾아야 할지를 알고 있는 사람들에게는 먹을 것들로 항상 가득 차 있는 곳이다. 이런 사실은 원주민 공동체 롬바디나(Lombadina)에 머무르는 동안 당신이 직접적으로 배울 수 있는 교훈이다. 꽃이 핀 관목들에 둘러싸인 오두막집들이 전부인 숙소는 단출하다. ② 그러나 전통적인 원주민 음식은 매우 훌륭하다. 잊지 못할 잔치를 위해서라면, 머드크랩을 잡으러 근처에 있는 맹그로브 나무숲으로 가보라. ③ 무릎 깊이의 물을 건너고 나면, 갈고리가 달린 금속막대가 당신에게 주어질 것이다. 이 금속막대로 머드크랩이 숨기 좋아하는 맹그로브 나무의 뿌리 안을 찌르면 된다. 크랩을 찾아내는 일은 쉽지 않다. 하지만 찾은 크랩을 끄집어내는 일은 그보다 더 힘든 도전이다. 머드크랩은 매우 몸집이 크고, 여간해서는 집 밖으로 나오지 않는다. ④ 다행스러운 점은 당신을 이끌어줄 이번 잔치의 호스트가 크랩을 잡는 일에 이골이 난 전문가라는 것이다. 호스트는 당신 일행 모두가 충분히 먹을 수 있을 만큼의 크랩를 잡을 것이다.

02 주어진 문장이 들어갈 위치로 가장 적절한 것은? 2018 국가직 9급

Some remain intensely proud of their original accent and dialect words, phrases and gestures, while others accommodate rapidly to a new environment by changing their speech habits, so that they no longer "stand out in the crowd".

Our perceptions and production of speech change with time. (①) If we were to leave our native place for an extended period, our perception that the new accents around us were strange would only be temporary. (②) Gradually, we will lose the sense that others have an accent and we will begin to fit in — to accommodate our speech patterns to the new norm. (③) Not all people do this to the same degree. (④) Whether they do this consciously or not is open to debate and may differ from individual to individual, but like most processes that have to do with language, the change probably happens before we are aware of it and probably couldn't happen if we were.

정답 ④

해설 주어진 문장은 어떤 사람들은 자신의 고유한 사투리를 고집한다는 내용이며 성격상 구체적인(particular) 내용이다. 그러므로 주어진 문장이 들어갈 바로 앞 자리에는 보다 일반적인(general) 진술이 적절하다고 할 수 있는데 ④의 바로 앞 문장이 모든 사람들이 이러한 일(사투리를 버리고 표준어에 적응하는 것)을 하는 것이 아니라는 내용이 나오므로 ④이 가장 적절하다.

어휘 **intensely** 매우, 강하게 **original** 원래의 **dialect** 사투리, 방언
accommodate 적응하다; 수용하다; 남의 부탁을 들어주다 **stand out** 눈에 띄다 **perception** 인식, 지각
extended 상당한, 긴 **fit in** 맞추다, 적응하다 **norm** 표준, 기준 **to the same degree** 같은 정도로
have to do with ~과 관계가 있다.

해석 말에 대한 우리의 인식과 행위는 시간에 따라 변한다. ① 만약 우리가 장기간 동안 우리의 고향을 떠나게 되면, 우리를 둘러싼 새로운 사투리가 낯설다는 우리의 인식은 단지 일시적이게 된다. ② 차츰, 우리는 다른 사람들이 사투리가 있다는 생각을 안 하게 되고 우리의 말투를 새로운 표준에 맞추기 시작한다. ③ 모든 사람들이 똑같은 정도로 이것을 하는 것은 아니다. ④ 어떤 사람들은 계속해서 자신의 고향 악센트와 사투리 단어, 구, 그리고 몸짓들에 매우 자랑스러워하는 반면, 다른 사람들은 그들의 언어 습관을 바꿈으로써 새로운 환경에 빠르게 적응하며 그 결과로 더 이상 무리 속에서 눈에 띄지 않는다. 그들이 이것을 의식적으로 하는지 그렇지 않은지는 논쟁의 여지가 있지만 개인에 따라 다를 수 있다. 그러나 언어와 관련 있는 대부분의 과정들처럼 그 변화는 우리가 그것을 인식하기 전에 발생하며, 만약에 우리가 의식한다면 그것은 발생하지 않을 것이다.

03 아래의 주어진 글이 들어가기에 가장 알맞은 곳은?

Scientists prefer to determine the age of fish by counting the growth rings on their scales.

There are stories of fish that are believed to have lived for a century or more. For example, in 1610 a pike that had caught a copper ring engraved with the date 1448 attached to its fin. (①) Another story tells of carp that were put into the pools at the French Palace of Versailles in the late 1600s. (②) In 1830, many people believed that the same carp were still in the pools. Scientists doubt such extreme claims. (③) They believe that in the case of the Versailles pools, for instance, the original fish could easily have died and been replaced by new fish. The date on the pike's ring could easily have been engraved incorrectly. (④) Using this method, scientists have found that a sturgeon caught in a Wisconsin lake was eighty-two years old.

정답 ④

해설 ④ 뒤의 this method가 주어진 문장의 counting the growth rings on their scales를 가리키고 있다.

어휘 **scale** 비늘 **pike** 강꼬치고기 **copper ring** 구리 반지 **engrave** 조각하다, 새기다 **fin** 지느러미 **carp** 잉어 **sturgeon** 철갑상어

해석 한 세기 또는 그 이상을 살았다고 믿는 물고기에 대한 이야기들이 있다. 예를 들어, 1610년에는 1448년 연대가 지느러미에 붙어 구리반지에 새겨져 있던 강꼬치고기가 잡혔다. 1600년대 말 프랑스의 베르사유 궁전의 연못 안에 들어 있었던 잉어에 관한 또 다른 이야기도 있다. 1830년에 많은 사람들은 연못 안에 아직도 똑같은 잉어가 살고 있다고 믿었다. 과학자들은 그러한 극단적인 주장에 대해 의심했다. 그들은 베르사유 궁전 연못의 경우에는 본래 물고기는 확실히 죽었을 것이고, 새로운 물고기에 의해 대체되었을 것이라고 믿고 있다. 또한 미늘창 고리의 날짜는 아마도 부정확하게 새겨졌을 것이라고 믿는다. ④ 과학자들은 물고기의 비늘에 있는 나이테 계산을 통해서, 물고기의 연령을 판단하는 것을 선호한다. 이 방법을 이용하여 과학자들은 위스콘신 호수에서 잡은 철갑상어가 82살이라는 것을 알게 되었다.

04 다음 주어진 글이 들어가기에 가장 알맞은 곳은?

Their narratives of slave life helped fire the abolition movement.

Writing helps us to record and communicate ideas. It is a definitive and essential part of daily human experience. Whether we write a shopping list or a great novel, we use a tool without which we would find ourselves isolated. Without writing we cut ourselves off from vital processes like the expression of political opinions, the description of medical emergencies, and the examination of our feelings in diaries and letters. Writing crosses many cultures. Whether we consider historic cave drawings or the transmission of fax messages after the World Trade Center disaster, we find evidence of the human instinct to communicate to other people. (①) In the past, writing brought about change. (②) African American slaves were frequently forbidden to learn to read or write, but some managed to find ways to gain literacy anyway. (③) Women in the nineteenth century used writing to advance the cause of suffrage, winning votes with passionate speeches and articles in newspapers. (④) Immigrants struggled to learn English in order to find a better life in the New World.

정답 ③

해설 주어진 문장은 노예들이 쓴 이야기가 노예해방에 도움을 주었다는 내용이며 대명사 their가 단서역할을 한다. 그러므로 주어진 문장 앞에는 노예들이 글을 배웠다는 진술이 나와야 한다.

어휘 **definitive** 결정적인, 최종적인 **isolated** 고립된, 소외된 **cut oneself off from** 차단되다, 분리되다 **emergency** 비상사태 **transmission** 전달, 매개; 전염 **instinct** 본능 **forbid** 금지하다 **suffrage** 투표권, 참정권 **cause** 대의명분 **passionate** 열정적인, 열렬한 **article** 기사; 물품; 항목 **immigrant** 이민자, 이주민 **abolition** 철폐, 폐지; 노예제도 폐지 **confine** 한정하다, 제한하다; 가두다

해석 글은 우리가 사유들을 기록하고 소통하는 데 도움을 준다. 글은 일상적인 인간 경험의 분명하고도 필수적인 일부다. 쇼핑목록을 작성하든 멋진 장편소설을 써 내리든, 우리는 그것이 없다면 우리를 고립시키게 되는 도구(즉, 글)를 사용한다. 만일 글이 없다면, 우리는 정치적 견해의 표현, 응급상황에 대한 설명, 일기와 편지에서 우리의 감정을 탐구하는 것 등과 같은 중요한 과정들로부터 우리 자신을 단절시키게 된다. 글은 여러 문화들을 넘나든다. 우리가 역사적으로 중요한 (선사시대의) 동굴 속에 그려져 있는 그림을 생각하든, 세계무역센터 참사 후에 전송된 팩스 메시지 떠올리든, 우리는 이러한 것들로부터 다른 사람들과 소통하고자 하는 인간 본능에 대한 증거를 발견한다. ① 과거에, 글은 변화를 야기시켰다. ② 미국 흑인 노예들은 종종 읽고 쓰는 법을 배우는 것을 금지 당했지만, 그들 중 일부는 어떻게든 읽고 쓰는 법을 습득하는 방법을 찾아냈다. ③ 노예들의 삶에 대한 그들의 이야기는 노예제도 폐지 운동에 불을 붙이는데 도움을 주었다. 19세기의 여성들은 열정적인 연설과 신문 기사를 통해 투표권을 획득하면서, 글을 이용해서 참정권 운동을 진전시켰다. ④ 이주민들 또한 신대륙에서 더 나은 삶을 찾기 위해서 영어를 배우려고 애썼다.

05 주어진 문장이 들어갈 가장 적절한 곳은?

Therefore in a just society the liberty of equal citizenship is taken as settled: the rights secured by justice are not subject to the calculus of interests or to political bargaining.

Justice is the first virtue of social institutions, as truth is of systems of thoughts. (①) A theory, however elegant and economical, must be rejected or revised if it is untrue; likewise, laws and institutions, no matter how efficient and well-arranged, must be reformed or abolished if they are unjust. (②) Each person possesses an inviolability founded on justice that even the welfare of society as a whole cannot override. (③) For this reason justice denies that the loss of freedom for some is made right by a greater good shared by others. It does not allow that the sacrifices imposed on a few are outweighed by the larger sum of advantages enjoyed by many. (④) The only thing that permits us to acquiesce in an erroneous theory is the lack of a better one; analogously, an injustice is tolerable only when it is necessary to avoid an even greater injustice. Being the first virtues of human activities, truth and justice are uncompromising.

정답 ④

해설 소수자들의 권리가 무시될 수 없다는 것과 모든 사람이 동등한 시민권의 권리를 가지고 있다는 것은 논리적으로 연결된다.

어휘 **virtue** 미덕 **social institution** 사회제도 **inviolability** 불가침, 불가침성 **override** 무시하다, 깔아뭉개다 **outweigh** ~보다 무겁다; ~보다 더 중요하다 **be subject to** ~에 예속되어 있다 **acquiesce** 동의하다, 묵인하다 **analogously** 유사하게 **uncompromising** 타협하지 않는, 단호한; 철저한

해석 진리가 사유의 체계에서 으뜸가는 미덕이듯 정의는 사회제도의 으뜸가는 미덕이다. ① 제 아무리 고상하고 간결하다 할지라도 이론은, 만일 그것이 진리가 아니면, 거부되거나 수정되어야만 한다. 마찬가지로 법과 제도는, 만일 공정하지 않다면, 제 아무리 효율적이고 잘 정비되어 있다고 할지라도 개혁되거나 철폐되어야만 한다. ② 각 개인은 저마다, 일반적으로 심지어 사회의 복지라는 대의명분으로도 무효화시킬 수 없는 정의에 기반한 신성불가침성을 소유한다. ③ 이러한 이유 때문에 정의는 일부 사람들의 자유의 상실이 타인들이 공유하는 더 큰 선에 의해서 정당화되는 것을 거부한다. 정의는 다수가 향유하는 보다 큰 이익들의 합이 소수에게 부과된 희생보다 더 중요하다는 주장을 용인하지 않는다. ④ 그러므로 정의로운 사회에서는 평등한 시민권의 자유가 확립된 것으로 여겨진다. 따라서 정의에 의해서 보장된 권리는 이해관계의 계산이나 정치적 흥정 등에 의해 지배 받지 않는다. 잘못된 이론을 묵인하게 허용해주는 유일한 것은 그것보다 더 나은 이론이 없는 경우다. 이와 유사하게 불의는 심지어 더 큰 불의를 피해야 할 필요성이 있을 경우에만 용인될 수 있다. 인간 행위의 으뜸가는 미덕으로서 진리와 정의는 비타협적인 것이다.

06 주어진 문장이 들어갈 위치로 가장 적절한 것은? 2015 지방직 7급

Both groups were then placed in the same escape-avoidance condition: they could avoid the shock if they jumped over a barrier after hearing a tone.

Perhaps the most dramatic evidence that organisms can be aware of the contingency (or lack thereof) between their behavior and reinforcement is found in the experiments on learned helplessness. In a prototypical experiment by Seligman and Maier, dogs were given painful shocks at unpredictable intervals. (①) A control group of dogs could avoid the shocks by pressing the lever, whereas the experimental group could have no means at all to escape the shock. (②) Thus one group of dogs learned a behavior that would eliminate shock, whereas the other did not. (③) Dogs in the control group, which could control their shock in the first phase, readily learned to jump over the barrier. (④) In contrast, the experimental dogs whined and yelped but made no attempt to escape the shock. They had learned that nothing they could do would prevent shock—that there was no contingency between their behavior and receiving shock.

정답 ③

해설 주어진 문장에서 말하는 두 집단은 실험 대상의 개들과 대조군의 개들을 지칭하므로, 그 두 집단을 모두 언급한 이 후에 주어진 문장이 나와야 한다. 또한 a barrier가 처음 나오고 나서 the barrier의 순서로 연결되어야 하므로 ③이 가장 적절한 위치다.

어휘 **organism** 유기체, 생물 **be aware of** ~를 알다 **reinforcement** (학습에 의한) 강화
contingency 우연성, 부수적인 관련 사건 **thereof** 그것의, 그것에 관한, 그것으로
prototypical 원형의, 모범인 **control group** 대조군, 통제군(실험 요건을 부가하지 않은 그룹)
whine 낑낑거리다 **yelp** 컹컹 짖다

해석 생물들이 그들의 행동과 강화 사이의 관련성(또는 그것의 결여)을 안다는 가장 극적인 증거는 아마도 학습된 무기력에 대한 실험에서 발견될 것이다. Seligman과 Maier에 의해 원래 이루어진 검사에서 개에게 불규칙적으로 고통스러운 충격을 주었다. ① 대조군의 개들은 지렛대를 누름으로써 충격을 피할 수 있었던 반면, 실험집단의 개들은 충격을 피할 수단이 전혀 없었다. ② 이와 같이 한 집단의 개들은 충격을 제거하는 행동을 습득한 반면 다른 개들은 그렇지 못했다. ③ 그런 다음 두 집단 모두 같은 도피 - 회피 상태에 놓여졌다. 만일 그들이 어떤 한 신호를 듣고 난 뒤 장애물을 뛰어 넘는다면, 충격을 피할 수도 있었다. 첫 단계의 충격을 통제할 수 있는 대조군의 개들은 장애물을 뛰어넘는 것을 쉽게 배웠다. ④ 대조적으로, 실험집단의 개들은 낑낑거리고 컹컹 짖을 뿐 충격을 벗어날 어떤 시도도 하지 않았다. 그들은 그들이 충격을 막기 위해 어떤 것도 할 수 없다는 것 즉, 그들의 행동과 충격을 받는 것에는 아무런 부수적 관련성이 없다는 것을 배웠었던 것이다.

07 글의 흐름으로 보아, 주어진 문장이 들어가기에 가장 적절한 곳은?

> The doctor also carries out some special tests to detect such dangerous diseases as cancer and diabetes, if necessary.

> Our bodies have the natural ability to fight off bacteria and diseases when they enter our bodies. (①) But there are other diseases that our bodies cannot successfully resist on their own. (②) In order to prevent such diseases, it is advised that everyone over the age of twenty-five should have a regular physical examination. (③) During a regular examination a doctor checks weight, vision and hearing problems, blood pressure, and so on. (④) The information from both check-ups and tests provides important insight into the patient's overall physical condition. Hence, the time spent on regular examinations is a sensible investment in good health.

정답 ④

해설 주어진 문장의 also를 볼 때 의사들의 검사에 대한 내용이 앞에 나와야 한다.

어휘 **detect** 탐지하다 **diabetes** 당뇨 **bacteria** 박테리아 **insight** 통찰력 **overall** 종합적인, 일반적인 **sensible** 현명한

해석 우리의 몸은 박테리아와 질병이 체내에 들어올 때 그것들과 싸워서 물리치는 타고난 능력을 가지고 있다. ① 그러나 우리의 몸이 스스로 성공적으로 저항할 수 없는 다른 질병들이 있다. ② 그런 질병들을 예방하기 위해, 25세 이상인 사람은 누구나 정기적인 신체검사를 받도록 권장하고 있다. ③ 정기 검진을 하는 동안에 의사는 체중, 시력과 청력 문제, 혈압 등을 점검한다. ④ <u>그 의사는 또한 필요하다면 암이나 당뇨병과 같은 위험한 질병을 찾아내기 위해 몇 가지 특별한 테스트를 실시한다.</u> 검진과 테스트로부터 얻은 정보는 환자의 전체적인 신체 상태에 대한 중요한 통찰력을 제공한다. 그러므로 정기 검진에 보낸 시간은 좋은 건강에 대한 현명한 투자다.

08 글의 흐름으로 보아, 주어진 문장이 들어가기에 가장 적절한 곳은?

For example, he dressed and bathed himself, and ate at the dinner table.

A pet chimpanzee, Travis had once appeared in television commercials. (①) He lived more like a person than a chimpanzee. (②) One day, however, he unexpectedly attacked a friend of his owner. (③) When his owner saw that her friend was being attacked, she called the police. (④) The police arrived and Travis was shot and killed. His victim was treated for serious injuries. (⑤) This tragic story shows that some animals don't make good pets.

정답 ②

해설 for example은 예시를 드러내는 순접의 연결사이므로 앞 문장에 이와 비슷한 일반적 진술이 요구되며 ②의 앞 문장이 침팬지가 사람처럼 행동한다는 일반적 진술을 담고 있다.

어휘 **commercial** 상업광고 **bathe** 목욕을 하다 **unexpectedly** 갑자기 **treat** 치료하다 **tragic** 비극적인

해석 애완 침팬지 트래비스는 일전에 TV 광고에 출연한 적이 있다. ① 그는 침팬지보다 인간과 더 유사하게 살고 있었다. ② 예컨대, 그는 혼자 옷도 입고, 목욕도 했으며, 식탁에서 밥도 먹었다. 그러나 어느 날 그는 예기치 않게 주인의 친구를 공격했다. ③ 트래비스의 주인은 친구가 공격당하고 있는 것을 보았을 때 경찰에 전화했다. ④ 경찰이 도착했고 트래비스는 총을 맞고 죽었다. 그의 희생자는 심한 부상으로 치료를 받았다. ⑤ 이 비극적인 이야기는 어떤 동물들은 좋은 애완동물이 되지 못한다는 것을 보여준다.

09 글의 흐름으로 보아, 주어진 문장이 들어가기에 가장 적절한 곳은?

Afterwards, the Chinese regularly celebrated their victory.

Many years ago, the Mongols ruled China. One day, the Chinese decided to drive them out. (①) To let everyone secretly know the date of the attack, the chinese used moon cakes. (②) They put secret messages inside the cakes. (③) The attack was successful and the Mongols left. (④) They gave each other moon cakes with messages in them every moon festival. (⑤) Many years later, Chinese workers in America didn't have moon cakes for the moon festival, so they used what they had and invented fortune cookies.

정답 ④

해설 주어진 문장은 중국인들이 승리를 기념한다는 일반적 진술의 표현이며 ④ 뒤의 문장이 이러한 진술의 보다 구체적인 내용이다.

어휘 moon cake 월병 fortune cookie 점을 치는 과자

해석 오래 전, 몽골인들이 중국을 지배했다. 어느 날, 중국인들은 몽골인들을 몰아내기로 했다. ① 공격 날짜를 모든 사람에게 비밀리에 알리기 위해, 중국인들은 월병을 이용했다. ② 그들은 월병 안에 비밀 메시지를 넣었다. ③ 공격은 성공적이었고 몽골인들은 떠났다. ④ 그 이후, 중국인들은 정기적으로 그들의 승리를 기념했다. 추석 때마다 사람들은 메시지가 들어 있는 월병을 서로에게 주었다. ⑤ 여러 해가 지난 후, 미국에 있던 중국 근로자들은 추석 때 월병이 없었고, 그리하여 그들은 그들이 갖고 있던 것을 이용해서 점을 치는 과자를 만들어냈다.

10 글의 흐름으로 보아, 주어진 문장이 들어가기에 가장 적절한 곳은?

But now that I am older, I realize that being "Big Sister" actually has its advantages.

When I was younger, I hated being the oldest child and the only girl in my family. (①) First of all, I get special treatment from my parents and brothers. (②) I get my own room, and my brothers have to do all the heavy work around the house. (③) Another benefit is that, being the oldest, I have learned to be responsible and dependable. (④) The experience I've had taking care of my brothers has prepared me for my own family in the future.

정답 ①

해설 주어진 문장에 강한 역접의 연결사 but이 있으므로 앞에 "큰언니"가 불리하거나 부정적 내용이 나오면 된다. 또한 뒤로는 its advantages의 구체적인 예가 나오면 된다. 그러므로 ①이 정답이다.

어휘 treatment 취급, 대우; 치료 dependable 의지할만한, 믿을만한

해석 지금보다 어렸을 때에 나는 집에서 장녀와 동시에 외동딸이라는 사실이 싫었다. ① 그러나 이제 나이를 좀 더 먹고 보니 장녀가 된다는 것이 실제로 이로운 점들을 가지고 있다는 사실을 깨달았다. 우선 나는 부모님이나 남동생들에게 특별한 대우를 받는다. ② 나 자신의 방을 갖게 되고 내 남동생들이 집 안의 힘든 일을 다 해낸다. ③ 또 다른 이점은 장녀이기 때문에 책임질 줄 알고 남에게 신뢰감을 줄 수 있게 되었다는 것이다. ④ 남동생들을 돌보면서 쌓은 경험이 미래의 내 자신의 가족을 위한 준비를 하게 해 주었다.

11 주어진 문장이 들어갈 위치로 가장 적절한 곳은? 2016 지방직 9급

But the truth is, after you successfully make it through this problem, there will be another problem to face.

Some people are convinced that life is simply a series of problems to be solved. The sooner they get through with the problem they are facing, the sooner they will be happy. (①) And after you overcome that obstacle, there will be something else to overcome and there's always another mountain to climb. (②) That's why it is important to enjoy the journey, not just the destination. (③) In this world, we will never arrive at a place where everything is perfect and we have no more challenges. (④) As admirable as setting goals and reaching them may be, you can't get so focused on accomplishing your goals that you make the mistake of not enjoying where you are right now.

정답 ①

해설 주어진 문장에서 접속사 but을 볼 때, 앞에 나온 문장에 대한 역접의 내용임을 알 수 있다. 따라서 문제를 빨리 해결하면 더 빨리 행복해진다고 믿는 사람들에 대한 언급 뒤에 나와야 한다.

어휘 make through with ~을 성취하다 get through ~을 끝내다 face 직면하다
convince 확신시키다, 설득시키다 a series of 일련의 overcome 극복하다 obstacle 장애물
journey 여행, 여정 destination 목적지 challenge 도전 admirable 감탄할 만한, 존경할 만한

해석 일부 사람들은 인생이 단지 해결해야 할 일련의 문제들이라고 생각한다. 그들에게 닥친 문제를 더 빨리 끝낼수록, 그들은 행복해진다는 것이다. ① 그러나 사실, 당신이 이 문제를 성공적으로 마쳤다 할지라도, 새로이 직면해야 할 다른 문제가 존재한다. 그리고 당신이 그 장애물을 극복한 후에도, 극복해야 할 또 다른 것이 있기 마련이며, 등반해야 할 또 다른 산이 있기 마련이다. ② 바로 이것이 목적지뿐 아니라, 여정 자체를 즐겨야 하는 이유이다. ③ 이 세상에서, 우리는 모든 것이 완벽하고, 더 이상의 도전은 존재하지 않는 곳에는 절대로 도착할 수 없다. 그 결과 당신이 지금 처한 상황을 감사하지 못하는 그런 실수를 하게 될 수도 있다. ④ 목표를 정하고 거기에 도달하는 것은 멋진 일이지만, 당신의 목표를 성취하는 데 너무 집중해서 현재 지금 있는 곳에서 즐기지 못하는 잘못을 저질러서는 안 된다.

12 다음의 문장이 들어갈 가장 알맞은 곳은?

Although this is somewhat generational, in fact, it is generally the case that the higher up in the organizational hierarchy an individual is, the less you will find online about that individual.

No matter what type of career you choose, work you do or what to do, managing your online reputation can be critical for both obtaining and maintaining employment. (①) It's important that you consider how you wish to "brand" yourself on the Internet — what perceptions you want others to have of you. (②) This may mean changing information about yourself that is currently available online, taking steps to publish and promote new information about yourself, and generally exercising care about what you say and do online. (③) Generally, the current rules follow the dictum that "less is more". (④) Try "Googling" a few individuals, and you will find this is the case. Additionally, the information that you do find about this individual is almost always the same, no matter what site you view it on.

정답 ④

해설 "조직의 위계에서 한 개인의 위치가 높으면 높을수록, 당신이 온라인상에서 그 개인에 대해 찾을 수 있는 정보가 더 적어진다는 것이 일반적이다".를 알아보기 위해서 행하는 것이 구글링이다.

해석 **hierarchy** 계급, 계층조직 **exercise care** 조심하다 **dictum** 격언, 금언 **take a step** 조치를 취하다 **this is the case** 사실이다

해석 당신이 어떤 종류의 직업을 선택하고, 당신이 하는 일 혹은 해야 할 일이 무엇이든지, 온라인상에서 당신의 평판을 관리하는 것은 직장을 구하고 유지하는 데 있어서 중요하다. ① 당신이 인터넷상에서 당신을 어떤 브랜드로 만들기를 원하는지 — 다른 사람들이 당신에 대해 어떤 인식을 갖기를 원하는지 — 를 고려하는 것이 중요하다. ② 이것은 현재 온라인상에서 이용 가능한 당신 자신에 대한 정보를 바꾸고, 당신 자신에 대한 새로운 정보를 공개하고 홍보하는 여러 조치를 취하고, 일반적으로 온라인 상에서 당신이 말하고 행동하는 것에 대해 신중해야 하는 것을 의미한다. ③ 일반적으로 (온라인상에서) 현재의 규칙은 "더 적을수록 더 많다"라는 금언을 따른다. ④ 비록 이것은 어느 정도 세대 간의 문제이긴 하지만, 사실상, 조직의 위계에서 한 개인의 위치가 높으면 높을수록, 당신이 온라인상에서 그 개인에 대해 찾을 수 있는 정보가 더 적어진다는 것이 일반적이다. 만일 당신이 몇몇 개인들을 대상으로 구글링(검색)을 시도해본다면 당신은 이것이 사실이라는 것을 발견하게 될 것이다. 게다가, 그 개인에 대해서 당신이 찾아낸 정보는, 당신이 다른 어떤 사이트에서 그 개인에 대한 정보를 찾는다고 해도 거의 항상 동일하다.

13 다음 글에서 전체 흐름과 관계없는 문장은? 2017 기상직 9급

The more digital and high-tech the world becomes, the greater the need to still feel the human touch, nurtured by close relationships and social connections. ① There are growing concerns that, as the fourth industrial revolution deepens our individual and collective relationships with technology, it may negatively affect our social skills and ability to empathize. We see this already happening. ② A 2010 study by a research team at the University of Michigan found a 40% decline in empathy among college students today with most of this decline coming after 2000. ③ According to MIT's Sherry Turke, most of the teenagers willingly unplug, while playing sports or having a meal with family or friends. ④ With face-to-face conversations crowded out by online interactions, there are fears that an entire generation of young people consumed by social media is struggling to listen, make eye contact or read body language.

정답 ③

해설 이 글은 온라인과 디지털 미디어 사회 속에서의 폐단에 대한 글인데 ③은 젊은이들이 온라인을 멀리하고 있다는 반대 주장을 담고 있으므로 글의 흐름에 적절치 않다.

어휘 nurture 영양분을 주다, 키우다 collective 집단적인 empathize 공감하다 unplug 플러그를 뽑다 crowd out 몰아내다 interaction 상호작용 consumed by 사로잡힌

해석 세상이 점점 더 디지털화되고 첨단 기술이 될수록 긴밀한 관계와 사회적 관계를 통해 커지게 되는 인간의 손길을 느낄 필요가 커집니다. ① 제4차 산업 혁명이 기술과의 개인적 및 집단적 관계를 심화시킴에 따라 우리의 사회적 기술과 공감 능력에 부정적인 영향을 미칠 수 있다는 우려가 커지고 있습니다. 우리는 이미 이런 일이 벌어지고 있는 것을 보고 있습니다. ② 미시간 대학의 연구팀이 2010년에 실시한 연구에 따르면 오늘날 대학생들의 공감도는 2000년 이후 40%가 감소한 것으로 나타났습니다. ③ MIT의 Sherry Turke에 따르면 대부분의 10대 청소년들은 플러그를 기꺼이 뽑고 스포츠를 하거나 가족이나 친구들과 식사를 하고 있습니다. ④ 온라인 대화로 인해 얼굴을 마주하는 대화는 밀려난 상황에서 소셜 미디어에 의해 사로잡힌 전체 젊은이 세대는 듣거나 눈을 마주 치거나 신체 언어를 읽는 데 어려움을 겪고 있다는 공포감이 있습니다.

14 다음 글에서 전체 흐름과 관계없는 문장은?

One suggestion for consumers is to buy no-brand items instead of famous brands. ① No-brand items in supermarkets come in plain packages. ② These products are cheaper because manufacturers don't spend much money on packaging or advertising. ③ You should find out the items that are on sale and decide if you really need those things. ④ The quality, however, is usually identical to the quality of well-known brands. In the same way, when buying clothes, you can often find high quality and low prices in brands which are not famous.

정답 ③

해설 유명 상표의 상품보다는 상표 등록이 되어 있지 않은 상품을 구입하라고 제안하는 내용의 글이므로, 할인 중인 상품 구매를 권유하는 ③이 글 전체의 흐름에서 벗어난다.

어휘 brand 상표; 낙인; 낙인찍다 item 항목; 상품, 품목 plain 평범한; 명백한 package 포장 identical 동일한

해석 소비자들을 위한 한 가지 제안은 유명 상표보다는 상표 등록이 되어 있지 않은 상품을 사라는 것이다. ① 슈퍼마켓에 있는 상표 등록이 되어 있지 않은 상품은 평범하게 포장되어 나온다. ② 제조업자들이 포장이나 광고에 많은 돈을 들이지 않기 때문에 이러한 상품들의 가격이 더 싸다. ③ 당신은 할인 중인 물건을 발견할 경우 그러한 물건이 정말 필요한지 어떤지를 결정해야만 한다. ④ 그러나, 그 물질은 유명 상표의 질과 대개 똑같다. 마찬가지로, 옷을 살 때에도 당신은 종종 유명하지 않은 상표 가운데 품질이 우수하고 낮은 가격의 물건을 찾을 수 있다.

15 글의 흐름상 가장 어색한 문장은? 2017 국가직 9급

Children's book awards have proliferated in recent years; today, there are well over 100 different awards and prizes by a variety of organizations. ① The awards may be given for books of a specific genre or simply for the best of all children's books published within a given time period. An award may honor a particular book or an author for a lifetime contribution to the world of children's literature. ② Most children's book awards are chosen by adults, but now a growing number of children's choice book awards exist. The larger national awards given in most countries are the most influential and have helped considerably to raise public awareness about the fine books being published for young readers. ③ An award ceremony for outstanding services to the publishing industry is put on hold. ④ Of course, readers are wise not to put too much faith in award-winning books. An award doesn't necessarily mean a good reading experience, but it does provide a starting place when choosing books.

정답 ③

해설 이 글의 소재는 아동문학상이다. 그런데 ③은 출판 산업의 기여에 대한 시상식을 언급하고 있으므로 글의 흐름에 적절하지 않다.

어휘 proliferate 급증하다 a variety of 다양한 contribution 기여 influential 영향력 있는, 중요한 awareness 인식, 의식 faith 신념

해석 최근 아동문학상이 급증하고 있다. 오늘날 다양한 기관에서 주는 100여 개가 넘는 다양한 상이 있다. ① 이 상들은 특정 장르의 책에 주어지거나 단순히 일정 기간 안에 출간된 모든 아동문학 중 최고의 도서에 주어질 수 있다. 상은 특정한 책이나 아동 문학 세계에 기여한 작가의 일생에 수여할 수 있다. ② 대부분의 아동문학상은 어른들에 의해 선택된다. 그러나 현재는 점점 증가하는 어린이들이 선정한 도서상이 존재한다. 대부분의 국가에서 주어지는 더 큰 국가적인 상은 가장 영향력이 있으며, 어린 독자를 위해 출간되는 훌륭한 책들이라는 대중적인 인식을 높이는 데 상당히 기여한다. ③ 출판 산업의 뛰어난 공헌에 대한 한 시상식이 보류되었다. ④ 물론 독자들은 수상한 책에 대해 너무 많은 신뢰를 주지 않을 정도로 현명하다. 상이 반드시 좋은 독서 경험을 의미하지는 않지만, 책을 선정할 때 훌륭한 출발점을 제공해 준다.

16 다음 중 글의 흐름상 적절치 않은 문장을 고르시오.

Virtual reality provides an open field for various and even multiple identities and identifications. In virtual environments, people are not confined to any one stable unifying subject position, but can adopt multiple identities (either serially or simultaneously). ① From the graphical avatars adopted to represent users in virtual environments, to the handles used in chat rooms, to something as simple as multiple e-mail accounts, all of these can be used to produce and maintain virtual identities. Identity in virtual reality becomes even more malleable than in real life, and can be as genuine and constitutive of the self as the latter. ② Whether Platonist, Cartesian, or Kantian in orientation, in all of these systems there is a shared notion of a unified and unifying subject whose existence provides a ground for knowledge, action, and personal identity. ③ Ongoing or adopted temporarily, identities can be altered, edited, fabricated, or set aside entirely. ④ Thus, virtual reality opens the possibility not only of recreating space and time, but the self as well. The subject is produced anew as it comes to occupy this new space.

정답 ②

해설 이 글의 소재는 가상 현실 내에서의 개인의 '주체성'에 관한 글인데 ②에서 말하는 주체는 철학적 주체를 언급하고 있으므로 ②는 전체적인 흐름에 맞지 않는다.

어휘 virtual 실제상의, 사실상의; 가상의 stable 안정된, 견고한, 견실한 unify 통합하다, 통일하다
serially 연속적으로, 계속해서 simultaneously 동시에, 일제히 malleable 순응성이 있는, 유순한
constitutive 구성하는, 본질의 fabricate 제조하다; 위조하다

해석 가상 현실은 여러 가지의, 그리고 심지어는 다중의, 정체성과 신분을 가지는 것에 대해 열린 장을 제공하고 있다. 가상의 환경에서 사람들은 단지 하나의 확정되고 통일된 주체로서의 자리에만 국한되어 있지 않고 여러 개의 정체성을 (차례대로 또는 동시에) 가질 수 있다. ① 가상 환경에서 사용자를 나타내기 위해 사용되는 그래픽 아바타로부터 해도실에서 사용되는 핸들에 이르기까지, 그리고 여러 개의 이메일 계정과 같이 아주 단순한 것들에 이르기까지, 이 모든 것들은 가상 신분을 만들어내고 유지하는 데에 사용될 수 있다. 가상 현실에서의 정체성은 실제 생활에서보다 훨씬 더 유연하고 실제만큼이나 자신의 진정하고도 본질적인 것일 수가 있다. ② 지향성에 있어서 플라톤식이나 데카르트식이나 칸트식이나 이 모든 체계에는 그의 존재가 지식, 행동, 그리고 개인의 정체성의 기반을 제공하는, 통일된 그리고 통일하는 주체라는 공통된 개념이 존재한다. ③ 지속적이거나 잠시 사용하거나 정체성은 변경되고, 편집되고, 조작되고, 완전히 버려질 수도 있다. ④ 따라서, 가상현실은 시간과 공간을 새로 만들어낼 뿐만 아니라 자신조차도 새로 만들어내는 가능성을 열어준다. 주체는 이 새로운 공간을 점하면서 새로이 만들어진다.

문덕 영어
독해

주제별 어휘

Theme 01 인체와 생물

Theme 02 사회생활

Theme 03 과학

Theme

01 인체와 생물

01 생물학(Biology)

amphibian	양서동물
animate	살아있는, 생기 있는
anomalous	불규칙한, 정상이 아닌
arboreal	수목의
barren	불모의, 불임의
bloom	(관상식물의) 꽃
blossom	(과수의) 꽃
botany	식물학
branch	가지
bud	싹, 눈
bunch	송이
carnivore	육식동물
cell	세포
cellulose	섬유소
ecology	생태학
eugenics	우생학, 인종 개량학
evolution	진화(론)
extinct	멸종한
feather	깃털
fertile	비옥한; 다산의
fin	지느러미
fledged	깃털이 다 자란, 날 수 있게 된
flock	동물 또는 새의 떼
flutter	퍼덕이다
fungus	균류
germinate	싹트다
herbivore	초식동물
herd	짐승의 떼
heterogeneous	이종의, 이질적인
homogeneous	동종의
horticulture	원예학
howl	울부짖다
inanimate	생명이 없는
larva	애벌레, 유충
lure	미끼새
mammal	포유동물
mammoth	매머드
membrane	얇은 막
metabolism	신진대사, 소화과정
metamorphosis	변태
mutation	변화
node	(식물의) 마디
optimum	최적(의)
organism	유기체
ornithology	조류학
parasite	기생충
paw	(발톱 있는 동물의) 발
pesticide	살충제
petal	꽃잎
photosynthesis	광합성
physiology	생리학
poach	밀렵하다
pollen	꽃가루
predatory	약탈하는

prey	사냥감, 먹이
proliferate	증식[번식]하다
prolific	다산의, 비옥한
propagate	번식[증식]시키다
protoplasm	원형질
reptile	파충류
roar	으르렁거리는 소리
rodent	설치류의 (동물)
sap	수액, 활력
scale	비늘
school	물고기의 떼
seed	씨, 종자
serpent	(크고 독 있는) 뱀
serpentine	꾸불꾸불한
shrub	관목, 키 작은 나무
snare	덫, 올가미
spawn	(물고기, 개구리의) 알
species	(생물) 종(種)
sprout	싹이 트다, 잎을 내다
stem	줄기
sterile	메마른, 불모의
sting	독침(毒針)
taxidermy	박제술
thorn	(식물의) 가시
transplant	이식하다
trap	덫, 올가미
twitter	(새가) 지저귀다
verdant	신록의, 푸른 잎이 무성한
wreath	화관, 화환

02 신체(Body), 오감(Five Senses)

acoustic	청각의, 소리의
askance	곁눈질하여
auditory	귀의, 청각 기관의
bald	(머리가) 벗어진, 대머리의
balmy	은은한, 부드러운, 위안이 되는
beard	턱수염
cardiac	심장의
choke	질식시키다
chubby	토실토실한
circumcision	할례(유대교 따위의 의식)
comely	잘생긴, 미모의, 아름다운
dimple	보조개
dorsal	등의
eavesdropper	엿듣는 사람
effluvial	악취의
exhale	(숨) 내쉬다, (말) 내뱉다
figure	용모
flesh	살, 고기, 근육
fragrant	냄새 좋은, 향기로운
gasp	헐떡거리다, 숨이 차다
glimpse	흘끗 봄
hoarse	목쉰, 쉰 목소리의, 귀에 거슬리는
inaudible	알아들을 수 없는
inhale	(공기 따위를) 빨아들이다, 흡입하다
malodorous	고약한 냄새가 나는
mustache	콧수염
nasal	코의, 콧소리의
obese	살찐, 뚱뚱한
olfactory	후각의, 냄새의
palpable	손으로 만질 수 있는
pant	헐떡거리다
profile	옆모습

pulse	맥박
raucous	목이 쉰
redolent	~의 향기가 나는, 향기로운
resonant	공명하는
respire	호흡하다
sigh	한숨 쉬다
slender	홀쭉한, 가냘픈
smother	질식시키다
stare	응시하다
stubby	땅딸막한
suffocate	호흡을 곤란하게 하다
tactile	촉각의, 촉각이 있는
tepid	미지근한
vapid	활기가 없는
visible	(눈에) 보이는
vociferous	큰 소리로 외치는
wrinkle	주름지다

03 의학(Medicine), 건강(Health)

aberrant	변태의
abortion	유산, 낙태
acupuncture	침술
affliction	(심신의) 고통, 질병
allay	고통 등을 덜다
alleviate	완화[경감]시키다
anatomy	해부학
anemia	빈혈증
anesthesia	마취, (지각) 마비
anesthetic	마취제
anodyne	진통제
anorexia	식욕부진
antibiotic	항생제
antidote	해독제
aseptic	무균의; 방부제
autopsy	시체 해부
bruise	멍, 타박상(= contusion)
buxom	(여자가) 건강하고 쾌활한
cadaverous	시체 같은, 창백한
callous	(피부 등이) 굳어진, 무감각한
carnal	육체의
cerebral	대뇌의
chicken pox	수두
cholera	콜레라
chronic	만성적인
claustrophobia	폐쇄공포증
coma	(의학) 혼수
complexion	안색, 피부색
conception	임신
contagious	(접촉) 전염성의
contraception	피임(법)
convalescence	(건강의) 회복
corporal	육체의, 신체의
corpulent	뚱뚱한, 살찐
cure-all	만병통치약, 치료법
deaf	귀머거리의
debilitate	쇠약하게 하다
decay	썩다, 쇠하다
deceased	사망한
decrepit	노쇠한, 늙어빠진
demise	사망, 서거
dental	치아의, 치과의
denture	틀니
diarrhea	설사
disability	장애, 무력
disinfectant	소독약
dissect	해부하다

dose	(약의) 1회 복용량
drug addiction	마약 중독
dumb	벙어리의
endemic	(병이) 풍토성인
enervate	기력을 빼앗다
euthanasia	안락사(= mercy killing)
excretion	배설(물)
exhale	(숨을) 내쉬다
exterminate	(병, 생각을) 근절하다
eye bank	안구 은행
feeble	연약한
fever	(병으로 인한) 열
flu	유행성 감기
frail	허약한
frostbite	동상
gallstone	담석
gastric ulcer	위궤양
gene	유전자
haggard	수척한, 말라빠진
hallucinogenic	환각(제)의
handicap	장애
headache	두통
heart attack	심장 마비
heart stroke	심장 발작
heart transplant	심장 이식
hemorrhage	출혈
hepatitis	간염
hereditary	유전성의
heredity	유전, 형질 유전
hiccup	딸꾹질(하다)
hygiene	위생학, 건강법, 청결
hypochondria	우울증
hypotension	저혈압
immune	면역(성)의
immunity	면역
impair	손상시키다
incurable	불치의
indigestion	소화 불량
inertia	무력증
infection	감염
influenza	인플루엔자, 독감
inherent	선천적인, 타고난
inherit	유전하다
injection	주사
inoculate	(예방) 접종하다
insulin	당뇨병 치료제
invigorate	기운을 돋우다
jaundice	황달
lame	절름발이의
latent	잠복한, 잠재적인
lethal	치명적인
leukemia	백혈병
lump	혹, 종기, 부스럼
lunacy	정신 이상, 광기
maim	불구로 만들다
malady	(만성적인) 병, 질병
malaria	말라리아
malignant	악성의
malnutrition	영양실조
measles	홍역, 마진, 풍진
mental asylum	정신병원
mental disease	정신병
migraine	편두통
miscarriage	유산
mold	곰팡이
monomania	편집증
mortality	사망률
mutilate	불구로 만들다

narcotic	마취제
nausea	메스꺼움, 구토증
nerve	신경; 용기
neuralgia	신경통
neurology	신경학
neurosis	노이로제
obesity	비만, 비대
obsession	강박관념
ocular	눈의, 시각적인
ointment	연고
operation	수술
optic	눈의, 시력의
organ transplant	장기이식
pain killer	진통제
pale	(얼굴이) 창백한
palliate	(병세를) 누그러지게 하다
panacea	만병통치약
paralysis	마비; 중풍
pathology	병리학
pill	환약, 알약(= tablet)
plague	역병, 전염병
plastic surgery	성형외과
plethora	과다; 적혈구 과다증
pneumonia	폐렴
polio	소아마비
posthumous	사후의
pregnancy	임신
prescription	처방전
pulse	맥박; 맥박이 뛰다
quarantine	(전염병 예방을 위한) 격리
rabid	광견병에 걸린
recuperate	회복하다
respire	호흡하다
revitalize	원기를 회복시키다
rheumatism	류머티즘
robust	튼튼한
salubrious	(기후가) 건강에 좋은
salutary	(심신에) 유익한
sanatorium	요양소
sanguine	혈색이 좋은, 낙천적인
sanitary	위생적인(= hygienic)
sanity	건전한 정신
scar	흉터, 상처, 자국
sedative	진정제
senile dementia	노인성 치매증
senility	노화, 노쇠
side effect	부작용
smallpox	천연두
soporific	최면제, 수면제
stalwart	키가 크고 건장한
stomach cancer	위암
stomachache	복통, 위통
stout	튼튼한
stroke	뇌졸중
sturdy	튼튼한
surgeon	외과 의사
tender	약한, 부드러운
therapy	치료, 요법
toothache	치통
transfuse	수혈(하다)
transfusion	혈관 주사, 수혈
trauma	외상, 정신적 충격
tuberculosis	결핵
tumor	종양, 종기
uncomely	아름답지 못한, 못생긴
vaccinate	예방접종을 하다
vertigo	현기증, 어지러움
vigorous	원기 왕성한

virulent	(독성이) 강한
vivisect	생체해부하다
vulnerable	상처를 입기 쉬운
wound	부상, 상처

04 스포츠(Sports), 오락(Entertainment)

amateur	아마추어
amusement	즐거움, 재미
arena	투기장, 경쟁 장소
arrow	화살
athlete	운동가, 경기자
award	수여하다, 상을 주다
basketball	농구
bound	튀어 오르다, 튀다
coach	지도하다
convivial	연회를 좋아하는
defeat	패배시키다
distraction	기분 전환, 오락
diversion	기분 전환
draw	비기다
exercise	운동
gamble	도박을 하다
gymnasium	체육관, 실내경기장
hilarious	명랑한, 들떠서 떠드는
javelin	투창
kinetic	운동의
leisure	여가, 자유 시간
match	시합, 경쟁, 경기
mischievous	장난을 좋아하는
outpoint	점수로 이기다
pastime	기분 전환, 유희
pavilion	(야외 경기장 등의) 관람석
pentathlon	근대 5종 경기
ping-pong	탁구
pitch	(공을) 던지다, 내던지다
prizeman	수상자
recreation	기분 전환, 오락
referee	중재인, 심판원
relaxation	긴장 완화
rivalry	경쟁, 대항
score	득점(기록)
stadium	육상 경기장
synchronize	동시에 일어나다
tennis	테니스, 정구
tie	(경기) 동점이 되다
tournament	경기 대회
umpire	심판, 중재자(= judge)
volleyball	배구

05 주거(Housing)

abide	머물다, 살다, 지속하다
abode	거주, 주소, 주거
accommodate	숙박시키다, 적응시키다
cohabitation	동거
cottage	(시골의) 작은집
denizen	주민, 거주자
domestic	가정의, 본국의
domicile	거주지, 주소
dormitory	(대학 따위의) 기숙사
dwell	살다, 거주하다
expatriate	국외로 추방하다
hamlet	작은 마을, 부락
hanger	격납고, 차고
household	가족, 세대, 한 집안

housekeeper	주부, 가정부
hut	오두막
immigrant	(타국에서의) 이주민
lease	임대차; 임대하다
lodge	숙박[하숙]시키다
migrant	이주자
nursing home	요양소, 진료소
occupation	거주, 점유
orphan's home	고아원
rent	지대, 집세; 임대하다
reside	살다
residence	거주지, 주택
slum	빈민굴, 슬럼가
tenant	(토지의) 차용자, 소작인

06 요리(Cooking)

acetic	(맛이) 신
acrid	매운, 쓴
alimentary	영양을 공급하는
antiseptic	방부(성)의; 방부제
appetite	식욕
cafeteria	카페테리아(셀프서비스 식당)
cloy	(단 것을) 물리도록 먹이다
condiment	양념, 조미료
cuisine	요리법
culinary	요리의, 주방(용)의
devour	게걸스럽게 먹다
dipsomania	음주광, 알코올 중독
edible	식용에 적합한
epicure	미식가, 식도락가
ferment	효소, 발효
gastronomy	미식학
glut	과식
glutton	대식가, 폭식가
gluttonous	많이 먹는, 게걸들린
gorge	게걸스레 먹다, 배불리 먹다
grind	(맷돌로) 갈다, 으깨다
hangover	숙취
ingredient	성분, (요리의) 재료
insipid	싱거운, 맛없는, 담백한
intoxicate	취하게 하다
jar	단지, 항아리
nutritive	영양이 되는
omnivorous	무엇이나 먹는, 잡식의
palatable	(음식 등이) 입에 맞는
peel	(과일 등의) 껍질을 벗기다
piquant	(맛 등이) 매운, 얼얼한
pot	단지, 항아리
potable	마시기에 알맞은
preserve	(설탕)절임으로 하다, (과일을) 저장하다, 보존하다
protein	단백질
rancid	썩은 냄새가 나는
ravenous	몹시 굶주린
recipe	요리법
roas	(고기, 감자를) 불에 익히다, 굽다
rot	썩다, 부패하다
savor	맛, 풍미
seasoning	양념, 조미료
sift	체로 치다, 조리질하다
squash	으깨다
squeeze	짜다
stale	(음식 따위가) 상한, 신선하지 않은
stew	천천히 끓이다
succulent	즙이 많은
surfeit	과식(하게 하다); 과다, 과도

tart	시큼한, 신맛이 나는
tray	쟁반
utensil	가정용품, 부엌세간, 도구
voracious	게걸스레 먹는, 폭식하는

07 감정(Emotions), 성격(Character)

abhor	몹시 싫어하다, 혐오하다
abject	비참한, 절망적인
abominate	지겨워하다, 혐오하다
acrimony	표독스러움, 신랄함
adore	숭배하다
affection	애정, 호의
aghast	어안이 벙벙한
agile	몸이 재빠른, 기민한
alacrity	기민함
ambitious	야망에 찬
amiable	상냥한, 호감을 주는
amicable	우호적인, 평화적인
animosity	증오, 악의, 적개심
antipathy	반감, 혐오
apathy	무관심
approbation	허가
astonish	놀라게 하다
audacity	대담무쌍, 뻔뻔스러움
auspicious	길조의, 경사스러운
averse	싫어하는
avid	탐욕스러운, 열심인
baffle	당황하게 하다
beatific	행복에 넘친
bemoan	슬퍼하다, 애도하다
blithe	즐거운, 쾌활한, 유쾌한
bravado	허세

buoyant	쾌활한, 낙천적인
chagrin	분함, 유감
charity	자비심
cherish	소중히 하다, 귀여워하다
circumspect	신중한
cloying	물리는, 넌더리나는
coax	감언으로 설득하다
commiserate	~을 가엾게 여기다
compassion	동정, 연민
complacent	자기만족의
composure	침착, 평정
conceited	자만에 찬, 건방진, 우쭐한
concerned	걱정하는, 염려스러운
conciliatory	달래는(듯한), 회유적인
condole	위로하다
congenial	마음이 맞는
console	위로하다, (슬픔 · 고통을) 달래다
cordial	따뜻한, 성심성의의
crave	열망[갈망]하다
deject	기를 죽이다
deplore	한탄하다, 애도하다
depression	침울, 우울; 불황
despair	절망, 자포자기
despondent	낙담한, 풀이 죽은
detest	몹시 싫어하다, 혐오하다
disappoint	실망시키다
discomfit	좌절시키다, 당황하게 하다
discompose	불안하게 하다
disgusting	구역질나는, 정떨어지는
dismal	슬픈, 우울한
dispassionate	냉정한, 공평한, 침착한
distress	고통, 빈곤
doleful	슬픈, 쓸쓸한
dolorous	슬픈, 마음 아픈, 괴로운

downcast	기가 꺾인, 풀죽인
dubious	의심스러운
effeminate	여성적인, 나약한
elated	의기양양한, 우쭐대는
elegant	우아한, 세련된
empathy	감정 이입, 공감
enmity	증오, 적의
enthusiastic	열광적인, 열렬한
erratic	괴상한, 이상한
esteem	존경(하다)
euphoria	황홀감, 도취감
exasperate	성나게 하다
exult	크게 기뻐하다
fanatics	열광자, 광신자
felicity	더 없는 행복
fervent	뜨거운, 정열적인, 열심인
fond	애정 있는, 다정한
forlorn	버려진, 불행한
fret	초조하게 하다
furious	성난, 맹렬한
gay	명랑한, 즐거운, 쾌활한
giggle	킥킥 웃다
grumble	불평하다
gullible	속기 쉬운
hedonist	쾌락주의자
hideous	무시무시한, 소름끼치는
hilarious	즐거운, 유쾌한
homely	친절한; 검소한, 수수한
hospitable	붙임성 있는
humiliate	창피를 주다, 굴욕감을 느끼게 하다
impassioned	감명적인, 감격한
impatient	인내심 없는, 초조해 하는
impertinent	버릇없는, 건방진
implausible	터무니없는
importunate	귀찮게 조르는
impudent	뻔뻔스러운, 건방진, 염치없는
incense	성나게 하다
indignity	모욕, 경멸
indisposed	기분이 언짢은
indolent	나태한, 게으른
indulgent	관대한, 멋대로 하게 하는
ingenuous	순진한, 솔직한
insatiable	만족할 줄 모르는, 탐욕스러운
insensible	인사불성의, 의식을 잃은, 무감각한
insolent	무례한, 거만한
intrepid	두려움을 모르는
invidious	비위에 거슬리는, 불쾌한
irascible	성마른
irritate	화나게 하다, 자극하다
jealous	질투심 많은
jocund	즐거운
jovial	쾌활한
jubilant	환호하는, 기뻐하는
lament	슬퍼하다, 애통해하다
lamentable	슬퍼할, 통탄할
lassitude	나른함, 권태
loathe	몹시 싫어하다, 혐오하다
malevolent	악의 있는, 심술궂은
malignant	악의에 찬
maudlin	감상적인, 눈물을 잘 흘리는
mawkish	역겨운, 혐오스러운
melancholy	우울한, 침울한
misanthrope	염세가
misogynist	여성 차별주의자
mollify	달래다, 진정시키다
mourn	슬퍼하다, 애통해하다
nonchalant	무관심한, 냉정한
obstinate	고집 센, 완고한

offensive	불쾌한, 무례한
ominous	불길한
outrage	격분시키다; 난폭
peccadillo	작은 결점, 가벼운 죄
peevish	성마른, 안달하는
perplex	당혹케 하다, 난감하게 하다
perturb	마음을 어지럽히다, 불안하게 하다
philanthropy	박애, 인자, 자선
phlegmatic	냉담한
plaintive	애처로운, 슬픈 듯한
pompous	거만한, 건방진
predilection	편애
prefer	~보다 좋다, ~을 좋아하다
presumptuous	주제넘은, 건방진
quandary	곤혹, 당혹, 궁지
querulous	불평을 하는
rage	격노, 분노
rancor	적의, 원한
rattle	당황한, 어리둥절한
relent	(마음이) 누그러지다
relentless	가차 없는, 무자비한
repugnant	비위에 거슬리는, 불쾌한
repulsion	혐오감
resent	원망하다
revere	존경하다
revolting	역겨운, 혐오스러운
scrupulous	양심적인; 신중한, 꼼꼼한
sensational	선정적인, 인기를 노리는
sensibility	감각, 감수성
sensible	분별 있는
sentient	감각이 있는
sentiment	감정, 정서
sentimental	감정적인, 감상적인
shrewd	영리한, 빈틈없는
sob	흐느껴 울다
stolid	둔감한, 신경이 무딘
sullen	시무룩한, 음울한
susceptible	감정에 좌우되기 쉬운
sympathetic	동정하는, 호의하는
tactful	재치 있는, 꾀바른
tenacious	고집 센, 완강한
timid	겁 많은, 두려워하는
toady	아첨꾼
tolerate	참다, 견디다
vainglorious	허영심 강한
vehement	격렬한, 열심인
venerate	존경하다, 공경하다
vim	(구어) 정력, 생기, 활기
vivacious	쾌활한, 명랑한
weep	울다, 눈물을 흘리다
wily	교활한, 잔꾀를 부리는
winsome	매력 있는
wretched	가엾은, 비참한
yearn	동경하다, 사모하다
zealot	열광자

Theme
02 사회생활

01 정치(Politics)

abdicate	퇴위하다
abeyance	중지, 미정
abrogate	폐지하다
accede	동의하다, 취임하다
actuate	개선하다
administration	통치; 행정부
ameliorate	개선하다
anarchy	무정부 상태
arrogate	(부당하게) 빼앗다
Attorney General	법무장관
autocrat	독재자
autonomy	자치(권)
bureaucrat	관료
cabinet	내각
campaign	(일련의) 군사 행동, (선거) 운동
candidate	후보자; 지원자
canvass	선거 운동하다; 조사하다
caucus	간부회의, 이익단체
cede	양도하다, 인정하다
clique	당파, 파벌
coalition	연합
collusion	공모
concordant	화합하는, 조화하는
confederate	동맹(하다)
congress	의회, 국회
consensus	일치, 여론
constituent	성분, 요소; 선거구민
convoluted	뒤얽힌, 복잡한
delegate	(권한 등을) 위임하다, 맡기다
democrat	민주주의자
denunciation	탄핵, 위협
deputy	대리인
despotism	독재정치
diplomat	외교관
dogmatic	독단적인
emissary	밀사, 간첩
empower	~에게 권한을 주다
envoy	(외교) 사절, 특사
exile	추방; 망명(자)
expel	추방하다
expire	만기가 되다
fidelity	충실, 충성
filibuster	불법 침입자, 혁명 선동자
foment	(반란 등을) 조장하다
harangue	열변, 장황한 이야기
hegemony	패권, 주도권
impeach	탄핵하다, 고발하다
imperious	고압적인, 긴급한
inaugurate	취임시키다
insurrection	반란, 폭동
intervene	끼어들다; 중재하다
intransigent	고집스러운, 비협조적인
inviolable	거역할 수 없는
local autonomy	지방자치

malfeasance	위법행위, 부정
mandate	명령, 통치의 위임
maxim	격언, 금언
mediate	중재하다
megalomania	과도한 권력욕, 과대망상증
oligarchy	과두제, 소수독재 정치
pandemic	전국적으로 유행하는 병
paradigm	보기, 범례, 모범
paramount	최고의, 탁월한
parity	동등, 유사
patronize	보호하다, 후원하다
plutocracy	금권정치
polarize	양극화되다
precept	가르침, 교훈
predominate	우세하다, 지배하다
prime minister	수상, 국무총리
promulgate	공표하다
proxy	대리(인)
puissant	힘센, 권력이 있는
realm	영역, 왕국
reconciliation	조정, 화해
regime	제도, 정권, 사회 조직
republican	공화국의; 공화당원
reshuffle	개각, 내각의 인물교체
Secretary of State	국무장관
Senate	상원
succumb	굴복하다, 지다
summit meeting	정상회담
Surgeon General	공중 위생국 장관
tenure	(관직의) 보유(기간), (땅의) 사용 (기간)
topple	전복시키다, 타도하다
tyranny	독재정치
unanimity	만장일치
uprising	반란
Vice President	부통령

02 사회(Society)

affiliate	가입시키다(하다)
akin	친척인, 유사한
alienate	소외하다
anthropology	인류학
assimilate	동화하다, (지식 등을) 흡수하다
banquet	연회
barbaric	야만인의
census	인구조사
clan	일족, 씨족
clannish	파벌적인
cognate	동족의; 친족
communal	공동체의
compatriot	동포
conception	임신
congregate	모이다, 모으다
conjugal	혼인의
connubial	결혼의
consanguinity	혈연관계
convention	모임; 전통
demography	인구통계
depopulate	인구를 줄이다
disperse	해산하다, 흩어지다
divorce	이혼
engagement	약속; 약혼
ethnology	민족학, 인종학
famine	기아, 기근
folk	(허물없는 사이의 표현) 사람들
forsake	(벗·가족을) 버리다

foster	양육하다, 육성하다
fraternal	형제의
heterogeneous	이종으로 된
indigenous	토착의
isolation	격리, 고립
marital	결혼의
maternal	어머니의
matriarch	여자가장
miscegenation	인종혼합
mulatto	흑백혼혈아
multiracial	다민족의, 다인종의
multitude	다수, 대중
ostracize	추방하다
overspill	인구과잉
polygamy	일부다처
populace	평민, 민중
pregnant	다산의, 풍족한; 임신한
progeny	자손
race	인종
racialism	인종차별주의
seclude	격리하다
segregate	분리하다, 격리하다
sinecure	(명목뿐인) 한직
starvation	기아, 굶주림
surname	성
tenet	(특정 집단의) 주의, 신조
throng	군중, 다수
unattached	약혼 하지 않은

03 경제(Economy)

accrue	(이자 등이) 붙다, (결과로서) 생기다
affiliate	부속시키다; 계열 회사
aggregate	합계; 총계가 ~이다
ancillary	보조의, 부수적인
appropriate	(돈의 사용처를) 책정하다
arrear	연체금
balance	(계좌의) 잔고
bater	물물 교환하다
beget	생기게 하다, 초래하다
bilk	떼어먹고 달아나다
boost	(값·삯을) 끌어올리다, (생산량을) 증가시키다
break-even point	손익분기점
broker	중개인
cache	은닉물, 저장물
cede	양도하다
clientele	소송 의뢰인
collaborator	공동연구자, 합작자
collateral	담보(물)
compensate	~에게 보상하다
confiscate	몰수하다
conglomerate	집합체, 복합기업; 응집하다
consolidate	합병하다, 강화하다
consumer price index	소비자 물가지수
counterfeit	모조품, 가짜, 모조의
customs	세관
customs declaration form	여행자 휴대품 신고서
debt	빚, 부채
default	채무 불이행
deficit	적자
deposit	입금(예금)하다
deteriorate	(가치를) 떨어뜨리다
disembarkation card	입국신고서
dividend	배당금
divulge	(비밀을) 폭로하다

embargo	(무역) 제재
embezzle	횡령하다
emulate	경쟁하다, 모방하다
endorse	배서하다, 승인하다
entrepreneur	기업가
executive	경영진, 기업가
exit	출구 전략
extravagant	낭비하는, 과도한
fasten	(벨트를) 매다
fluctuate	변동하다
forge	(문서 따위를) 위조하다
frugal	검소한
gain and loss	이익과 손실
GDP(Gross Domestic Product)	국내 총생산
GNP(Gross National Product)	국민 총생산
goods and service	재화와 용역
gratis	무료로, 공짜로
gross profit	총이익
headquarters	본부
incorporate	합병하다
indemnify	변상하다
inflation	인플레이션, 통화팽창
insurance	보험(계약)
lavish	아낌없이 주는
lay off	해고
levy	세금을 부과하다; 징집하다
liquidate	(빚을) 청산하다, 숙청하다
loan	빌려주다; 대출
lucrative	수지맞는, 유리한
M&A(Merger and Acquisition)	합병과 인수
marginal cost	한계비용
monopoly	독점(권)

mortgage	담보 대출
net profit	순이익
operating expense	운영비
opportunity cost	기회비용
parcel	소포
patent	특허
patron	후원자, 단골손님
peculate	횡령하다
pecuniary	금전상의
peddler	행상인
penurious	가난한
plummet	급락하다
plunge	폭락; 급락하다
pragmatic	실용적인
price freeze	물가동결
prodigal	낭비하는
production and consumption	생산과 소비
profuse	사치하는, 풍부한
prohibitive	엄청나게 비싼
propel	추진하다
proxy	대리인
quarantine	검역소
quid pro quo	(~에 대한) 보상으로 주는 것
reap	거두다, 수확하다
reasonable price	적정가
receptionist	접수 계원
recession	경기후퇴, 불황
reciprocal	상호간의
redeem	되찾다, 보상하다, 갚다
reimburse	변상하다
remiss	태만한
remittance	송금
remuneration	보상, 급료

requisition	(문서에 의한) 요구
reserve	예약하다
retail	소매, 소매의
retail price	소매가
retrench	긴축하다
scapegoat	남의 죄를 대신 지는 사람
secondhand	중고의
spinoff	파생적인
stable	안정된
status quo	현재의 상황
stockholder	주주
subordinate	하위의; 좌천시키다
subsidiary	자회사
subsidize	보조금을 지급하다
subterfuge	구실, 핑계
surveillance	감시, 감독
tariff	관세 (제도)
telegram	전보, 전신
transaction	처리, 거래
unemployment rate	실업률
usury	고리대금, 폭리
valuables	귀중품
vender(or)	상인
via	~을 매개로 하여
virtual currency	가상 화폐
wholesale price	도매가
withdraw	인출하다, 출금하다

04 법률(Law)

abet	부추기다, 선동하다
abscond	도망하다
accessory	(범행의) 종범[방조자]
accomplice	공범자
acquiesce	묵인하다
acquit	무죄석방하다
adjudicate	~로 판결하다
annul	무효로 하다, 폐지하다
arbitration	중재 재판, 조정
arraign	기소하다
attest to	증명 · 입증하다
aver	단언하다
bail	보석(금)
breach	위반, 파기
capital penalty	극형
capital punishment	사형
castigate	징계하다
clientele	소송의뢰인, 고객
clue	단서
collude	공모하다
concede	인정하다, 시인하다
confiscation	몰수
connive	묵인하다, 공모하다
conspire	공모하다
constitution	헌법; 체질, 구성
convict	유죄평결하다; 죄인, 범인
corroborate	확증하다
culprit	죄인, 범인, 원인
de facto	사실상의, 실질적인
deception	사기, 속임수
defraud	편취하다, 사취하다
delude	속이다
demur	이의(를 제기하다)
disinterested	공정한, 사심 없는
enact	(법을) 제정하다
epochal	획기적인
exculpate	무죄로 하다

extirpate	근절시키다
fraud	사기
gravity	중죄
illegitimate	불법의
impugn	비난하다
incriminate	고소하다
indict	기소하다
infraction	위반, 침해
infringe	(법규를) 위반하다
inquest	조사, 사인 규명
intrigue	음모(를 꾸미다)
inveigle	(남을 속여서) 꾀어 들이다
jury	배심원
life imprisonment	무기징역
machination	음모
malefactor	범법자
malice	악의
menace	협박
misdemeanor	경범죄
negligible	무가치한, 사소한
nolo contendere	불항쟁의 답변
ordinance	법령
outlaw	무법자
parole	가석방
perjure	위증케 하다
perjury	위증
perpetrate	(나쁜 것을) 범하다
phony	가짜의, 위조의
precedent	선례, 판결례
probation	집행유예
procure	획득하다, 조달하다
proponent	제안자; 변호사
proscribe	인권을 박탈하다, 법률의 밖에 두다
prosecute	기소하다; 수행하다
purloin	절취하다, 훔치다
recidivism	상습적 범행
refute	논박하다
reprieve	집행유예
respite	유예, 연기; (사형)집행유예
retroactive	반동하는, 효력이 소급하는
sedition	난동, 선동, 치안방해
sequester	몰수하다, 격리하다
statute	법령
stipulate	(조항 등을) 규정하다
substantiate	성립시키다
surrogate	대리인
testimony	증언
the condemned	사형수
transgress	위반하다
validity	(법적인) 효력
verbatim	축어적 보고
verdict	평결, 판결
vindicate	정당성을 입증하다
warrant	영장
witness	증언; 증언하다, 목격하다

05 군대와 전쟁(Military Affairs)

air force	공군
align	정렬시키다
armistice	휴전
army	육군
bellicose	호전적인
census	인구조사
command	명령하다
commando	특공대
conscript	징집하다

decimate	(인구를) 격감시키다
decode	암호를 해독하다
demilitarize	비군사화하다
demobilize	제대시키다
deport	추방하다, 처신하다
detach	파견하다
draft	징집하다
drill	군사훈련
encode	암호로 쓰다
enlist	입대하다
espionage	간첩행위
exservice	퇴역한, 전역한
garrison	수비대
guerrilla	유격대
liaison	섭외, 연락
marine corps	해병대
militant	호전적인
mobilize	(전시에) 동원하다
navy	해군
Post Exchange	군대매점
reconnaissance	정찰, 수색
recruit	신병
reinforce	강화하다
the Reserve	예비군
vigilance	경계, 불침번
volunteer	지원병

06 예술(Art)

acclaim	~를 환호하며 맞이하다
apotheosis	신격화, 숭배
applaud	박수갈채 하다
artisan	장인, 기능공
authenticate	진짜임을 증명하다
autograph	자필 서명(하다)
bent	구부러진; 성향, 소질
caricature	풍자적으로 묘사하다
censor	(출판물, 영화 등을) 검열하다
climax	절정
comedy	희극
conductor	지휘자, 안내자
connoisseur	(미술품 등의) 감식가
depict	묘사하다
drama	극, 연극, 희곡
effigy	형상, 초상
elaborate	정교한
ensemble	전체적 조화
exhibit	전시하다
exposition	노출, 전시
extemporize	즉흥적으로 하다
fodder	(작품, 예술의) 소재
formative	모양을 형성하는
garnish	장식
genuine	진짜의
imitation	모방, 모조
immortal	불멸의, 불후의
impromptu	즉흥적인
improvise	즉석에서 ~하다
inborn	타고난, 본래의
innate	타고난
inscribe	새기다, 쓰다
intermission	중지, 휴식
iridescent	무지개 빛깔의, 진주 빛의
libertine	자유주의
licentious	파격적인, 방종한
mellifluous	감미로운
mimic	모방하다

mundane	현세의, 세속적인
nostalgic	옛 시절이 그리운
obscene	음란한
occult	신비로운, 불가사의한
ornate	잘 꾸민, 화려한
ostentatious	화려한
paean	찬가
pariah	(사회에서) 추방당한 사람, 부랑자
perspective	전망
plagiarism	(문장 등의) 표절
proficient	능숙한
rehearse	예행 연습하다
repertoire	상연목록, 레퍼토리
replica	사본
rhapsody	서사시, 열광적인 말
scenario	각본, 시나리오
screen	심사하다, 가려내다
soap opera	드라마, 연속극
spurious	가짜의
tenor	취지, 성질
versatile	다재다능한, 다용도의
vilify	비방하다

07 문화(Culture), 대중문화(Popular Culture)

aboriginal	원주민의
adjacent	인접한
alienate	소외시키다, 멀어지게 하다
alimony	위자료
amenity	예의
antique	고대의
apparel	의복, 옷을 입히다
appliance	기구, 전기제품
archaic	고대의, 오래된
array	의상; 정렬하다
assimilate	동화하다, (지식 등을) 흡수하다
attire	복장, 차려입다
bachelor	총각; 학사
capacious	널찍한
communal	공동체의
customarily	습관적으로, 관례상
denomination	이름, 명칭
disband	해산하다
embellish	장식하다
emigrate	(외국으로) 이민하다
engaging	매력적인, 마음을 끄는
ennoble	품위 있게 하다
evacuate	대피시키다, (집·장소 등을) 비우다
exquisite	아주 아름다운, 정교한
flamboyant	화려한
garment	의복
gaudy	지나치게 화려한, 야한
gorgeous	멋진
gregarious	(사람이) 사교적인
immature	미숙한, 덜 발달된
incongruous	어울리지 않는
lure	매력; 미끼
melee	격론
multiracial	다민족의, 다인종의
neat	단정한, 깔끔한
occidental	서양의
odds and ends	잡동사니, 허드렛일
odorous	향기로운
ornamental	장식적인
ornate	화려한
philanthropist	박애주의자
propriety	예절; 적합성

relish	즐기다
sloppy	단정치 못한, 엉망인
slovenly	단정치 못한, 부주의한
sober	술 취하지 않은, 진지한
superego	초자아
tenet	주의(主義), 신조
thoroughfare	주요 도로, 큰길
tranquilizer	진정제
uncongenial	마음에 맞지 않는, 적합지 않는
unkempt	단정치 못한
vogue	유행, 인기

Theme

03 과학

01 물리(Physics)

acceleration	가속도
acclivity	오르막길
amplify	확대하다, 상승하다
concrete	물체의, 구체적인
crude	자연 그대로의, 가공되지 않은
decompose	성분으로 분해하다[되다]
dynamic	동력의
electron	전자
fission	(원자의) 핵분열, (세포) 분열
inflexible	구부릴 수 없는, 불굴의
lever	지레, 레버
magnet	자석, 자철
magnetize	자기를 띠게 하다
pulley	도르래, 활차
stiff	빳빳한, 딱딱한, 굳은
stuff	재료, 원료, 소재
the law of gravity	중력의 법칙
velocity	속도

02 화학(Chemistry)

analyst	(화학상의) 분석가
apogee	최고점; 원지점
blaze	불꽃, 화염
catalysis	촉매작용, 촉매반응
coagulate	응고시키다[하다]
compact	빽빽한; 간결한
diffuse	흩다, 발산하다, 퍼지다
dilute	(액체, 빛깔을) 묽게 하다
dissolve	(액체가) 녹다, 용해되다
emission	(빛, 열, 냄새 등의) 발산
evaporate	증발하다[시키다]
flash	섬광, 순식간; 번쩍이다, 비추다
fluorescent	형광을 발하는, 형광성의
fusion	융해(물)
glow	빨갛게 불타다, 홍조를 띠다; 백열
incandescent	(가열하면) 빛을 내는, 백열의
laboratory	(화학의) 실험실
melting-point	융점, 녹는점
microscope	현미경
organic	유기의
reagent	시약, 반응물(력)
rust	녹
sediment	앙금, 침전물
smelt	(광석을) 용해하다, (금속을) 제련하다
soluble	잘 녹는, 용해되는
sparkle	불꽃, 섬광; 불꽃을 튀기다, 번쩍이다
sticky	끈적끈적한
tarnish	광택을 잃다, 더럽히다
test-tube	시험관
thermal	열의, 열량의, 온도의
tripod	삼각대
volatile	(액체가) 증발하기 쉬운, 휘발성의

03 공학(Engineering)

apparatus	(한 벌의) 장치, 기계, 기구
appliance	기구, 기계
civil engineering	토목 공학
gadget	(기계의) 소형 장치, 도구
hammer	망치
implement	도구, 연장
maul	큰 망치; 혹평하다
mechanic	기술공
mend	수선하다, 고치다
mill	공장, 제조소, 제작소
nail	못, 징
recondition	수리하다
renovate	쇄신하다, 수리하다
saw	톱
screw	나사(못)

04 천문학(Astronomy)

apogee	근지점(近地點); 정점
asteroid	소행성
astrology	(중세의) 점성술
astronaut	우주비행사
astronomer	천문학자, 천문대장
blaze	불꽃, 화염
celestial	하늘의
comet	혜성
constellation	별자리, 성좌
cosmos	우주, 천지만물
eclipse	일식, 월식; (명예의) 실추, 초월하다
emit	방출하다
galaxy	우주의 성운(= nebula)
interstellar	별과 별 사이의
lunar	달의
macrocosm	대우주; 전 범위(= gamut)
meteor	유성, 별똥별
nadir	천저(天底), 최하점
nebulous	성운의, 구름 같은
observatory	천문대, 기상대, 측후소
orbit	궤도
stellar	별의
twilight	(해 지기 전의) 황혼
wane	(달이) 이지러지다
zodiac	12궁도(별점)

05 지질학(Geology)

alluvial	충적의
brass	황동, 놋쇠
bronze	청동
cartography	지도 제작술
chaotic	혼돈의
clay	점토
clod	(흙 등의) 덩어리
coal	석탄
contour line	등고선
copper	구리
crust	지각, 땅껍질
deluge	대홍수; 쇄도, 폭주
disaster	재앙
earthy	상스러운; 흙의
erode	좀먹다, 침식하다
excavate	~에 구멍을 뚫다
fossil	화석
inundate	범람시키다

landslide	산사태
maelstrom	대혼란
mercury	수은
mineral	광물, 광석; 광물성인
petroleum	석유
slate	점판암, 석판
stratum	지층, 사회적 계층
tin	주석
undermine	밑을 파다, (명성을) 손상시키다
undulate	요동하다
unearth	발굴하다, 발견하다

06 컴퓨터(Computer), 인터넷(Internet)

access	접속하다
boot	시동시키다
computer	컴퓨터
desktop	탁상용 컴퓨터
display	화면 표시기
e-commerce	전자 상거래
hacker	컴퓨터 침입자
hardware	하드웨어(컴퓨터 기계 설비)
input	입력
laptop	휴대용 컴뮤터
operating system	운영체계
output	출력
password	비밀번호
printout	프린트 출력
shut down	다운되다
storage	기억장치
upgrade	업그레이드하다
upload	업로드하다
web browser	웹브라우저

Theme

04 학문과 교육

01 문학(Literature)

abridge	줄이다, 요약하다
acronym	두문자어
aesthetics	미학
alexia	독서 불능증
allegory	우화, 풍자
anagram	철자 바꾸기
anecdote	일화
annotate	주석을 달다
anonymous	익명의
antagonist	적, 상대편
anthology	명시전집
appreciation	(작품의) 감상
autobiography	자서전
avant-garde	전위, (예술, 문학의) 선구자
banal	진부한
bibliophile	애서가, 서적수집가
biography	전기
calligraphy	서예
chronicle	연대기, 편년사(編年史)
cliche	(진부한) 상투 어구
climax	(소설 · 극 등의) 절정
clique	동인, 파벌
cogent	설득력 있는
compendious	요령 있게 간추린
compendium	개요
compile	편찬[편집]하다
concise	(말 · 문체가) 간결한
concoct	(이야기 · 소설을) 구상하다
construe	해석하다
critique	평론
debunk	(정체를) 폭로하다
decadence	(문예, 도덕의) 타락
didactic	교훈적인
draft	초고, 초안, 밑그림
dyslexia	난독증
elegy	애가, 비가
ellipsis	생략
emend	교정하다, 고치다
epic	서사시
epigram	(짧고 날카로운) 풍자시
epilogue	맺음말
epitaph	비문
epitome	(책, 연설의) 요약
eponymous	이름의 시조가 된
excerpt	인용구
extract	인용[발췌]하다
fairy tale	동화
fake	꾸민 이야기
fictitious	가짜의
folk tale	민화
hackneyed	진부한
illegible	읽기 어려운
illiterate	문맹의, 무식한
impressionism	인상주의
inkling	암시하다
innuendo	암시

insinuate	넌지시 비추다
interpolate	고쳐 쓰다
irony	아이러니, 이상한 일
laconic	(말 · 표현이) 간결한
libel	비방하는 글
literally	글자 그대로
lyric	서정시
manuscript	원고
memoir	전기, 실록
metaphor	은유, 비유
mimic	모방의, 흉내 내는
miscellany	여러 종류의 모음
omission	생략
omnibus	염가판 작품집
parable	우화
paradox	역설
paragon	모범, 전형
parody	패러디, 풍자적 모방
peruse	정독하다
plagiarize	표절하다
platitude	진부
plot	줄거리, 비밀 계획
plotter	공모자
prosaic	단조로운
prose	산문
protagonist	주인공
pseudonym	가명
quandary	곤혹, 궁지
recapitulate	개괄하다
redundancy	쓸데없는 반복
reference	참조, 언급
revise	교정하다
saga	대하소설, 중세 무용담
sarcasm	풍자, 비꼼
sardonic	냉소하는, 빈정거리는
scathing	(비평이) 통렬한, 가차 없는
scrabble	갈겨쓰다
scrawl	휘갈겨 쓰다, 낙서하다
simile	직유
skim	대충 읽다
syllabus	(학과의) 개요
synopsis	요약, 개요
terse	(문체 등이) 간결한
transcribe	베껴 쓰다
travesty	서투른 모방
trite	진부한
verse	운문

02 어학(Philology)

accentuate	강조하다, 주의를 끌다
adage	격언, 속담
allusion	암시, 간접적인 언급
ambiguous	둘 이상의 뜻을 가진, 모호한
anagram	철자를 바꿔 만든 낱말
antonym	반의어
aphorism	금언, 격언
bilingual	2개 국어를 말하는
circumlocution	완곡어법
clause	절
collocation	연어, 배열
colloquial	구어체의
comparative	비교급
connote	(뜻을) 함축[내포]하다
context	문맥
cuneiform	설형문자
derive	기원[유래]하다

dialect	방언
dictum	격언
entry	표제어, 항목
epigram	경구, (짧은) 풍자시
equivocal	둘 이상의 뜻을 가진
equivocal	애매한, 두 가지 뜻을 가진
etymology	어원학
euphemism	완곡어법, 간접적으로 돌려서 말하기
exaggeration	과장
grandiloquent	과장된
hieroglyph	상형문자
hyperbole	과장법
implicit	함축적인
insinuate	넌지시 말하다
ironic(al)	반어법의
jargon	특수 용어
juxtapose	나란히 놓다
lexicon	전문 용어, 전문 용어 목록
locution	말투, 어법
magniloquent	(표현이) 과장된, 허풍떠는
maxim	격언
minuscule	소문자; 아주 작은
modify	수식하다
neologism	신조어
nuance	미묘한 차이, 뉘앙스
paragraph	단락
paraphrase	바꾸어 말하다
parenthesis	괄호; 삽입어구
parlance	말투, 어법
participle	분사
phonetics	음성학
pithy	간결한
platitude	상투어
plural	복수(複數)
polyglot	수 개 국어를 아는
positive	원급
precept	격언, 가르침, 교훈
predicate	술부, 술어
prefix	접두어
punctuate	구두점을 찍다
rhetoric	수사(학), 웅변술
semantics	의미론
sententious	금언 같은, 교훈적인
singular	단수(의)
slang	속어
solecism	어법위반
subordinate	종속절
suffix	접미어
superlative	최상급
syllable	음절
synonym	동의어
syntax	구문론
tense	시제
terminology	술어, 전문용어
thesaurus	유의어 사전
understate	불완전하게 말하다
vague	막연한
verbatim	말 그대로

03 철학(Philosophy)

abnegation	자제, 금욕
aesthetics	미학
agnostic	불가지론자, 불가지론의
altruism	이타주의
anarchism	무정부주의
ascetic	극기의, 고행의

atheism	무신론
autonomy	자율(성)
axiom	자명한 이치
confute	오류를 입증하다
deduction	연역법
deviant	(도덕적 기준을) 벗어난
dialectic	변증법, 논리, 논법
empiricism	경험론
extrinsic	비본질적인, 외부로부터의
fallacy	잘못된 생각, 착오
grotesque	터무니없는
hedonism	쾌락주의
induction	귀납(법)
inferential	추리상의
integrity	성실, 정직, (인격의) 완벽함
intrinsic	본래의, 고유한, 내부의
intuition	직관
materialism	유물론
meditation	명상, 숙고
metaphysics	형이상학
muse	숙고하다
natural right	자연권
nihilistic	허무주의의
optimism	낙관주의
pessimism	비관주의
philosopher	철학자
postulate	가정, 조건
pragmatism	실용주의
premise	전제
preposterous	불합리한, 터무니없는
queer	기묘한
rationalism	이성주의
realism	실재론
recondite	심오한
relativism	상대주의
sophism	궤변
stoical	극기주의자의
transcend	초월하다
utilitarian	공리적인, 실리적인
validity	타당성
verification	검증

04 종교(Religion)

ablution	목욕재계
abyss	심연
altar	재단
anathema	저주, 악담
apostate	배교[배신]자
apostle	사도, 주창자
apotheosis	신격화, 이상형
ascetic	금욕적인; 금욕주의자
atheist	무신론자
augury	점, 전조, 징조
avatar	화신
benediction	축도, 축복
blasphemous	신성모독의
buddhism	불교
celestial	하늘의, 천국의
clergy	목사, 성직자
cloister	수도원
consecrate	신성하게 하다
creed	신조
demon	악마
desecrate	신성 모독하다
devout	독실한, 경건한
disciple	제자

divine	신의
dogma	교의, 교리, 독단
ethereal	탈속적인
fabulous	전설적인, 굉장한, 멋진
foresee	예견하다
heresy	이교, 이단
hermitage	암자, 은자의 거처
holy	신의, 종교상의, 신성한
iconoclast	성상파괴자
idolize	우상화하다
infidel	무신론자
irreligious	반종교적인
malignant	악의 있는, 악성의
martyr	순교자
mundane	세속적인
neophyte	초보자, 신개종자
occult	숨은, 신비한, 비밀의
omen	징조, 길조, 흉조
omnipotent	전능한
omniscient	전지의
orthodox	정통의
pantheism	범신론
persecute	박해하다
pilgrim	설교하다, 전도하다
pious	경건한
portend	예언하다
preach	설교하다
profane	세속의, 속세의
prophesy	예언[예고]하다
puritan	청교도
recluse	속세를 떠난 사람, 은둔자
reincarnation	화신, 재생
religious	종교의
renegade	배반자, 배교자
resurrection	(예수의) 부활
sabbath	안식일
sacrilegious	신성모독의
sanctity	성스러움
sanctuary	신성한 장소, 사원, 성당
sect	종파, 교파
superstition	미신
temporal	현세의
tenet	주의, 신조, 교리
theism	유신론
theology	신학
vicious	사악한
villain	악인, 악한

05 역사(History)

aboriginal	원시의, 토착의
Agricultural Revolution	농업혁명
archaeology	고고학
armor	갑옷과 투구
capitalism	자본주의
chauvinism	국수주의
chivalry	기사제도, 기사도
citadel	피난처
civilization	문명화
colonialism	식민주의
crusade	십자군
dethrone	폐위시키다
emancipate	해방하다, 자유를 주다
enthrone	왕자에 앉히다
extricate	해방하다, 풀어주다
feudal	봉건제도

Great Depression	세계 대공황
hierarchy	계급조직
imperialism	제국주의
independence	독립, 자립
Industrial Revolution	산업혁명
Medieval Age	중세
Modern times	근대, 근세
Prehistoric Times	선사시대
primeval	태고의, 원시의, (세계사에서) 초기의
pristine	원시의
reformation	(16세기) 종교개혁
regal	제왕의, 제왕다운
regime	정권, (정치) 제도
remains	유물
renaissance	문예부흥(기)

06 교육(Education)

acquaint (with)	~에게 알려주다
apprentice	견습생, 초심자
awkward	서투른, 어색한
berate	(호되게) 야단치다
callow	경험이 없는, 풋내기의
chide	꾸짖다
clumsy	어색한, 서투른
diploma	졸업증서
disseminate	유포하다, 보급시키다
edification	지덕의 함양
edify	교화하다
encyclopedia	백과사전
enrollment	입학, 등록(된 인원수)
erudite	박식한, 학자다운
expostulation	충고, 훈계
expound	상세히 설명하다
extol	칭찬하다
faculty	재능, 학부, 학부의 교수단
foster	기르다, 양육하다
gauche	어색한, 서투른
governess	여자 가정교사
graduate	졸업생
harbinger	선구자
hooky	학교를 빼먹기
illuminate	조명하다; 계몽하다
impart	알리다, 주다
inculcate	(사상 따위를) 가르치다
indoctrinate	(신앙, 이론을) 주입하다
inspire	격려하다(= instill), (사상 따위를) 스며들게 하다
intricate	난잡한, 난해한
laudatory	칭찬의
maladroit	서투른
novelty	새로움, 신기함
novice	초심자
pedagogue	학자티를 내는 교사
pedant	현학자
potential	잠재적인
pundit	(인도의) 학자
pupil	학생
rebuke	질책하다
reproach	질책하다
rudimentary	초보의, 기초의
tutelage	보호 감독, 후견, 지도
tutor	가정교사
undergraduate	대학생
upbraid	(심하게) 야단치다
upbringing	양육, 교육
vanguard	선구자
verbose	말이 많은, 장황한

문 덕

20년 넘도록 영어를 연구하고 강의해 온 국내 최고의 영어 전문가이다. 김영 대학 편입학원과 위드유 편입학원, 그리고 www.ybmsisa.com의 온라인 강좌를 통해 백만 명 이상 그의 강의를 수강하였다. EBS라디오와 TV, 재능방송을 통해 일반 대중들에게도 널리 알려진 인기 강사이다. 저술활동으로도 이름을 떨쳐 『MD vocabulary 33,000』과 『웃지마! 나 영어책이야』 등은 국내 베스트셀러를 넘어 중국, 일본 등 해외에까지 수출되고 있다.

약력

서울대 영어영문학과 졸업
MD 영어 연구소 소장
現, 박문각 남부고시학원 교수
前, 김영 대학 편입학원 전임교수
With U 편입학원 전임교수
YBM시사 강사
EBS radio 〈문덕의 어휘 대첩〉 진행
EBS TV 〈문덕의 어휘보감〉 진행

저서

문덕 영어 독해 (박문각출판)
문덕 영어 어휘 (박문각출판)
문덕 영어 문법 (박문각출판)
MD 중학 영단어 (지수출판사)
MD 수능 VOCA (지수출판사)
MD Vocabulary 33,000 (지수출판사)
MD Grammar (지수출판사)
MD Reading (지수출판사)
웃지마! 나 영어책이야 1,2 (뉴런출판사)
문덕의 뜨금있는 영어 회화 (뉴런출판사)

MD 영어연구소 http://www.moonduk.com

문덕 영어 독해

초판인쇄 | 2021. 7. 12. **초판발행** | 2021. 7. 15. **편저자** | 문 덕
발행인 | 박 용 | **발행처** | (주)박문각출판 **등록** | 2015년 4월 29일 제2015-000104호
주소 | 06654 서울시 서초구 효령로 283 서경 B/D **팩스** | (02)584-2927
전화 | 교재 주문·내용 문의 (02)6466-7202

저자와의 협의하에 인지생략

정가 15,000원 ISBN 979-11-6704-134-0